W9-ACY-611

wrong

6

DRAWN TO TROUBLE

Confessions of a Master Forger

A MEMOIR BY
ERIC HEBBORN

RANDOM HOUSE

New York

ACKNOWLEDGMENTS

For help in the long task of getting my story into readable form, I wish to thank the following: Paul Binding whose early interest and encouragement was largely responsible for getting the project underway; Barry Cole who went over the childhood chapters and offered invaluable suggestions; and Edgar Alegre both for helpful revisions and for practical assistance at all stages of the work. In addition, my thanks are due to Orazio Amato, Danny Lao, Marlene Manuel, and Janice Viarnaud for preparing the typescript, and Raimondo Luciani for photographing most of the works illustrated.

It would be gratifying to be able to add to this list the names of the various dealers and museum people whom I have approached in the hope of tracing the present whereabouts and status of some of my "Old Masters," but unfortunately, my enquiries have almost invariably met with the sternest of answers—silence.

Originally published in the United Kingdom by Mainstream Publishing Projects Ltd. Edinburgh, in 1991.

Library of Congress Cataloging-in-Publication Data
Hebborn, Eric
    Drawn to trouble: confessions of a master forger : a memoir/Eric Hebborn.
        p.   cm.
    ISBN 0-679-42084-3
    1. Hebborn, Eric-   .   2. Art forgers—England—Biography.
I. Title.
N8791.H43A2   1993
741'.092—dc20
[B]   92-56818

Manufactured in the United States of America
98765432
First U.S. Edition

Fig. 1: *Self-portrait*, 1984, etching touched with grey wash

Our priests are not what simple folk suppose
Their learning is but our credulity...
Let us trust to ourselves, see all with our own eyes;
Let these be our oracles, our tripods and our gods.
                                                    VOLTAIRE

CONTENTS

PROLOGUE

There once was a poor artist named Vincent Van Blank. Vincent was so poor he lived in a garret. He had little or nothing to eat, and when the weather was cold he burnt his unsold canvases to keep himself warm.

Although Vincent was a genius nobody had noticed the fact, and the art critics, dealers and collectors were unanimous in their total disregard of him and his masterpieces. Then one day Vincent decided to take his revenge on the ignorant people who governed the art world by painting yet another masterpiece, but this time in the style of a recognised master. And so it came about that he painted a picture in the style of Leonardo da Vinci, and instead of burning the painting he baked it until it was covered with fine cracks, into which he rubbed the dirt of centuries.

This done, Vincent set about discovering his Leonardo in the outhouse of a lady of title to whom he promised a percentage of the proceeds.

An expert was called in to examine the find, and to everybody's delight declared that here was a genuine Leonardo of the highest quality, and certain to realise a high price.

The day of the sale came and Vincent's masterpiece fetched the gratifying figure of a million pounds. It was sold to a great public gallery where it was exhibited for over a decade to adoring crowds who never failed to fall for the magic of the expensive picture.

Alas, poor Vincent (I am sorry, rich Vincent, for by now his garret had been remodelled and called a penthouse) had made one silly slip in his otherwise perfect Leonardo. He had inadvertently introduced a telephone in the background, and this anachronism was spotted by an eagle-eyed journalist who checked the facts and found that the telephone was about the only device that Leonardo had not invented. The journalist was now determined to track down Vincent and unmask him (I had forgotten to tell the reader that Vincent always wore a mask and this habit made him easily recognisable). Faced with the journalist's irrefutable evidence, Vincent broke down. 'Yes,' he confessed, 'I painted the Leonardo to avenge myself on the ignorant critics who failed to recognise my genius.'

The story made headlines and Vincent was hailed as the prince of forgers. One scurrilous Sunday paper suggested he was the queen of forgers, but everyone agreed that he must be a genius to have fooled the experts. Very soon, however, there was a change in opinion, and then everybody said that Vincent was a talentless old hack who couldn't draw or paint to save his life, and how his horrible daub in the manner of Leonardo had passed undetected for so long was beyond understanding.

Many writers hinted that they themselves had always known that the picture was a miserable fake but had kept the secret to themselves for fear of being accused of showing off. As for Vincent, he took to drink and lived happily ever after.

effect, and sometimes my father would return from work, or from looking for it, to find me still sobbing; whereupon he would ask with casual interest, 'What's up wiv lightoles (I suggest that etymologically speaking this uncommon name derives from lightning, an epithet I may have earned by a remarkable ability to dawdle and daydream) this time?' To which my mother would answer: 'Don't take no notice of 'im. Yer know what e's bleeding well like, always 'owlin' over nuffing.' It was good of her to protect me from an application of my father's belt by concealing my naughtiness from him, but as I have said, she loved me dearly, and for my part I can truly say that no other woman has ever held the same place in my affections.

In spite of her being a Marchant, I suspect my mother's interest in the arts was really not very great, and yet it was she, curiously enough, who first impressed upon me, and in no uncertain manner, the prime importance that is attached to the correct attribution of a work of art. The incident arose from a drawing I had made at the infant school. We had been given crayons and were let loose upon paper to draw anything that we pleased, in any manner that we pleased. In my opinion, most of the children made an awful mess both of their drawings and themselves, wildly expressing themselves in a proliferation of images of spiky suns, dolls-houses, and cabbage-trees, as coarse in colour as they were foul in drawing: the sort of drawings that doting parents love, and which famous modern artists despair of ever being able to emulate however much they are paid to try. Such childish stuff would not, however, do for a descendant of the artistic dynasty of Marchant who had a totally different self to express. Much to my teacher's surprise I began to draw the likeness of a stuffed owl which happened to form part of our schoolroom's meagre furnishings. Perhaps it served for the teaching of natural history, or as a symbol of the knowledge imparted in that seat of learning but for whatever reason, there it stood, glassy-eyed, wise and inscrutable. And there stood I, pushing five, making my first essay in the language of line. I hate to think what my effort looked like, but one thing I can guarantee: it was not delightful, or charming, or any of the other things that children's drawings are supposed to be. And yet to its author it was at the time an object of wonder, and I am quite certain that my satisfaction with my study of an owl (present whereabouts mercifully unknown) was infinitely greater than Michelangelo's on the completion of the Sistine Chapel. Off I ran clutching my masterpiece, anxious to display it to the whole world except, for some reason, my mother, from whom I tried to hide it by sticking it up my jumper.

'What yer got there? Pinched sumfing 'av yer?' said my suspicious parent on observing me holding my jumper at its lower edge to stop the drawing from falling out. 'And it over.'

'Shan't.'

'We'll soon see about that,' said she, gripping me round the neck, lifting me up and giving me a good shake. And sure enough, no length of time passed before my hands moved instinctively towards my throat and my treasured drawing floated down to the floor. My mother retrieved the study of an owl and scrutinised it for a moment before asking in some bewilderment: 'What the 'ell is this?' 'What I done at school,' I replied. Again she glanced at my study. Surely few works of art have ever roused such emotions in the human breast. I doubt if ever Rodin's Balzac, which on being unveiled raised the cry of '*la patrie en danger*', ever moved anybody to the wrath that my mother showed on viewing my owl.

What she really objected to was the attribution – on what grounds, like many a scholar and expert of greater erudition than Rose Molly Marchant, she did not care to make clear. Instead, she abandoned objectivity in favour of a subjective approach. Indeed, it is not too much to say that she quite lost control of herself, and falling into a paroxysm of rage shouted: 'You bleedin little liar you never drawed it that good, I'll learn yer to come ome ere wiv yer bleeding lies; take this for a start.' 'This', was what she herself would have termed 'a swipe round the lugoles' (much is lost in translation but the phrase may be rendered as a blow struck with some violence to the head in the region of the ears). The blow was quickly followed by others, but I shall not give a blow by blow account; let it suffice that the spirited encounter ended as usual with her permission for me to stop 'owlin'. Whether or not she was aware of the clever pun she was making I am not at all sure, because unlike my father, my mother was not given to making witticisms. This was not from any want of humour, far from it, but hers was of a kind that found its expression more readily in action than in words.

In September 1939 the Prime Minister, Neville Chamberlain, announced the declaration of the Second World War in a café in Charing Cross Road. I have that curious piece of information on the authority of the late Kenneth Clark, Lord Clark of Saltwood, who writes: 'I heard Mr Chamberlain's tired old voice announcing the declaration of war in a café in Charing Cross Road.' But perhaps I misunderstood, and Lord Clark meant the Prime Minister was announcing the declaration of a war that was shortly to be waged in a café in Charing Cross Road. With the death of Lord

Clark perhaps I shall never know for certain, but have little doubt that a war did in fact then take place.

By now my parents had moved to a house in Station Road, Harold Wood. With eight windows, the house was considerably larger than the one they had occupied near Gallows Corner, but the advantages of its extra size were somewhat diminished by its position and condition; nor were the two matters unrelated. Black with grime, the dilapidated residence stood in a terrace running parallel to the tracks of Harold Wood Station's shunting yard, over which it commanded views as unspoiled as they were unenviable.

The station was at the time an enemy target and although the Germans seldom hit their targets, it was little consolation for those who received near-misses, as with some of my parents' neighbours, whose homes were in need of doors and windows.

Being so close to destruction was at the time my keenest source of pleasure, for I stood a better chance than the other boys in the area of collecting shrapnel and other souvenirs so generously showered on us by our enemy in what appeared to me to be a super war (most children at the time thought of the war as the status quo).

But my first impression of the house in Station Road was not altogether favourable. My mother reminded me that 'there was a bleedin' war on' and that she was in need of my 'bleedin ration book'. And it was the rationing of food stuffs which brought about the first of a sequence of differences between us.

I had been taught how to make tea (one teaspoon for each person and one for the pot), and to please my mother, I told her I would like to make the afternoon brew. Off I went to the kitchen, and having boiled the water and heated the pot, I put in the tea, which I believe was called Mazawatee. So in it went: one for mum, one for Keith, one for Rosemary, one for me, one for . . . and so on until the pot probably contained more tea than water.

It seems that I had not taken into account two important factors. First the teapot was not large enough for ten or eleven cups of tea; second, only three of the people for whom I was preparing it were actually home. Needless to say, the tea as poured out was as black as treacle and almost of the same consistency; neither of these details was lost on my mother who, realising that I must have made deep inroads into her precious supply of rationed tea, treated me to a good 'swipe' or two to 'learn' me, and sent me into solitary confinement in an upstairs room.

Both the door and windows were locked, and as the room was on the top floor and the living room was on the ground floor, I could not communicate my basic needs to the outside world. After a few hours the satisfaction of those needs became desperate and I was obliged to empty my bladder on the floor and watch with satisfaction its contents seeping between the floorboards into the room below, from where it apparently continued to drip.

The occupants of the downstairs rooms, getting less satisfaction from my urine's arrival than I from its departure, eventually drew my parents' attention to the matter, for I soon heard animated conversation outside the very door I had earlier wanted open but would now prefer to be doubly locked.

'I'll slawter the bugger!' asserted my mother.

'What you expect the bloody kid to do?' said my father. 'He ain't made of bloody cast iron.'

'You wait till I've finished with 'im. You ain't seen nuffink yet,' she replied.

'You bloody well keep your paws to yerself; you'll get us bofe inter trouble, you will, if you ain't careful,' he said.

Thus by carefully chosen words of reason, my father managed to pacify my mother, and led her back down the stairs.

I once again found myself, apart from the chuffing of the trains, in silence. Although an outside observer would have said little untoward could occur in such a solo-occupied room, I became aware of a further and more serious requirement of nature which only a lavatory could or should supply.

The consistency of the substance I excreted upon the floorboards was this time such as to deny me the satisfaction of watching it disappear through the cracks, and for a while I toyed with the idea of what to do with it. Could it be hidden in the pockets of the old overcoat that served as blanket and bedspread? But that would certainly have been inadvisable (I slept there). Was it to be hidden under the bed itself? That too would have been olfactorily unpleasant. Had the window been open I could have thrown it out – but where would it have landed?

Freud has said that artists as children are led to their calling by manipulation of their calls of nature. And writing to Vanessa Bell, Roger Fry thought Freud's theory might amuse her by its indecency, adding in a subsequent letter: 'Anal-erotic complexes appear to account for everything one does or doesn't do. But it's a fine corrective to nobility and edification to realise that our spiritual nature is built on dung.'

Could it be that playing with my excrement in the house in Station Road led, by degrees, to my mature works being exhibited in Bond Street and housed in the leading galleries around the world? Had my mother foreseen that upon such unalluring foundations, the whole superstructure of my life's work (so far) was to be erected, she might have looked more kindly on this early product of my promise. As it was, she didn't know what to make of the untitled sculptures that decorated my nascent atelier. Those on the floor were in the round; those on the walls in high or, more appropriately, low relief.

Whatever my mother's limitations as a connoisseur may have been, as an art-lover no one could accuse her of insincerity. Unlike so many visitors to a 'difficult' art exhibition she did not pretend to 'understand' the works on show, still less did she feign to like them (though a hundred years earlier she would no doubt have liked my Wilkie – more of which later). On the contrary she openly attacked such works, describing them with one of the four-letter words which, while strictly accurate, was offensive.

Understandably I did not want to pursue these earlier manifestations of my career as a sculptor and instead branched out into the then unknown (to me) fields of lettering and calligraphy. In this I was assisted by the art teacher appointed in 1941 to Harold Wood Junior School. Her name escapes me but I shall call her Miss Serif.

I believe I owe more to Miss Serif for my skill as a calligrapher than to anyone else, and have since come to the supposition that she was a one-time pupil of Edward Johnston. He was a first-rate calligrapher who, hoping to bring about a general improvement in

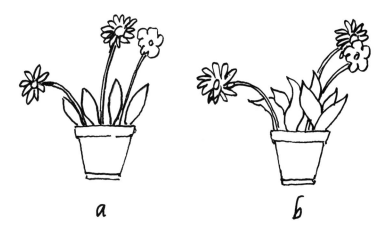

Fig. 2: *Vase of Flowers*. Diagram illustrating the principle of overlapping lines. Because some leaves appear to be partially hidden by others, B implies a certain amount of depth, whereas A is totally flat

everyday handwriting had designed a skeleton or 'stick' alphabet which, while retaining the splendid proportions of the lettering on, for example, Trajan's column, would be simple enough for children.

Miss Serif went further, and taught the elaborate geometrical structures that she and many others before her, notably Albrecht Dürer, believed to underlie the Roman form. Some might think this very early exposure to fine lettering was premature, and perhaps it was. But I shall always be grateful to Miss Serif for providing me with the rudiments of a skill (as it became) which was to prove invaluable in my future career. How often have I increased the interest in an 'old master' with an inscription in a contemporary hand requiring me to: 'Limn the classic letter's form / And urge the careful pen.'

It was about this time that I made a big step forward as a draughtsman, and here again I was indebted to Miss Serif, who made what seemed to me a perceptive observation concerning a vase of flowers I was attempting to draw. I imagine that I must have lined up the leaves and flowers on one plane with no sugges-tion of depth, rather in the manner of the following reconstruction (Fig. 2), because she said: 'Look, Eric, how some leaves lie behind, and are partially hidden by others.' She was, I remember, wise enough not to show me how I could achieve the effect of depth she was speaking of, and it was while wrestling with this problem that I discovered for myself a fundamental relationship of line I was to dub many years later: 'the principle of overlapping lines'.

This early interest in drawing, an innocent occupation on the face of it, led to my departure from Harold Wood Junior School under a cloud – a cloud of smoke.

As every compulsive draughtsman knows, if one lacks normal drawing materials, one improvises in producing them, using any-thing remotely suitable that may come to hand. I had, as an inqui-sitive child, long discovered that a burnt match, being tipped with charcoal, could be used to make some sort of sketch. Furthermore, that when the charcoal tip had been consumed, the stick itself might, in the absence of a knife, be sharpened to a point on sand-paper (such as that on a matchbox), then stuck into a school desk's inkwell and charged with ink to provide a very agreeable line. And it was these experiments in the methods and materials of the draughtsman's art that led to the headmaster's discovery in my desk of a match-stick and a piece of sandpaper.

Whether the headmaster, Mr Percy, had any knowledge of the craft of drawing I do not know, but if he did it was not uppermost in his mind at that moment. When he saw the improvised tools of my future trade he came to the not unreasonable conclusion that a match in close proximity to a piece of sandpaper meant the imminence of one thing only – fire. And fire was something his pupils should be dissuaded from creating.

The method he chose to use was the traditional 'six of the best': six whacks with the cane (caning in England was then a commonplace). Such punishment could be taken on the hand or backside – as the pupil wished. Denied the opportunity (traditional) to pad my trousers, I elected to receive the punishment on my hands. But far from being persuaded by Mr Percy not to play with fire, I resolved that at the next opportunity I would commit the crime for which I had peremptorily been punished.

I was in a dilemma over Mr Percy's conscience. Would it not be a relief to him to have his suspicions confirmed and know for certain that, originally, arson, and not art, was on my mind? And that his whacking of my hands was totally justified?

Some time elapsed, however, before I could resolve the headmaster's supposed conscience. This unfortunate delay was not the result of any weakening of my resolve, but due to the fact that my caning took place on Monday and payday was Saturday. If my WREN, or WRAF or WAC or whatever my uniformed customer was, had known to what a noble cause her eagerly awaited sixpence was to be put that week, no doubt she would have paid her shoeshine boy in advance, praising him for his moral rectitude and rejoicing in being party to such a virtuous enterprise. But as it was, the buying of the matches was delayed, as was their employment, until the following Monday.

Arriving at school even later than usual on that significant day, I was hopeful of being able to carry out my plan unobserved. The corridors were empty and silent but for the muffled roar of the classrooms where, as Blake has said: ' . . . under a cruel eye outworn / The little ones spend the day / In sighing and dismay. . . .'

I made my way unseen to the cloakroom, which I knew contained sacks of wastepaper awaiting collection. I carefully hung some of the sacks among the caps and satchels, bags and coats. I also emptied sacks, scattering the contents about the floor, and began to ignite as much as I could by dropping lighted matches. Mr Percy's disciplinary action vindicated at last, I retired to the doorway to view the spectacle.

Nero, strumming his lyre as he watched the burning of Rome, knew no greater satisfaction. The live thing that roared and raged about me held me spellbound. I was transfixed, struck by awe at a monster which only moments before had been innocuous sticks in a box.

But exactly what passed through my mind in those enchanting moments can, now, only be guessed at. Had I known the story of Prometheus I might perhaps have reflected with Max Beerbohm that 'time, which has civilised man and domesticated his animals, has not tamed fire.

'Fire is just as wild, as fierce, as terrible now as when Prometheus snatched it from the gods. Of all the elements fire alone was brought from heaven, the others were here from the cold and dismal start. And this is why, for all its savagery, fire has nobler connotations. By "earthy" we impute cloddishness, by "watery" imply the insipid, by "airy" the inconsequential; but "fiery" is associated with faith, courage, genius, and all the finer qualities of the human spirit. Fire is also the symbol of purity, of triumph over corruption, and wheresoever there is flame there too is innocence.'

Yes, there I was, innocence itself. As innocent of the fact that my bootlaces had caught on fire, as I was unaware of the power I had unleashed. The fire took hold, roared and glowered, licked its crimson lips and noisily and indiscriminately devoured caps and satchels, coats and paper, scarves and gloves. The smoke became dense and I began coughing, my eyes cried but still I was unable to move.

Could one, at eight years of age really be so innocent? Like the fire, I was angry and savage. That caning hurt more than my hands. And yet I did not want to be merely malevolent. I wanted to have the fire's finer qualities too – to be noble, just, courageous. But I must have been none of these. The flames were now playing with the ceiling, blistering the cheap paint of the walls, and cracking the window panes.

And then, at last, I moved.

'Ouch!' I yelled unstoically as the burning bootlaces, like fuses, propelled me into action.

I knocked on the headmaster's door.

'Come in,' he called cheerfully. I put my scorched face round the door and stammered:

'Please Sir, please Sir. . . .'

'Well, Hebborn, don't just stand there like a moonstruck monkey. Say something!'

At which I began to recite: 'Fire fire Mrs Dire,/Where where Mrs Clare?'

Never have I seen a grown-up move with such alacrity. In less time than it takes to tell, Mr Percy had bounded from his desk, snatched a fire extinguisher from its wall-bracket and, thrusting me aside, begun to combat the enveloping flames.

Moments later came the fire alarm. Since fire-drill was a regular part of the school's curriculum it is a wonder that anybody took any special notice of it, but in the event it was not long before every pupil was assembled at the far end of the playground to enjoy the sight of Mr Percy and his staff ineffectually attacking the flames and smoke brought about by my behaviour – they loved the distraction.

There were cheers when the red fire engine appeared with its bells and uniforms. The firemen had helmets and hatchets, and the engine was decorated in brass fittings, none of which, it seemed to us, had any particular purpose other than to look resplendent.

The ladders were extended and hoses hissed and the fire faded. To the disappointment of most of the children the ultimate damage was not great. Not, that is, great enough to prevent resumption of lessons. I, however, was delivered into the unwanted custody of my mother.

Having, as I believed, been already punished in advance for playing with fire I imagined I would hear no more of the incident. And it did seem to me that Mr Percy was prepared to forgive and forget. For he made it known that I need never again attend his school; that I was, indeed, and for the very first time, a *persona non grata* – a recognition I very much appreciated.

My mother was much less forgiving and, cornering me, said that she would 'learn me to bleedin well play with fire', guidance on which, I felt, I needed little instruction. To begin the lesson she lit several matches, each of which she stubbed out on my flesh. As the matches in the box dwindled so did her enthusiasm for teaching. She thereupon used the last to light a cigarette, told me that my ''owlin' got on her 'bleedin nerves' and it would be better if I not only went to my room but stayed there for the rest of my life.

How long I actually stayed in confinement is hard to say. The room would get light and go dark. Food arrived at irregular intervals – bread and dripping, a mug of tea, water. My chamber pot was reluctantly removed at what I assume were regular intervals. I began to develop boils and recall one on the edge of my anus which was particularly painful. My sister Rosemary, who did most to alleviate my discomfort, treated them with warm water, and I remember to this day the relief when the worst of them burst. It was almost better than collecting shrapnel.

Moves, however, were afoot, and a day of judgment lay ahead. Curiously, my mother released me from my bondage, gave me food in the kitchen, clean clothes; she even brushed my hair and, from time to time, gave me a smile. All this was unprecedented. She also asked me never to forget my 'mum', particularly after all she had done for me.

We were soon on a bus heading for a town the name of which I forget – Romford? Ilford? At a sweetshop I was treated to a rare bag of sweets called, appropriately, 'humbugs'. From there we made our way to an enormous building with what seemed to me doors more suited to giants than an errant schoolboy. There followed a maze of green and cream corridors ending in a large room lined with pews.

I was given to a policeman and my mother was placed on a pew. To my surprise, sitting next to her was Mr Percy. Was this simply a coincidence?

A man whom I took to be the priest wore a wig and a gown and sat between two other seeming clerics – one of whom was a woman. The service began by the priest asking me if I would like to plead 'guilty' or 'not guilty'. I stayed silent until the policeman at my side whispered, 'Own up, son; say guilty.' So I said, 'Guilty.'

The priest then asked my mother and Mr Percy some questions concerning my behaviour at home and at school. Mr Percy answered indirectly, saying, if I remember correctly, that it would have been better had I been strangled at birth. Yet he found a word of praise for my mother, complimenting her on her long sufferance and lauding her ability to bring up so many children without – with one notable exception – aberration.

My mother's statement to the court, as may be imagined, was not wholly in my favour. She more or less confirmed Mr Percy's view and seemed to complement his assault on my character.

Then came the crunch. To my mother I was the devil incarnate. How she had come to give birth to such a walking iniquity she would never know, or so she said.

After some deliberation those in power decided that I should, as a juvenile delinquent, spend two years confined to what was then called a 'Borstal'. In fact, Borstal is a place near Rochester where the first prison expressly for errant youth had been opened in 1902, but by 1940 it had already become the eponym so many would-be-bad boys have attended. And most of my generation will see or hear the name with an emotional shock.

The idea behind the institution was that one should be given a technical or otherwise appropriate education – thus reforming one into becoming a useful and upright member of society. That is: one would, as a result of Borstal training, prefer honest labour to theft

and deceit. One such Borstal, known as Longmoor, was in operation in Harold Wood – not far from my enforced atelier in Station
Road.

The courtly business had not yet ended, and the lady priest (or
magistrate) spoke sternly to me. She said that I would go to 'prison'
for some few months, and that I shouldn't cry.

I sat on a bench next to a boy who had been found guilty of
something more dramatic than my arson, and was impressed by
the fact that the policeman – the one who had apparently been so
kind to me – offered him a cigarette. I was dismayed to note that
the policeman didn't regard me as a grown-up boy. He and the
older boy were soon in deep conversation over a photograph of a
woman which was pulled from the policeman's pocket. 'You won't
see a bit of skirt like that where you're going,' he said.

Being excluded from their conversation I gave myself up to more
profound thoughts. Why, for example, was tea or cocoa less hot
than the rim of an enamel mug? Another policeman entered, bearing two pairs of handcuffs. 'We won't be needing them,' said the
first. 'These two are no trouble.'

We were then escorted from the room into a yard and loaded into
a van resembling it: there were hard benches on either side and
bars at the small windows. The two policemen sat on the benches
and continued the conversation concerning women which had
earlier so fascinated the older boy. 'What,' said one, 'happens when
a WREN goes for a swim on a winter's day?' There was no reply.
'Two blue tits emerge! Ha! Ha! Ha!'

He wore his learning lightly, and after discussing birds for some
time he switched to cooking, and crumpets were discussed. Many
recipes for cooking and eating them were talked about but the finer
details escaped me. I feel certain, however, that Mrs Beeton would
not have approved. I should add that at the court I saw my mother
for the very last time. A poignant moment for most, perhaps, but to
me a relief I have never regretted.

I learned during our drive that Jimmy (the older boy) had been
convicted of stabbing a knife into his uncle's groin. Jimmy explained that the unusual extenuating circumstances were that the
uncle had actually requested the assault. Or in his own words, his
uncle 'had been asking for it'. Later, when I knew Jimmy's distressing story more fully, I realised that the magistrate had been a
shrewd judge of human nature. For Jimmy had felt too humiliated
to tell the court that he had on several occasions been sexually
abused by his uncle. And yet the magistrate must have suspected
something of the sort to have given the seventeen-year-old boy no

more than a few months in a reformatory school for his assault and battery.

Eventually the van driver honked his horn and the gates of Longmoor opened. It is said that architecture speaks, and I imagine that that place, though not vociferous, spoke Edwardian English with a Victorian accent. It had once been a private dwelling, but one hesitates even to imagine its original occupants. No tree or shrub or flower mellowed its bricks or attended its curtainless windows. It possessed the charm of a warehouse (which it resembled).

Our first task was to bathe and exchange our clothes for the reformatory's uniform of grey flannel. Jimmy's body was pearly white and smooth, firm and fit – for the first time I was aware of physical beauty. Quentin Crisp (whom many years later I was to know) refers in one of his books to the penis as being merely part of a plumbing system. But I felt, looking at Jimmy's, feelings totally different from those with which I regarded the taps of our separate baths. And with a splendid indifference to the laws of gravity his penis was pointing to the ceiling.

'What yer starin' at?' he said. 'Ain't yer ever seen a 'ard-on before? Wanna give me a wank?'

Whatever a 'wank' was I knew I couldn't give him one because all my personal effects had been taken away.

'Sorry,' I said, 'but I can't.'

'That's all right. I didn't mean it. You're only a nipper. You probably don't even know what a piece of skirt is.'

I would have complimented him on his perspicacity had we not been interrupted by a master. 'Master' was the euphemism for warder. For although Longmoor was called a reformatory school, little or no schooling actually took place and 'master' therefore doubled as 'warder'.

The directions and exhortations were as monotonous as they were uninventive: 'Get a bloody move on!' 'Move your bloody arses.' It struck me, without a pang, that my mother, had she not been of the gentler sex, would have made an efficient warder.

Our dormitories were not in the main building but had been purposely built, pre-fabricated, and resembled the army barracks that seemed to sprout towards the end of the war.

The army analogy was continued in the bugle call we received for reveille at six o'clock in the morning. This was followed by a compulsory cold shower and the brushing of teeth with a toothpowder called Eucryl. Then we had 'morning prayers' – followed by a speech from the 'headmaster', who would also administer punishment for those caught attempting to escape the previous evening. The punishment took the form of a beating with a traditional birch: a bundle of thin twigs bound together with a leather thong. The 'owlin' of those so beaten put my own laments to shame.

Before breakfast we were occupied in cleaning windows or scrubbing floors already pristine from the previous day's exertion. Breakfast was at eight o'clock, and comprised a bottle of milk and two slices of greyish bread spread thinly with a bright yellow margarine. On Sundays, for no doubt some God-given reason, this fare was augmented with half a boiled egg.

After breakfast we returned to our dormitories for the regular 'morning inspection'. Each putative criminal stood to attention at the foot of his bed, and all his equipment – clothes, shoes, toilette – had to be laid out just so. One of the masters (warders) would then carry out an inspection. The folding of blankets was particularly irksome. If out of range from the prescribed ten inches, and if not complete with 'hospital corners' one was doomed to summary punishment. The warder (master) carried a cane with which he could carry out instant retribution. Should a bar of soap be a millimetre out of line, down would come the cane and up would go the 'owlin'.

After this inspection we were divided into groups or classes. One set would continue with the repetitive chores, which had apparently gone on since time began, while another would be set to peeling potatoes. Yet another would go into the playground and 'exercise' on its cinder surface. A final group would make its way to the schoolroom where there were games – snakes and ladders, Ludo, table tennis, jigsaw puzzles – in abundance, but little of educational value except Bunyan's *Pilgrim's Progress*, which I read avidly, and a history of England which was to have a profound influence on my subsequent career.

This book greatly affected my drawing and posed a problem of perspective that I was to struggle with for years. The book contained a drawing of Sir Francis Drake. I cannot recall who did it, but I was so struck by it that I decided to make a copy. The result was creditable enough but for one detail: the mariner's feet in my copy were not flat on the ground, and to see such a hero precariously balanced on his tip-toes offended even my sense of propriety. After a number of sessions of rubbing out and re-drawing I took what I considered to be the easiest way out. This consisted of drawing a box – made plausible by calling it a sea-chest – and placing it in front of the offending feet (Fig. 3).

Many well-known paintings and drawings might well be improved by such simple means. One that comes to mind is Augustus

Fig. 3: *Portrait of Sir Francis Drake*

John's mural in the Tate Gallery, *A Summer Idyll*. This contains a number of charming gypsy characters, many with apparently un-anchored limbs. I half-seriously suggest that the trustees commission me to paint in some carefully placed sea-chests or bales of straw – I'm always open to suggestions.

Now I am going to tell the story of Eric and Jimmy. Ever since Gilgamesh and Enkidu, David and Jonathan, Achilles and Patroclus, there have been grand tales of friendship between men. Boys whose parents can afford the fees for 'public' (elsewhere 'private') schools come – or came, as it were – early to these heroic stories, and tend (or tended) to see such relationships as made of noble stuff. It is hard for me to accept, even in retrospect, such an idealisation. Longmoor, though its library included such gems as *The Water Babies*, was short on the sort of literary material which might well have made my slide into the adult world a little easier. True, some of the comics in the library alluded to friendship. I am thinking of *Lord Snooty and his Pals* – a seminal creation for those of my generation. But one might look in vain for hints of high-minded hanky-panky.

My own sexuality was in a confused state. I could appreciate that women ('ladies') could be beautiful – art told me that. But the fact is, that like most other children of my time, I had no official sex education. Furthermore the era was still suffering from the Victorian repression of homosexuality (repressed, significantly, by the homosexuals themselves of that lengthy era). Disraeli described school friendship thus:

> At school, friendship is a passion. It entrances, it tears the soul. All loves of after-life can never bring its rapture, or its wretchedness; no bliss is so absorbing, no pangs of jealousy or despair so crushing and so keen! What tenderness and what devotion; what illimitable confidence; infinite revelations of inmost thoughts; what ecstatic present and romantic future; what bitter estrangement and what melting recon-ciliations; what scenes of wild recriminations, agitating explanations, passionate correspondence; what insane sensitiveness, and what frantic sensibility; what earthquakes of the heart and whirlwinds of the soul are confined in that simple phrase, a schoolboy's friendship!

What a lot of 'what's! And yet how true. It is obvious that Disraeli went to a better school than Longmoor. And no doubt it was a school where 'little pretty white-handed, curly-haired boys . . . petted and pampered by some of the big fellows', received their extra-curricular sexual education.

It is my experience, however, that *Le Paradis des amours enfantins* is known to 'young criminals' in penal institutions as well as it is known to young gentlemen at Eton or Harrow: boys without girls will seek boys – expressing feelings which in different circumstances might have been given to members of the opposite sex.

Perhaps so, but I still do not know what these things had to do with seeing Jimmy naked. I know that the effect of that sight caused me to dream of him. I was still incapable of an erection and yet I grew so fond of Jimmy that I would become miserable if I didn't see him at least once during the day.

Although older than I, he was illiterate and my admiration got him interested in reading and writing. We would sit side-by-side and I would coach his hand in the right direction.

I did not want him to think of me as a sissy, and as I found none of the other boys attractive this was no difficulty. It must also have been, even at that age, a manifestation of true love, because – sweets apart – I would have given him anything, even my premature life.

Jimmy, in his own way, returned my affection and would occasionally even put his arms around me and say that I was 'nice', and that if I had a fault it was that I wasn't a 'piece of skirt'.

One night, towards the end of my stay at Longmoor, he crept into my bed. I was in that drowsy state between sleep and wakefulness when I felt Jimmy's hand upon my mouth and heard him whisper, 'Be quiet'. There was a different smell about him and he breathed heavily upon my neck and made sudden, urgent, thrusting movements against my body. I tried to free myself from his grip. He pulled down my pyjamas. Frightened by the energy of his passion I consoled myself with the thought that this attacker was my very best friend, Jimmy, and not a nightmare. When he'd finished, he apologised, and said he hadn't wanted to hurt me, and that he would 'make up for it'.

Although I loved him still, I somehow loved him less. No one, not even Longmoor, was to blame. One day I would love again with the same intensity as I loved Jimmy. But long before that could happen, the difficult and often despairing days of my childhood would have to end.

CHAPTER II

THE DEATH OF BILLY BUCKLE AND OTHER TALES

Eric has developed into a quick very willing lad. He is keenly interested in dramatics, athletics and physical training. His attainment
in art is of a high standard. I have found him honest and trustworthy.

A. V. Horner (Headmaster of Maldon Secondary School – in a school
report for 1949)

After a year of schooling at Longmoor I was judged to be sufficiently reformed to be set free on probation and was sent by the
Essex County Council to live with foster parents in a charming
little town, once a fishing village, called Maldon.

To the average educated English person Maldon's name brings
to mind the *Battle of Maldon* – a famous old poem which gives an
account of a battle fought between Danes and Saxons on the town's
hill. But how many know that Maldon, which had long since
slipped from the front pages of history, rose again to prominence in
the nineteenth century, this time as the birthplace of an illustrious
British artist named John Rogers Herbert? Never heard of him?
Ah, how fickle is fame! And yet Herbert was in his day mentioned
in the same breath as Reynolds, Lawrence, West, Turner, Landseer, Wilkie (they drew long breaths in Herbert's day), Gainsborough, Copley and Stothard; not to mention Owen, Thomson
and Pickersgill. I quote John Sherer, the editor of *The Gallery of
British Artists*, London, *circa* 1890:

John Rogers Herbert was, in 1810, born at Malden (sic) in Essex. He
became a student in the Royal Academy; and having passed through
the various branches of practical study pursued in that institution, he
set himself up as a portrait painter, and for some years followed this
department of his profession. In 1835, however, he exhibited in the
Academy a picture entitled 'Prayer'; but it did not attract much

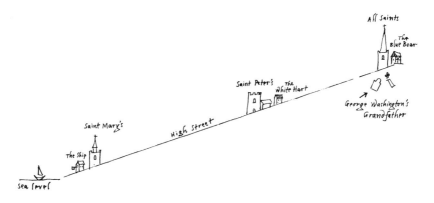

Fig. 5: *Spires of Maldon.* Diagram representing the elevation of the principal monuments in the ancient town of Maldon on the river Blackwater in Essex. Professor Fulldim attributes this drawing to the author, and points out the similarity between the treatment of Saint Mary's and the undoubtedly authentic drawing of the church in Fig. 4

forty years of my absence, but it was quite clear to me as a boy that Maldon's hill was bewitched: and the situation was totally unlike that of the noble Duke of York's ten thousand men, for when one was up one was down, and when one was down one was up, and when one was only halfway up one was really halfway down.

Naturally, Maldon's High Street contained more than pubs and churches. Squeezed in between them were to be found a handsome town hall with a fine clock sticking out over the street, a Woolworth store, an Odeon cinema which boasted a Wurlitzer organ, stationers, butchers, bakers, and in the place of the candlestick makers of yore, the establishments of Madam V. Tunbridge, Milliner, and her husband John H. Tunbridge, Gentleman's Outfitter, outside of which houses of fashion we shall not linger. Instead, I invite the reader to follow me down/up a turning off High Street on the left called Wantz Road. It is a bitterly cold evening in the year 1941. Halfway along Wantz Road we turn into an alley of frozen puddles, and then again into a sizeable yard, in the centre of which, on a bandaged pipe, is a tap dripping icicles. The wintry air is delicately perfumed with the smell of freshly baked cakes; following our noses, we press them against a tiny window through which we can see in the mellow light of a gas lamp a little old woman greasing a baking tin. Her blind, and even older, husband sits beside a cheerful coal fire which heats a tin oven above it. Eyeing a batch of cooling cakes with more than casual interest is a grubby boy of about eleven. He is sitting at a table which, although of no great size, occupies almost a quarter of the cosy, if shabby, interior. Without unduly straining our ears or our consciences, we eavesdrop and overhear the following dialogue:

Old Woman: ''E oughta be 'ere bar nar.'

Old Man (with feeling): ''E'll be froze ter the marrer 'e will, poor little bugger.'

Old Woman: 'You ol sinner you! 'Ow many times do I 'av to tell yer not ter use them there words in this 'ere 'ouse. I'll wash yer marf out wiv carbolic if yer ain't 'arf careful.'

Grubby Boy: 'Can I 'av a cake nar?'

Old Woman: 'No yer bloomin can't! Keep your bloomin 'ans off till 'e's 'ere!'

Although I am absolutely certain that such a scene really did take place, I was not there to see it. The grubby boy was Ron. I was the awaited ''e' who, while the cakes were being baked, was being motored by a probation officer at top speed – probably as much as twenty miles an hour – from Longmoor towards them; being as it were their destiny.

Ron and I were known as 'Council Boys'. This is because the council gave Mr and Mrs Buckle a pittance for our maintenance; and never did so little money provide so much discomfort. Not for us – Mrs Buckle did wonders, and we were looked after far better than we deserved. No, the discomfort was for our neighbours. Ron and I were a formidable combination of naughtiness, if that is not too mild a term; our forces joined for the purpose of making as much nuisance of ourselves in the neighbourhood as possible without Mrs Buckle finding out about it. At home we took every care to be models of obedience and helpfulness. We cheerfully ran errands, washed dishes and helped with the housework. We even learned to darn our socks and mend our shoes. And we vied with each other in politeness of the 'Hafter you, Herrick', 'No, hafter you, Ron' variety. All these things led our foster parents to believe that they were housing two little angels. Thus, should an irate neighbour come to call bearing complaints of let us say a broken window, not an uncommon occurrence at the time, Mrs Buckle would defend us stoutly, saying in astonishment something like: 'What my little Ron and Herrick do a wicked fing like that! Not on your bloomin life they wouldn't. Don't you come 'ere casting no "nasturtions".'

When Ron reached his fifteenth year he was the inordinately proud owner of 'long 'uns'. That is to say he wore trousers that reached down to his boots, whereas my own hose, as his before, scarcely covered my knees. Unfortunately, the increase in the length of his trousers had a number of alarming side effects. His voice deepened, fluff began to sprout on his cheeks, he was forever combing his hair which he smeared down with Brylcream, and he grew noticeably less grubby. This last because he was given to the madness of washing himself under the tap in the yard even without being told to do so. But most alarming of all was his shift in interest from the footballers on his cigarette cards to a girl of his own age, whose real name I have forgotten but whom I shall call by the not altogether improbable one of Mary.

All boys have a girl next door and Mary was ours. Like Mrs Mills she lived either to our right or to our left, whichever the reader prefers. In the good old days there was nothing that Ron liked better than to tear the limbs off Mary's dolls, pull her pigtails, steal her lollipop or indulge in some other not over-subtle tear-inducing stratagem; but now he was no fun at all. He was under one of Maldon's spells and went about in a kind of trance from which he emerged only in her sight.

One day he commissioned me to draw the likeness of Mary in pencil, full length, in the nude, and showing 'everyfing'. The terms of the commission posed a problem – I had never seen 'everyfing'. Here Ron proved to be both an understanding and resourceful patron. What he proposed was that we ask another young lady of our acquaintance, a 'tomboy' called Jean if she would be so kind as to show me her 'everyfing' which we assumed would closely resemble Mary's in its broadest outlines. The suggestion was made to Jean on a lonely stretch of the seawall; as she was not at all keen on the idea, she took flight, hotly pursued by artist and patron. Catching up with her, Ron lifted up her dress over her head, and I pulled down her knickers. What a shock! No wonder poor Jean had been reluctant to co-operate. Instead of the expected 'everyfing' I saw 'nuffing', absolutely 'nuffing'. Unless, of course, one calls a miserable little slit for peeing through something. Thoroughly dejected by the uninspiring sight, I was about to abandon the commission, when Ron again showed his resourcefulness, suggesting that I drew Jean's slit on Mary's full length portrait and then decorated it with a 'hartistic' border of hair. Happy with this solution, I set to work and much to my patron's satisfaction, I completed Mary's portrait in time for him to peruse that very evening in bed. The matter did not, however, end there.

The twentieth century had caught up with the yard. Each of the four rooms of our cottage now had a five-watt light bulb, and a welfare worker had installed a wireless. Although principally for the benefit of Mr Buckle, I would eagerly run home from school to listen to a radio programme called *Dick Barton, Special Agent*. Dick was a detective with two assistants: a Cockney called Snowey and a Scotsman called Jock. At precisely a quarter to seven every evening, except for Sundays, Dick, Snowey and Jock would escape some perilous situation such as hanging over a cliff by their fingertips on which a crook happened to be stomping, and at precisely seven o'clock they would have managed to get themselves into another potentially fatal predicament – perhaps bound and gagged in a cellar which is being slowly filled with water and is already up to their chins. Together with thousands of other children, I would be left for a whole day in agonising suspense wondering how on earth the three heroes could possibly escape this time. One memorable evening, not long after the taking of Mary's likeness, Mrs Buckle, knowing when to expect me home for *Dick Barton* stationed herself outside the kitchen door. She stood with arms akimbo to accost me with: 'I've called the police. They'll be 'ere any minute nar; better pack yer fings an go quietly; I wouldn't be surprised if this ain't an 'anging matter. Not that 'anging ain't too good for some people as I knows.'

'What's up now?' I asked innocently.

'What's up now?' mimicked Mrs Buckle. 'What's up now? says 'e as if bloomin butter wouldn't melt in is bloomin mouf. I spose you don't know nuffing about this 'ere filf do yer?'

My foster mother produced from her apron pocket the likeness of a naked Mary which she had discovered in Ron's bed. In spite of the misleading provenance and the poor condition of the drawing, which was by now grubby, torn, and crumpled, with considerable rubbing and vigorous reinforcing of the pubic hair by a later hand, Mrs Buckle had not been deceived as to who the draughtsman was. There was no signature or inscription to guide her, no reference books or experts at hand to consult, and yet the speed and certainty with which she came up with the correct attribution to Herrick would have been worthy of Bernard Berenson.

'So this is what they learn yer at school! Yer ain't never seen me like that, yer aint!' asserted my angry foster mother. At which I was ungallant enough to secretly praise the Lord.

The police were unaccountably delayed, and I was sent without supper to await their arrival in bed. Ah, the things I haven't sacrificed for art! Even now, I sometimes find myself wondering how Dick, Snowey and Jock escaped with their lives that evening, bound as they were to chairs under which sticks of dynamite with lighted fuses had been placed.

After Longmoor my education continued, first at Maldon's Junior

School and then, after failing my Eleven Plus, at Maldon's Secondary School. My school report for the academic year ending in June 1948 has, by some miracle, survived, and tells me that I came top of the class in English as well as in art. But it is not, however, to draw undue attention to my early academic achievements that I mention this particular school report, but rather because it contains my first essay in the diabolical art of deception.

These reports were given to the pupils to take home for the perusal of their parents or guardians who would append a signature as proof of them having actually seen it. As a poor report from school might get a boy into trouble at home it was not unknown for pupils to keep their report to themselves and imitate a parent's or guardian's signature, and this is what I did with Mrs Buckle's. This was not because I was ashamed of my report, although five out of a hundred for maths is not exactly brilliant – but because in that year, for reasons I shall speak of below, my guardian was in no condition to be worried by such trivia. A comparison of my hesitant scratchy effort compared with the bold sweep of Mrs Buckle's copperplate shows how far I had to go before I would later write attributions and even lengthy inscriptions on 'old masters' in the hand writing of distinguished artists and collectors such as Vasari, Reynolds, and the Richardsons, most of which still remain undetected in the great museums of the world. But as the Chinese philosopher says, 'A journey of a thousand miles begins with the first step,' and Mrs Buckle's signature was mine (Fig. 6).

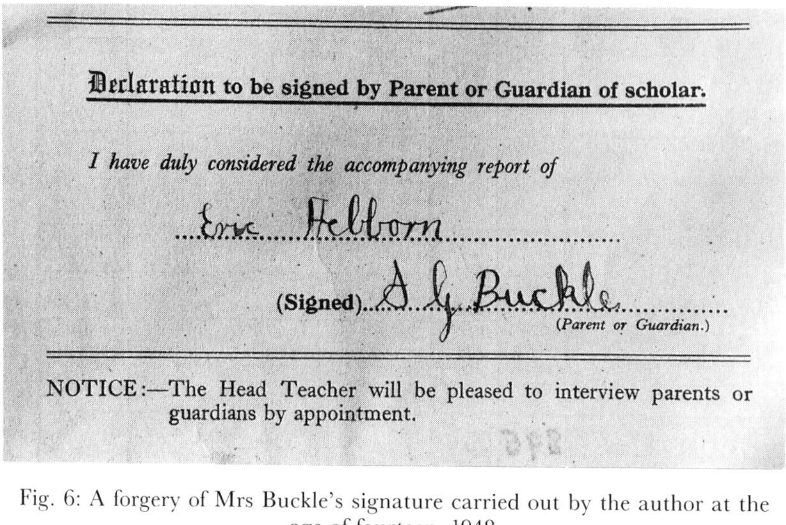

Declaration to be signed by Parent or Guardian of scholar.

I have duly considered the accompanying report of

Eric Hebborn

(Signed) A. G. Buckle
(Parent or Guardian.)

NOTICE:—The Head Teacher will be pleased to interview parents or guardians by appointment.

Fig. 6: A forgery of Mrs Buckle's signature carried out by the author at the age of fourteen, 1948

The art master at Maldon's Secondary School was a Mr Tait, and a very good art master he was. He possessed the two essential qualities of all good teachers – enthusiasm and the ability to convey it to others. A landscape painter with an eye for a view and a vigorous manner in both oil and watercolour, Mr Tait was an indefatigable worker and would be out and about in all seasons painting *en plein air* or, as we English say, more prosaically, 'on the spot'.

On many an occasion he let me go with him. Perhaps it would be more truthful to say that he failed to stop me from going with him. I would waylay him as he left his house and would plead along these lines: 'Please Sir, can I carry yer sketchin fings Sir; go on Sir, be a sport Sir.' If he had not planned to meet his fiancée somewhere *en route*, he would sigh, not exactly a lover's sigh, and say: 'Oh, all right.' No squire of old ever carried the arms of his knight more proudly than I would carry Mr Tait's paint box and easel to the selected view. Once there, the easel set up and the palette laid, my teacher would go through the strangest antics: screw up his eyes, make 'L' shapes with his thumbs and forefingers, pretend to attack the view with dry paintbrushes, stand with his back to the subject, and bend down to view it through his parted legs. On being questioned about the last part of his curious behaviour, Mr Tait would say that it helped him to see the landscape in a 'fresh' way, but when I tried it myself, I saw the landscape in the same old way but upside down, which made drawing it even harder. Results are, however, what count, and in about two hours Mr Tait had conjured up on his canvas what I considered the 'spittin' image' of the scene before him.

In the early summer of 1949 the following article appeared in *The Essex Chronicle*:

15, HAS PAINTING IN EXHIBITION

Among the hundreds of exhibits of landscapes, portraits and other forms of art exhibited by local artists at the Friends Meeting House this week are several which are the work of 15-year-old Eric Hebborn of Wantz Road, Maldon.

Eric, a keen and promising artist at present at Maldon Secondary School, is too young to be a member of Maldon Art Club, but because of his skill and enthusiasm he is permitted to take part in its activities and meetings in an Honorary capacity. He has been accepted by and will commence studies at the Chelmsford Art School in September.

This is the third exhibition of drawings and paintings held by the club, and was opened on Saturday by the Mayoress.

The club's tutor and chairman (Mr. W. A. Cuthbertson) presided, and the exhibition included pen and ink, pencil and pastel drawings, watercolours and oils.

It was Mr Tait who introduced me to the Maldon Art Club. Members of the club met once a week in a building belonging to the Quakers and called, naturally, the Friends Meeting House. It was a modest building, something like a small church or chapel except that it lacked the trimmings of the kind to be found in All Saints' or Saint Mary's. No candlesticks, sculptures, paintings, candles and so forth. Everything was of the simplest materials, and in the place of pews were straight-backed wooden chairs. On Thursday evenings one chair was placed in the middle of the room for a model to sit on, and at a distance of about ten feet, two circles of chairs were set up around it. The backs of the chairs of the inner circle were used for the members to rest their drawing boards on, while they themselves sat on the chairs of the outer ring. The model was clothed, and the meeting took the form of a portrait drawing class.

The teacher was the club's president, Mr Cuthbertson. His method was the traditional one of going from one student to the next, pointing out failures in observation, saying such things as 'Ye're a wee bit too short here' or 'Ye're a wee bit too long there'. The problem is that we 'Sassenachs' have invented for our amusement a type of Scotsman to which Mr Cuthbertson in a sense approached – he was careful about money. I do not mean by this that he was avaricious, or stingy. Nobody could have been less greedy, and no one knows better than myself how generous he was with his time. But it cannot be denied that in money matters he was, as I have implied, careful; and this carefulness gave to Mr Cuthbertson a unique approach to the craft of painting.

Members were always welcome to bring to the drawing class any painting they may have produced at home for his criticism and guidance, and when they did so, they learnt things of a most practical nature. Their first lesson would begin with being given the address of an artist's colourman in Longacre, London, called Corneillison and Son, where one only had to mention Willy Cuthbertson's name to get a 'wee discount'. This would be followed by an eulogy on the virtues of the earth colours. We all know how beautiful the earth colours are: the glowing ochres, the radiant siennas, and noble umbers that have been the backbone of classical painting from the cave painters to Braque. As venerable as time itself, as stable as the ground we stand on, their very names evoking the history and romance of the places where they are excavated: Venetian red, Naples yellow, Roman ochre – of all colours the most aristocratic. But how many of us have stopped to consider with Mr Cuthbertson, that of all colours, the earths are the cheapest? In the days before everything an artist happened to use was considered a

Fig. 7: *Beleigh Lockgates, Maldon*, 1957, oil on canvas

luxury item and taxed accordingly, the earths were as cheap as their humble relation, dirt. Then what a bonnie bonus their beauty was!

My early master would continue by speaking of a number of sacrifices that the careful painter will make for the good of his pocket without detriment to his picture. I need give only one example: turpentine. Pure turpentine brings with it into the studio the pleasant invigorating perfume of the pine woods from where it comes. The canny artist will, however, shun this self-indulgence and accustom himself to the less costly odours of paraffin, which will dilute his paints and clean his brushes equally well at a fraction of the cost.

Mr Cuthbertson was a stickler for a good likeness, and I know it would have warmed his Highland heart to learn that the facility gained from his insistence in this respect has earned me more than enough to indulge myself in just a wee drop of turpentine from time to time.

At fifteen, I was far and away the youngest member of the Art

41

Fig. 8: *Self-portrait, aged fifteen*, 1949, oil on board (Collection of the artist)

Club, just as a very skilful artist who had made drawings for the *Illustrated London News* on the battlefields of the Boer War, a Mr Kemptebby, was, at eighty-five, far and away the oldest.

Strictly speaking, like Churchill, who was an Honorary Member of the Academy, I was an Honorary Member of Maldon's Art Club. I paid no fees, and became, as it were, the club's mascot. The kindness with which I was treated made the hours spent in the Friends Meeting House some of the happiest in my life. Mr Cuthbertson gave me every encouragement and even invited me to take my work to him at his home for advice, where he could devote more time to teaching me. And so it was, a self-portrait (Fig. 8) in hand, that I found myself one spring morning in the boatyard where my teacher and his wife lived on a converted motor launch. Their vessel was named *Grace II*, Mrs Cuthbertson herself being *Grace I*. To board the boat I had to walk across a precarious cat-walk constructed of loosely connected planks supported by tall slimy posts. The tide was out and I zig-zagged my way high above what an old lady friend of mine would have termed the black mud's 'naughty' smell, inhaling a more wholesome breeze coming from the open sea. *Grace II* was about thirty feet long, had been built for the Royal Navy, and was captained during the First World War by its present owner. She had seen action again in the Second World War when Mr Cuthbertson courageously sailed her, single-handed, across the Channel to take part in the famous rescue operation from the beaches of Dunkirk. Now she never left her moorings, and con-fined her movements to rising and falling with the tide.

Mr Cuthbertson was on deck, dressed in a paint-splattered over-all of blue denim, holding a spatula. He was not working on a painting, but on *Grace II* herself.

'Come aboard, shipmate,' he welcomed, and then called down the hatchway leading to the galley, 'Grace, wee Eric's here.'

'Good morning, Eric dear,' said Mrs Cuthbertson as her head and shoulders appeared on deck. Over sixty, she was still a hand-some woman with a fine carriage; she held her head high and pre-sented herself to the world in perpetual profile. Those familiar with Augustus John's portrait of Madame Suggia in the Tate will under-stand the sort of bearing I mean.

'Come along in, I've just made coffee,' she continued. 'You too, Willy darling. You mustn't overdo things, you know what the doc-tor said.' Adding, in a whispered aside to myself: 'Heart trouble, Eric, heart trouble. Please don't tire the poor darling, will you?'

The old sailor-artist and his young pupil did not, however, go down to the galley at once, but stood in silence to look about them, as united in what they saw as a duo of musicians in what they could hear. They were surrounded by a host of sailing craft, great and small, from the black Thames barges of hefty tonnage to little cheerfully painted single-masted hulls that a strong man might conceivably carry on his shoulder. All these boats had flopped at different angles in the cradling mud, and where they lay the thickest, they created a forest of masts. Then, suddenly, Maldon cast another of its spells. Legions of dense purple thundered across the delicate wash of sky. The morning's silver trembled and its gold fled. Rudely awakened boats bristled in a silhouette of oaken spears, as distant incoming waters glared and glittered, and a metal ruler drew a horizon of frozen steel.

'The Surrender of Breda,' murmured Mr Cuthbertson as though reluctant to intrude his voice upon the scene.

Presently we joined Mrs Cuthbertson below deck, and her husband explained to me what he had meant. He opened a monograph at a reproduction of Velázquez's masterpiece, and there stood the spears against the sky just as we had seen them a few minutes before – but now organised into art.

This was the first of many times that I sat in the cramped space of the galley, with its fitted copal-varnished furniture bolted to the deck, and its two small portholes – one casting shadows from the port side and one from starboard to join in a central area of gloom. We sipped strong, freshly brewed coffee, the aroma of which was as palpable a presence as ourselves, and talked, and talked about art. Or, rather, my hosts talked and talked about art, and 'illustrated' what they had to say with pictures, books and artefacts they had on board. Nor were they lacking in examples. Even our severely restricted area contained innumerable objects: ushabti figures from Egypt, terracotta figurines from Tanagra, an African mask and many other exotic things from all times and parts, all jumbled together with the down-to-earth pots and pans of the gentle old couple's existence. From where I sat I could see into the boat's largest cabin. It was impossible to see how large because it was so packed with things that it looked as if one could not even enter it, let alone pace its length. From time to time the Cuthbertsons would somehow manage to disappear among the piles of things as if they had been sucked into them and totally absorbed – to emerge clasping some treasured object. They knew where everything was and the disorder was only apparent.

Many of their possessions were of real artistic value and some of them, even then, of considerable monetary value. They owned, for instance, a thick album of original photographs by Lewis Carroll, with inscriptions in the photographer's own hand. They also possessed a series of drawings by Capability Brown, and a collection of etchings by Rembrandt – all good impressions in early states. These were kept between tissue paper in a box, wrapped in oil cloth, and tied with knots that only a sailor could tie or loosen. In the same box as the Rembrandts were etchings by James McBey. This was a reflection of Mr Cuthbertson's conviction that the Scottish etcher was 'right up alongside' the great Dutch artist.

Clearly my hosts had known better days, and the reason for their present genteel poverty lay in a black and gold deed box that would from time to time be opened with some ceremony to reveal a sheaf of shares in a privately owned railway company which, with nationalisation, had become totally worthless. Why the Cuthbertsons held on to those useless pages I didn't know, for even those unworldly people could not have entertained any hope of their regaining value.

After the coffee cups had been cleared, Mr Cuthbertson asked me to show him my self-portrait. He held it close to the porthole and after saying, 'It's nay sa bad', began to give a constructive criticism of the kind that is as useful as it is rare. He pointed out errors of construction, the coarsely drawn ear, the lack of form given to the hair, and went on to speak of the quality of the paint; that is to say, how the paint had been handled. 'It looks as if ye're a hoosepainter,' he said, referring to the flat uninteresting way I had treated the background. 'The trouble is ye're still a wee laddie and never seen a bonnie portrait.' This was certainly true. I had never been to a picture gallery, and knew great paintings only from reproductions, which in the forties were unreliable. Even today there is no way of reproducing a painting that can truly convey the quality of its handling. This is mainly because the quality I am speaking of is a tactile one – one that cannot be captured by optical means alone. It depends on a variety of touch and texture, impasto, scumbling, and glazed transparencies, all of which are painterly qualities.

At this point Mr Cuthbertson told me of his own training. How as a young man he had studied at the Royal Academy in Scotland, where he won a travelling scholarship to Spain to study his favourite painter, Velázquez, from the originals in the Prado. His method of studying was the time-honoured one of making copies. On one occasion he set up his easel before Velázquez's *Infanta* and, using the dateless earths with such touches of the more expensive colours as were necessary, he made a thorough study of it.

My host disappeared for a few minutes into the densely packed regions of the main cabin and brought his copy out to show me. It was brilliant. I thought so then when I saw it for the first time, and I thought so when I saw it again recently. It was a coloured photograph occupying an entire page of one of those prestigious art magazines which consist of a thinly spread layer of learning sandwiched between two thumping great slices of publicity. Willy Cuthbertson's copy of the Velázquez had gone up in the world – it was now by Manet; or at least it bore the question 'Is this the lost Manet?'

The painting had been the subject of a book called *The Infanta and the Lost Manet* by Andrew Brainerd, a lawyer who had bought the picture in 1967. The book includes a foreword by Albert Boimé, an art historian, and a report by Walter McCrone, a scientist. According to the publishers it was printed from 'the manuscript no university press dared print for fear of academic reprisal'. It

> details a lawyer's and a scientist's inquiry into the authorship of an unsigned, aged portrait of a little girl, the most famous secular girl subject in the history of art. Here logic, science and probability theory challenge the often arrogant mystique and the *intuitive* foundations of traditional authentication practice, raising fundamental questions of objective, intellectual integrity of very great relevance to the intelligence-orientated and financially involved segments of the international art community.

It was, so the blurb continued, 'Important reading in an explosive, jealously protected area.' How the old Scotsman would have chuckled! But the reader may well wonder how, after the passage of so many years I can remember a copy of a much copied picture with sufficient clarity to feel certain that the 'Manet' copy is one and the same as Mr Cuthbertson's. To be quite honest, I doubt whether I would be sure, if it were not for a minute detail that the painter pointed out to me as a lesson in craftsmanship. Mr Cuthbertson explained to me that for reasons of economy he had prepared the ground for his copy of the *Infanta* himself, and, as is customary, he had first laid on a coat of glue to prevent subsequent 'sinking' of the colours. Being keen to get on with the work, he had made the mistake of drying this glue in the fierce Spanish sun. Glue, my teacher warned, if dried out too rapidly becomes brittle and causes a premature, and very distinctive kind of cracking to the picture surface. He pointed to such cracks in his copy of Velázquez and said that in his opinion those crossing the Infanta's face were disturbing and he had thought of touching them out. Then he showed me a crack on the forehead which he had rather clumsily retouched. The fresh paint had not filled the crack but had gone over the edge slightly on either side. Finding this more disturbing than the crack itself, Mr Cuthbertson had decided to go no further with the touching out. It was the single retouched crack, plainly visible in the magazine reproduction, between the Infanta's brows that convinced me that I was not looking at a possible Manet, but a certain Cuthbertson.

When on that spring day over forty years ago, I came to take my leave of Mr and Mrs Cuthbertson on the deck of *Grace II*, my teacher looked again at the masts of the surrounding boats and said, not without melancholy, that he had often thought of painting a picture of them. One day he would get round to it, and try to give it some of the formal virtues of his beloved Velázquez. Until then . . .? Well, there was scraping, repainting, caulking, tarring, and a host of other chores if *Grace II* was to remain buoyant.

Somehow I knew the dream picture would never be painted. What I did not know then, however, was that metaphorically speaking every artist, including myself, has a boat of some kind to keep afloat, and painting pictures seldom does it for them.

For two weeks of every summer the Maldon Art Club held an exhibition. The Friends Meeting House was cleared of chairs, tidied and swept and its walls were filled with members' work. The paintings shown were extremely varied both in size and quality, the larger ones not always being the best.

One year exhibited with the pictures was a collection of hand-potted tableware created by Pamela Diamand, the daughter of the art critic Roger Fry, and it was through this exhibit that I got to know her. Pamela had difficulty in finding transport for her pieces from her home in Heybridge, a short way out of Maldon, and I agreed to run along and collect them, and run I did.

I was proud of my strength and energy and, as nobody had told me to conserve them or channel them in different directions perhaps, I ran up High Street, turned right at St Peters and ran down Cromwell Hill, which is so steep that, as my body gained momentum, I feared I might move too fast for my feet and roll head over heels to the bottom. Fortunately this did not happen and once safely at the bottom I ran across a bridge that spanned the Blackwater. Leaving Maldon behind, I raced the mile and half to Heybridge where I stopped to catch my breath and look at the water mill that I had sketched in the company of Mr Tait. There on the bank and there in the flood stood a tree of light, gently moving against the sky. Reflections of cloud hurried along with the current down stream. In the glassy green pond the surrounding willows met in the depths of the water, and made a new world. Looking down into the limpid quiet, where the familiar mill was now so alien, my eyes saw beyond those mysterious glades of blurred replicas and impossible perspectives. No Hylas was to be charmed into the green silence, nor any Excalibur to be raised above the mere, yet there was magic in those reflections; and looking down into the mill pond I realised that as far as the limits of the finite allow, it was a mirror of the infinite, a shadow of eternity. The sketch I had made of the mill was in oil and showed it reflected in exact mirror image. It was at that very moment hanging, the right way up, in the Friends Meeting House. There were advantages to being on the hanging committee.

In spite of a factory called Critalls which manufactured steel window frames, Heybridge was still little more than a hamlet and there was a strong atmosphere of being really and truly in the countryside. And the countryside that one felt oneself to be really and truly in was that most English of English countrysides known as Constable country. Strictly speaking, Constable country is on the border between East Anglia and Suffolk, but one could not look upon Heybridge Mill across the mill pond without thinking of Constable's paintings, the *Haywain*, *Glebe Farm*, *Boys Fishing on the Stour*, and many others. Here was 'the sound of water escaping from mill-dams, old rotten planks, shining posts and brickwork' – those scenes that Constable had said made him a painter, and for which he was grateful.

Separated from the mill pond by water meadows was what, since memory fails me, I shall call Mill House, the home of Pamela Diamand. To me, Mill House was large and had enormous white gates which one only had to pass through to leave Constable's England, and enter into Monet's France. France of the Impressionists, where in a world of dappled sunlight, tinkling water, and the smell of jasmine, was a real live French artist, complete with beard, bow tie, and smock. He was a handsome man with all the charm of his race.

'Good morning,' he said putting the accent on the 'ing' in the best Maurice Chevalier manner.

'You're the *garçon* for Pamela's pots, aren't you? Pamela, *le garçon est arrivé pour porter tes céramiques à l'exposition.*' At this his wife emerged from behind a clump of ivy. Over forty, with grey untidy hair, covered from head to foot with mud and laughing, she said something in French that I did not, of course, understand, but perhaps it was something like: '*Mon Dieu, je suis en un état épouvantable, et juste alors qu'un de mes jeunes ensorcelants admirateurs vient me rendre visite.*'

In any case it made Monsieur Diamand laugh as well, and still laughing, he himself dived into another clump of ivy. I discovered later that the ivy bushes concealed the entrances of their respective studios; hers contained bins of clay, a kick-wheel and a kiln, but his?

'You're Eric, aren't you? Mr Cuthbertson has told me all about you. You look as if you could do with a little refreshment. I'll just put on the kettle and while the water boils we can look at the house.' She sat me in a wicker chair and went indoors. When she returned she had removed her overalls, washed her hands and face and was wearing a floppy straw hat.

It was a Georgian house, simple and charming, with nothing of the Cuthbertsons' clutter about it. The whitewashed walls would have told a more travelled person than myself that we were still in France; what was on the walls, to a more cultured person, made it seem like a part of France inhabited by foreigners from Bloomsbury. Among the well-spaced paintings was a charming portrait by Duncan Grant of my guide as a young girl, sitting in the sunlit garden, a number of still-lifes by Vanessa Bell and landscapes by Roger Fry. The *Anglais* had also painted the panels of the doors and window shutters with bottles, apples, guitars, headlines of French newspapers and harlequins, all in the most discreet colours.

Exhibited on the walls of the stairway was a series of drawings of European architectural views made by Roger Fry, and the entire space of a bedroom was given over as a store-room for the pictures which lacked wall space. Most of these were also the work of Roger Fry. I remember one with particular clarity: it was a portrait of the artist's mother, Lady Fry, painted full-length, seated and toying with the idea of turning herself Cubist. Years later I was to see Rembrandt's moving portraits of his mother, Whistler's exquisitely tender treatment of the same theme, and the no less touching *Artist's Mother* by Van Gogh (proving that photographs can serve as the basis for good as well as for bad paintings), but Roger Fry's picture had none of the humanity of these great works. Dry, hard, unsympathetic, it was, in short, totally intellectual, and for that reason exactly what I needed as an antidote to the undisciplined, excessively romantic, and all too often sentimental paintings to which I was accustomed.

Pamela Diamand was wonderfully kind to her grubby little visitor. She served me tea with cakes on the lawn, and eagerly showed me her father's notebooks and sketchbooks. As I have said, I knew nothing about the Bloomsbury Group. Indeed, there had been nothing whatsoever in my background to prepare me for this cultural encounter, and yet there was something about this slight middle-aged lady in her flowing summer dress and floppy straw hat, something so charming, so eager, I felt I could never tire of looking at her treasures. Perhaps it was because they meant so much to her that they began to mean something to me.

Roger Fry had died in the year of my birth and yet I swear that he was alive on that lawn. His daughter brought the spirit of the dead man to have tea, and for half an hour we sat in the company of one who had passed beyond death. I could smell the clean dusty smell of his old tweed jacket with leather patches on the elbows and edgings on the cuffs and look into the blue of an intelligence stripped of eyes. Freed as he was from time and flesh, I knew him in youth, as a frail energetic mixture of artist and scholar visiting re-mote churches of difficult access to study the then almost totally neglected Italian 'primitives'. Somewhere he might easily have en-countered an unknown American of his own age, called Berenson, also scribbling notes. I saw him in middle-aged maturity as a man capable of love and devotion beyond the ordinary measure and in-spiring them in others. I saw him writing a lecture on his knees while waiting for the train to take him to where he would speak within the next two hours. A man who, like Socrates or Leonardo, preferred eternal questions to temporary answers. A man who had dreamt of a time to come when the artist might again play a practi-cal role in society.

Mrs Diamand's tea party was a far cry from Herrick's usual intellectual fare and it gave him mental indigestion for years, but it also whetted his appetite and strengthened his stomach for feasts to come.

Monsieur Diamand did not really join us for tea, but would, as the whim took him, suddenly emerge in his French artist's uniform from the ivy bush to dash to the table, grab a cake or 'gulp' down a drop of tea, and then, just as suddenly, dive back. From behind the ivy bush he produced a clattering noise, and this, his wife explained, was the noise of a printing press, adding proudly that her husband was a very busy man, engaged in important work.

Before I left, with a cardboard box full of thick rimmed earthen-ware cups and saucers, all carefully wrapped and packed in straw, Pamela Diamand asked me if I would like to come to the art classes she gave every Saturday morning for local children. Nothing could have pleased me more and I ran back to Maldon with her box of pottery on my shoulder without stopping, breathless as much by excitement as by running. So it was that, instead of going to Saturday morning cinema for children at the Odeon, I went to art classes in the South of France.

Pamela Diamand's method of teaching differed greatly from that of Mr Tait or Mr Cuthbertson. In the first lesson each pupil was supplied with a large, round hog's hair brush, and powder colours to be mixed with water. We were then told to listen to a record of music by Stravinsky and allow the music to sink into the very depths of our being, and then express our feelings about it by giving room for our unconscious minds to expand and overflow through our dripping brushes on to the huge rolls of paper spread out on the floor to collect them, this paper having something to do with Monsieur Diamand's mysterious printing activities.

If Jung's theory of a universal unconscious is sound, then the productions of Pamela Diamand's pupils should have had much in common. This was almost, but not exactly, the case. Broadly speaking, the pupils could be divided into two groups: the first having a universal unconscious crammed with dolls houses, cabbage-like trees, pin figures, and spiky suns, and the second, very much smaller group, a universal unconscious dominated by a single obsessive image. In this latter group was a boy from the depths of whose unconscious Stravinsky could bring forth nothing but aeroplanes decorated with swastikas and dropping bombs; a little girl who drew again and again a Scottish terrier wearing a plaid waistcoat, and myself whose unconscious refused to release anything except Sir Francis Drake standing behind the ubiquitous sea-chest.

All in vain would Pamela Diamand try to stimulate my creative impulse by getting me to close my eyes and let my mind drift along with the music. Be as a leaf borne on the wind, swept hither and thither, now soaring above the clouds, now floating gently down to earth to arrive in some strange new land where I was to paint the fresh marvels surrounding me. Alas, wherever I fell there stood the admiral on his undrawable feet.

It was at this point that my teacher showed her resourcefulness. She gave me a ball of plasticine to model Sir Francis in the round, thereby if not solving the problem of perspective, at least circumventing it. This, however, led to other problems. In pencil, on paper, the noble features of my illustrious subject could be swiftly indicated with four shrewdly placed shadows. Not so in sculpture. The features had to be patiently modelled. Furthermore, in a drawing or painting Sir Francis could only threaten to fall over. These problems were soon solved in an ingenious way. The great man was put in a diver's suit. A helmet covered his face, and weighted boots kept him anchored vertically to the table. A thinly rolled sausage of plasticine, stuck upright on to his helmet to indicate a breathing tube, completed my first piece of sculpture in conventional materials.

During one of my visits to Heybridge I was let into the secret of what Monsieur Diamand was printing behind his ivy bush. Lithographs in limited edition for Picasso? *Livres d'Artiste*? Banknotes? No, none of these things. He was printing toffee papers.

In 1979, I had a one-man show of my sculpture in a West End gallery. One day, a lady who had seen the show advertised, phoned the gallery to ask if I was the same Eric Hebborn whom she had known over thirty years before in Heybridge, and, if I were the same person, would I come to have tea with her?

Pamela Diamand was now in her eighties, but time, which had taken from her Monsieur Diamand and moved her from Mill House to a tiny flat in town, had proved powerless to take away her spirit. Her panelled doors were still Bloomsbury bright, her walls still covered with pictures by Roger Fry, and she still treasured, now in a trunk under her only table, her father's sketchbooks and notebooks.

She made tea which we drank from the thick-rimmed earthenware cups that I remembered having carried in the cardboard box. She spoke of the magical Mill House and its garden and showed again her treasures, all with the same infectious enthusiasm of those distant days in Heybridge. When I noticed the absence of her father's portrait of Lady Fry, she explained that she had donated a number of Roger Fry's paintings to various museums, adding with a not very convincing note of practicality: 'In the future I must insist that they pay me for them.'

Thus we spent a happy hour together in the past. As I was leaving she pressed upon me two handsome volumes of Roger Fry's *Letters*, edited by Denys Sutton. Now I have only to open these volumes inscribed in a firm hand: 'To Eric Hebborn from his first teacher, Pamela Diamand,' and I again find myself running happily down Cromwell Hill, through Constable country and Bloomsbury to find myself in a sunlit garden in the south of France.

Mrs Buckle had difficulty in clothing a growing boy on the money she received from the Council. When she had taken me in I scarcely reached up to her shoulder; now I was fifteen and she scarcely reached up to mine. My old pal Ron had left school over a year before and moved to live with other guardians in Chelmsford where he had found work. This meant that I could no longer be fitted out with his 'hand-me-downs'. So Mrs Buckle struck on the idea of dressing me in a discarded battle-dress. She realised, of course, that if it was not disguised, I would be mercilessly teased at school by the better-off boys, and she took the trouble of dyeing the uniform what nobody at the time thought twice about calling 'nigger' brown. She had overlooked the fact that Italian prisoners of war were also dressed in British battle-dresses dipped in the same dye; and when I appeared on the playground in my new clothes, I was greeted with a chorus of: 'I-tie, I-tie, / Dirty little I-tie.'

The name stuck, and to save me from what she wrongly imagined to be my embarrassment a member of the Maldon Art Club – a Mrs Foster, who painted in the manner of her namesake, Miles Birket – very kindly gave me a Harris Tweed jacket which had belonged to her own boy who had been killed in action. The old jacket was in good condition except for the lining which, when explored produced an envelope containing two hundred foreign stamps. Fortune had smiled on me, and on the very next day half of the Herrick Collection of Highly Important Stamps went up for auction on the playground, to be knocked down to the highest bidder in cash or kind.

In substance the auction went like this:

'Am I offered five shillings for this outstanding collection of foreign stamps?'

(Silence)

'Half a crown?'

(Silence)

'You're a stingy lot aren't you? All right then, two bob?'

'A jar of tadpoles.'

'A jar of tadpoles to my right! Any advance, any advance on a jar of tadpoles!'

'A bundle of *Beano* comics!'

'A bundle of *Beano* comics! Going to the young gentleman with the snotty nose, going for a measly bundle of *Beano* comics! Any advance, do I hear a nearly full packet of Woodbines?'

'A compass!'

'A compass ... any advance on a compass? Going then for a compass, going, going ...'

'I'll give yer a bike.'

This extraordinary offer came from a boy called Tom Harris, known for his no less extraordinary ability to defecate, standing up, fully dressed, and with such adroitness as to deposit the evacuated material on to the ground without soiling his clothes. Tom did not have the bicycle with him – simply because it had no wheels. In other respects I had to admit that it was a sound if somewhat rusty Hercules, fitted with such conveniences as handlebars and pedals;

but I was of the opinion, and the intervening years have not caused me to change my ideas on the subject, that wheels make all the difference in the world to a bicycle, and I said so.

'Wheels?' queried Tom, as though he had never heard the word before. 'Wheels?' he repeated as if repetition might jog his memory.

'Yes,' said I. 'Wheels.'

'Oh, *Wheels*, yeh wheels; them's hextra, them is.'

'Hextra?' I asked.

'Yeh, them's hacksessories if yer know what I mean.'

I did not know in the least what he meant, and if by 'hextra' he intended more stamps, it was out of the question. Then began the haggling:

'Tell yer what, Herrick, yer can 'av it fer ninety stamps honely.'

'Honely! Without wheels it ain't worf nuffing!'

'Haul right, haul right, keep yer bloomin 'air on. Give me heighty stamps and it's yours.'

'Wivout wheels yer can keep it mate!'

'Tell yer what. Give me fifty stamps, take the bike 'ome and when I find some wheels give me the ovver fifty. OK?'

'OK.'

Although I had agreed, it was not without reservations that I parted with a quarter of my capital and carried the old rusty Hercules frame home to the yard. Supposing Tom did not or could not keep his word?

In the event, my fears turned out to be groundless. Less than a week passed before Tom bowled into the yard with two vital 'hacksessories'. They seemed new, and the tread on the tyres unworn.

'Where did yer get 'em?' I asked, handing over the stamps.

'Contacks, contacks.'

Naturally I was delighted but, as the old saying might just as well go: 'It's a good wind indeed that blows nobody any ill.' And it turned out that my good luck in acquiring the wheels for my Hercules coincided with Mr Horner's (headmaster of the secondary school) bad luck in losing those of his.

The poor man was very concerned about his loss and made it the subject of several of the little talks he would give after morning prayers. At first he let it be known that he knew very well who the thief was, but it would be in the best interest of the boy concerned were he to own up of his own accord.

When the culprit failed to respond, Mr Horner promised that if the wheels of his bicycle were restored to their rightful place, he was prepared to overlook the incident. Even this generous offer had no effect, and the headmaster, who had by now, it seems, forgotten who the thief was, offered a reward of five shillings to anyone who could give information leading to the return of his property. But his efforts were all in vain.

I sympathised with Mr Horner. One can get very attached to bikes. For a few weeks my own became the very centre of my existence. I cleaned it and polished it with even more enthusiasm than Mrs Buckle's brassware – and oiled it almost hourly. I named it 'Lightning' after my old nickname of 'lightoles'.

Mr Buckle was more than a guardian to me, he was a friend and a confidant and I gave him a detailed account of how I had acquired Lightning and what progress I was making with its cleaning and restoration. There were, I explained, a number of accessories beyond wheels to be acquired before it would be roadworthy, such things as a saddle, a pump, and a dynamo, to power the front and rear lights.

''Ow can yer do all that on two bob a week?' the old man asked. I explained my arrangement with Tom. For ten stamps he would use his 'contacks' to find me a pump, for twenty a saddle; but for the dynamo he would be obliged to take me for all I was 'worf'.

'Better watch out, son,' warned my foster father. 'Yer don't want no more trouble wiv the law, do yer?'

Fortunately, the local police constable did not come to call, and after a few weeks of work, and two or three lucky 'finds' by Tom, the blissful day arrived when Lightning was ready for the road. There it was leaning against the wall of the air-raid shelter, as good as new, waiting to take me to the furthest corners of the earth, viz., Mill House, Beleigh Abbey, Mr Cracknell's allotment, and the Cuthbertson houseboat.

I leapt into the saddle, turned the front wheel towards the open gate, applied myself to the pedals, and fell off. Time and time again I repeated this pathetic performance. Try as I might, control over Lightning did not come at once, and that afternoon I was obliged to confide in Mr Buckle a secret that I would not have shared with my school fellows for all the ice-cream in High Street, almost as close and shameful a secret as the fact I had never kissed a girl – I did not know how to ride a bike.

'Don't worry, son, I'll learn yer,' came my guardian's helpful response, adding: 'Ain't I biked all over England?' I knew the answer was no, but I did not dare to give it. Mr Buckle claimed that before he was struck blind he had perfect vision, X-ray in fact. Nor did his resemblance to Superman stop there, and curiously enough, his former prowess lay in precisely those areas of interest that had attracted me.

'Yer know that big pitcher up in your room? I done that when I was 'alf yer age.' The work of art referred to depicted a little boy blowing bubbles; it was painted in a style closely resembling that of Millais, and Mr Buckle had modestly hidden his authorship under the name of Pear's Soap.

When I told my foster father that I was training for sports day, it reminded him that he must ask the missis whatever happened to the medal he had won in the Olympics. And when I won a fountain pen in a boxing tournament he told me the story of how he knocked out Jack Dempsey in the first round of an off-the-record fight – adding that Joe Louis, the Brown Bomber, could count himself lucky that Bruiser Buckle had hung up his gloves when he had. How he had done all these things and still found time to 'show Sir 'Enry Irvin' a fing or two on the boards', I could not guess. And now he was telling me he had cycled all over England; it was too much!

'Cor yer never did,' I said, expressing my true opinion, and then perhaps a little less sincerely: 'Bet yer still could, couldn't yer?'

'Cors I could. Between you, me and the doorpost, I feel like a spin in the fresh air. But yer gotta cross yer 'eart an promise yer won't tell the missis.'

And so it was I found myself leading my foster father into the yard and getting him seated on Lightning. For security I held on to both the saddle and the handlebars, but when the old man had found a wobbly kind of balance (by which I was, and for good reason, enormously impressed), I removed my hand from the handlebars, and a greatly amused Mr Buckle began to pedal with vigour. Now, as all cyclists know, the faster one pedals, the faster one proceeds, and the faster one proceeds, the less one wobbles; and Mr Buckle's greater velocity gave him the false impression that he was in control of the machine.

'Yer can let go now,' he laughed. 'I'll be on me way.' With this he began to pedal with a sudden frenzy that jerked Lightning's saddle out of my hand, and sent the machine careering madly towards the open gate with me in close pursuit. Through the gate rushed Mr Buckle on the runaway bike into the lane towards a wall on the other side.

'Turn left!' I yelled.

'Turn what?'

When I picked him up, my guardian, far from being hurt, seemed rejuvenated by the experience and said with a chuckle, 'That showed yer, didn't it, life in the ol dog yet! I told yer I could bike, didn't I?'

Mrs Buckle returned from shopping to find a by now dusted down spouse wearing what I suppose he imagined to be an enigmatic smile of the *Mona Lisa* kind.

'What yer grinnin about yer ol fool?' said his wife. 'Smokin yerself to death I spose.'

'No I ain't,' said Mr Buckle in an offended voice. 'Ain't 'ad a fag all afternoon, 'av I Herrick?'

That night Mr Buckle died of a heart attack. A weeping Mrs Buckle woke me up a little after midnight with: ''E's gone, 'e's gone.' My first thought was that my foster father had borrowed Lightning and had gone on a cycling tour of England; but when his widow told me to remove the stove from their bedroom, saying, ''E don't need it no more,' I knew things were otherwise.

The old Valor lamp threw a pattern of circles on to the bedroom ceiling and cast a shadow over Mr Buckle's body. The warm stuffy air stank of death. I felt physically sick and wanted to seize the lamp and run; but my legs trembled, a terrible dryness gripped my throat, and movement was for a time impossible. Transfixed, my sight grew accustomed to the gloom, and making out the dead man's head, sunk in the pillows, I saw that he had died with his eyes open, and wore a smile. It was as if in death blindness had forsaken him and what he saw of eternity was pleasing.

But no such pleasure was mine. I was suffering pangs of remorse for having grown impatient with Mr Buckle's harmless boasting, and suspected that by encouraging him to ride Lightning I had been instrumental in bringing about his death. Before I left Mr and Mrs Buckle's bedroom I forced myself upon my knees beside my foster father's corpse and prayed a tearful earnest prayer: 'Please God, 'oo art in 'eaven, forgive this day my awful sins, an look after Mr Billy Buckle of 31 Wantz Road, Maldon, Essex, 'oo is on 'is way up now. An tell 'im that Herrick didn't mean 'im no 'arm. Fanks ever so much, and I promise you'll be 'earing from me again soon, eiver 'ere or at All Saint's on Sunday.'

Of the funeral I only remember seeing Mr Buckle's coffin placed on rustic trestles in the 'best' room for the inspection of the neighbours and relatives. The coffin was of the plainest. It was simply a box made of the cheapest pine without a single moulding or dovetail joint to dignify it. The lid was closed, and therefore one could not see if any silk or satin cushioned the corpse, but I very much doubt if there was anything inside more comfy than a cotton winding sheet. There was, however, a particular of that otherwise economy-class container that showed it had been chosen personally by the widow, and at some cost. The tell-tale detail lay in the choice of huge brass handles, of intricate workmanship, the sort we might now call executive class, and clearly intended for a far more expensive coffin. How well they looked among the glitter of Mrs Buckle's brass collection! She had done her Billy proud, and yet I could not stop myself from wondering how she would bear the loss of those glorious baroque handles which were for two short days her collection's crowning glory.

In the event, it seemed to me, as well as to certain gossipy neighbours, that my foster mother took the loss of her husband, together with the brass handles, rather well. Perhaps too well, for scarcely three months after her husband's burial, another man, Mr Cracknell, entered the life of the widow Buckle.

The family atmosphere I had enjoyed when Mr Buckle was alive had vanished with him. Mr Cracknell and I were distant with each other, and although I was really very fond of my fostermother, she was too involved in her new relationship to pay as much attention to me as before. And without my pal Ron to share my woes I began to mope – but not for long.

Now that it was my turn to wear 'long uns', grow fluff on my chin, and speak in lower tones, my own growing fancy did not turn to thoughts of the girl next door, but directed itself to a classmate from the nearby village of Danbury. His name was Anthony, and he had riveting eyes of cerulean blue framed by black eyelashes so thick and long that they seemed false. But I was fickle in my first amorous affections, and although thoughts of Anthony gave rise to a series of nocturnal emissions, it was not long before I had a new crush, this time on a fellow council boy with black curly hair, olive skin, thick eyebrows, and what I imagined was the body of Adonis himself. Stan was sixteen years old and an orphan. He lived under the thatched roof of a Mrs Jackson in Tolleshunt Major, a hamlet about five miles from Maldon in the same direction as Heybridge. Although we soon became close friends, our relationship was strictly platonic. Stan was as straight as a laser beam and to humour him our conversation mostly centred on girls. Occasionally, however, we would speak of other things, and finding out about my ambition to become an artist, Stan once gave me to understand that his guardian owned an original painting by Vincent Van Gogh, and suggested that I might like to cycle home with him to see it. Van Gogh was my favourite artist, and I was beside myself with excitement at the prospect.

Mrs Jackson's cottage was scarcely larger than Mrs Buckle's but it was much more charming. Its builder had eschewed the use of plumb line, spirit level, and set square, with the result that the eye was everywhere soothed with the gentlest of slopes and curves. Its thatched roof, white-washed walls, and low-beamed ceilings were the embodiment of tranquillity, and it was with some dismay that one turned from the contemplation of such simple serenity to note that it stood next door to the clutter and clatter of a canning factory called 'Snowkist'.

Mrs Jackson herself was an eminently clean little woman, of pleasing plumpness, in her mid-fifties. Her hair was neatly brushed back to form a bun, and she wore a spotless pinafore. Both she and her immaculately kept home had something pleasantly antiseptic about them, and had she said she was a nurse, her assertion would have gone unchallenged.

Looking me over with a critical eye she asked me to please be very careful not to touch the walls. Mrs Jackson made tea, and as she did so she talked, and talked, and talked. So that by the time I was actually sipping from my cup I knew the greater part of her history. As a young woman she had worked for a number of years as a nanny in France. That, I thought, explained how she came into possession of the Van Gogh; perhaps she had even known the great artist. Returning to England, she met and married Mr Jackson, a handsome man who gave the appearance of being a 'real' gentleman.

It just shows, don't it, you can't judge the book by the cover; 'andsome is as 'andsome does, is what Mrs Jackson said. For her husband deceived her 'sumfing terrible', and after getting his hands on her life savings he left her in the lurch, wherever that may be. And it was in the lurch that a model of chivalry called Mr Denny swept her off her feet and took her away from it all to Tolleshunt Major where he was the manager of the above mentioned canning factory. Snowkist had given the manager the use of the cottage in which Mrs Jackson now told her tale, and where the unfortunate Mr Denny had but two years before died of a heart attack in his mistress's arms. In eighteen months' time she would have to leave, but in the meantime she was making ends meet by cooking lunches for some of the workers and looking after Stan. She had room for another council boy, and had applied for one to the Essex County Council, and . . .

'Can yer show Herrick your Van Gogh picture?' asked Stan.

'What Van Gogh picture?'

'You know, that one wiv them there birds.'

'Oh, yer mean that coloured picture what my bruvver sent. It's in that drawer over there. Yer can show it to yer friend, but don't muck it up.'

Stan got up from his chair, and opening the drawer indicated, took from it a postcard. True, it was a picture postcard, and what the picture reproduced was really and truly by Van Gogh, but still it was only a postcard. I tried to hide my disappointment, and looked at the postcard with what was soon to be real interest.

The paintings by Van Gogh known to me in reproduction then were, of course, those that had been most widely circulated. *The Potato Eaters* of 1885 and *Sun Flowers* of 1888 were those I knew best because large Skira reproductions of them hung in the secondary school's dining room. But I also knew paintings of boats, bridges, a postman, the artist's doctor, his room, his chair, and portraits of himself.

The painting on the postcard was, however, new to me. It depicted a flock of crows flying across a corn field; the corn field at Auvers-sur-Oise, where in 1890 the artist took his life. Such is the power of the picture that much of its strength survived even in the poor coloured print I held in my hand, and I was moved by this frenzied emotional release, disturbed to see the anguished grain tearing itself up by its roots rather than bend to the oncoming storm, to hear the flapping and cawing of the startled crows, prophetic of the pistol shot to come. For a few minutes I was totally engrossed in the drama of that magic postcard.

I belonged to an evening drama group organised by Mr Edmunds at the secondary school, whose main hall was furnished with a reasonably well-equipped stage. Once every three months we would give a performance for a captive audience of parents. My own roles included Inspector Rough in a Victorian melodrama called *Gaslight*, and Lord Loam in *The Admirable Crichton*; in both of these parts I succeeded in getting laughs in the most unlikely places.

Mrs Buckle had ruled that I must be home and in bed by nine o'clock. The drama group held its meetings between seven and nine, and consequently on the evenings of my attendance I would arrive home late by the few minutes that it took me to walk from the school. This irritated my foster mother and one evening the matter came to a head.

Mr Cracknell had gone to the Jug and Bottle and, alone in the kitchen, his wife greeted me with:

'Late again, always bloomin late. How many times do I 'av ter tell yer to be 'ome before nine? I might as well speak to the bloomin mantlepiece, for all the good it does talking to you. Get up them bloomin stairs sharp or . . .'

'But, Mrs Buckle,' (I never got used to calling her Mrs

Cracknell) I began.

'Don't you bloomin but me!' retorted my guardian. 'Rules is rules, an that's all there is to it.'

By now I was annoyed myself, and flared up:

'I've 'ad just about as much as I can stand of you and your stupid ol rules; I'm clearin off.'

'Over my dead body, you're bloomin clearin off.' And so saying, Mrs Cracknell threw herself dramatically against the door to bar my way. Now it will be remembered that she was a short woman, and as she leaned back on the door her head rested at a height scarcely above the latch, which Mr Cracknell, choosing that very moment to return from the Jug and Bottle, sharply lifted.

'Ouch!' cried his wife as the swiftly rising bar of iron struck the base of her skull. Hearing the cry of pain, Mr Cracknell hastily, forcibly, and inadvertently, thrust open the door to send his screaming spouse sprawling before him. Whereupon, standing astride the fallen body and taking up the stance of a prize fighter, he challenged me with: 'Strike Mrs Cracknell would yer? We'll soon see about hitting a lady, you blaggard.' Having no wish to waste time in futile explanation, the blaggard ducked a right hook and fled through the open door.

It took me half an hour to cycle the five miles to Tolleshunt Major.

Mrs Jackson was listening to the ten o'clock news. News which must have paled before the news that I had for her: 'Yer know that council boy you're looking for? Well, your prayers have been answered!'

CHAPTER III

WORK OF THE UTMOST IMPORTANCE

'No gentleman would be so rash as to have a taste of his own'

Goldhanger, the Essex village through which I was pushing Lightning at a little after one o'clock on a summer afternoon in 1949, was the picture of drowsy rusticity. On entering it from the direction of Tolleshunt Major, I could hear only the sound of the village blacksmith shaping a horseshoe on an anvil beneath a chestnut-tree. I would gladly have stopped to share the tree's generous shade with the waiting carter and his horses, but I was late for work, and continued to push my bicycle with its flat tyre past the smithy, past the dairy, past the manor house with its sleepy lawns and ivy-covered chimney-stacks, the home of Lord and Lady Jenkins, into the brightness of the village square. Here was a drinking fountain, and pausing to wet my mouth, I reflected on the joys of a home-made water-ice, sold at the local post-office, of which, by a scarcity of time and money, I was being at that very moment deprived.

Leaving the square, I trundled my machine down Fish Street, a narrow and, at this hour, apparently deserted thoroughfare. It was flanked at its upper end by the most modest of two-roomed thatched cottages, behind whose lace curtains I knew many a curious housewife lurked, muttering something to the effect of: 'There he goes, that good-for-nothing boy from Tolleshunt Major, late for work again. He'll come to no good, he will!'

Fish Street led to two places: the sea-wall where I longed to cool myself – in the waters of the Blackwater estuary; and Page's fruit farm to which I was obliged to turn my unwilling steps to earn ten shillings a week. It was possible to earn as much as three pounds a week there, but it was 'piece work', that is, one was paid

63

for how much fruit one picked, and since my mind was seldom on my work, I picked little and was paid little.

In the middle of Fish Street, on the right-hand side going down, and just before the turning leading to the sea-wall, stood Sea View, the name, and only banal feature, of a singular residence, with which, unknown to me then, I was soon to become closely acquainted. My attention was drawn to the figure of a man, crouching in the road and apparently engaged in the repair of two bicycles standing upside-down before him. In those days it was not uncommon to see in the byways of Essex a little notice tacked on to a tree or gate bearing the legend: 'Punctures Repaired', and thinking that I had perhaps chanced upon the answer to my problems of transport, I determined to enquire. Stopping beside the crouching figure I discovered him to be a grubby old man with off-white hair, as unruly as its limited quantity would allow, a frosty bristle on his chin, and, as for clothes, nothing more than a pair of khaki shorts that had clearly spent their long life in the same innocence of soap and water as their owner. Paint-brush in hand, he was diligently applying gold paint to one of the bikes. In doing this he did not neglect the smallest part, metal or otherwise: tyres, saddle, handle-grips, front and rear lights all shining bright now with gold. Nor had the shopping basket and its contents escaped his magic touch. The other cycle and its accessories had been just as scrupulously completed in silver. Having taken in these details I felt less inclined to make my enquiry, but since the strange fellow had looked up from his work, I thought it would be impolite not to give a reason for hovering over him.

'Excuse me,' I ventured, 'but do you mend punctures?'

'Certainly not!' came the slightly offended reply in the unmistakeable accent of a public school. And then – as though he had suddenly recognised an acquaintance – he continued in a kindly tone: 'But if you would care to borrow one of these' (indicating his bicycles with the sweeping gesture of magnanimity), 'please do!'

The thought of arriving for work on a machine seemingly touched by the hand of Midas, and of the coarse hilarity it would have provoked among my fellow fruit-pickers led me politely to decline the well-meant offer, and gripping my black Hercules bicycle as tightly as one might sanity itself, I took my leave of the eccentric gentleman to trudge the short distance from Sea View to Page's Farm.

The tedious hours of work happily over, I found myself again pushing my bike along Fish Street. The shadows that had earlier kept strictly to the sides of the street were now spreading themselves unrestrainedly. But scarcely had I taken a homeward step than the peacefulness of that early summer evening was disturbed by the angry shouts of two men. What they were shouting about was not at first clear, but as I advanced up the road the voices grew nearer and I was able to make out: 'Look here, Frost, I don't care a tinker's cuss about your bloody foot, and if you don't clear up your place, you'll be hearing from my solicitors, and that's all there is to the matter – good night!'

To which the said Mr Frost rejoined: 'I shall show it to you, Page, yes, I shall show, you shall see, tanks and guns!' With this, Mr Frost, who turned out to be no other than the gentleman of my afternoon encounter, came hopping out of Sea View clasping his right foot in both hands with the clear intention of displaying it to his adversary and next-door neighbour, Major Page.

Major Page was a familiar figure to regular users of Fish Street such as myself. He was an elderly man, long since retired from the army and keenly interested in gardening. Thus he was to be seen outside in all weathers engaged on one or another of the endless chores attendant on a well-kept garden: trimming hedges, weeding borders, forking among shrubbery, mowing the lawn, sprinkling weedkiller on to the paths, or whatsoever it happened to be the time to do. The Major and his garden were of the same stuff: his box trees trimmed to the shape of a pair of joyless birds sharing a single tail seemed to have found their inspiration in the immaculate symmetry of his own moustache, and his hollyhocks stood smartly to attention on either side of a crazy-paving path. The path led to a low but large thatched and beamed cottage built in the style known as 'stockbroker's Tudor'. Olde English characters burnt into a slice from a tree-trunk and hung from a wrought-iron scroll at the front gate advertised the Major's property as 'Thatch End'.

By the time I arrived on the scene, Mr Frost was preparing to thrust his uplifted foot through the gate of Thatch End, shouting: 'Here are your tanks and guns. This is what comes of them. Look, look here!'

But he was outmanoeuvered by the Major who had marched briskly to his gate, not to examine Mr Frost's foot at close quarters, but firmly to lock that member and its owner out. This achieved, he retreated to his house, leaving Mr Frost, foot in hand in the middle of the street with none to address but myself:

'I say, young man, you would not paint pictures of guns and

tanks, and leave them where children might see them, would you?' Although I cannot claim that this was a question to which I had given previous consideration, I felt that the answer most likely to please was no, and no I said. 'I knew it,' said he, putting down his foot next to its fellow, 'I knew you were an artist.' This puzzled me. How did he know I was an artist? (At least an artist in embryo.) How could he possibly have known of my interest?

Before I had time to reflect on the matter, Mr Frost had gripped my elbow and was propelling me towards Sea View, muttering, apparently more for his own ears than mine: 'No, no, artists should not pick plums!' And, 'That dreadful Page, I shall show him, I shall show him yet!' Arriving at his gate, he said to me: 'I've got work for a clever artist, work of the utmost importance. Do it well and I shall pay you handsomely. Wait here for a moment, and I shall show you what I have in mind.'

With this he disappeared into his house by a side-entrance leaving me in the street. I noticed in the failing light, that the house, for all its air of neglect, was probably not more than twenty years old, and that it was unique in Fish Street, insofar as it rose above one storey. Indeed it was virtually three storeys, for above the second floor a kind of look-out tower had been attached. This I later discovered to be designed for the watching of seabirds, one of Mr Frost's many interests. Out of the downstairs windows issued the flourishing branches of well-established trees, indicating that the lower rooms were used for horticultural purposes, a fact that seemed to explain the quantities of rotting furniture arranged among, and half-hidden by, the weeds of what I could see of the garden. The front porch was occupied by a large company of swollen cats that had fallen asleep. In their midst, completely blocking the front entrance, stood the cause of their somnolence, a half-eaten mountain of stinking fish.

Mr Frost returned carrying a roll of enlarged photographs of his own making, and a box of watercolours. The object was, he explained, to colour these photographs, return them to him, and should they prove satisfactory, I would be handsomely rewarded. Thrilled by the commission, I set off for home, running as fast as the simultaneous pushing of a bicycle allowed. Arriving at Mrs Jackson's, I gulped down my supper, then borrowed Stan's puncture outfit and mended the flat tyre, by which time it was about nine o'clock. This was bed-time in the country, but I was determined to stay up and colour the photographs that very evening, and thus gain the rewards of my labour as soon as possible, that is, the next morning. Spreading the prints out on the kitchen table, I stopped them from rolling themselves up again by holding them down at the corners with tea-cups. There were six prints in all: one was a photograph of an owl surprised in its nest, a reflection of the photographer clearly visible in the bird's startled eyes; another represented a haywain creaking its way up Fish Street, while a third was an underexposed interior of a church. I no longer recall the subjects of the other photographs, but from what has been said it will be understood that the great importance of my task was not immediately evident. I was nevertheless determined to do the colouring as well as I possibly could.

The first obstacle was to get the watercolour to spread evenly on the glossy surface of the prints. Here one of Pamela Diamand's lessons came in useful. I remembered that she had instructed her pupils in printing from patterns cut into potatoes, on to shiny toffee-paper. The ink we used was water-based, and yet because of its combination with the potato, it printed perfectly evenly on a surface that would not otherwise have taken it. Bearing this in mind I took a potato, cut it in half, and rubbed it thoroughly over Mr Frost's photographs. This done, the watercolour took moderately well, and by a little after midnight the 'work of utmost importance' had been completed, and my studio transformed back into Mrs Jackson's kitchen.

Next morning saw me again at Mr Frost's door with his roll of photographs tucked under my arms. 'No, no!' he said on seeing me, 'you could not conceivably have done the work properly in so short a time. Take the prints home and colour them as you should.' With this admonition the interview was over, and carrying the unopened roll of photographs I continued my way to Page's farm.

Two dreary weeks of fruit-picking had crawled by before I had the courage to present myself again to my patron. In the meantime I had not even looked at the photographs, much less retouched them, so it was with some trepidation that I unrolled them for his inspection. But I need not have worried. 'I say,' he exclaimed on seeing the church interior, 'it's exquisite; you have captured the magic of light coming through stained glass wonderfully well.' Thus each print as he came to it elicited some laudatory comment. 'Splendid hues!' 'Magnificent effect!' 'Wonderful tones!' and so on. The virtues giving rise to these raptures being entirely hidden from myself, I received each compliment in embarrassed silence, merely reflecting that Mr Frost must have been blessed with a vision from which all imperfections were miraculously excluded.

Having heaped me with praise he turned his attention to the matter of remuneration. Here, I thought, might be the rub. Would he treat me as the Vicar of Tolleshunt Major had? That gentleman had urged me to make a watercolour of his church, promising that he would purchase the result, but on being presented with the work, had begun the meeting by saying: 'I know, Eric, that you are far too proud to accept money!' and had ended it by pressing a bag of sweets into my palm. But my present patron soon put my mind at rest by saying: 'I said I shall pay you handsomely, and so I shall,' with which he disappeared along the side of his house (the cats and their slowly subsiding stench still forbidding entrance by the front door) to return shortly with a crisp five-pound note which he thrust upon me, repeating over and over again something about artists and plums, tanks and guns, his foot and the future of Africa. 'Important matters, my boy, in which I trust I can continue to rely on your invaluable assistance.'

Thus began my employment by Mr Frost. My duties were to give concrete expression to my employer's artistic dreams, and my wages would reflect the extent of his satisfaction. Artwork was by no means lacking from Sea View. It took the form of dozens and dozens of identical rabbits cast in cement from a single jelly mould; these Mr Frost had scattered about his property as fancy dictated. But with the assumption of a 'real' artist more ambitious plans were to be realised. The first was a mural above the front porch executed in oils in the manner of the well-known naturalist, Peter Scott. The subject-matter consisted of a flight of ducks rising from marshland and silhouetted against a sunset. The sunset owed much of its notable brilliance to Mr Frost's insistence that no expense should be spared in the plastering on of chrome yellow and vermilion red in the hope that the pattern of the underlying brickwork might disappear. But no matter how much colour was applied, the disturbing pattern continued to grin through, and it would certainly have spoiled the whole effect were it not for my patron's happy decision that far from being detrimental, the brickwork in reality added both unity and distinction to what he called a 'capital work', and on no account was it to be got rid of. Not all the commissions, however, were of such a lofty nature, and my next work at Sea View was to carve in chalk a number of gigantic duck eggs. These were solemnly shown to Mr Frost's ducks as examples of what they themselves should aim for.

Duck and chicken eggs were an important element in Mr Frost's economy. Should his birds lay more eggs than were sufficient for his own needs, he would hire a certain Mr Cash, and have himself driven to London in a smart limousine. Once there he would sell his eggs, and with the proceeds (augmented no doubt by other funds) he would buy fish and oranges. These were bought by the sackful, and on Mr Frost's return to Sea View, the sacks of fish replenished the odours of the porch, and the sacks of oranges provided the antidote that made the odour supportable. For myself I was constantly to be seen with an orange at my nose.

Fish and oranges were not the only purchases that Mr Frost made in London, and I am sorry to say that he was an occasional collector of early books and manuscripts. Sorry because the state of mind that lent such distinction to his life-style rendered him incapable of taking proper care of his precious acquisitions. Several items of beauty were simply abandoned to the mercy of the English climate to perish in the same manner as his furniture. A beautiful handwritten gospel served for many years in the capacity of a doorstop. Fortunately it was rescued from this situation by a caprice of its owner who got it into his head to send the book as a gift to the Spanish ambassador. His purpose was to cement the Anglo-Spanish relations that Mr Frost, independently of any official opinion, had decided were needed. What connection, if any, the book had with Spain was never made clear. But if Mr Frost was a vandal, he was an unwitting one, and on at least one occasion he was firmly convinced that he was greatly adding to the artistic value of an acquisition. This particular item was a fine illuminated initial letter from the fourteenth century. It stood at the top left-hand side of an otherwise empty sheet of vellum, the scribe never having completed the page. The gilded letter was combined with a miniature painting representing a saint standing on a magical little island made to the measure of his feet, its shores lapped by waves of lapis lazuli. It was this blue sea that worried Mr Frost. The real sea, he argued, was not blue. Had he not seen it often enough from the sea-wall, and was it not very definitely green? Of course it was; obviously the ancient illuminators had never seen the sea. But Mr Frost could, and would, remedy the fault, and seizing on a can of green house-paint, he slopped it over the lapis ocean, and with his fingers drove North Sea waves furiously over the violated page.

Perhaps it would be charitable at this point to draw a veil over my employer's activities as a collector, and return to the more noteworthy commissions with which at various times he entrusted me. Mr Frost was of philanthropic bent, and having inherited that sufficiency of wealth as in the eyes of the world distinguishes the eccentric from the mad, was free to indulge in good works without troubling other people either for their money or their opinions. He had, for instance, presented the local church with a splendid organ, making only one condition to the gift: that he himself should retain the right to practise on the instrument whenever he pleased. The vicar, I recall, had reason to regret having accepted this condition, for when Mr Frost was pleased to play the organ, this invariably coincided with when he himself was pleased to preach a sermon. It was true, to judge from the amusement of the congregation, that Mr Frost's music was popular; equally true that it formed a kind of sonic illustration to his own discourse – *piano* when his voice was low, *forte* when it was louder, and swelling to a great *crescendo* to underscore the more telling phrases. Nevertheless it was apparent from his sometimes less-than-Christian expression that on the whole the Vicar would have preferred the unadorned word.

It was this fiercely independent spirit of philanthropy that set my patron on the course of helping the Africans. According to his analysis of the situation, the problems of the natives in the Dark Continent stemmed from their diminished interest in artistic matters. Where were now the woodcarvers of Africa? Perhaps they lacked carving tools. If that was the case, Mr Frost would write to Harrods and arrange for a large shipment of the finest chisels and gouges to be dispatched to them at once. But what would the savages carve? None of those horrid heathen idols, hoped Mr Frost; no no, that would not do at all: they must be encouraged to carve something essentially Christian and spiritually uplifting. And since example was better than precept, the gift of the tools should be accompanied by carvings that would be to the natives of Africa what the chalk eggs had been to the ducks: inspiring models.

This is, of course, where I came into the matter. The execution of these stirring expressions of the Christian spirit was to be left to me. The iconography involved, however, was to be decided upon by Mr Frost.

Three trunks of wood, each twelve feet in length and of daunting girth, were delivered by Sadd's, the local timber-merchant, and after much deliberation the subject-matter was decided upon. The sculptures were to symbolise the temptations of Crawshay-Frost (my patron's surname in full). Each work was to stand for a sin that he had overcome during his life. Thus it was that I found myself

Fig. 9: *Portrait of an Insane Man*, after a painting by
Géricault, 1982, pencil (Collection of the artist)

carving a twelve-feet-long rifle representing the wickedness of war,
a twelve-feet-long champagne bottle standing for the evils of drink,
and a twelve-feet-long woman, naked and in a most seductive pose,
symbolising a vice I would never have suspected my employer of
knowing about, let alone overcoming. Such was the trinity with
which Mr Frost added to the symbols of Christian art and to my
pocket money.

The sculptures bore no inscriptions to indicate their intentions,
and it occurred to me that the natives of Africa might be forgiven
were they to mistake them for a glorification of, or even an in-
citement to, violence, drink and sex. It would perhaps have been
proper to communicate my fears to Mr Frost, but I thought it
better not to meddle in matters beyond my understanding and,
with a slightly uneasy conscience, kept my silence.

In due course huge crates clearly inscribed 'To Whom It May
Concern, The Congo, Africa' left Sea View never to be heard
of again, and with the passing of time I was able to soothe my

71

conscience with the reasonable assumption that the influence of my carvings for good or bad on the natives of Africa had not been decisive.

I worked for Mr Frost on an average of two days a week for three years, after which my studies were to take me to London. During that period the war between the occupants of Thatch End and Sea View would from time to time flare up. The hostilities usually took the same course: Major Page would launch a verbal attack from behind the trimmed half of the hedge dividing the two properties, informing the hedge that a certain person of his acquaintance should be put away for his own good, and the good of the rest of society. This he would follow with an account of the various tactics employed by his enemy's weeds to infiltrate themselves into Thatch End. These included a vigorous underground movement, a network of roots that was undermining his lawn, and bombardment by air with seedlings. According to the Major's statistics, thousands and thousands of these undesirable aliens were being flown on the wind from Sea View and parachuted into his territory every minute. The Major's opening shots would elicit a furious rustle from the untrimmed side of the hedge as the owner of Sea View prepared to mount a counter-attack. It was not what Major Page had to say that angered Mr Frost. He was as indifferent to the distinction between cultivated plants and weeds, tidiness and untidiness, cleanliness and dirt, as he was to the distinction between the inside and the outside of his house. What made him angry was Major Page himself.

The Major had become for him the embodiment of an otherwise intangible evil. The mere sound of his hated voice would send Mr Frost literally hopping mad, as he took up his right foot which he judged to be his strongest weapon against the Major. Certainly Major Page appeared defenceless against it, and would beat a hasty retreat whenever it was advanced towards his gate, much in the same way as vampires are said to retreat from garlic or the sign of the cross, and the little pantomime enacted in front of Thatch End mentioned earlier in this chapter would bring each skirmish to an end.

Whatever it was that the Major stood for in the mind of Mr Frost, it was the antithesis of the spirit that led him to the passionate pursuit of sculpture, painting, music, ornithology and photography. To this list I should perhaps add archaeology, because in the museum in Colchester Castle are preserved the remains of a Roman galley excavated by Mr Frost in Goldhanger Creek. Although these various interests were pursued in a totally haphazard and amateurish way, Mr Frost's efforts were the reflection of a truly independent spirit that was not afraid to question generally held views, to have its own taste, or make mistakes in a vigorous quest for something beyond mundane existence. I would like to think that a little of this quality rubbed off on my youthful self, and whether it did or not, I owe a great debt of gratitude to Mr Frost. In retrospect it is my belief that he knew before our meeting (probably through the Maldon Art Club of which I discovered he was also a member) both of my own interest in art and my poverty, and had embarked on the 'work of the utmost importance' to help me financially, without it appearing as an act of charity.

My last visit to Mr Frost and to Goldhanger was in the summer of 1955. Sea View had not changed its appearance, or its smell, during the three years of my absence. It was the middle of the afternoon, and remembering that Mr Frost had taken to having afternoon naps, I glanced up in the direction of his bedroom, looking for the unmistakeable sign of its occupation. Mr Frost's doctor had told him that fresh air was good for his foot, and thus it had become a habit with him to sleep with it sticking out of the window with a string hanging from the big toe. Attached to the bottom of the string was a note asking visitors to pull only in cases of emergency.

In the absence of this sign I called out Mr Frost's name. Getting no response I entered the gate and made for the chicken run where one might on occasion find the master of Sea View sitting cross-legged in a hole scooped out of the ground with his hands, in imitation of a brooding hen, and engaged on the writing of his *magnum opus*. This consisted of writing in between the lines of a copy of Churchill's history of the war what had really happened. I never had the pleasure of reading these revelations, but one day, peering over the author's shoulder, I was impressed by the fact that they were written first with blue ink and then gone over again with red ink, these colours combining with the white page to give a most patriotic appearance.

But Mr Frost was not to be found in the chicken run, or anywhere else in the garden, and I was resigning myself to the idea that perhaps he was in London selling eggs, when I heard his voice coming faintly from the direction of a cornfield that adjoined both his and Major Page's properties. Making my way to the cornfield, I found a corner of it flattened down with blankets upon which a splendid picnic had been laid. The silver ice-buckets contained bottles of champagne, the plates the appetising pink and yellow of smoked salmon garnished with lemon, while savoury aromas arose from covered serving dishes that were later found to contain a variety of delicious foods quite unlike any I had seen or tasted before (I shall speak of my hungry art-school days in the following chapter). Standing near this feast, spread for several people, was Mr Frost. He was munching, not smoked salmon, but leaves and berries picked from an overhanging bush. Every now and again he would stop munching to say: 'I suppose it would have been all right for the gentlemen, but not for the ladies!'

'What,' said I, 'would have been all right for the gentlemen but not for the ladies?'

Receiving no response whatever to this question, and judging myself both inaudible and invisible to my unwitting host, I turned my attention to the delicacies before me, making a bulging sandwich from the salmon and filling a glass to the brim with Dom Pérignon.

Mr Frost continued to be oblivious of myself and the inroads I was making on the picnic lunch. He simply went on munching his own frugal meal, muttering to himself, constantly returning to the phrase: 'I suppose it would have been all right for the gentlemen but not for the ladies!' But as the afternoon drew on, and the champagne had begun to have its effect, I found myself party to a strange communication. I became conscious that Mr Frost's isolation from myself and what I thought of as reality was largely due to the fact that I had not recognised where he was. Now I remembered the cornfield, I had seen it on Mrs Jackson's postcard; it was the selfsame field that Van Gogh had painted.

Beating their way across it came ladies with parasols on the arms of crisp-collared gentlemen to call on Captain Frost, 'such a charming young man'. The company strolled in clarity on immaculate lawns, then struggled in vagueness against encroaching weeds, solid in sunshine on the whitest wicker, dissolving on the rotting sofas. 'What a delightful surprise. I insist you stay for lunch. I shall send Cash to Fortnum's, only the best will do.' 'The Captain was wounded, you know, shell-shock, poor fellow!' 'The lavatory is the first door on the right.' 'What are you doing with those tombstones?' 'The disgusting creature does his business on the floor just outside the lavatory.' 'One of his toes is gangrenous, frost-bite in the trenches.' 'Full of photographic equipment, couldn't get in!' 'Well, why don't you go to the churchyard and relieve yourself there?' With this the company would fade away leaving Mr Frost muttering again: 'I suppose it would have been all right for the gentlemen,' etc.

It was early evening when Mr Frost returned, at least in part, to his fragile senses, surveying the scant remains of the once splendid picnic and observing: 'To judge from the amount they ate and drank, they had a far better time than I imagined.'

CHAPTER IV

THE FORGING OF AN ARTIST

Judge Tindle sits in Tindle Square, Chelmsford, judging the merits of a neo-classic façade belonging to a courthouse. He frowns in disapproval. At least, that is how it seemed to me as I cycled past his plinth on my way to and from Chelmsford Art School during the years 1949 to 1951. My hands, in youthful disdain at touching Lightning's handlebars, were usually thrust into my pockets, but as I passed the judge I would take one out, stick its thumb to my nose, and waggle my fingers at his bronzeship. At this I imagined his frown to deepen into a scowl, but careless of his displeasure, I would go whistling on my way. The first time Judge Tindle suffered this impudence, my other hand was also out of its pocket to clutch a portfolio containing, among other treasures from my juvenilia, a splendid watercolour of Maldon's promenade bathed in the ruddy glow of evening, a pastel drawing of a collie-dog with a look in its eye that might have done credit to Landseer, and a lino-cut of a sailing ship that had sailed straight off a chocolate box. I was on my way to meet an unsuspecting member of the Technical College's teaching staff for an unscheduled interview. The art school was in fact attached to the technical college, but – the complex being called the Mid Essex Technical College and School of Art – somehow I got into the wrong building and having cornered the first adult I came across, the following dialogue took place:

'Please Sir, I want to be a draughtsman, Sir.'

'Are you good at maths?'

'I know my tables up to twelve, Sir.'

'Can you read?'

'Yes, Sir.'

'What does that sign say?'

'Way out, Sir.'

'Clever boy, very c-l-e-v-e-r.'

Then looking me up and down, 'Cheer up, it's not the end of the bloody world, here's a shilling, go and get yourself something in the canteen.'

Judge Tindle must have been gratified to note a great improvement in my behaviour as I biked past him on my way back to Tolleshunt Major. I was not whistling, I did not waggle my fingers at him, nor did I carry the hazardous portfolio which I had absentmindedly left in the canteen.

Then came the letter. It was from the art school;

> Dear Mr Hebborn,
>
> A portfolio of drawings with your name and address on it has found its way to the school. It was brought to us by Mr Evans of the Technical College who tells us that you wish to become a draughtsman; by which he at first thought you were hoping to train as a technical draughtsman, where an aptitude for mathematics would have been a requirement, but as it is . . . if you would care to come for an interview . . .

It was signed – Charles Archer. Mr Archer was absent when I went for my interview some time in the spring or early summer of 1949. In his place was a Mr Halliday who I later discovered to be a calligrapher who had received his training at the Central School under Edward Johnston, the man who had, almost single-handed, revived the art of the scribe and illuminator in this century. Mr Halliday began by telling me that my drawings had been looked at with interest by the teaching staff who were unanimous in the opinion that they were remarkably bad. The school, however, was desperately in need of students to justify its continued existence, and in the circumstances they had agreed to meet the challenge that a student such as myself would present. Naturally I would be expected to work twice as hard as my more gifted *confrères* and must not be surprised if I should be asked to leave before the end of the course. It was on these unflattering terms that I continued to be a burden to the tax-payer and a growing threat to the art market.

Chelmsford Art School was housed in a few modest rooms on the third and fourth floors of the original Edwardian Technical College. The largest of the rooms was known as the Life Room because here the students drew from life, that is to say, from a naked model.

Bertha (Fig. 10) was the first naked woman I had ever seen.

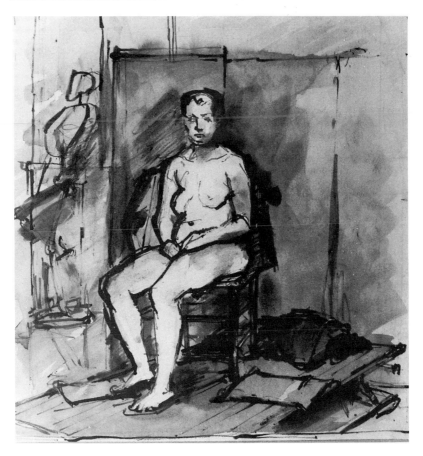

Fig. 10: *Bertha*, 1957, pen and wash (Collection of the artist)

Flanked by electric heaters, she sat on a chair placed on a raised platform called the model's throne and was surrounded by students mounted on donkeys (small benches with a T-shaped neck on which to rest one's drawing board). Head high, back straight, breasts and belly thrust forward, fingers dimpling her parted thighs, Bertha held court.

I was a few minutes late. My fellow students had already jockeyed for the best positions, and the only place left for my donkey gave its rider an unparalleled view of Bertha's private parts. I blushed, I gaped, I gawked, and fumbling for my pencil began ever so tentatively to draw her toes, her hair, her eyes, her knees, but, try as I might, all courage fled as I approached that unmentionable organ. 'Don't forget her fanny.' It was Mr Archer, who seized on my pencil, and boldly tackled the central problem; a few magic lines and there was Bertha complete in her majesty.

Mr Archer was a volcano. Beard of flaming ginger, sparks for eyes, now smouldering, now flaring; never spent. And what a draughtsman; with what strength he grappled with a line, with what tenderness caressed a form or coaxed a hidden axis into view (Fig. 11). He was my hero, the champion who came to my aid in the daily battle I waged with the problems of learning to draw.

Problems involved in learning to draw? Is not drawing like all art a gift of nature? If it is, then it is not unsolicited. Nature's arm has to be well and truly twisted before she will part with a mite of ability. Furthermore, she is forever snatching back what she has given. Learning to draw requires an immense amount of application. It is only by working, by drawing, by practising long and regularly that a draughtsman develops his eye, that is to say that sense which eventually enables him or her to see where the power of a line lies. The last sentence is a paraphrase of one I recall from a writing manual. I have simply exchanged ear for eye, hear for see, and word for line. It still makes sense because drawing is itself a language, and what Epictetas said of writing applies equally well to it: if you wish to be a good draughtsman, draw. But if drawing is a language, it is also a dead one; it died after a decline brought on by exposure to photography. True it was old, thousands and thousands, if not millions of years old, yet we should mourn its passing; for the ancient tactile meaning once attached to line, and understood by our whole anatomy – our physical and our subtle bodies – has been replaced by a mechanical copying of shape and shadow which speaks only to the eyes. Few indeed are the people in our time who can read and write the language of line – Mr Archer was one. If I could sing, I would sing the praises of this man, laud in song his skill as a painter, draughtsman and maker of violins; but I would have to follow with a dirge, bewailing a talent trampled by the hobnailed boots of circumstance, and who would cry over crumbs of crushed genius?

So let us return to Mr Archer as a drawing master happily running his one-man Renaissance surrounded by eager students. Eager? Everyone knows that students reserve their enthusiasm for leaving their studies, not pursuing them.

True, but it should be remembered that the year was 1949. Mercifully the Second World War belonged to history and the demobbed servicemen were planning a peaceful future. Some of them had returned to their interrupted studies. Those that were completing their art training at Chelmsford, being anxious to make

Fig. 11: Charles Archer, *Life Study*, 1950, chalk (Collection E. Hebborn)

up for lost time, created an infectious atmosphere of enthusiasm and diligence which, much to the benefit of our artistic organs, we younger students greedily inhaled.

We were studying to take what was shortly to be called the Old Drawing Examination, for in 1951 the Ministry of Education decided that it would be fairer to reduce the difficulties presented by this examination rather than increase the students' capacity to meet them. In this way it could ensure that the hardworking would have no advantage over the lazy, or the talented over the untalented. The new drawing examination would be so easy that nobody need fail it, and each and every student who took it would be given a diploma called the Intermediate Diploma of Arts and Crafts to prove that he or she was no more competent than anybody else, and was warranted never ever to stir the murky waters of mediocrity. Here are two items from the Old Drawing Examination, the examination I nearly had the honour of failing.

Artistic Anatomy

1. Draw from memory a tennis player in the act of serving a ball.
2. Draw a skeleton in the same pose and from the same angle as your first drawing. The skeleton should be complete as to the number of bones, and the articulation of the joints clearly rendered.
3. Again using the same pose and point of view as in your first drawings, draw the superficial muscles of the body.
4. Name the origins and insertions of the following muscles: sterno-cleidomastoid, deltoid, pectoralis, trapezius, obliquus externus, sartorius, and gastrocnemius.

Perspective

You are standing at an open window on the fourth floor of a building in a busy thoroughfare. Directly across the road is a building identical to the one you are in yourself. On the ground floor of this building, Mrs Smith is leaning out of a window to look down the street in the middle of which both Mrs Smith and yourself can see a monument in the form of an equestrian statue on an oblong plinth. At the very end of the road is a church with a spire.

Make two drawings; one showing what Mrs Smith sees, and the other what you yourself see. The drawings must be drawn to the same scale, show a variety of vehicles, and include architecture from three different periods. Both drawings are to be accompanied by technical drawings showing how you have arrived at their construction.

We also studied Sculpture, Calligraphy, Architecture, and Art History. It was in connection with the last subject that I made my first drawing after old masters. One of these exercises has survived (Fig. 12). It is after Thomas Rowlandson (1756-1827), an artist to whose already large oeuvre I was later to add a number of works among which may be mentioned one in the Witt Library, but we shall come to that below, and mention here the first time I was commissioned to make a drawing in the style of another artist.

It was given to me by a lady of Indian extraction whom I shall call Mrs B. Mrs B paid for her tuition out of her own purse, and being financially independent was judged to be well-off. In any case she was as assuredly the richest student in the school as I was the poorest, and being good-natured could always be counted on to lend me half a crown. The only snag about the arrangement was that she could seldom count on me to pay it back. This led her to suggest that I repay her in kind, the kind being two drawings in the manner of Wyndham Lewis (1882-1957), to me a harsh unpleasant draughtsman. She had two sheets of paper that she claimed came from a Wyndham Lewis sketchbook and I made the drawings in the slightly less disagreeable style of the artist's youth.

They were not copies or adaptations from known works, but original drawings reluctantly following his manner. Whether Mrs B. ever passed them off as really being by Wyndham Lewis I do not know, but I do hope she did and reaped some reward for the faith she put in my growing ability. The seed of my future career was sown.

Well, the time for the Old Drawing Examination came, but not for me. It was taken after a two-year course, and I had only been studying for one. As I mentioned above, in 1951 it was exchanged for the Intermediate Examination of Arts and Crafts, and it was this exam which I had the distinction to fail. Who, one may ask, could possibly fail an examination especially tailored for all to pass? The answer is: any student who dares to think for himself. Such

Fig. 12: *A Domestic Scene*, after Rowlandson (1756-1827), 1949, pen and wash, made at the age of fifteen (Collection of the artist)

people cannot accept the formulas prescribed for success, and in my own case I could not entertain the idea of having a predetermined size for the life drawing. 'The drawing must fairly fill a half imperial sheet of cartridge paper,' said the powers that be. Unfortunately for me, I had noticed that master draughtsmen vary the size and proportions of their drawings to match their ideas, and believing that the example of Rembrandt (who had taken over from Van Gogh as my preferred master at the time) was better than the precept of the Ministry of Education, I produced a drawing much smaller than the regulations called for. How wrong I was!

My early art career ended in ignominy. I could no longer lift my head among the clever young people who were now going forward to take the National Diploma of Design, and then the Art Teacher's Diploma . . . oh the mind boggles! For myself I would soon be conscripted into the army and, on being demobbed, marry a girl, no more original thinking, work at Critall's making metal window frames for ten pounds a week, buy a punch-bag and a new bike, have insurance and a retirement plan: such were my reduced aspirations. The National Gallery and many similar institutions may now wish I had achieved these modest aims but it was not to be. Mr Archer again came to my rescue. My champion spoke so highly of my abilities to the Essex County Council that it decided to renew my grant to study for a further year. During that year I must have made some progress (Fig. 13), inasmuch as Mr Archer decided that I was sufficiently advanced in drawing to start to learn to paint.

'Well, Hebborn, and what would you say to painting a still-life in oils?'

'What, real oils Sir! Thanks ever so much Sir, when can I start Sir?'

'Contain yourself boy. Before you rush into it you must be sure you have the right subject and limit your palette. Now what I suggest, and it is only a suggestion,' (here he put his hand to his chin in the gravest manner, to indicate that he was giving the matter the most serious consideration) 'is, let me see, yes, I've got it: a cup, a saucer, and a . . . uhm, a sugar bag. How does it sound?'

'Cor, smashing Sir, I'll run down to the canteen . . .'

'No need, boy, I think we may find what we are looking for closer at hand.'

With this he took a key from his pocket, opened a locker, and lo and behold, drew forth, already arranged on a drawing board, and covered with dust and cobwebs, miracle of miracles, a cup, a saucer and a sugar bag!

'Scuse me Sir, but ain't it a bit dull Sir?'

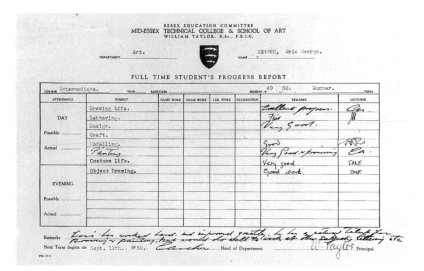

Fig. 13: Progress report from Chelmsford Art School, 1949-50

'A bit dull?!' exploded Mr Archer. 'I know what's a bit dull around here, boy, and it's between your ears! Ah, could you but see the nuances of warm and cold colour in this humble china, feel the tactile contrast of its smoothness with the crisp creases of this crumpled bag . . .' And so saying, pointed his beard of flame at the ceiling and marched off.

Long and hard I stared at the dusty old cup searching for nuances, long and hard at the sugar bag for tactile values, but they had all marched off with Mr Archer. At length, I decided to paint a still-life of my own choosing. And so it was that when my mentor returned he found my easel set up before a Chianti bottle that had long since been obliged to exchange the company of wine for that of candles, a folded cloth with a knife laid upon it, a bread roll, and six apples with a bite taken from their backsides. Mr Archer with great solemnity began to count the objects, and being as good at counting as everything else he turned his hand to he soon arrived at the total. He then turned his attention to the number of colours on my palette. 'Ten and nine,' he said, adding sadly, 'ah, youth ever was ambitious,' and went his way.

No time was wasted in painting the apples and the bread roll which were then greedily and speedily devoured. This was better for my stomach than for my painting. As painters will appreciate, take one element from a still-life and all the other elements are altered. This is because colours have only a notional existence, and this depends on the relationship that the artist judges them to have with their fellows. For instance, place a lemon on a purple book and the apparent colours of both objects are made stronger by the contrast. Remove the lemon, or the book, and the remaining object will appear to have changed colour. Suffice it to say I got myself into difficulties. No amount of over-painting would cover up the faulty start, and many coats of many colours soon turned the once bright canvas into a muddy rag. My champion refused to come to the rescue. Three days passed by, and then a fourth, a fifth, and yet a sixth, and then, upon the seventh, the volcano erupted. My daub was hurled into a corner to be swiftly followed by a Chianti bottle, six apple cores, a folded cloth and a table knife. The humble cup, saucer and sugar bag were again produced from the locker. Colours: black, white and burnt sienna, were squeezed on my vacated palette, and Mr Archer gave me a lesson which, because the basics of painting are not elementary but elemental, is with me to this day.

Although in later life I was to take up sculpture, it was decided by the staff of the Chelmsford School of Art that my natural ability, if I had any, was probably for painting. This being so, if I should pass the Intermediate at my second try it would be necessary for me to attend a school that specialised in teaching that craft – and so it came about I was to go to Walthamstow.

By now I had left Mrs Jackson's cottage in Tolleshunt Major. Stan was doing his military service, and Mrs Jackson herself had moved to Welwyn Garden City.

I was staying in Chelmsford with an elderly couple called Mr and Mrs Gibbs, kind, well-meaning people who had until recently been housing my boyhood friend, Ron, who – according to them – had 'gone to the bad', and was now behind bars.

The Essex County Council found lodgings for me within walking distance of Walthamstow Art School, and so, having no further need for a bicycle, I gave Lightning away to a young man called Peter who, to have been deemed worthy of such a gift, must have meant much much more to me than I now recall.

Walthamstow is not in itself an attractive town. It is just another drab suburb of London, a place that gives more pleasure to leave than to visit. But it does stand near Epping Forest, which must be one of the most beautiful spots in the whole of England, and it does boast a close association with the arts. It was the home of William Morris, and has a charming little museum largely devoted to the works of the Pre-Raphaelites.

The façade of the then South West Essex Technical College and

School of Art, was as long as its name. Its tedious length was split in two by a Greekish temple-type entrance, through which I marched to meet the head of the art school, Mr Stuart Ray, who gave me an interview:

'Well, Hebborn, and which department of painting interests you in particular?'

'I'm a landscape painter, Sir,' I replied in the tones of the country bumpkin I was.

'And so am I, Hebborn, so am I. O for the smell of new mown hay! The taste of the morning air as to a chorus of birds, a copy of *The Times* under my boots, and the muse at my shoulder, I set up my easel to catch the first glimmerings of dawn! Welcome to a kindred spirit.'

'Thanks very much Sir.'

Mr Ray was a tall bony man in his mid-thirties, with the face and figure which in Art are normally given to Don Quixote (Fig. 14). And there was indeed something Quixotic in the nature of Stuart, as I was later permitted to call him, for like the Don he dreamed an impossible dream, and fought an invincible foe. He dreamt of transporting Camden Town to Walthamstow, or more precisely, he wanted to recreate in his art school the Camden Town of Walter

Fig. 14: Stuart Ray, *Self-portrait*, slipware bowl made at Walthamstow, 1952 (Collection E. Hebborn)

Sickert (a painter's painter best known to a wider public for his painting in the Tate entitled *Ennui*).

His invincible foe was the encroachment on his Camden Town world by alien influences originating in the modern art movements of America. But Stuart put up a good fight before his school finally, perhaps inevitably, succumbed to the pressures of Op and Pop, and for a decade or so Walthamstow School of Art flourished. I quote from Stuart's obituary in *The Times* written by Roger de Grey, PRA:

> In 1951 he [Stuart] became head of the School of Art at Walthamstow, and it was here that his capacity to teach came in full flower. Within a few years Walthamstow was transformed into one of the leading art schools – particularly for painting, fashion, photography – and included on its staff, Olwyn Bowey, Peter Blake, William Bowyer, Fred Cuming, Anthony Eyton and Ken Howard [now all Academicians] and Daphne Brooker and Joanne Brogden [now both Professors].
>
> Its distinguished students include Ian Drury, Peter Greenaway, Bill Jacklin, Shirley and Ken Russell and Tuffin and Foal.

The first bit of Camden Town appeared in the life-room at Walthamstow in the form of a sofa, which was shortly followed by a dressing table, a foot bath, an enamel water jug, and a wall-papered screen – all from the time of Sickert's Edwardian heyday. The model's throne was banished and the new props were arranged to create an 'authentic' setting for the ubiquitous Bertha. Sometimes younger, sometimes older, but always Bertha, for she was the typical female art school model. Now we were to see her in her natural habitat engaged in her everyday activities; at her toilette, preparing for bed, waiting for a gentleman caller, who if he had ever shown up would no doubt have been wearing a bowler hat, and at the end of his visit would have left *A Little Check* (the title of an etching by Sickert). Bertha had, it seemed, only one way of going about her daily activities, and that was to sit down, bolt upright, hands clutching her thighs, with her feet firmly planted sometimes on the floor and sometimes in the foot bath. In short, just as I had first seen her in Chelmsford and was later to see her in Burlington House. The fact is that Bertha was not a subject to draw or paint, she was an art form in herself, an art form invented by Degas and ferried across the English Channel by Sickert.

Once this is understood her value as an exercise becomes clear. Bertha is to the student of painting what the sonnet or the sestina is to the student of poetry – a virtually obsolete form practised for the challenge it offers, and then placed on the shelf of experience.

Fig. 15: *Portrait Study*, after a painting by Rembrandt,
together with a study of a kitchen corner, 1957, pencil
(Collection of the artist)

Stuart was well aware of the thread connecting Sickert's London
to Degas' Paris and fell deeply under the influence of the French
master. He even went as far as to paint the ballet dancer. The views
Stuart held about drawing strongly reflected this influence, and he
was keen to impress upon his students the first importance of
shape.

Here lay the underlying difference between Stuart's teaching of
drawing and that of Mr Archer, who insisted on the prime importance of the exploration of volume, and would have preferred a
drawing by Andrea del Sarto to one by Degas. Thus the basic doc-
trines of my two early teachers seemed to be in conflict, and I had
neither knowledge nor experience enough to resolve the dilemma.
Was it merely a conflict of opinion based on nothing more tangible
than a divergence of taste? I did not think so. I could not prove it
then, but I felt that the two contrasting notions were not really in-
compatible, and lying behind and beyond them is a third concept

nearer to the source of art, and from which they both stem.

At Walthamstow School of Art in the fifties, our bible was Sickert's *A Free House*. As far as I know none of us had actually gone so far as to read the book, but it was an article of faith that, sealed between its covers, lay painting's most jealously guarded secrets. The high priest of the Sickertian cult was, of course, Stuart Ray who would on occasion divulge some gem of the master's wisdom, but on the whole we had only the vaguest ideas of the Camden Town painter's doctrine. By studying his paintings, however, rather than his words, many of us grasped something of Sickert's method, and a number of our productions might easily have passed as works by the master himself. As we shall see below, one of my own eventually did.

Fig. 16: *Portrait of a Man*, 1955, pencil (Collection of the artist)

Fig. 17: *The Social Realist – Self-portrait*, 1952, pencil
(Collection of the artist)

There were also other forces at work upon us. One was an 'ism' known as 'Social Realism'. And at one point we were so far under its influence as to call ourselves social realists, although in fact none of us was very realistic and the majority of us were very definitely anti-social – we stank.

The kind of painting we did belonged to what is called the 'Kitchen Sink School'. John Bratby made the style, and himself, famous, by paintings that were used in the film of Joyce Cary's book, *The Horse's Mouth*.

For myself I still held in theory to the Buckle system of weekly ablutions, but without Mrs Buckle or a bathroom in my lodgings to keep me up to the mark I seldom managed to put it into practice. In addition, being social realists meant that we painted the people. Not nice, clean, neatly dressed people; they didn't count. It was the dirty, scruffy derelicts of society, the real people that we had to paint, and to understand real people we had to live that way. This was easy enough for me with my propensity for poverty, and soon I was as foul and filthy as the best of them.

I recall that my landlady, an Irish woman called Mrs Whittle, did not fully appreciate having a social realist as a lodger. Whether it was the stench of rancid sweat and unwashed clothes that crept beneath the social realist's door to take possession of the rest of her home, or whether it was his appearance – his scraggly beard, his unkempt hair snowing dandruff on his threadbare shoulders (Fig. 17), his nails like talons, his paint-covered rags, his lacklustre shoes of flopping soles and absent heels – something was not altogether to the liking of Mrs Whittle.

'I'll be having something to say to you, Mr Hebborn,' said she. 'For sure it is you're a shabby genteel, too decent to beg, too honest to steal, but you'll be finding yourself another place, or I'm not Mrs Whittle!' And as there was no question of her not being Mrs Whittle, the social realist was forced to live rough for a while in Epping Forest.

I made no effort to ensure a good night's sleep – I simply chose a tree and slept under it. It was September, not a time for running naked, and each morning found me cold and damp – but far from unhappy. On the contrary, it was a great pleasure to awake in such

Fig. 18: *My digs, seen through the trees of Highbury Fields,*
1955, pen and wash (Collection of the artist)

a room. The gnarled trunks of the ancient elms were my home. They were also my teachers: both master and masterpiece, example and precept. Epping Forest became a sort of school and I made many studies there, and some progress.

All too soon foul weather and the need for regular food drove me from the woods to seek refuge in a rooming house recommended by a fellow social realist. This establishment was in Highbury Grove, Islington (Fig. 18).

The owner modestly called himself the manager, and what he managed was truly extraordinary. He had managed to turn a house of eight rooms into a house of twenty-four rooms; and having done this not once but thrice, boasted an establishment of seventy-two rooms.

Each room had at least two walls of hardboard, a bed, a sink, and a gas meter. Some rooms had more than one bed, and these special rooms, the landlord would explain, were intended for 'three or four gentlemen sharing, by Christ already!' Rents were paid to him in his bedroom-office under the doorstep of No 42. 'Thirty bob a week single and two quid 'sharin'' was the rate. Translating these sums into pounds sterling we can estimate his takings to have been in the region of £450 a month. And when one considers that a house in Highbury Grove could at that time be bought outright for less than £2,000 it is clear that he was doing very good business indeed. Such a house today would fetch £200,000.

If I recall correctly a gentleman called Rachman, then doing similar good business, suffered the indignity of going to prison for it. Even so, thirty shillings a week was as low a rent as one could find in London at the time, and while I might have wished better value for my money, I was grateful for my hardboard haven.

Apparently not all of the tenants were as content with their lot as I, and during the years of my stay, six of them surrendered their lease – their lease on life. The passage to the underworld normally cost two shillings and sixpence, payable in advance to the gas meter, but it was not unknown for a passenger to cheat on the fare by breaking the lock on the meter and passing the self-same six-pence five times or more through the slot. In these cases the deceased party would usually leave in arrears with their rent, and regardless of their sex, the doubly grieved landlord would mourn their passing with: 'By Christ, and I thought they was gentlemen already!'

Before leaving Stuart Ray's painting school, mention should be made of one of the most gifted teachers on his staff. Mr Kurt Roland had learnt the art of wood engraving from a distinguished

German engraver called Imre Reiner and was himself a first-class craftsman. His influence on our work is interesting in the present context because he taught that the design for a wood engraving should be made directly on the box-wood in pen and wash. Pen and wash is one of the principal techniques of the old masters and we were urged by Mr Roland to study their work closely so that we might learn how to translate the various tints or tone values of their washes with the graver, the tint tool, the *spitzsticker*, the scorper, and other exotic tools. His method was essentially the same as that of the reproductive engravers of yore, save that we mostly reproduced our own drawings, merely using the old masters for guidance in the initial stages of learning (Fig. 19).

We were studying for the National Diploma of Design. For myself I took painting as my main subject, and wood engraving as my craft.

In addition to producing evidence of our practical skills we were called upon to write a thesis – mine was called *The Science of Drawing*. It was basically an unlearned lope through the history of European draughtsmanship from Leonardo to Van Gogh, with many a slip between, but it did contain an idea that was later to be developed as a full dress theory. This germinal notion was not, however, contained in the text, which was of unrelieved banality, but in the illustrations. These were copies after the various masters discussed, and at the top of one double-page spread, I made a drawing after a Leonardo landscape on the left-hand page, the movement of which seemed to be continuous with a landscape after Van Gogh on the right hand page. Since the originals are separated in time by several centuries, and were made by an Italian and a Dutchman of totally different temperament, according to present artistic theory, they should have no stylistic affinity whatsoever. And yet as I drew from them, I became more and more aware that both Leonardo and Van Gogh were tapping a common source. Defying time and space, they were working in some shared dimension, exploring a world of universals common to all great art. My course was set, I might never set foot in that world myself, but I was determined to look for its pointers, and if I were lucky enough to find them, I was going to show them to others. Had I known then how audacious (I imagine some might say presumptuous), and how arduous the direction I had taken, I might have abandoned it.

Although a student of painting and engraving, I took an evening class in sculpture and it was at this class that I met a handsome young man named Graham Smith. Graham was to be my companion for fourteen years. He was posing for a portrait sculpture by a gifted student from Australia called Mary Frazer. Thinking that her portrait captured Graham's Greco-Roman looks excellently, I complimented her, at which Graham seems to have thought that by admiring his likeness, I was making overtures to him himself. In actual fact I would have been far too shy to have made the first move. But as it was we were soon involved in an emotionally intense affair. And as I could not take him back to my lodgings and he could not take me to his home, we found ourselves making love where we could. Once we were spotlighted with our trousers down outside a row of garages. The torch-bearing policeman unaccountably, but fortunately, mistook us for a boy and a girl, otherwise we would have been in serious trouble. Homosexuality was against the law, even for consenting adults.

Two friends of ours, Sam and Jerry, aged nineteen and twenty-three respectively, were reported by their neighbours to the police who raided their flat and took away their bed sheets to be examined for traces of sperm. The couple were eventually convicted. Jerry was sent to prison. Sam committed suicide!

The NDD was a graduate course, and having successfully completed it I could now advance to a post-graduate course. To do this meant being accepted by one or another of the three august

Fig. 19: *The Massacre of the Innocents*, after a painting by Peter Breughel the Elder, 1956, wood-engraving (Collection of the artist)

95

The gas meter was at hand, but so, thank God, was Stuart Ray. Stuart kindly offered to put me on his part-time staff, and so it was I became an evening lecturer at Walthamstow on anatomy, life drawing and, with my old teacher Kurt Rolands, engraving. With easier hours I could keep awake, and try to keep my students awake with me.

Furthermore, part-time teaching was relatively well paid and consequently my financial position was sufficiently eased for me to view the feeding of my gas meter as leading to certain comfort on earth rather than speculative comfort elsewhere. In addition, by not falling asleep at the Academy, I was able to win a number of scholarships and prizes: the Leverhulme Scholarship, the David Murray (Fig. 7) Landscape Prize, and a good many more. No large sums of money were involved, but every penny was most gratefully received.

As for the teaching at the Academy, it generally consisted of leaving us alone, the teacher offering advice only if called upon by the student to do so. I suppose it was rather naïve of me, but I had imagined that the more important the art school, the greater would be the ability of the teachers, and hence the higher the standard of instruction, but I cannot honestly say that there was any teacher at the Academy Schools of greater ability than Charles Archer of Chelmsford, or Stuart Ray at Walthamstow. And it may be significant that when the Academy later increased the number of its teachers, the new additions were largely drawn from the stable formed at Walthamstow: Margaret Green, Jack Millar, and John Bryne being the names that first come to mind. However that may be, in my first year as a student at Burlington House our teachers (called Visitors) were few and rarely seen. This can be explained by the fact that instruction in the schools was confined to that given by members of the Academy themselves; and because membership of the Academy appears to be the passport to longevity, the average age of the Academicians was about seventy-five – the age of the President, Sir Gerald Kelly.

Peter Greenham was the teacher, or Visitor, we saw most of. He struck one as being retiring, courteous and amiable, with a gentle wrinkled face looking somewhat older than his forty-odd years (Fig. 21). He smoked heavily and when drawing or painting would leave a cigarette in his mouth from which the smoke would rise to curtain off his kindly eyes and let ash drop where it would.

Peter once said to me that one could tell an artist whose work had deteriorated by the smart clothes he would be wearing. If true,

Fig. 20: *The Pieta*, from a plaster cast of Michelangelo, 1957, pen and ink
(Collection of the artist)

it was clear from his old grey suit of crease and crumple, ash and
splash, that his own talent was yet intact.

He was a portrait painter of some distinction who had painted
many important people, including the Queen, and in the Summer
Exhibition of 1978 his portrait of Lady (Charlotte) Bonham Carter
was to be judged the most distinguished exhibit of the year.

During the time I am speaking of he exhibited an enormous canvas representing the Duke of Wellington and his grandson. This
picture was not, it appears, very well received. Peter had had problems painting it, which he himself was not certain had been satisfactorily solved. He revealed his disappointment to a group of
students of which I happened to be one. We were chatting and
cleaning our brushes at the sinks in the cloakroom, when he said
sadly and to no one in particular: 'I'd give ten shillings to anyone
who could find something appreciative to say about my picture.'
We fell silent, rubbing our brushes even harder in the bars of soap.
Then came my unkind whisper: 'Make it a pound, Peter, make it a

Fig. 21: *Peter Greenham*, 1958, red chalk (Collection of
the artist)

pound.' A thoughtless remark which I regretted as soon as I had
made it.

The Professor of Architecture was A. E. Richardson, who was to
be elected President of the Academy in December 1954 and
knighted in January 1956.

Richardson has been dubbed as 'probably the most genial President of the Academy of all time'. He was over seventy, yet full of
vigour, and his lectures, all impromptu and illustrated with hand-
drawn slides, were delivered with unforgettable verve and humour.

They were given in the Architecture School, a mysterious, otherwise unfrequented place, hung from floor to ceiling with grimy
casts of classical mouldings.

Professor Richardson, who had been Professor of Architecture at
London University for over twenty-five years, had developed his
own approach to lecturing. Over his paunch was spread an expanse
of embroidered silk, with pleats, pockets, and buttons of mother of

pearl. It was a genuine eighteenth-century waistcoat of exceptional quality, in superb condition. He would begin his discourse by taking from one of its copious pockets a gold watch on a golden chain, both from Georgian times.

All this was indicative of the man and his ideas. Professor Richardson still breathed the air of the well-to-do English gentleman of Georgian England. His Georgian home at Ampthill was lit with candles and oil lamps, and stuffed to overflowing with paintings, sculptures, costumes, books and furniture from the period.

Incidentally, he believed one of his paintings to be by Gainsborough, and on being asked if he had ever consulted an expert on the matter, snapped back: 'I don't need any damned expert to tell me a Gainsborough is a Gainsborough!'

He sometimes travelled in a sedan chair, and this habit of his once got him into trouble with the law. He had gone to dine at a friend's house, and had thoughtlessly parked his conveyance in a manner for which he was given a ticket and charged in court for having parked a vehicle without lights. The Professor defended himself vigorously, pointing out that a sedan chair does not qualify as a vehicle, the definition of which is: 'any kind of carriage or conveyance for use on land, having wheels or runners'. He carried the day.

It was rumoured that on another occasion our Professor shinned up an old street lamp that local authorities had decided to replace with some cement horror, and refused to come down until he had a written promise that the lamp-post would be spared. Again he won the battle, but it is all too plain today who won the war.

But to return to Professor Richardson glancing at his pocket watch before his first lecture for the academic year 1955-1956 and beginning in grandiloquent tones: 'In Rome we have the Colosseum; in Paris we have the Arc de Triomphe; and in London what do we have? (looks around for effect) Why, a sailor on a stick and a couple of squirts!'

He continued his discourse by pointing out, more seriously, the vital importance of preserving what was left of London's skyline as seen from the Thames, a skyline that was once dominated by the dome of St Paul's. He gave examples of buildings that might be sacrificed or redesigned to that end. He was, if I recall correctly, also very keen on the idea of continuing with a general plan for the city that had been conceived by Nash.

His deeply felt condemnation of modern architecture, which, of course, prefigured that of Prince Charles, was nevertheless delivered with good humour. Suburbs sprouting bungalows were said to be suffering from a disease known as 'bungalitis', and high-rise blocks of flats earned the epithet of 'breeding boxes' . . . 'maggotries full of pale and squirming people'. His earnest desire was to see a return to the gracious living of his beloved Georgian times. And this not only for the gentry.

Once every now and again we held in the Schools what was known as an exhibition of the 'Sketch Club'. In this exhibition (not open to the public) the students showed work which had not been drawn or painted on the premises of the Academy. An artist of distinction, whether associated with the Academy or otherwise, was called in to give a little talk, discuss the works on view, and award the Sketch Club Prize which consisted of a very modest sum of money – I seem to remember five pounds.

One of the artists invited was John Minton, then a lecturer at the Royal College of Art. He was brilliantly talented and very much interested in drawing. He had made beautiful illustrations and having a literary turn, wanted to see a return to the narrative picture, a kind of painting illustrating scenes from history, even going so far as to exhibit a picture in the Academy called *The Death of Nelson*. But for all this he was a 'modernist'. He hoped to inject new life into the old themes.

The picture I had submitted for his consideration was a painting of trees in Epping Forest. It was painted in a style perhaps reminiscent of Courbet, but really very much in my own manner. And of all the pictures on show, Minton singled mine out, not for the prize, but for a most savage attack. He could not believe, he said, that as late as the fifties an artist could be so old-fashioned, so banal, so – untouched by modern movements, so . . . in short so unoriginal.

At the end of his talk he asked if we had any questions; and as he had thought fit to talk at length of the shortcomings of my performance, I thought I might be permitted to ask on what grounds he had based his damning criticism. He replied (obviously not thinking of his own work) that an artist today should tackle contempoary problems, from a contemporary point of view, using contemporary techniques.

'Why?' I asked. 'What weakness makes us so fear the influence of the past? And even if there is real danger in taking our inspiration secondhand, is the remedy for all contemporary artists to paint as much like each other as possible? You criticise me for being unoriginal, but you must admit that, insofar as I am the only unoriginal painter in this room, I am unique!'

After his talk, Minton approached me in a most friendly manner, and asked me if I would like to continue our discussion over a drink. We went to a pub, and then got drunk at his expense in a gay club in Greek Street called the 'Neptune', all without, as far as I recall, solving any of the big questions of aesthetics.

John Minton had a boyfriend with the very grand name of Spencer Churchill. This man was extraordinarily handsome with a muscular frame. He was a wrestler and an occasional art school model. He posed for my life class at Walthamstow, and it was there that I made a number of drawings of him. I made them in pen and blue fountain-pen ink, which was the same medium in which Minton worked, and this, combined with the subject-matter, was sufficient for people to mistake this group of drawings for Minton's. The Piccadilly Gallery, the Redfern and Roland Browse and Delbanco have all at one time or another handled them. And I suspect because of the handsome model, my drawings are among Minton's most popular works.

Another Visitor to give a talk to the School's Sketch Club was Sir Stanley Spencer. He turned up wearing a suit that for artistic shabbiness upstaged even Peter Greenham's, and a pullover badly in need of darning, to tell us that he had no idea why he had been asked to speak, as he knew nothing about anything except Stanley Spencer. He continued by giving us an account of his day since he had woken up. How he had put his cat out, emptied his teapot, throwing the leaves as nourishment to a favourite hydrangea, and so on. Then, almost by the way, he said something illuminating about how he designed his paintings. He said that the designs sprang from the actions of the figures involved, and that he began by going through the motions of his figures himself. And it was while acting out the gestures of his characters that he conceived of the simplest and clearest way of communiciating them to the viewer. This I believe explains the link that has often been noted between his work and that of the early Italian masters. His pictures, like theirs, tell a story through meaningful gestures that function on two planes – one the narrative level and one the formal level, being rather like good poems where each word has a two-fold significance, i.e. its literal meaning and its musical or poetical value.

Sir Stanley liked my work better than John Minton had, and awarded me a prize for a large drawing that I had made, again in Epping Forest. He also invited me to visit him in Cookham. When I turned up he pretended that he had never ever judged a Sketch Club exhibition and that I must have been awarded the prize by his brother, Gilbert. He was nevertheless very charming, and kindly showed me over his modest little terraced house, which was unremarkable except for his bedroom which doubled as his studio. It was tiny and yet he painted enormous pictures in it. This he managed to do by having the canvases rolled up, unrolling only the portion that he was actually working on. At the time of my visit he was painting a picture of Christ preaching from a boat on the Thames. He was at work on the central area which filled one entire wall. Both ends of the great canvas being rolled up, he could not see the rest of the composition, and had to rely on his remarkable ability to keep the whole tonal and chromatic design before him in his mind's eye.

It had been a tradition at the Schools to present each probationer with a substantial ivory disc engraved with their name and the year of their admittance. This custom had long been in abeyance, but it was one of Professor Richardson's first acts as President to revive it. Thus we each received an ivory plaque, paid for and presented by the President. The presentation was followed by a grand dinner – also paid for out of Richardson's own pocket.

Since the foundation of the Academy, every Academician, besides presenting a Diploma Work, had been expected to make a gift of a piece of plate, with the result that the Academy possesses a fine assortment of silver tableware. This valuable collection was brought down to the Schools, the central corridor of which was transformed into a great banqueting hall. The linen-covered table was well over a hundred feet long and lit by countless candles set in splendid Georgian candlesticks. The glasses were of cut crystal.

A waiter was appointed to each student and his two personal guests and the food (catered by Fortnum and Mason) was brought in on silver trays. Doing what it is supposed to do, but all too seldom does, the claret flowed. Then came the toast to the Queen, followed by cognac, cigars, and, of course, speeches.

Sir Henry Rushbury thanked the President on the students' behalf for his liberality, let him know of the high esteem in which he was held by all present, and proposed a toast to his good health and to the success of his presidency.

The President, wearing his familiar waistcoat, responded in his best Churchillian manner, perhaps a trifle slurred, and likened the Academy to a great ship, saying that he himself was the captain of that ship which under his command would sail in safety across troubled seas to reach as yet unchartered waters. Then, perhaps reflecting that he was probably better as an architect than as a sailor, he changed metaphor in mid-ocean, as it were, and said that the Academy was really a cathedral with a well-stocked cellar. Saying: 'Above' (here he pointed to the ceiling to indicate Heaven and the

Fig. 22: *Portrait Group, c.* 1957 (Graham is third from left), oil on canvas
(Collection of the artist)

Academy's *piano nobile*) 'we have the spirits divine, below' (looking at his brimming glass) 'we have the spirits of wine', at which everyone cheered, and sang: 'For he's a jolly good fellow, for he's a jolly good fellow . . .'

The sumptuous feast was followed by the boogie, a form of dance which to my mind, and I suspect Professor Richardson's, tended to spoil the Georgian-type fun. But our genial septuagenarian host made no objection. He simply withdrew into a sedan chair of the mind, from where he continued to sip his cognac, smile and wave graciously until, the evening grown late, he drew the blinds and was carried home.

Among the many prizes and scholarships I won as a student was the Hacker portrait prize, and with it the Royal Academy silver medal for painting. The prize came from funds given to the Academy in 1920 by Miss Hacker in memory of her brother, Arthur Hacker RA, who had died the year before. Strictly speaking, the award was intended for a head and shoulders painted from life, but I won it for a life-size, full-length portrait. Sir Henry Rushbury told me that my picture had been greatly praised by Augustus John. All this made me feel inches taller and gave me confidence to under-

Fig. 23: *Study for a Portrait of Graham*, 1957, pencil
(Collection of the artist)

take more work on a large scale.

It was my fondest wish to win the Rome Scholarship, which
would allow me to spend two years studying in Italy, thus putting
off the problem of what to do when my student days came to an
end. The competition was very stiff, and I thought I should paint
something particularly ambitious for it; and this was how I came to
paint a large portrait group – 10′ × 8′ (Fig. 22). The idea behind
the picture was to paint a group of my friends and fellow students,
mostly in their everyday clothes, and to give them some of the dignity of formal portraits of important people in what is known as the
'grand manner'.

A full-length portrait of mine with a similar idea behind it was
accepted for the annual exhibition of the Royal Society of Portrait
Painters in 1957. Its title, *The Young Edwardian*, indicated the notion

involved. It was the time of the 'teddy boys', when young working-class men dressed themselves up in what they imagined to be the clothes of the Edwardian era. They sported jackets with velvet collars, 'drainpipe' trousers, 'boot-lace' ties, 'winkle-picker' shoes, and had shirts with tucks and ruffles and upstanding collars. Being a teddy boy was an expensive matter, and for that reason my painted version only alluded to the fashion. It was a portrait of Graham, who posed for it wearing tight jeans, a simple white shirt with its collar turned up, and a duffel coat thrown over his shoulders in the manner of a cape. The drawing illustrated in Fig. 23 is a study connected with, but not directly for, this picture, and gives some idea of the casually dignified pose I was aiming for. And this was my point. 'Ordinary' young people feel a need to enhance themselves and their lives. They have not yet succumbed to the idea that they have to accept the dreary fact that they are 'nobodys'. A young working-class man dressed up according to his fancy can feel like a prince, and it is this feeling, and not his actual appearance, that I tried to capture in my portrait.

The portrait of Graham was well received, and the President of the Portrait Society, James Gunn, who at the time was perhaps the most successful portrait painter in the country (and was exhibiting his portrait of George VI) wrote me a letter telling me how highly he and the other members of the Society thought of the picture. And Edward Halliday, who was the President of the Royal Society of British Artists, asked my permission to use the work to illustrate a magazine article he was writing.

But to return to my large portrait group. As with the portrait of Graham, it was supposed to express the dignity without pomp which is natural to the young. My friends were painted in front of a wall on which I copied the menacing figures of Picasso's mural *War*. We were living in the relatively early years of the Cold War which has only just ended. Later we were to grow to accept the constant threat of nuclear and chemical warfare as the status quo, but in the late fifties we were not so insentient as to lack fear of the ghastly prospect, or so lacking in hope as to think that politicans could not be persuaded by the ban-the-bomb arguments of the greatest thinkers of our time such as Einstein and Lord Russell. Picasso's figures with their weapons raised above the heads of my friends symbolised for me the frailty of our optimism.

Graham was again in the picture, now standing in a pose that Van Dyck had once used for a king. Other people in the picture included my two closest friends in the Academy, Patrick and Derek.

It should be remembered that abstract painting was all the rage among young artists of the time and that whatever the merits or demerits of my large picture, it was for somebody of my generation an extraordinary performance. It was very definitely and very deliberately swimming against the tide of taste.

Abstract painting is no longer in fashion, and it is hard now to imagine the grip it had on the minds of my contemporaries. Intellectually it was an attractive idea. Painting was to be freed from the shackles of representation and like music, be unsullied by reference to anything outside of itself. But I realised even then that there is a flaw in the argument upon which the intellectual acceptance of abstract painting rests. The truth is that no painting can truly be abstract. To abstract is to separate the universal from the particular. Thus it was hoped, for instance, that colour could be separated from coloured things, such as the representations of blue skies, green fields and so on, and this to a limited extent is true. Unfortunately, however, one is only exchanging one particular for another. Instead of a particular blue sky or green field one gets a particular blue or green shape. This is because an actual shape is always a particular, a particular triangle, a particular square, or whatever. The abstract or the 'ideal' shape as it was once called, can only exist in the mind. And the failure of 'abstract' painting comes about for the very same reason as the failure of those much maligned artists of the past who sought to represent 'ideal' beauty – it's a marvellous thought, but it can't be done! The ideal must remain in the realms of the ideal, the abstract in those of the abstract. This does not mean that there are no good 'abstract' paintings, far from it, but it does mean that they are good in spite of being based on an intellectual fallacy. We may still like them, but they do not offer the mind the new horizons that the style seemed to promise.

The judges responsible for choosing the Rome Scholars for 1958 did not approve of my big non-abstract picture, and my attempt to win the Rome Scholarship failed.

It looked as if my student days were almost at an end, and that I would have to prepare myself to do national service, and on being demobbed, consider how I was going to earn a living. Teaching was the obvious choice, partly because I was already earning part of my livelihood in that way, and partly because it was the usual way that artists survived. Selling one's work was not a realistic proposition, and even such a highly successful artist as Henry Moore had taught until his fortieth year.

I could not, however, resign myself to failure and made up my mind to compete again for the Rome Scholarship. Having failed with my gigantic painting, this time I went to the other extreme, and submitted a number of miniature works – tiny engravings on wood, smaller than the palm of my hand. These works were liked by Sir Henry Rushbury who, as much to my embarrassment as pride, introduced me to perhaps the most famous wood engraver of the day, Blaigh Hugh Stanton, as: 'Eric Hebborn, the finest engraver on wood since Thomas Bewick'.

As it happened, Sir Henry was one of the judges that year, and I felt that with his support I stood a good chance of succeeding. Nevertheless, I thought it prudent not to postpone any further the problem of easing myself out of the limited environment of art schools. And it was this consideration, combined with an urgent need of money, which led me to make what may be described as a false start.

CHAPTER V

HAUNCH OF VENISON
YARD

'Vandevelde – I can't paint like him.'
J. M .W. Turner.

The life painting class was over, Bertha dressed and on her way
home. The cleaners were trying their best to sweep the floor
of the studio without disturbing either the easels or the model's
throne whose positions were marked on the floor in chalk so that
they would remain exactly as the students had left them until the
following session.

Patrick and myself had just finished washing our brushes in the
cloakroom. This we had done by rubbing the bristles on bars of
soap provided for the purpose and worn through in the middle
by the process. We walked down the long vaulted corridor of the
Academy Schools towards the plaster *Laocoön* – the very cast that
had once been drawn by William Blake. We discussed financial
matters. The question was, did we or did we not have enough
money to buy two beers at the Cricketer's Arms in Piccadilly?
Leaving *Laocoön* and his sons to their deathless struggle with the
snakes, we passed the porter's lodge, said good evening to George
and Ernie, mounted the short flight of steps to the Schools'
entrance and stepped into the dingy alleyway that separated our
cultural aspirations from the commerce of Burlington Arcade.

There in the alley we found a friend and fellow student, Sidney,
engaged in conversation with a short middle-aged man wearing
tweeds, a hat of the same material, an ochre tie, a thick shirt – all of
excellent quality – and expensive brogue shoes. From his bluff and
prosperous appearance I took him for a gentleman farmer.

'Maybe,' said Sid, 'my mates here, Paddy and Eric, might be
interested as well, Mr, excuse me, what did you say?'

'Aczel,' replied the supposed gentleman farmer, opening a fat wallet, and taking therefrom, and handing out, three visiting cards which read:

George Aczel
Picture Restorer to the Trade
Haunch of Venison Yard
Brook Street
London W.1.

Sidney explained that Mr Aczel had visited the Academy in the hope of meeting art students who might be interested in becoming apprentice restorers. His business was flourishing and he had more work than he and his two assistants could manage. His offer was to train us for two days a week and pay us a nominal fee of one pound a day until such time as we were skilled enough to be an asset to the business, when our wages would be raised accordingly.

It seemed a fair, even generous, offer, and after having made a rapid calculation of how many pints of bitter the nominal fee would

Fig. 24: *Patrick*, 1957, pencil (Collection of the artist)

buy at the Cricketer's Arms, Patrick and I decided to join Sid as the restorer's apprentices.

So it was that at nine o'clock the very next morning I strolled along Old Bond Street into New Bond Street and, crossing the road in front of Sotheby's, turned into Brook Street to find that Haunch of Venison Yard was a turning to my right.

It was a small irregular enclosure that in my imagination still preserved the atmosphere of a cobbled courtyard of a Tudor coaching inn. Coaches and cobbles gone, beams and timbers long since plastered over, and yet the asymmetry of the whole, the irregularity of its parts, the lowness of the doors and pokiness of the windows spoke to me of the past, and presaged days of good business.

Today the yard houses the offices of Phillip's, the auctioneers, but in 1957 part of their present premises was given over to the restoration of Old Master paintings, and one could see, perched high in the furthest left-hand corner, a sign advertising the studio of my employer, George Aczel, Picture Restorer to the Trade.

From the yard I took a stairway which wound its way up in narrow gloom, as though it would end in some ancient tower. I knocked on a shabby door bearing the same wording as the sign outside, and was admitted to a strong smell of turpentine and dammar varnish by Sid who, with Paddy and two female recruits from the Academy, had arrived a few moments earlier.

Mr Aczel was reiterating the nature of our agreement in accents that suggested he had left his homeland to avoid the unpleasantness of a concentration camp. As I listened I inspected his studio. It was on the top floor and had a skylight patched here and there with waterproof paper. Its shape, unknown to geometry, seemed to have been the result of demolishing the connecting walls of a number of once separate rooms. If this were true, it accounted for certain abrupt changes of floor level. The exact architectural nature of the workroom was, however, obscured by its contents. Apart from the large tables necessary for cleaning and varnishing, the chairs and easels for the retouchers, and shelves of materials and tools employed in the restorer's art, the oils, varnishes, solvents, stocks of cotton wool, paint rags and so on, the room was furnished with racks. These were full of paintings, some newly arrived, others in the process of restoration, others again bright and shiny, awaiting collection. Good, bad, new, old, large, small, quantities and quantities of paintings. Mostly they were without frames, and this gave them the appearance of being naked and vulnerable; defenceless objects, like the sick in an overcrowded hospital.

Mr Aczel started our training by getting us to make pencil copies from photographs. The photograph given to me was of a horse grazing in a field. This exercise was designed to show our master that our eyes and hands were not unco-ordinated.

Having satisfied himself that we had the basic manual skill, he set us to work on the paintings set up on the easels. Mostly these pictures had been relined, that is, they were worn or damaged canvases that had been re-backed. This work had been carried out by workers in a studio specialising in this highly skilled and delicate operation. Where there had been tears or holes, our teacher had prepared them for retouching and we were given the job of filling in these damaged parts with colours to match the surrounding areas of paint. Unlike the scientific picture restorer, who likes to maintain a distinction between the new and the old, we endeavoured to match the original colours so exactly as to make the mend invisible. We were given *mahl* sticks with which to steady our hands, the smallest of sable brushes, and colours from the selected lists of the best makers to mix with dammar.

It may seem that Mr Aczel was being rash in setting absolute beginners to retouch the old paintings entrusted to his care, and perhaps he was. But not irremediably so. Paint mixed with dammar is very easily removed with turpentine and consequently errors committed with it are just as easily rectified.

Our teacher was a good one and as we were not entirely new to the handling of paint, it was not long before we became proficient in mixing up the correct tints to match the original colours. The girls were quicker at this matching of colours than the boys. They also had more patience with minute work. But it soon became apparent that each one of us brought a slightly different talent to the craft of restoration. The best all-rounder was Sid, who in fact was to take up restoration as a profession. Only Paddy seemed unsuited as a restorer. He was an extremely talented artist, and had won the Academy's coveted Turner Gold Medal, but his manner was broad and painterly and it was not in his nature to produce the tiny precise touches necessary for fine inpainting. As a result he left the studio in Haunch of Venison Yard after only a few days.

Mr Aczel soon discovered that my own special gift was for painting-in large areas of missing colour in the style of the original artist. This pleased him, because for all his knowledge and craftsmanship he was severely limited as a draughtsman, and when it came to painting in large lacunae, the clumsiness of his drawing made the repair all too obvious. Thus when the damage was large Mr Aczel would gratefully put the picture on my easel.

Before he did so, however, he would make a stopping, or a filler, with flake white (white lead) mixed with *gesso* powder (plaster of Paris) into a paste. He would apply this mixture to the missing area with a flexible palette knife and allow it to become partly dry, though still soft enough to take an impression. He would then take a piece of unprimed canvas of the same texture as the old part of the painting, and press it firmly on to the stopping, leaving it in position long enough for the stopping to take the impress of the grain of the canvas, and then carefully remove it without disturbing the imprint. Then he would leave it for three or four days to harden, when of course the filling would have a texture closely resembling the surrounding canvas. This he made even more like the original areas by drawing a needle along the underside of the impression of the horizontal threads to deepen them. When I had painted over them, these lines cast shadows like the threads of canvas.

After the completion of my inpainting the newly painted detail had to be 'cracked'. Mr Aczel taught me to do this by waiting until the retouched surface became tacky and then, again taking up the darning needle, to draw it along a genuine crack which stopped short at the edge of the stopping. On reaching the stopping I was told to press harder to continue the crack across the damage. I continued all the cracks leading to the filling across it in this way until its surface appeared to be cracked all over. Where necessary, colour was rubbed into the new 'cracks' to give them exactly the same appearance as their older companions.

Thus it was that under Mr Aczel's guidance I began, little by little, to develop my abilities and improve my knowledge of the materials and methods of the Old Masters until I would one day be able to 'restore' a whole painting – from nothing at all. It is a well known fact, however, that the alteration of old pictures is a much more common practice than the making of old masters' *ex novo*, as indeed it was in Haunch of Venison Yard.

The borderline between what is restoration and what is simply repainting is not always clear. Nor should it be thought that old pictures are necessarily spoiled by modern alteration. This attitude arises from a scientific approach devoid of any aesthetic judgment. Would we return the Sistine Chapel to what it was before Michelangelo exchanged the Perugino frescos for his own? Well, no, but it would be nice to have the Peruginos as well. Would we remove the retouching with which Rubens was in the habit of improving his collection of mediocre Old Masters? No. The truth is that age in itself is obviously no guarantee of quality, and many old pictures are bad old pictures, some so bad it would be difficult to make them worse.

Even good pictures may on occasion be improved by some deliberate alteration. An example could be the well known case of Joshua Reynolds's portrait group showing the Payne sisters at the spinet accompanied by their mother. This picture, now in the Lady Lever Art Gallery, once had the girls' mother painted out. Precisely why is not known, but it was a vast improvement. With the mother, the composition is overcrowded. Without her, it is spacious and charming. I would not go so far as to suggest painting the woman out again. Her memory would persist, and our pleasure would be impaired by knowing that the old busy body was still lurking under the new paint. Nevertheless, the art historian's gain in having the mother as Reynolds left her is the aesthete's loss in having to endure her.

Less happy results of altering fine paintings are recorded. Friedlander and Rosenberg in their monograph of *Lucas Cranach* (1932, p.82) speak of a painting by Cranach of Salome holding the head of Saint John the Baptist which had the Saint's gory head overpainted, and transformed into a heap of precious ornaments. The outcome was that Salome, bearing a silver salver dripping with jewels instead of blood, was obliged to change her name, and appeared in respectable society as *The Goldsmith's Daughter*. Such is the lamentable fate of Salome in art. She is, however, more fortunate than Saint Joseph, who does not merely change his identity, but is often removed from 'The Holy Family' altogether to leave behind a more saleable 'Madonna and Child'. And this is the point. Art is business. Dealers are businessmen, and as such prefer pictures that sell. To give an example, the famous picture dealer, Duveen, had bought a Masaccio on the advice of Bernard Berenson. Berenson had not, however, taken into account the saleability of the picture, and in spite of its great virtues, and Duveen's fabled ability as a salesman, the picture was judged by his clients as being too dull for them. Seeing the unsaleable item month after month on his walls, the 'king of art dealers' grew to loathe the masterpiece, and one day summoned his assistant Boggis. 'Get me an axe,' he said. 'I want to chop that picture up.' 'Don't do it, Joe,' advised Boggis, 'B.B. likes it.' The Masaccio, it is said, was saved from destruction by Boggis presenting Duveen with a more commercially attractive painting to contemplate. It is very doubtful whether Duveen would in fact have destroyed his investment, but it is perfectly clear from his little joke what his attitude towards pictures really was.

Pictures that are unsaleable are bad business; and by some warped kind of logic become bad art. Nobody wants bad art, so dealers have it 'improved' and that was how Mr Aczel made most of his money.

Should a painting be unsaleable because it represented an ugly woman, the ugly woman would become a pretty young girl. If it represented a saleable young man contemplating an unsaleable skull, the offending skull was changed into a brimming glass of wine, or some other object with commercially viable associations. A cat added to the foreground guaranteed the sale of the dullest landscape. Dogs and horses enlivened otherwise unsaleable pastures. Balloons floated into commercially deficient skies at once became immensely important (i.e. expensive) documents in the history of aviation. Popular signatures came and unpopular signatures went. Sullen-faced individuals left our easels wreathed in smiles. Poppies bloomed in dun-coloured fields. Unknown sitters transformed themselves into illustrious statesmen, generals, admirals, actors, actresses, musicians, and men of letters. So, like Gilbert's king whose heart was twice as good as gold, we '. . . to the top of every tree promoted everybody'.

The Old Masters that left Mr Aczel looking as good as new (if not better) would soon be presented in the galleries of the well-respected dealers for whom they had been doctored. These gentleman-owners and experts would be explaining their pictures' finer points in sumptuous surroundings: the paintings in a golden frame placed on a velvet covered easel whose base sank into a costly carpet. When he had successfully persuaded the prospective buyer of what an unrepeatable bargain he was getting, he would seldom have made less than 100 per cent profit – and more often than not 500 per cent and more. Though he might, if asked, give a discount, in which case he would consult his stock book saying something like: 'Let me see. Well, I'm afraid competition was keen and I had to pay quite a stiff price. Pictures of this quality don't come on to the market every day, you know, sorry to see it go, but as it's going to a good home, shall we say *pounds* instead of *guineas*?' This meant he was offering a discount of almost five per cent, but he would have argued it was better to be generous than to lose the sale. It is fair to point out that the dealer has overheads and expenses: costly home, wife with a taste for furs and jewels, a Bentley or a Rolls or both, business trips to expensive cities, a country home and much much more. Without these luxuries he could not impress his clients, and if he did not impress his clients he could not ask exorbitant prices, and if he did not ask exorbitant prices he could not pay for his luxuries. The sympathetic reader will realise at once what an enviably vicious circle the poor man was in.

We humble craftsmen in Haunch of Venison Yard had few of the dealers' problems. True, Mr Aczel had the outward signs of affluence: the car, the house, the life-style (I'm not sure if a wife counts as a luxury, but he had one); and so on, but we apprentices could not buy many problems on a pound a day.

Even so, I did have one that caused me some anxiety. It occurred to me that fusspots might argue that the way we came by our relatively modest earnings was not strictly honest. Was not 'restoration', as the word was understood in London's West End, something akin to forgery? And was not forgery something akin to fraud? And was not fraud a punishable crime? Thinking that my employer had not perhaps given much thought to this aspect of his trade, and hoping to save him and myself from any conflict with the law, I decided to acquaint him with it.

'Do you think,' I asked bluntly, 'that what we are doing is ethical?'

'Yes, it is a very good trade, you won't regret becoming a restorer, Eric. Take myself for example, nice house, car . . .'

'No, what I mean is, are we really being honest?'

'Look at my hands, my friend, what do you see?' Being interested in palmistry, and having noted his deep money line, I was about to give him a reading when he answered his own question: 'Paint, my friend. And look here.' He was showing callouses between his index and middle fingers caused by long years of holding brushes. 'Worker's hands are honest hands,' he concluded.

'Well, I'm worried,' I said, and remembering Mr Buckle's advice of long ago, I continued: 'I don't want any trouble with the law.'

'The law?' said Mr Aczel incredulously.

'Yes, the law.'

'What's the law got to do with it?'

'I thought maybe some people might think that we were faking pictures for the dealers to deceive their clients with, that's all.'

'Eric,' began Mr Aczel with the air of a man who is offended, but feels he must make it clear there has been some slight misunderstanding, 'do you think that George Aczel would do anything crooked? Just use your brains, my friend: my customers would not deal with a crook – they are highly reputable dealers with everything to lose.'

My employer went on to explain the distinguished nature of his customers, some of whom had been in business for generations (how they live so long has always puzzled me).

Furthermore the majority belonged to the British Antique Dealers Association (BADA), which, as the association itself tells us, has, since its foundation in 1918, established and maintained the highest ethical standards by which its members are bound in all their transactions. Memberships of BADA, Mr Aczel explained, are restricted to the most reputable antique and picture dealers in the country – those dealers in whom the collector may place implicit trust. This being so, we could be quite sure that none of his customers belonging to that august body would ever commission him to do anything that was not morally – and of course legally – irreproachable. Convinced by my employer's argument, my doubts assuaged, I returned with a clear conscience to my restorer's easel.

One day a picture dealer came into the studio carrying a canvas and a large brown paper envelope. He was an impressive middle-aged man of aristocratic bearing. His long white hair somehow suggested a powdered wig. His eyes were as lacking in humour as his cheeks were wanting in colour. He was slim and his expensive clothes hung well upon him. He wore striped trousers, morning coat and wing collar with a white silk cravat held together by a gold and diamond pin. His whole being contrived to suggest a fashionable survival from the late eighteenth century – a period upon the English portraiture of which he considered himself an authority. The canvas under his arm was not, however, a portrait, a landscape, a still-life, or for that matter anything else – it was completely blank. Nor did the blank canvas belong to England or even the eighteenth century. It had an original Dutch seventeenth-century stretcher, a Dutch seventeenth-century canvas, and a Dutch seventeenth-century ground. All it lacked was a Dutch seventeenth-century picture to make it worth a small fortune.

It would seem that I was alone in noticing the want of a picture, because the picture dealer said: 'Aczel, old boy, I've made an exciting discovery, what do you think of this Vandevelde?'

'Very interesting,' said Mr Aczel, turning the empty canvas this way and that to get a raking light on it: 'Very interesting indeed. Looks like a job for Mr Hebborn here. What do you say, Eric?'

'Uhm, very, uhm, interesting,' said I, following my employer's example. 'What did you say it was, Vanden what?'

'It, Eric, is a *Vandevelde*, and a very fine one I should say, wouldn't you?' He addressed the dealer.

'Not too fine, not too fine. Something for the small collector I imagine. After all it needs fairly extensive restoration and the museum people might be finicky. Then there's the problem of attribution. On the other hand if a signature should appear during the cleaning . . .'

'More than likely it will,' said my employer, as the dealer took from his large brown paper envelope a bundle of photographs of more readily discernible paintings by Vandevelde. They were sailing ships of all sizes, put together so that the large would indicate the scale of the small, the small the scale of the large. Thus massive three-masted galleons, men-o-war with great forecastles, portly poops and bristling with cannon, would overshadow little rowboats plying between them and an unseen shore upon which the viewer looked over the artist's shoulder; the larger vessels were nearly always at anchor, the sea calm, their sails slack, as they waited for a favourable wind.

The dealer pointed to a ship in the photograph on top of the pile and said that it looked very similar to one in his, to me invisible, painting.

'Not exactly like,' said he, 'but very similar.'

And taking the photographs one by one, he found something or other in each to remind him of a detail in his own Vandevelde: a certain kind of rigging, a flag, the handling of the reflections, the figures in a rowboat and much else. All of this seemed to confirm him in his belief that he had in his possession a genuine Willem Vandevelde the Younger (1633-1707).

These things were said with such a deadpan expression that I wanted to laugh. Had it not been for a grave look of warning from Mr Aczel, I probably would have done so, in which case the dealer would have lost face, we a customer, and some collector a Vandevelde.

As it was, when the latter day Beau Brummell had left the premises and his 'Vandevelde' behind, my employer sent me to look at the great marine artist's work in the museum at Greenwich.

I returned with some pencil sketches and colour notes, plus some observations on Vandevelde's way of handling paint. This material, together with the photographs left, provided the inspiration for a detailed preparatory drawing in Vandevelde's manner. This was shown to the dealer for him to judge whether or not it was an accurate copy from his picture. The dealer scrutinised the drawing for some time, and then exclaimed: 'What a pity!'

'Why? Is something wrong?' asked Mr Aczel.

'Wrong! Wrong! What a blockhead you are. If you had taken the trouble to give your assistant here a sheet of seventeenth-century paper we would now have two Vandeveldes instead of one!'

Then began the lengthy process of 'restoration'. After making some very minor alterations to the design, I transferred it to the canvas. There are mechanical ways of doing this but I preferred to do it freehand. First I drew it in charcoal, and then went over the drawing with a fine brush charged with raw umber, much diluted with turpentine. When this was dry I brushed off the charcoal.

The old ground was cracked all over. The cracks were a sign of the picture's age, and could not be filled in with new paint without giving the game away. Fortunately my employer had taken the trouble to fill the crevices with a jelly of his concoction which tended to resist the application of oil paint, and, being soluble in water, could be removed when the painting was finished.

When the drawing was complete except for the fine lines of rigging, which were to be painted over the sky, Mr Aczel gave the picture to another assistant to 'lay in'. That is, to paint in the general effect which acts as an underpainting and gives unity and substance to the painting. I was rather upset by this because I was enjoying the work and looked upon the Vandevelde as my creation. This is, of course, why my teacher took it away from me: he was afraid I might impress too much of my own style on it. The picture was on two other easels before it came back to mine. By now it was very nearly complete, and a very creditable and credible performance it was.

Mr Aczel had taken the precautions to forestall scientific examination of this restoration *par excellence* by having his assistants use only colours that were known in Vandevelde's time. He knew that the chemist in his laboratory had only to make a tiny prick in the painting with a hypodermic needle to get a sufficiently large sample of paint to study under his microscope. And if, for example, he were to find zinc white or Prussian blue he would know that the Vandevelde could not have been painted before the first part of the eighteenth century. A very late work, made on the artist's deathbed? Perhaps, but better to avoid the unlikely proposition. Worse still, supposing the expert called in to make a scientific examination were to find artifical ultramarine, cobalt blue or the cadmiums? In that case the attribution to Vandevelde would have to be abandoned altogether on the grounds that these colours were not discovered until the nineteenth century.

Mr Aczel told the story of Van Meegeran, a Dutch painter who, on being accused at the end of the Second World War of collaboration with the enemy by selling a painting by the seventeenth-century master, Vermeer of Delft, to the Nazi general Goering, had been able to demonstrate that he had in fact painted the Vermeer himself. Whereupon the charge of collaboration was changed to one of forgery and other Vermeers of his making came to light. Van Meegeran, after going to all the trouble and expense of obtaining and using pure ultramarine, was told by the experts at his trial that his so-called pure ultramarine was adulterated with cobalt blue. The man who had fooled experts had been fooled by a money-grubbing colour merchant! Our mentor went on to explain that Van Meegeran was also somewhat careless about his grounds. Naturally he used genuine old grounds, but did not bother (as somebody had in my opinion done for our customer's Vandevelde) to remove all traces of the original painting. His *Last Supper*, for example, was painted over a hunting scene by A. Hondius, which was of course revealed by X-ray. He might have added that Van Meegeran was neither a skilled painter nor a good draughtsman. No painter of new Old Masters, Mr Aczel counselled, need fear having his work X-rayed if he had taken proper care with his preparations.

The Vandevelde back on my easel, I was instructed to check the drawing, put in the rigging on the boats, and add a little freshness and crispness which my employer termed 'half-crown touches'. This done, I was given a photograph of a signature by Vandevelde and asked to 'discover' it, on the canvas. The restoration did not, however, end there.

Two or three days passed, during which time the painting dried and I was away studying at the Academy. When I returned to Haunch of Venison Yard it was at the request of Mr Aczel who asked me to come to the studio after working hours, as he had something to discuss, and would like to invite me out to supper.

The Vandevelde was yet again on my easel. 'Isn't it complete?' I asked Mr Aczel.

'Yes,' he answered. 'But I want to let you into a little secret.' With this he asked me to press my thumbnail into the surface of the marine painting. 'What do you feel?' he asked.

'The paint is still soft, I've made a dent in it.' I answered.

'Now press your nail into this picture,' my teacher invited, offering me an eighteenth-century portrait. 'What do you feel now?'

'It's hard and resilient.'

'Do you know how long it would normally take before you could no longer press your nail into the Vandevelde?'

'A year?' I hazarded.

'Multiply that by forty and you'll be nearer the mark. Our problem, Eric, is that collectors and experts also have thumbnails and most of them know how to use them. Unless we harden the surface of our nice little seascape here our customer will end up refunding somebody their purchase money.'

Naturally I asked how we were going to do this. He explained that he had in fact half done it. 'Did you notice anything strange about the medium I gave you to paint with?'

'Yes, it smelt of benzene.'

'Why do you think I put benzene instead of turps?'

Thinking back to my early lessons from Mr Cuthbertson I answered: 'Because it's cheaper?'

'Don't be silly, my friend. It's because benzene is more volatile, and doesn't leave an oily residue. What else did you notice about the medium?'

'It wasn't as sticky as usual, and didn't smell of dammar.'

'That,' said Mr Aczel, 'is because there was no dammar.'

At this point my mentor revealed to me that he had not only chosen colours known in the time of Vandevelde, but had ground them not in the usual linseed oil or nut oil, but in some special oil, a clearer, less viscous oil which would somehow confuse any tests made to discover its age by measuring its refractive index. Then he had made a medium for us composed of benzene and an artificial resin.

'What is the resin called?' I asked.

'Eric, I told you I would reveal to you a secret, and George Aczel is a man of his word.' Here he paused as though debating with himself as to whether or not it would be wise even for a man of his word to divulge a secret of such momentous importance. Lowering his voice to a scarcely audible pitch, he whispered: 'The secret is, my friend, never, ever, give away your secrets. At least not your important ones!'

'Thanks,' I thought.

Although he did not actually tell me what the mysterious ingredient was that I mixed with my paint, what was to follow makes me suspect that it was in all probability phenolformaldehyde, the resin used by Van Meegeran.

Having promised that the next time I saw the Vandevelde I would no longer be able to dent it with a thumb nail, he took it off the easel, put it under his arm and suggested that we went for supper.

His car was parked nearby, but after putting the painting in the boot, it was decided that we should walk the twenty minutes or so to Soho where Mr Aczel knew of a good *trattoria* belonging to a friend of his.

The restaurant owner-friend greeted him: '*Ciao, Giorgio, amico mio. Buona sera. Come stai?*' Whereupon, to my British horror, Mr Aczel called him 'Angelo' and the two middle-aged foreigners fell to embracing and kissing. So this, I thought, was the reason my employer had invited me to a candlelit supper in Soho.

Happily I was mistaken, and as we were eating a *primo piatto* of *tortellini*, and drinking a bottle of Orvieto, Mr Aczel made me a more attractive proposition. According to him, I was an exceptionally talented young man. In all his long years of experience he had never come across a painter with such an ability for working the style of another artist, and compared me with Pietro della Vecchia (1605-1678) of whose versatility the contemporary art-historian Marco Boschini wrote (my translation):

> His skill is such, that should it cross his mind
> To paint a picture by Correggio, say,
> He will adopt that artist's finest way;
> And all will in his work that master find.
> The same with Palma Vecchio and Giorgione,
> The same with Pordenone and with Titian.
> Be ever blessed those hands of erudition
> Whose virtuosity makes experts phony.

All I lacked, according to my host, to reach the pinnacle of success in the realm of making new Old Masters was the technical knowledge he himself possessed. Why should we not combine abilities? George Aczel was old and would like a good sum to retire on. I was young and needed capital on which to build a future. Why should dealers make most of the money when between us we not only knew an equal amount of art-history, but also had the manual skill to make use of it? As for selling our products we could put them into sales and let the dealers bid against each other for their possession.

For obvious reasons the new firm of Aczel and Hebborn would have to have premises distinct from the '*bona fide*' practice of 'restoration' in Haunch of Venison Yard. My present employer would put up the capital. Otherwise everything would be on a fifty-fifty basis.

The prospect of such a partnership was attractive, and I would certainly have gone into it with enthusiasm except that I had submitted work to the competition for the Rome Scholarship, which if I were successful, would take me out of the country for two years.

Mr Aczel was not pleased with me for turning down his offer, and from then on our relationship began to deteriorate.

When the Vandevelde was returned to Haunch of Venison Yard it was absolutely impervious to the thumbnail test. How had Mr Aczel done it? He was evasive. He did not want me to learn his secret, but, as Leonardo said: 'It is a poor pupil who does not excel his master', and I was determined to find out.

That the picture had been baked seemed the most likely answer.

This was Van Meegeran's way and since my teacher had, it seemed, followed the Dutchman's method in the initial stages, there was no reason to suppose that he had not done so to create the Vandevelde's hard resistant surface now identical to a genuine Dutch painting of the seventeenth century.

Mr Aczel would not, however, admit to it, and when I suggested that he had put the picture in an oven he said that I was a fool. Anyone, he argued, who has stripped old paint off a door with a blow-lamp knows that the application of heat does not harden paint, it softens it! 'What about a steady heat of let us say 100 to 105 degrees centigrade for a period of two to three hours?' I countered. This was the temperature and length of time I knew Van Meegeran had used for his 'Vermeers', and the exactness of the information caught Mr Aczel off guard. He muttered something in German, but his expression told me all I wanted to know.

Now came the preparation of the Vandevelde for the expert's examination under ultra-violet rays. Although it cannot determine the age of the painting, such an examination is useful for detecting retouches. It also requires much experience to interpret correctly what appears under the ultra-violet lamp. This is because certain resins become fluorescent themselves, and if they are mixed unequally throughout the painting medium, parts of the picture may erroneously be judged as retouches.

Naturally, the skilful painter of new Old Masters uses this know-ledge to his advantage, and Vandevelde's name was reduced to a shadow visible only under magnification. Then using a medium with a carefully calculated quantity of varnish, I was instructed to add the highly important, but also highly improbable attribution to Jan Brueghel. Examining the name under the ultra-violet lamp, Mr Aczel satisfied himself that the signature was really and truly false and must have been added in relatively modern times. Had he cleaned it off, and examined the area it had occupied under magni-fication he would have had the joy of discovering the obliterated signature of Vandevelde – a joy he left for others.

After this the Vandevelde was surfaced with dirty 'old' varnish, which was promptly cleaned off except for in the crevices of the im-pasto. It was then stressed and damaged but not enough to decrease its value, and ended up on the easel of one of the girls, who retouched it.

As a preparation for retouching, Mr Aczel had 'varnished' out all over with mastic varnish thinned with turpentine but left just strong enough to dry shiny. The young lady from the Academy Schools treated the picture with all the respect due to an Old

Master. Using the finest sable brushes, Nos. 00 and 0, she was very careful not, on any account whatever, to touch the existing surface of the picture, and confined her work entirely to touching out 'stains', 'damages', 'pinpoints' and 'freckles' all of which Mr Aczel had thoughtfully prepared for her. Much to her credit, her re-touching did not encroach by so much as a hair's breadth on the surrounding 'original' paint. The cracks, because they showed the period of the work, were left untouched except for some little black triangles here and there where they crossed one another. These occur often in late-seventeenth-century work but, being unsightly, are usually touched out.

The final operation on the Vandevelde was the varnishing. In this it was treated in the same way as all the other paintings before being returned to their owners. Mr Aczel laid it on the large table he reserved for the purpose. Before applying the varnishing, he gave it a coat of size. Although not necessary for the Vandevelde, this was the standard practice for ensuring that new paint would pass the alcohol test. Fresh paint readily dissolves in alcohol, whereas old paint is much more resistant. A layer of glue ('the size') on a freshly painted surface shields it from the alcohol and all the jolly changes and additions that the restorer may have made go undetected.

Not until the size was thoroughly dry did Mr Aczel apply the varnish. Any trace of damp would have made the varnish 'bloom'. The term comes from the appearance of a bluish haze caused by the imprisonment of damp by the varnish which resembles the bloom on fruit.

Varnishing day in Haunch of Venison Yard was something of an event. In the first place it was supposed to be a fine dry day. The windows were closed, the premises were warmed to an even temperature, and everybody in the studio moved about as little as possible. Dust, damp and draughts are the enemies of the varnisher.

Taking care not to make it more than lukewarm, Mr Aczel heated his mastic varnish in a jam jar. Then with a flat brush, about four inches in width, he worked quickly and surely; first with horizontal strokes right across the picture, which had also been slightly warmed, and then with rapid strokes where he might have missed an area. Thus, 'restoration' of the picture was happily concluded and a delighted customer carried off his discovery.

Shortly after the invisible Vandevelde had been brought to light, and for reasons I shall explain in the following chapter, I was to leave Mr Aczel's employ. Nevertheless, I kept in touch with him for two or three years afterwards. This was because I had left with him a collection of about twenty paintings for cleaning. Cleaning was Aczel's forte. It was also the cause of our falling out.

How I came into the possession of the collection of old paintings that I left with Mr Aczel is a story which belongs to another chapter, but I must just mention it here to explain how the rift between my former employer, which had its beginnings in the *trattoria* in Soho, was to widen beyond repair.

My landlord in Highbury had heard that old paintings were a good investment, and since he had accumulated large sums from Rachmanism he decided to consult me on the matter of becoming an art collector. It was agreed that I should give him the benefit of my growing knowledge, and receive nothing in return. This apparently showed the application of sound business principles on his part. But as I say this is a story for elsewhere. Suffice it to say that it was really part of the collection of paintings I was forming for my landlord that I gave to Mr Aczel for restoration.

My employer naturally concluded that, since I was buying pictures at a rate which the amount I earned in his studio combined with my modest earnings from teaching and Academy prizes could not possibly have permitted, I must have been dealing profitably on the side, and he was determined to get his hands on part of the money I was making.

As it happened Mr Aczel was also a dealer on the side, and when restoration work for the traditional gallery clients left him time, he undertook restoration of pictures he had bought in bad shape from minor sales at Sotheby's, Christie's, Phillip's or Bonham's. He would retouch them in the inimitable manner of his studio, and return them to the rooms. In this way he would on occasion make a genuine find, hidden only by dirt. Once he bought a very fine little David Cox for three pounds, which he sold to me for eighteen. I did not begrudge him his profit because I was, in a way I shall explain below, making money on the deal myself. On another occasion I bought from him an attractive portrait in the style of Corot.

These various transactions with Mr Aczel led to a regrettable incident involving a painting by or attributed to Sir David Wilkie (1785-1841), one of Britain's finest artists. It was painted on panel and corresponded to the description of lot 131 in Sotheby's sale of 22 November 1961: Sir D. Wilkie, *The Marriage Contract*, signed with initials and indistinctly dated, on panel, 13 ¼ in. by 11 in. I had bought the picture from Appleby and Son Ltd. in St James's, and taken it to Haunch of Venison Yard to have the old varnish removed. Mr Aczel's method of cleaning was the traditional one of using a solvent (alcohol) and a restrainer (turpentine). Many years of experience on all kinds of paintings had given him immense skill in this branch of the restorer's art. He shook together in a bottle seven parts of turpentine and one part of pure alcohol, and taking a wad of cotton wool he dampened it with the mixture and tested it on a small area of the edge of my David Wilkie. He held the wad for a moment very close to the old varnish, to see if the fumes of the mixture alone would be sufficient to soften it. Finding that the varnish remained unaffected he took up a bottle containing the stronger mixture of one part alcohol to four parts turpentine, and after shaking the contents thoroughly together repeated the test. At this point he explained that it is better to increase the strength of the solvent even to equal parts of alcohol and turpentine rather than to rub harder with a weaker solvent. A solvent which is found to be too strong will do no harm if it is not touched; it will simply evaporate. It is rubbing, however delicate, which removes paint. But even to a restorer of Mr Aczel's experience, the unexpected can happen.

With the wad of solvent he began lightly but firmly to peck and lick at the old varnish. He started at the upper left-hand corner, and frequently examined his wads of cotton wool for any tell-tale sign of colour or paint that would have warned of the mishandling of the picture. He used each wad only for the tiniest area. Different parts of a picture need different strengths of solvent, for some colours are more easily damaged than others. Vermilions, pinks and pale reds are, said Mr Aczel, particularly vulnerable, especially if they have been applied as glazes. Burnt umber, Van Dyck brown and ivory or lamp black also come away easily. So sensitive was the cleaner's touch that he claimed he could feel when he was nearly through the old varnish and so leave just the very thinnest layer where there seemed to be glazed colour underneath.

Then the first danger signal appeared under his wad in the form of streaks of lighter colour on the dark brown background. This was a sure sign that the painted surface was being disturbed and Mr Aczel quite correctly, it seemed, took up a wad of cotton wool and applied the restrainer. Since the restrainer is harmless Mr Aczel spread it beyond the area where the streaks had appeared. Imagine my horror, on returning to his work, to see that where he had passed the supposedly innocuous restrainer the picture was covered with bubbled and blistered paint, for all the world as if a paint stripper had been used on it.

My lovely little Wilkie was a total wreck. When the blisters were removed all one could see below was the artist's first lines in pencil.

Mr Aczel was not, however, unduly put out by the destruction of the picture. He pretended to have known that this was likely to happen, and explained that in the process of cleaning one often uncovers traces of former restoration. Sometimes a darker background has been applied, or a tree or ornament added to hide a bare patch made accidentally in cleaning. If this retouching or overpainting is recent then it comes away with the solvent; and should it have been carried out by a modern restorer using a varnish medium with his colours, such as mastic or dammar, then it will come away even with turpentine.

According to Mr Aczel he had, of course, known from the beginning that the Wilkie was largely repainted, and had undertaken to clean it simply to demonstrate that I did not have enough experience to buy old paintings on my own judgment, and would be wise to consult him before making further purchases.

It was clear to me that he had deliberately destroyed the picture, and I was furious. But the damage had been done. I took all of my landlord's paintings away, and never saw or spoke to Mr Aczel again.

The destruction of the Wilkie shocked me. Not because of its monetary value. The picture was not mine, and whether it was worth ten pounds or £10,000 was a matter of total indifference to me. What hurt was to think that a fine old painting had been destroyed by a person entrusted with its conservation. It was like watching a surgeon cut his patient's throat.

Naturally, I repainted the Wilkie, but I sincerely wish that I had been spared the effort.

CHAPTER VI

THE OLD CURIOSITY SHOP

'People who don't know much about art should either not start a collection or, if they do, shouldn't complain about the cost of the lessons
it teaches them!'

Karl Kusenberg.

Rembrandt knelt upon a sack outside the National Gallery,
drawing with coloured chalks upon the paving stones. It was
1959 and yet his beautiful boozy face was exactly as it had been
in 1659. Unfortunately, however, reincarnation which had been
so punctilious in returning to the great artist each hill and hollow,
each blotch and blemish of his former features, had overlooked
giving back to him any of his former talent, and his sack was adrift
on the slimy sea of a vast and unbelievably bad version of his
Polish Rider.

'Hello Remby,' I hailed across the waste of chalk, 'How's
business?'

'I've just got back from Amsterdam, ain't I? They paid my fare,
didn't they?'

'Who did?'

'The bleedin Dutch, of course. This Buggermaster bloke meets
me off the boat wiv a bleedin brass band and big banner wiv WEL-
COME HOME MASTER written all over it, don't 'e? And then 'e
gives me a bleeding banquet in the town 'all, gets me all Brahms
and Liszt (Pist, i.e. drunk), and then shoves a bleedin tenner in me
pocket an' sends me packin on the next bleedin boat back to
Blighty, don't 'e?'

Although I dearly wanted to believe that some Dutchman, as
jolly as kind, had really humoured Remby in the way he claimed, I
knew from past experience that the old artist's tales were based less

131

Fig. 25: *Portrait of an Old Man*, after a painting by
Rembrandt, *c.* 1959, pencil. (Although not a
Rembrandt self-portrait, the face is similar to Remby's)

on truth than on conviction, and like the statements in a Sotheby's
or Christie's sale catalogue, were not to be taken as statements of
fact, but of opinion. He was of the opinion that he was Rembrandt,
and if artists could themselves be sold at auction, Remby would
certainly have insisted on being catalogued as Rembrandt
Hormenszoon Van Rijn in full – the fullness of his name being a
reflection of the fullness of his faith in being the genuine article.
Speaking of the genuine article reminds me that on another
occasion Remby confided in me as a colleague that he had been
approached by the then director of the National Gallery, Sir Philip
Hendy, to 'authenticate' the paintings in the Rembrandt Room.
On learning from the great painter's own mouth that 'arf of 'em
was bleeding duds', the sadly disappointed Sir Philip, for fear of
there being 'all bleedin 'ell to pay' if the truth was ever made
public, pressed a substantial sum of money into Remby's curiously
unwilling hand, and very improperly muttered, "Ere take this and
keep yer bleedin north an south (mouth) shut. Don't 'e?'

Fig. 26: *Louis Meier*, 1971, pencil. This is one of a
number of studies for the bronze shown on p. 324
(Collection of the artist)

But it was not to chat with Remby that I had passed by
Trafalgar Square – I had an appointment to keep. So having
dropped a coin in my colleague's hat, I said a hurried goodbye and
quickly turned my steps into Charing Cross Road, crossed over and
entered a narrow turning leading to Saint Martin's Lane called
Cecil Court. It was flanked with dingy shops, most of them selling
second-hand books and old prints, and there among them, on the
right-hand side, was number twenty-one, the shop with which I
had an appointment. Given good eyes, the time and patience to
penetrate its many layers of London grime, one could just make out
on the sign above the door: Louis Meier Antiques, Greek,
Egyptian, Ceramics, Paintings, Drawings, Prints, Old Maps, Etc.
The glass of the shop's small window was no less grimy than its

sign, but I had cleaned a tiny space between the bars of the iron grid by which it was protected to use as a peephole, and had been rewarded with intimations of: a Roman terracotta figurine, an Apulian vase, a Piranesi print, an African mask, a fragment of an Egyptian sarcophagus and many other, to me, highly exotic items. They were heaped together with no pretence whatsoever at display. On the contrary, they seemed to have been hidden there and long forgotten until I intruded my sight on them. Now, veiled in semi-transparencies of dust and web, these art objects from the past worked so forcibly on my fancy that they whisked me away in spirit to the very when and where of their creation. I longed merely to handle them and dreamt of the day when I might afford to own such wonders myself.

I am aware that one normally makes an appointment with a shopkeeper rather than his or her premises, but clearly this was no ordinary shop, and I had for several weeks arranged to visit it at all hours in the hope of one day finding it open. On more than one occasion I had sensed rather than known that somebody had been inside, but it was always stoutly locked and barred. Today was different. To my joy the rusty railing which normally fenced off the doorway had been moved aside, and chained to the grating covering the window was a penny-farthing bicycle. At last I was to touch the magic objects, and who knows what other marvels lay behind the door I was pushing open! Or rather, trying to push open, for something on the floor inside prevented me from opening it more than was enough to cause the shop bell to tinkle, and allow my head inside.

My nostrils were greeted with the musty smell of unaired antiquity such as I imagine met the noses of Carter and Lord Carnarvon on entering the tomb of Tutankhamun. As my eyes grew accustomed to the dim light, I saw that on either side of the narrow shop were floor to ceiling shelves sagging under the burden of bulging portfolios and cardboard boxes, each one labelled according to what it purported to contain: Old Master drawings, Pinelli prints, Roman lamps, English watercolours, Rembrandt etchings, old coins, ancient weapons, Egyptian jewellery, etc. The gap between the shelves was barely large enough for a person to pass. I heard a movement and, from the gloomy recesses of the back of the shop, there emerged the figure of a man who shambled towards me through the restricted gap. As he approached the light from the open door, I made him out to be advanced in years. He had long white hair which on one side of his head shot upwards and backwards to cover a balding pate, and on the other side flung itself

Fig. 27: *Marie Grey*, 1961, pencil. Drawn in Torrington
Place *c.* 1963 (Collection of the artist)

recklessly forwards and downwards in a shaggy lock to effectively
curtain off an eye. His facial bags and sags were surmounted by an
impressive brow. He was lean and his baggy tweeds hung upon him
as they would a peg. I supposed him to be Mr Meier and judged
him handsome in his decay (Fig. 26).

'Vot is it you vont?' he asked gruffly.

'May I look around?' I responded.

'No you mayn't! I know your sort, vonting for only two shillings
to buy Rembrandts. Get zat face out of my shop! Out! Out! Out!'
Whereupon he slammed the door with such surprising vigour that
the owner of zat face was lucky to remove his property from Mr
Meier's premises intact. I could scarcely have guessed from this
first encounter that Louis, as I came to call him, was to become one
of my closest friends.

It came about like this. It was a cold winter evening, and I had
decided to warm myself up with a double brandy in the Salisbury, a

pub in St Martin's Lane. Thinking I might again peep at the beloved antiques, I walked through Cecil Court. There was a light in Louis' shop. It came from a single unshaded light bulb and it shone down on a head of white hair. The head was not Louis', but I would not have known this were it not for the fact that the glass of the shop's door had to some extent been cleaned. The window too had gained in transparency and the dusty objects were slightly rearranged. The owner of the illuminated hair was a woman whom I judged to be stout and somewhere in her sixties. Doubtless she had been responsible for the improved visibility. Would I dare to enter once again? Supposing the dreadful Louis was lurking some-where behind her? Or maybe he had put her there, some fearful harpy, to guard the shop from unwelcome customers. I decided to risk it, and pushed upon the door, which on this occasion opened wide. The tinkle of the shop bell, accompanied by a freezing draught, caused the lady of the snow white locks and generous girth to look up from the electric fire at which she was warming her hands. She had large handsome brown eyes set in a powdered face with two circles of rouge to indicate the points where I fancied her cheek bones to lie, and from where her face fell in a fulsome pouch to rest upon a scarf surmounting a quantity of tweed, cladding what appeared to be a giant ball (Fig. 27). The ball bounced on to its feet and its owner asked in the friendliest way if she could be of assistance. On being told that I would like to examine the contents of the shop window, she kindly launched herself into the narrow space between the shelves. The contents of these shelves seemed to adjust themselves to her circular contours, much in the same way as the brushes of a car-washing machine adjust themselves to the contours of the vehicle driven through them.

'Are you interested in anything in particular?' she asked as she slid aside a panel to gain access to the objects in the window.

'Yes,' I replied. 'I would very much like to look at the Apulian vase.'

The vase was an impressive object about eighteen inches high and potted in the form known as 'Bel krater'. Vases of this shape were used in antiquity for mixing wine, and this one was appro-priately decorated with a border of vine leaves and bunches of grapes framing the figure of a youthful Bacchic figure with an erect penis in hot pursuit of a maiden who, perhaps at the idea of one day being caught, threw back her lovely head in ecstasy. It was really much the same scene as Keats pictured in his *Ode on a Grecian Urn*: 'What mad pursuit? What struggle to escape? What pipes and timbrels? What wild ecstasy?'

The form of the krater and the decoration on it was by no means original. The ancient vases from southern Italy of the type I was gingerly turning around in my hands are in reality only imitations of the finer ones made in Greece known as 'Attic' vases. So in a sense it could be argued that the object I was so respectfully handling was an ancient fake. Was I supposed to dislike the krater for not being Attic and dismiss it as a miserable imitation? Perhaps I was, but I did not. In fact it gave me immense pleasure. I knew the vase was not as fine as its Greek prototype, but it had a quality of its own. The very fact that the krater was coarser in workmanship lent it an air of rusticity, conjuring up a rural scene far from the marble halls of fifth-century Athens, and one rather more suitable for youths to chase maidens about in. And what was lost in Attic grace was gained in lusty vigour. In short, I was enjoying the vase for what it was, rather than concerning myself about what it was not.

'How much is it?' I asked as I handed the precious object back to whom I supposed might be Mrs Meier.

'Thirty-three pounds,' said she, reading from a label attached to the foot of the base which in fact read: £cc nett. This was a great deal of money to me at the time, but for reasons I shall explain below I actually had enough in my pocket, and I counted out the money at once. I had no idea what the commercial value of the vase might be, nor did I care. What I did know was that the contemplation of the ancient artefact gave me infinitely more pleasure than the contemplation of thirty-three pounds. When the supposed Mrs Meier made out the receipt she signed it M. Grey, and made a point of introducing herself as *Miss* Grey.

Marie, as I may now call her, took a pile of old newspapers and started to crumple up the sheets and throw them into a cardboard box. When she had thickly covered the bottom of the carton she put the Apulian vase into it and proceeded very slowly to pack more crumpled paper in and around the krater for its protection. To speed up the packing process I helped to shred and crumple newspapers, and while we were thus engaged Marie told me a little of the history of Louis and the Old Curiosity Shop. Mr Meier was Swiss, and as a young man had read philosophy and was, as Marie put it, 'very deep'. His interest in philosophy did not, however, earn him a living and being as deep in debt as he was profound in thought, he decided to work in Zurich as a bank clerk. He continued in this work until a little before the Second World War when, at the age of forty-five, he grew weary of handling other people's money and decided to go into business on his own. He had always had a liking for artefacts from the past and decided to invest his savings in opening a shop in London – then the world's centre for trading in antiques. His business flourished, and this, explained Marie, was largely due to the war. People were not very keen on owning goods that might be destroyed any minute by enemy bombing, and Louis was able to accumulate vast quantities of antiques at virtually give-away prices. His stock was, she said, enormous, and quite apart from the amount I could see in the shop, he had three warehouses and a large apartment all crammed full of the old and the ancient. Her account was interrupted by Louis' coming in. He scowled at me fiercely, and I was afraid that I was about to be ordered out of the shop again. But Marie gave him what she herself described as a 'certain look', and introduced me by saying in a firm voice: 'Louis, Mr Hebborn here has just spent thirty-three pounds with us,' adding, 'Mr Meier likes money, don't you, *dear?*' At the mention of money old Louis' face lit up, he shook my hand and our friendship began.

Speaking of money, I must now tell the reader how a poverty-stricken art student came by enough of it to acquire a valuable Apulian vase. It will be remembered that I had taken a room in a slum building in Highbury. At first I rented one of the smaller hardboard enclosures, but when Graham and I decided to live together, we took one of the grander rooms, which our landlord said was really intended for 'four gentlemen sharin already'. It was the greater part of a front room on the ground floor with a window overlooking Highbury Fields, and originally must have been rather attractive. The broken mouldings of the cracked and flaking ceiling, and the imposing marble fireplace spoke of a former, and to use one of Marie's phrases, '*better*-type' of owner. Now from the ceiling's central panel, designed I imagine for a crystal chandelier, a naked light bulb dangled. In front of the sealed up fireplace stood a shabby gas fire connected to a coin meter. The generally bare floor boards had a few strategically placed tatters of gaily coloured linoleum, and as for furnishings, there were two beds with lumpy mattresses (of no great cleanliness), a chair of sorts, a dilapidated dressing table, and an old and largely empty food cupboard which bore a similar relationship to the vertical as the famous Tower of Pisa.

Like Marie and Louis, Graham and I were not a tidy couple, and our home was, to put it mildly, in some disorder. Canvases, crockery, clothes, books, papers, paints, brushes etc., were allowed to find their own accommodation where they would, and one was just as likely to discover a pot scourer on the bed as a pillow in the sink.

Furthermore, the room ordinarily stank of a mixture of oil paint, turpentine and stale cigarette smoke, more rarely of cooking. Graham and I were very much in love, and would have been happy together almost anywhere. Even so there were moments when it was hard for us to keep our spirits up, and sometimes our squalid surroundings and perennial poverty got the better of us. It was on one such occasion, hungry and broke, that desperation drove us to break open the gas meter and remove the contents to an inexpensive Chinese restaurant. Cheap as the meal was, it came to somewhat more than the pile of six pences we left on the table when we took to what was left of our heels.

We had intended to put the money back in the meter, but

Fig. 28: *The Food Cupboard*, 1957, pencil
(Collection of the artist)

Fig. 29: *Ruby*, one of my fellow tenants in Highbury Fields, 1958, pencil
(Collection of the artist)

fortunately, as it turned out, before we had discovered the means to
do so, our landlord came to call. He found me alone making a
drawing of the old food cupboard (Fig. 28). Examining the meter's
broken lock and surmising its significance, he cried: 'What's all this
by Christ! I thought you was gentleman already!' Somehow I managed to soothe him with promises of repaying him as soon as
humanly possible, and asked if he would like a cup of tea while we
discussed repayment plans. Returning from borrowing the tea and
sugar from our neighbour, Ruby (Fig. 29), (the milk had been borrowed earlier from the vicar's doorstep across the way), I found the
landlord nosing among our belongings, and as he sipped tea from a
filthy cracked cup, he remarked on the number of paintings in the
room and asked:

'This lot must be worf sumfing, ain't they?'

'Yes,' I said, indicating a painting I had made under the
guidance of Stuart Ray at Walthamstow, and continued, 'and if
you would be prepared to take this as settlement of our little debt

you would be doing very good business. It's worth many times the four and sixpence we owe you.' The slum landlord's eyes lit up, but he was hesitant to accept my offer and replied suspiciously: 'Ow can I be sure you're not 'avin me on, by Christ?' So I explained to him that the canvas and stretcher the painting was on had in themselves cost ten shillings, then there were the colours and my time to consider. After procrastinating for an hour or so he agreed to accept the painting on the condition that I would allow him to have it valued by a junk dealer friend of his, and if it was not worth at least five shillings, I was to take it back and repay him in cash, with ten per cent interest added for every week he may have had to wait. Exactly what the junk dealer's opinion of the painting was, I do not know, but apparently he liked it enough to offer four pounds for it. But our landlord, suspecting that if his friend had offered four, the painting must be worth eight, had refused. Whereupon it seems that the dealer proposed that he buy a half share in the picture for two pounds and should he manage to sell it he would share the profit. My landlord made no secret about the transaction, and even showed me the agreement he had drawn up with the junk dealer, but made no offer to give me some of the already considerable profit he had made. This no doubt he considered business – I judged it as rapacity. Eventually he and the junk dealer must have done very well indeed on the deal, because shortly afterwards I saw my painting in the window of a gallery in Cork Street. It now bore the signature of Sickert – how it got there I can't imagine – and was priced at forty pounds. Fair enough for a Sickert, but on the high side for a Hebborn.

From then on the landlord gave me no peace. Feigning friendship, he would call on me at all times of the day. Very occasionally when he was feeling generous he would treat me to a meal at a local café called Mick's, where, over egg and chips, he would continue his incessant talk about money and try to pick my brains as to how it could be made out of art. He would ask such questions as: Why were Picasso's pictures worth a fortune when he himself could paint better with his eyes shut? Or, did I think that I would become famous and, if he bought my pictures, then would he be making a sound investment? The vulgar avaricious creature had precisely the same attitude to art as the vulgar avaricious creatures with better backgrounds, smarter accents, higher education, and infinitely greater pretentions who control the art trade from the top, and for whom a work of art is as good or bad as the amount of money it fetches.

Why did I not throw the plate of egg and chips into the slum landlord's loathsome face? Well, let me make my attitude plain – if I were hungry enough I would eat out of the hand of the Devil himself but the Lord of Darkness should not imagine from this that I would be grateful, let alone that by eating his food I was tacitly subscribing to his ideas. But a more important reason for denying myself the pleasure of seeing my landlord's features dripping with egg or happily smashing shop windows in Bond Street was that I knew physical action can do nothing to solve a problem which is essentially one of the mind. Somehow, I have no idea how, the people who equate everything with money, judging even human beings by what they are worth, have got to be made to realise that important as money is, and none of us can do without it, there are equally important things that can only be sacrificed on the altar of capitalism at the expense of everything that makes life worth living. Such things as love, friendship, kindness, learning, and above all, because it embraces all, civilisation.

It was while securing the survival of my body at the risk of losing my soul in Mick's Café in Highbury that it became clear to me that I need have no scruples in dealing with the unscrupulous, and decided to pretend to play along with the landlord, and treat him to some of his own medicine. Little by little I sowed the seeds in his greedy mind of investing money in art on a larger scale than he had perhaps envisaged. I spoke of the enormous profits that clever people were making out of art, sometimes thousands of pounds. Especially, I said, when they made a find such as recognising a Raphael in a junk shop, buying it for a song, and thus making a fortune overnight. To prove my contention that there was easy money to be made out of art, I suggested that my landlord give me ten pounds. I would scour the junk shops and flea markets, and with my knowledge buy something that he could sell at once for a hundred. 'Give me the money in the morning,' I said, 'and if I fail to make a find, I will return the sum intact in the evening.' My slum landlord was a little nervous at parting with as much as ten pounds, but when I pointed out that the room I shared with Graham was full of paintings of the kind he had already made money on, paintings which could be used as security, he finally agreed.

I suggested Saturday as the best day for going in quest of a 'find'. There were more markets open then than on any other day. What I really meant was that Saturday was the day he collected rents, and he would, therefore, be too busy to accompany me on my search for a bargain. When Saturday came, Graham and I went on a spending spree and splurged the ten pounds on two substantial meals

Fig. 30: 'Augustus John', *Dorelia Standing*, 1957, pencil. The stains are on the
old photograph not on the actual drawing

and an evening out in the gay club where I once got drunk with John Minton – the Neptune Club in Greek Street. We came home at about two in the morning and at seven were woken up by an anxious landlord.

'By Christ!' he hollered into our hangovers, 'I was expectin you back when the shops shut yesterday, and was kept hanging about 'ere 'til after midnight already.'

'Don't worry,' I said, 'we went to have some drinks with useful contacts in the art world and I have found a real bargain.' With this I showed him a pencil portrait I had made for the purpose.

'And what d'yer call *that* for ten quid by Christ already!' he exclaimed with a note of derision.

'This,' said I, 'appears to be an Augustus John.' (Fig. 30)

'A bloody what?'

'A portrait of his wife, Dorelia, by Augustus John, one of England's most distinguished draughtsmen. And if you can find the time to take it to the West End I imagine you will turn your ten pounds into a hundred and ten pounds.'

The very next day the landlord took the drawings to various West End dealers whose names I had given him as having handled John's drawings in the past: Roland, Browse and Delbanco, Agnew, Arthur Tooth, the Piccadilly Gallery, etc. Although every one of these dealers expressed interest in the drawing, the highest offer that my landlord could get for it was from Agnew at ninety pounds. It was a blow, but he took it philosophically. In the first place he argued that an 800 per cent profit was not too bad and, secondly, if a West End dealer offered ninety pounds, the drawing was presumably worth more. It was this last consideration that made him decide to keep the John for himself as an investment. Thus it became the first item in what was to become the sizeable, if largely unenviable, landlord's collection. Again there was no mention of giving me a commission for helping him to obtain what was to all intents and purposes a first-class drawing at a tenth of its market value. Perhaps he considered that as he had been offered only ninety pounds, instead of the hundred and ten that I had predicted, he was the loser by twenty pounds – a loss he would have to make good from any commission he might be tempted to offer me in the future.

Gradually, he came to trust me with larger sums of money to make 'finds' with, but I could not literally make all the 'finds' myself and so pocket all the money without arousing suspicion. The slum landlord normally wanted receipts for what I spent of his money, and so it was that by buying for him I began to get to know

Fig. 31: *Morning Walk*, after Gainsborough, wood
engraving. (One of a number of studies made in
connection with the author's Gainsborough-ing)

the world of art dealing as a customer. The first dealer I bought
from on my landlord's behalf was a Mr Appleby whose son now
carries on the family business in Ryder Street. Mr Appleby had a
very large stock of old English watercolours, as well as oil paintings. He knew that as a collector I was a novice and was most helpful. 'I'll tell you which are the good names,' he said. 'Yes,' I
thought, 'but who's going to tell me which are the good drawings?'
Many of the watercolour drawings that I bought from Mr Appleby
for the landlord's collection were in fact very fine indeed. Excellent
examples of Sandby, the Varleys, Cotman, Cox, Rowlandson,
Girtin and many other important British artists. If I was particularly struck with a drawing I would make one or more copies of it.

That is why, for instance, John Varley's *High Street in Conway* is known in many more versions than the artist ever saw. The same is true of a portrait of a lady in a fanciful hat by Rowlandson. Some of the copies I made at the time were so precise that when I later saw one reproduced in the *Burlington Magazine*, I had to study the reproduction for about ten minutes before I was certain that I was looking at my own handiwork.

Having got to know and to like Marie and Louis of the Old Curiosity Shop, I began to spend more and more of my landlord's money with them; and it was from them that I bought two drawings that were indirectly responsible for a number of 'Gainsboroughs' coming on to the market. The drawings were in black chalk on blue paper heightened with white. On the back of them was an old attribution to Gainsborough. Marie told me not to take any notice of the inscription, and I did not in fact take the attribution seriously. Nevertheless, I had a theory as to who might have made the drawings. I had once seen a similar study in reproduction that had been attributed to Sir Peter Lely. Not only was the style and technique of my drawings close to the Lely I remembered, but they, like it, were framed by a single black line. Furthermore, there is a stylistic link between Lely and Gainsborough. They were both under the influence of Van Dyck, Gainsborough going as far as to say that it was Van Dyck who had made him a painter. Wishing to test my theory, I took the drawings on blue paper to the British Museum for an expert opinion. There I showed them to an elderly scholar who was as courteous and helpful as one can imagine.

'Ah ha,' he said, 'what have we here? Two Gainsboroughs by the look of it.'

'Are you sure?' I asked in surprise.

'I think there can be very little doubt, but perhaps we should compare them with drawings by the artist in our collection.' The expert then sat me at a desk with my drawings before me and went to fetch a box containing some very beautiful Gainsboroughs.

I had made no special study of the Suffolk artist's work, but I could see at a glance that my two landscapes were not by the same hand as those that came out of the box. It was not a question of their not being as good, but their having a different calligraphy, they were less tender in their touch. The expert I was consulting did not, however, seem to notice this difference and upheld the attribution to Gainsborough. When I tentatively put forward the name of Lely, he said that Lely was a century earlier – a piece of information I did not need. My reaction was mixed. Modesty argued for accepting the expert's opinion; an opinion which greatly enhanced the value of my acquisitions (in a matter of minutes their monetary value had risen from fifteen shillings to somewhere in the region of a hundred pounds each). On the other hand I felt certain that the scholar was wrong. With a piece of chalk, a suitable sheet of paper, and a year or two to teach him the rudiments of the draughtsman's art, I might possibly have been able to point out his mistake to him, but as it was, I was powerless. As I have indicated above, this experience with the two 'Gainsboroughs' led to a number of other 'Gainsboroughs' suddenly appearing on the London art market, but before speaking of the most important of them I should like to mention another visit I made to the British Museum.

It came about as a result of a purchase I made in the famous flea market in Portobello Road. Some of the things I have acquired there over the years have been really quite extraordinary. On one occasion, for instance, I bought for a few shillings a 'buckle', which in reality is a Renaissance relief in bronze. Another genuine find I made there is a unique proof of Schiavonetti's engraving after Philip's portrait of William Blake which was used as the frontispiece for Blair's *The Grave*. Perhaps Schiavonetti's only claim to being remembered is his collaboration with Blake on the splendid illustrations to his book. The proof I discovered differs from the published print in only one small detail. Whereas the published state is inscribed in straightforward English: 'Painted by Philips R.A.' and 'Engraved by Schiavonetti', my proof bears the words 'Philips R.A. *pinxit*' and 'Schiavonetti *incidit*'. In this minor change I can see the hand of Blake himself. The poet-painter disliked using Latin when plain English would do, and the existence of the Portobello proof strongly suggests that Schiavonetti's engravings after Blake's designs were closely supervised by the great artist himself, and probably owe much of their beauty to the fact. But the discovery I made in Portobello Road which sent me hurrying off to the British Museum was an engraving in the style of the great fifteenth-century Mantuan master, Andrea Mantegna. The subject was *The Battle of the Sea-gods*. Mantegna's engravings are among the finest ever made, and I was thrilled to find what at first sight appeared to be an exceptionally good example.

At the museum I saw the same elderly scholar to whom I had shown the Gainsboroughs. 'I say,' he said, recognising the print at once, 'that's as fine a specimen as we ourselves possess!' with which he went off to get the Museum's print and put it side by side with mine. He spent several minutes making a scrupulous comparison between the two engravings with a magnifying glass. At length he discovered that one of the lines in my print was very slightly different from the Museum's print. 'Ah,' he said, 'I am afraid that yours is a copy, a most extraordinarily faithful copy, but a copy nevertheless.' He then put what he thought to be the Museum's Mantegna back in its box, but in actual fact he had absent-mindedly put my print in the place of the original. Even in those days the engraving that he had left with me was worth tens of thousands of pounds, and I was sorely tempted to let matters stand as they were. But knowing that I could not have lived with my conscience, I reluctantly drew the scholar's attention to his oversight. 'Good heavens!' he exclaimed. 'What a silly Billy I am!'

To return to the Gainsboroughs. By now I had become a close friend of Louis and Marie, and would frequently be invited to 65 Gordon Mansions, Torrington Place, the couple's home which, in its jumble of antiques, greatly resembled their shop in Cecil Court. Among the pictures on the crowded walls of the hallway was a watercolour of my own that I had given them as a gift. One evening, while we were sitting sipping sherry among the piles of old black and white prints which Marie was colouring in a forceful style all of her own, she mentioned that I might be amused to know that my drawing was now a valuable old English watercolour. When I asked how that could possibly be she explained that a certain authority on the subject had seen it and come to the conclusion that it was by David Cox (1783-1859). We laughed and wondered how the expert could possibly have deceived himself, when the drawing was on modern paper and clearly inscribed: 'For Louis and Marie with best wishes, from Eric'. Obviously he had not taken the drawing off the wall and had been misled by the hall's poor light, but even so Marie was impressed, and suggested that I might try putting some of my work (unsigned of course) into a sale of English watercolours. When I pointed out that unless the drawings I made were catalogued by the same expert who had turned the watercolour in the hallway into a Cox, the modern paper might tend to lower the price. Marie made no comment, she simply handed me a portfolio of old paper. Among the various unused sheets were several from the eighteenth century of the kind and colour that Gainsborough had sometimes used. And remembering the 'Gainsboroughs' that I had had 'authenticated' at the British Museum, and thinking that perhaps the experts were not as expert on that particular artist as they might be, I decided to try my hand at Gainsboroughing.

First of all I bought a number of books on the artist – not so much for the text as for the reproductions. Some of these books were costly, but by what I thought to be cheerfully cheating my landlord, money was becoming slightly less of a problem, and in any case these books were soon to pay for themselves time and time again. None of the twenty or so drawings I made in the Suffolk artist's style was a copy, and only a very few were adaptations from known drawings. My aim was to analyse Gainsborough's manner and then draw something original in it. It must be remembered, however, that in those days I was only a beginner, and faking, like every other art, requires an enormous amount of study before proficiency is gained. Although these Gainsboroughs were among my very first attempts at drawing in the style of an Old Master, using old materials, and I could do far better now, they were remarkably successful. Much of this early success was, however, largely due to the helpfulness of the experts and I am particularly indebted to a highly distinguished scholar called Ellis Waterhouse.

Professor Sir Ellis Waterhouse (1905-1985), CBE, was one of the most distinguished art historians of his generation. His interests ranged from Byzantine manuscripts to Karel du Jardin, from Antiveduto Grammatica to Gainsborough and Reynolds. He studied at Marlborough, New College, Oxford, and Princeton. While at Princeton, he made his first real contribution to the literature of art history, *El Greco's Italian Period*, which appeared in *Art Studies* in 1930. Among a number of important positions he held at various times may be mentioned: Director of the National Gallery of Scotland, Director of the Barber Institute of Fine Arts in the University of Birmingham, London Director of the Paul Mellon Centre for Studies in British Art, and Kress Professor in Residence, National Gallery of Art, Washington. His publications included: *Sir Joshua Reynolds* (1941), *British Painting 1530-1790* (1953), *Gainsborough* (1962), *Italian Baroque Painting* (1964), and *The Catalogue of the Pictures at Waddesdon Manor*.

Ellis, who was later to become a friend of mine, was in 1963 known to me only by reputation as the leading authority on Gainsborough. So when I wrote to him care of the Barber Institute enclosing a photograph of what seemed to me the best of my Gainsboroughs, I received a formal answer, which to my immense satisfaction told me that my drawing was a preliminary study, with considerable variations, for no less a masterpiece than Gainsborough's *Blue Boy*. Armed with Ellis's letter I wasted no time in taking the 'Gainsborough' along to Sotheby's, who were delighted to put it into a sale and catalogue it in full as being by Sir Thomas Gainsborough RA, thus indicating that they believed the work to be absolutely authentic. My study 'for' the *Blue Boy* was sold in their rooms on 16 April 1963, and if I recall correctly, fetched £200. This was a sizeable sum for a drawing at the time and it was good to know there were more 'Gainsboroughs' where it came from. At this point I must apologise to the reader for getting a little confused with my chronology. Between my first purchases and fakes for the landlord's collection and my sale of the 'Blue Boy' there was a two year gap in my dealing activities caused by taking up the Rome Scholarship.

During my *dolce vita* years I had left my landlord's collection of oil paintings in the care of Mr Aczel of Haunch of Venison Yard, who was to undertake any necessary restoration, and it was after my return from Italy that the destruction of the Wilkie described in Chapter V took place. Among the paintings I left with Mr Aczel were a number that the landlord had bought on his own initiative. This came about because of his suspicion that by buying from Louis and Marie I was making him pay too much for his acquisitions. Why, he wanted to know, did I buy from the old couple when I could buy directly from the great auction houses where much of their stock came from in the first place? It was the principle of cutting out the middleman. 'Alright,' I agreed, 'but in that case you don't need me to advise you.' I then went on to suggest that he attend a picture sale by himself. There would, I told him, be a catalogue compiled by recognised experts which he could consult telling him what the various paintings were, and he could ask the auctioneers for their expert valuation (this was before reserves were printed in the catalogue) and not bid much beyond it – thus assuring himself that he was buying authentic works at their true market value. The idea appealed to him and he decided to attend a sale at Sotheby's in New Bond Street.

The slum landlord could not have chosen a more reliable firm. Sotheby's have been in business since 1754. True, there was no firm of auctioneers actually called Sotheby's in that year, and the founding of the firm was left to a bookseller called Samuel Baker who on 11 March auctioned off the library of Sir John Stanley. But in 1767 Baker entered into partnership with one George Leigh, who on Baker's death in 1778, only thirty-three years after the sale of Sir John Stanley's books, did really and truly associate himself with a Sotheby. John Pendred's *Directory* of 1785 does not, however, speak of Leigh and Sotheby as auctioneers, experts and valuers, but rather as 'Stationers, Bookbinders, and Booksellers'. Nevertheless, one should not be hair-splitting, and it is really rather touching to note with what pride members of the grand old firm trace the tenuous line of Sotheby's history back to Samuel Baker's second-hand book sale, a line which in their eyes would seem to be scarcely less illustrious than that of the House of Windsor. Confident that he was in good hands, I waited with some interest to see what splendid purchases my landlord would make with the guidance of the renowned dealers.

My landlord returned from the sale in a mini-van from which he unloaded a dozen or so canvases. He had an air of triumph about him, but was clearly angry with me.

'Look here gentleman!' he yelled. 'Raphael, Rembrandt, Goya, Constable, the 'ole bloody lot of 'em, and all for three hundred and fifteen quid!'

'Hold on a minute,' I said picking up the 'Raphael', 'let's have a look at them.' Taking the paintings one by one, I examined them carefully and came to the conclusion that there was not a picture among them that I would have given more than ten pounds for. They were all of very dubious quality and highly uncertain date. When I told him of my opinion, he put it down to professional jealousy. Furthermore, he probably thought it was in my interest to disparage the collection because I was getting a rake-off from Marie and Louis.

'Take this 'ere Rubens,' my landlord argued. 'It's ten times bigger than that sketch thing that you bought the other day, and bleedin 'arf the price.'

'Yes,' I countered, 'but are you certain it really is by Rubens?' In answer, he took Sotheby's sale catalogue from his pocket and pointing to the lot number said:

'Read that, there it is in black an white – *Rubens*! You can't get no clearer than that, can yer?' He then reminded me that I myself had said that Sotheby's were reliable experts, and as for himself, if they said the picture was a Rubens, then a Rubens it was.

'No,' I began to explain, 'when Sotheby's or Christie's catalogue a picture as a Rubens, or any other artist, using only the artist's surname they mean the opposite. That is to say by cataloguing your painting as a Rubens, Sotheby's meant you to understand it is not a Rubens.'

'Don't talk bleeding daft,' said he perplexed. Whereupon I explained that auction houses have a code, and should for instance a painting or drawing be catalogued in full as 'Sir Peter Paul Rubens', then in the salesroom's opinion the work really is by that artist. If, however, the work is catalogued as 'P. P. Rubens', then it is held by the auctioneers to be of the period of the artist and may be wholly or in part by him. But if, as in the present case, the work is simply catalogued 'Rubens', then it is thought to be of the artist's school or by one of his followers, and of uncertain date.

'So what you're saying is Sotheby's 'av taken me for a muggins an sold me a van load of duds already.'

'No,' I said, 'I am not saying that, but Sotheby's do not guarantee the authenticity of what they sell. Look here,' I continued, pointing to some small print in his catalogue: 'All lots are sold as shown, with all faults, imperfections and errors of description. Neither the auctioneers nor the vendors are responsible for errors of description or for the genuineness or authenticity of any lot, or for any defect in it. No warranty whatever is given by the auctioneer to any buyer in respect of any lot.'

'What kind of experts are they then by Christ,' queried the crestfallen slum landlord, 'if they can't even promise they ain't selling fakes? A bloody rip off I call it!'

He never mentioned by-passing Louis and Marie or other dealers again.

Another of the grander firms I had dealings with while forming the landlord's collection was Agnew's, who, like Colnaghi's, have premises in Old Bond Street. The basis of Agnew's fortune was made from selling Guinness. They did not, of course, sell the beer themselves, that would be beneath their dignity; they left that to Lord Iveagh who used the proceeds to buy through Agnew's agency the famous collection of Old Masters at Kenwood House in Hampstead. The drawings I recall having bought from Agnew's are a portrait drawing by John Edridge and a group of drawings by Paul Sandby. The latter were very minor works but they served me as study material for making more important 'Sandbys', some of which were to make an appearance on Agnew's walls in later years. As were some 'Augustus Johns', but in the early days I was buying from Agnew's rather than selling to them. In these transactions I was not permitted to deal directly with Mr Agnew, who was far too grand to speak to ordinary folk, and we did our haggling through an intermediary called Mr Plummer. This poor man, who was no lightweight, would convey my offers upstairs to the head of the firm and come panting down the plushly carpeted staircase with the great man's replies.

Many years later, sometime in the eighties, I returned physically to Agnew's. I make the point of saying physically because I had made my artistic presence felt on their walls a number of times during the interim. Under one arm I carried a portfolio of watercolours I had made of Italian views, and tucked under the other was a framed 'Sandby'. The frame was one of those in which I had bought an authentic Sandby from the firm. Hence the frame had Agnew's label on the back, bearing their attribution and stock number. Mr Plummer was, I believe, no longer with the firm – in any case I spoke with an attractive young lady, telling her that I had bought 'this' (referring to the frame and not its contents) from Agnew's some years previously and would they care to buy it back. The young lady said she would consult Mr Agnew (a different Mr Agnew by now I imagine) and disappeared upstairs for a few minutes to show my 'Sandby' to the powers above. She came down with the news that Mr Agnew had agreed to buy the Sandby back and had made an offer. Beyond recalling that it showed the new Mr Agnew to be a chip off the old block, I do not remember exactly what the offer was. I was not, however, interested in the money and accepted it without argument. When I had Agnew's cheque safely in my hand, I said to the young lady that I understood Agnew's occasionally dealt in contemporary art of a traditional nature, and I wondered if they might consider showing some of my water-colours. She kindly looked into my portfolio, and apparently liking what she saw, told me that she thought Mr Agnew would probably be pleased to consider putting my drawings on exhibition. 'That,' I thought as I watched her climb the staircase carrying my portfolio, 'is what *you* think, young lady!' As I stood in the showroom clutch-ing my cheque and waiting for the illustrious dealer's pronounce-ment, it was all I could do to stop myself from laughing out loud at the scene I imagined to be going on above my head. By now the scandal in *The Times*, concerning the long series of 'Old Masters' that Colnaghi's and other important dealers had bought from me over the years, had already broken and Mr Agnew certainly knew all about it. Consequently, my name was only too familiar to him. Now here he was, looking at a group of watercolour drawings all signed E. Hebborn. Was this the person to whom the firm had just made out a cheque for an early English watercolour? 'Oh no,' he was groaning inside, 'let me have a closer look at that "Sandby".' And to the young lady, 'Would you be kind enough to tell Mr Hebborn that Agnew's is very definitely *not* interested in handling his work!'

But let us return to my dealings with Louis and Marie. Marie would sometimes take me to Louis' warehouse in Drury Lane, a once handsome Tudor building, then built around and dwarfed by later constructions which robbed it of light. The barn of a place was cheerless and uncared for, with small cracked and broken windows patched here and there with paper, as ineffective in keeping out the weather as they were of keeping out the thieves. Everything was broken down and ramshackle, but among the thousands of badly cared for paintings and prints the warehouse contained, were some of really fine quality. On one visit I noticed that most of the better paintings had a P chalked on the back of them. Marie told me that these pictures were reserved by an Italian dealer called Peretti. I had never met this dealer, but I knew him by reputation as a clever young man and he clearly had a good eye for paintings. It seemed to me, however, that it was unfair that he had earmarked all the best things in the warehouse so I took to surreptitiously rubbing out the P's on anything I particularly wanted. In this way I acquired a painting which has given me a great deal of pleasure over the years. It is a fragment of a painting by one of the Bassanos. The best of the Bassano family of painters was Jacopo, and my painting representing the animals entering the ark, known in several versions, may possibly have been designed by him and executed by Francesco, one of his sons. Nobody could be certain. One can only judge by quality. So it is possible that some of Francesco's better work is given to Jacopo, and some of Jacopo's less good work attributed to Francesco or some other member of the family. But whether my picture is by one or both or neither of these artists does not matter to me in the least. Indeed, I am glad of the uncertainty, for if it were possible to give my Bassano a firm attribution, even as a fragment it would be too valuable for me to own. My enjoyment of it would be marred by such considerations as fearing it might be stolen, or wondering whether I had it sufficiently well insured. In short, I would have bought as much of a problem as a pleasure.

Among other pictures I snatched from Peretti by wiping off his initial were two life-size, full-length portraits in elaborately carved and thickly gold-leafed frames. These pictures had once belonged to Lord Kitchener of Khartoum whose monogram was incorporated in the design of the frames. Both of these portraits were remarkable; one remarkably bad and the other remarkably good. The bad one was of James I and painted by some anonymous hack of his day. The other was of a Spanish nobleman, perhaps a royal personage, which looked to me as though it might be by Coello, a Spanish court painter prior to Velázquez. When I had the latter cleaned, I was so pleased by its quality that I decided to put it into a sale and hoped that somebody with money would be as impressed with it as I was. By taking the picture to a dealer's I learnt my first hard lesson about dealers. I once asked an ex-dealer why he had left the picture business. His answer was: 'I woke up one morning and decided to go straight', and it does seem to me that to speak of an 'honest art dealer' is to fall into a contradiction in terms. At the time of selling the Spanish portrait, however, I was blissfully unaware of the dodges that the pretentious rogues get up to, and I fell

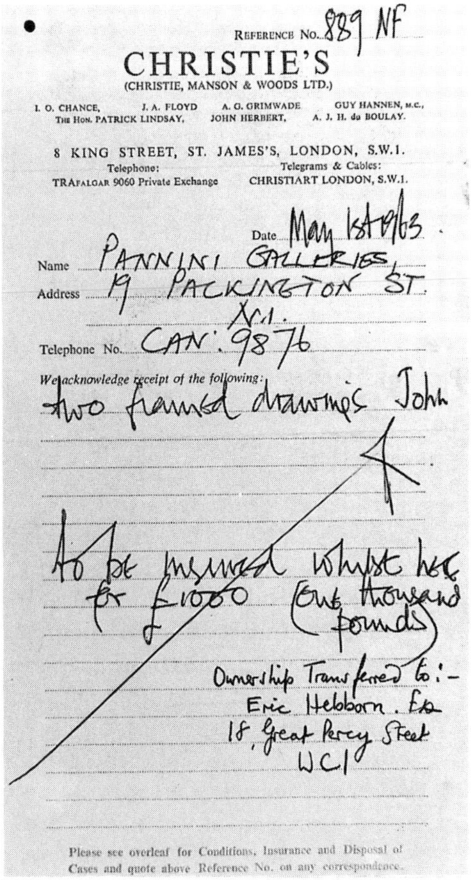

REFERENCE No. 889 NF

CHRISTIE'S

(CHRISTIE, MANSON & WOODS LTD.)

I. O. CHANCE, J. A. FLOYD A. G. GRIMWADE GUY HANNEN, M.C.,
THE HON. PATRICK LINDSAY, JOHN HERBERT, A. J. H. du BOULAY.

8 KING STREET, ST. JAMES'S, LONDON, S.W.1.

Telephone: TRAFALGAR 9060 Private Exchange

Telegrams & Cables: CHRISTIART LONDON, S.W.1.

Date May 1st 1963.

Name PANNINI GALLERIES,

Address 19 PACKINGTON ST. N.1.

Telephone No. CAN: 9876

We acknowledge receipt of the following:

two framed drawings John

To be insured whilst here for £1000 (One thousand pounds)

Ownership Transferred to:- Eric Hebborn. Esq 18, Great Percy Street WC1

Please see overleaf for Conditions, Insurance and Disposal of Cases and quote above Reference No. on any correspondence.

Fig. 32: Christie's receipt, dated 1 May 1963, for two 'Johns', issued by Brian Sewell

for one of the oldest tricks of their trade. As mentioned above, my portrait of a Spanish nobleman was an oil painting, but the auctioneers decided to overlook this fact, and instead of putting the picture into a sale of fine Old Master paintings, they put it into a sale of second-hand furniture where naturally enough it was not seen by anybody competent to appreciate its worth and where it was bought at an absurdly low price.

The reader unacquainted with the devious ways of the art market may be wondering how it could possibly have been in the auctioneer's interests to get a low price for my picture, when they were to earn a percentage of the sale price. Well, what happened was this. The picture expert to whom I showed the painting had realised that the picture was of considerable value and because I had trustingly asked him for his opinion as to who painted it and what it was worth, had correctly assumed that I was ignorant of the painting and its monetary value and would be content with a low price. He therefore suggested to me a reserve of £300 and putting the portrait into the furniture sale with only a general description such as 'Portrait of a Nobleman, Spanish School,' bought it for exactly that price himself. Once the painting was his own property he could pat himself on the back for having made a brilliant discovery, and resell it at an enormous profit. It was years later that I found out I had been cheated. A former prints and drawing expert at one of the larger salerooms played the same trick on an unsuspecting client so successfully that he had the capital to start himself up in business on his own. In this case the expert put an album full of valuable etchings into a second-hand book sale, rather than a sale of important prints and drawings, where, of course, he cleverly discovered it at a low price. In such cases it is not the salerooms that are guilty of defrauding their customers but their employees: a nice distinction but little consolation. Understandably some may see in my criticism of the dealers a classic case of the pot calling the kettle black. This humble pot differs, however, from the hypocritical kettles of London's West End in one very important particular – I do not pretend to be white.

No spotless purity is mine. Take for instance my endlessly wicked deceptions of Christie's experts which started as long ago as 1963 with the highly improper use of some sheets of old Whatman paper to make some more 'Augustus Johns'. Incidentally, the curious thing about the eighty or so drawings I have made over the years in this particular artist's manner is that they have proved more popular than the greater part of John's authentic works, and the collector is able to buy several genuine examples for the money they would now have to pay for a single 'John' of my making. To be precise my first dealings with Christie's began on 1 May 1963. On that day I went to them with two framed 'Johns' for the perusal of their then drawing expert, Brian Sewell, an attractive, highly intelligent young man with curly hair and a voice which reached heights to remember. When writing out Christie's receipt for the drawings (Fig. 32), I recall Brian saying: 'I suppose they're about as good as John gets, although you might just as well have made them yourself.' These particular 'Johns' came up for auction in Christie's sale of *Fine Barbizon, Impressionist, and Modern Drawings, Paintings and Sculpture*, 5 July 1963, lots 10 and 11, and were catalogued as follows:

10. Augustus John O.M. R.A.
    A small boy leaning on a staff
    pencil 42 × 29 cm
11. Augustus John O.M. R.A.
    A clothed female model with a broad brimmed hat
    pencil 54 × 32.5 cm

I seem to remember them fetching somewhere between one and two hundred pounds. As we shall see below, John is by no means the only modern artist whose style I have adopted, but on the whole I have preferred to meet the greater challenges offered by the making of 'Old Masters'.

One of the essential requirements for the successful creation of new 'Old Master' drawings is a sound knowledge of period paper. Most of my own know-how on this subject was acquired by handling prints and drawings in Cecil Court. Because of the vast quantities in stock and the limited space available, Louis and Marie could not display their wares properly and left their customers to sort out what they wanted from the floor-to-ceiling piles as best they might.

Fig. 33: 'Bartolomeo Pinelli', *An Episode from Roman History*, 1969, pen and wash. The inspiration for this drawing came from the story of a Roman senator who was instrumental in passing a law which his own sons transgressed. The penalty was death, but on principle the father refused to intercede, and the drawing shows him on the extreme right impassively watching their execution. (Sold to Plinio Nardecchia, 1969)

The sorting through of prints and drawings is, even in the best of circumstances, tiring work, and an experienced hand, as I may now claim to be, has developed a number of ways of conserving his energy. Let us imagine, for instance, you are faced with a pile of miscellaneous prints and you are looking for etchings by Piranesi. You know the large size of the great etchers' prints, so looking down the pile of papers you dismiss all those that are not of that size from consideration. But you do not necessarily have to unstack the pile to find out if those large sheets really are Piranesis. With your knowledge of paper and style you simply have to look at a corner of each print to know if it is on the right paper for Piranesi and if the etched line, however little you may be able to see of it, is in his manner. If in this way you have judged the prints to be by Piranesi, the paper will also have told you to what edition of the master's work they belong. Mostly, however, I was not looking through Louis' stock for a specific type of print or drawing, and would patiently work my way down pile after pile, handling thousands of prints, maps and drawings of all periods, thus acquainting myself with the feel of old paper. This kind of experience can teach one an immense amount about paper, much of which would escape even the scientific investigator with his microscope and chemical testing. The unaided eye, hand, and sometimes even nose of a practical paper expert such as myself will often come to a quicker and more reliable assessment of the age and physical qualities of a given sheet than the scientist in his laboratory.

This may be due to the very nature of a scientific examination. For the scientist is restricted by the rules of his discipline. Forbidden to be unscientific he must go through the most elaborate procedures to determine what you or I might find out with the simplest of tests. Take for instance the judging of the ink-resisting property of paper. The scientist might employ the Schuttig and Neumann solutions, the composition of which is:

Solution A

100 cc Distilled water
2.9 gms Ferric chloride
1 gm Iron
1 gm Gum arabic
0.2 gm Phenol

Solution B

1% solution of Tannic Acid containing 2% Phenol

The sample of paper to be tested is arranged on an apparatus the shape of a roof, held in a tray, with sides sloping at 60 degrees. Then, taking a few drops of solution A, the investigator trickles it down the sheet in three places simultaneously. Waiting for fifteen minutes he then turns the sheet over and allows three trickles of solution B to trickle down at right angles to the trickles he made on the reverse side. The scientific investigator then measures the time required for the tannic solution to penetrate and cause a black stain through contact with the iron salt. He compares this time with a comparative table compiled from tests on various other papers and thus arrives at the relative ink-resisting value of the sample. And when the poor fellow has done all this work he knows no more than you or I could discover in a moment by simply drawing a line in ink on the paper and noting to what extent, if any, it spreads out.

Speaking of paper, Marie's gift of a portfolio of old unused sheets was soon exhausted, and I was to expend a lot of time and money in collecting more. But one day in 1969, while looking through my piles of period paper, I came across Marie's long since empty portfolio and realised that it was itself a possible support for a new 'Old Master'. It was simply a large sheet of stout paper folded in half, which, although old, appeared to be machine-made. Until the close of the eighteenth century paper-making was essentially a hand-process, at least so far as the actual formation of the sheets was concerned. It was not until 1798 that a certain Nicolas Louis Robert invented a machine for making paper in lengths of 12 to 15 metres. Thus a drawing on a large sheet of machine-made paper such as Marie's portfolio would excite suspicion if it purported to be earlier than the beginning of the nineteenth century and I had to look about for an artist active in the first decades of the nineteenth century. The draughtsman I chose was Bartolomeo Pinelli whose dates (1781-1835) fitted my paper's age perfectly.

Pinelli lived and worked in Trastevere, and is to nineteenth-century Rome what Rowlandson is to eighteenth-century England – an indefatigable depictor of the manners and customs of his day, which he recorded in a long series of brilliantly executed drawings and etchings. He is also the unsung source of inspiration for a number of Géricault's compositions, the most obvious being the French artist's rendering of a horse race along Rome's Via del Corso. This is not the only link between Pinelli and Géricault, because in a sense they are both followers of the French painter David who sought to treat contemporary subjects, such as his famous *Death of Marat*, with some of the formal dignity usually associated with classical art. The problem proposed by David was not, however,

satisfactorily solved by either of them. In Pinelli's work the stereo-
typed neoclassical features of his characters removes them too far
from the lusty flesh and blood of the everyday scenes of Roman life
he depicts and which are more convincingly described in the poems
of another Trasteverian of the time, Giacomo Belli. Géricault, on
the other hand, falls down not from any over-stylisation of his
figures, but from too self-conscious an application of classical lore,
as far as composition is concerned. Nevertheless, they are both important artists and at his best Géricault is a great one – their
failures can be attributed to the largeness of the problem they
tackled. Apart from his scenes of everyday life in Rome and its environs, Pinelli also illustrated the Eternal City's ancient history and
it is this type of Pinelli that I made on Marie's portfolio (Fig. 33).

Twenty-two years later, my Portfolio 'Pinelli' is still considered
to be among the Trastevere artist's major works. In 1981, the bicen-
tenary of Pinelli's birth was celebrated with a highly important exhibition of the artist's drawing, watercolours, and etchings in the
Galleria Rondanini in Rome. Visiting the show, I was pleased to
note that my effort had been considered good enough to be
honoured with a wall to itself, and looking it up in the richly illustrated catalogue read the following (my translation):

> 41. *An Episode from Roman History with a Scene of Decapitation in the Centre*
> *– c. 1815-1820*
> pencil and watercolour on paper, 96 × 58, signed in the bottom
> right-hand corner *Pinelli* (this signature was added after the draw-
> ing had left my hands).
> The dimensions of the work and the consequent development of
> the composition consonant with the individual elements of the
> subject, make of this previously unrecorded work an authentic
> Pinelli masterpiece, and not only in the context of his neo-classic
> productions. The composition is clearly the result of the support
> and absolute mastery of vast erudition. It evokes memories of
> Raphael and the frescos of Domenichino and Guido Reni in the
> chapel of Sant'Andrea in San Gregorio al Celio in Rome, as well
> as quoting from the 'barbarians' on the Arch of Constantine, all
> wonderfully combined to create a setting in which the ancient
> buildings in the background with their generally Poussinesque
> mood unite with the three zones of figures to tell a story in which
> they themselves are equally important protagonists.

The next time my Portfolio 'Pinelli' is catalogued, I imagine the
entry will be rather more succinct: 'Forgery by Eric Hebborn of a
drawing by Bartolomeo Pinelli'. This will not, however, be a fair or
even accurate description, and the new catalogue entry should
read: 'Original drawing by Eric Hebborn in the manner of

Bartolomeo Pinelli.' The new entry should also get the medium right. The drawing is in fact in pen and wash, not pencil and water-colour. I suppose it is too much to expect the scholar responsible to recognise which episode from Roman history is represented, is it not?

To return to Cecil Court. One of the things that I remember with affectionate amusement about my old friends of Cecil Court is their one-sided conversations. Being 'deep' as Marie had said, Louis was not given to shallow talk, indeed he was hardly given to talk at all, unless it were about how much antiques were currently fetching at auction, and it is not too much to say he was normally taciturn. Thus Marie would do the talking and Louis would punctuate her words with grunts: 'Listen, Louis, to what it says in the paper.'

Grunt.

'A silver chalice valued at £4,000 has been stolen from Saint Martin-in-the-Fields.'

Grunt.

'What have you got in that sack, Louis?'

As it turned out Louis did really have the chalice in the sack. He had bought it only minutes after the theft from the escaping thief who had rushed into the first junk shop on his way. Louis had paid thirty shillings, which is what he thought the chalice was worth, and it was with some difficulty that he was persuaded to hand the stolen object over to the police.

My friendship with the old couple lasted for over twenty years. Now they and their Old Curiosity Shop are no more. They died within a year of each other. Being abroad at the time, I learnt first of Louis' death at the age of ninety-four in a letter from Marie, and then of her own, aged eighty-five, from a mutual friend. Where their graves actually are I do not know, nor shall I try to find out, because I treasure a memory of Marie telling me of the place where she would have liked to be buried:

'It's a secluded churchyard in a very good area. The church itself was destroyed by the Nazis, wasn't it Louis?'

Grunt.

'There are some beautiful moss and ivy covered tombstones. The newest of them goes back to Dickens's day, but the majority are much older. The place is so wonderfully peaceful. In the old days we used to go there for picnics, don't you remember, Louis?'

Grunt.

'In the spring it's full of the fragrance of wild flowers and the song of birds who have turned the old elms into a sanctuary.'

Here Marie paused to give Louis one of her 'certain' looks before continuing with: 'And it's only twenty minutes from the shop. You'll find that a great convenience, won't you dear?'

CHAPTER VII

LA DOLCE VITA

'How I shall freeze after all this sun! Here I am a gentleman, at home
a parasite.'

Albrecht Dürer.

Letters terrify me. I am as scared to write them as to receive
them. Mine is perhaps an irrational fear, but none the less real
for that. Letter writing is for me a fearful torture which I invariably
postpone, and sometimes fail to undertake at all. How many friendships lost, how many marred by my inability to conquer this unreasonable fear – even unwritten letters are dangerous! It is no use
telling me that letters convey good as well as bad tidings. That is
like saying tigers are sometimes as tame as pussycats. Letters, like
tigers, have a fearful potential. Mostly they hide their claws, call
you dear so-and-so, and tell you how truly and sincerely they remain yours faithfully, while in between they are quite likely to have
mauled your heart or in some other way torn your life to shreds.
Letters can destroy nations, raise up and cast down religions, and
with what contemptuous ease alter our personal histories. But like
all dangerous things there is something fascinating about them. To
me even the most ordinary letter has a fascination about it that no
other form of writing has. Take for instance these few lines from the
British School at Rome:

21 April 1959

Dear Sir,

   I have the pleasure to inform you that upon the recommendation
of the Faculty of Engraving you have been awarded the Rome
Scholarship in Engraving for 1959.
   I enclose a copy of the General Regulations and would explain
that ordinarily a Scholar is expected to arrive at the School in

Rome at the beginning of October in the year of the appointment. The Scholarship stipend is payable in advance and is ordinarily dated from 1st September. May I suggest that at some time convenient to yourself you might call and see me at this office to discuss the award.

Would you be kind enough to acknowledge the receipt of this letter.

Yours sincerely,

W. D. Sturch
Hon. General Secretary

This matter-of-fact communication altered the entire course of my life. No wonder I stand in awe of it. My first reaction was to jump for joy, seize Graham around the waist and waltz round and round the room and out into the street. Then I celebrated by getting hideously drunk – it was not until three days later that I was sober enough to grasp the immediate implications of Mr Sturch's letter. I was to live among strangers in a foreign land and speak a foreign tongue. I saw it as a great adventure, but something hurt inside. I loved Graham, I loved my friends, I loved London, and did not know how I could bear to part from them for two long years. But there was no time for dewy-eyed sentimentality. There were practical matters to be attended to. First on the list was to apply for a passport. This was connected with the wish to avoid immediate conscription into the army. The authorities had postponed sending me my call-up papers so that I could complete my studies at the Academy, but would make no further postponement, and it seemed very likely that I would see military service long before seeing the Eternal City. I knew, however, that the British army would be powerless to conscript me on foreign soil and I might yet avoid going into the army by getting myself abroad as soon as possible. But would Sir Henry Rushbury approve of my shirking my duty to Queen and Country? More important still, would the British School at Rome pay the scholarship stipend to someone who was in effect a deserter? The problem was solved less by telling lies than by anticipating truth. When I visited Mr Sturch at his office in Lowther Gardens to discuss the award, I told him of the imminence of my conscription and the plan I had for avoiding it, adding that I had already discussed the matter with the head of the Faculty of Engraving and Sir Henry had said that whereas he would not, and could not encourage me to avoid my obligations, were I to actually show up at the School in Rome, faced with the *fait accompli*, he would see no objection to paying me my stipend. 'Well,' said Mr Sturch, 'if Sir Henry says it's alright, I suppose it is.' Whereupon I went to see Sir Henry at the Academy and told him the same story, except of course I changed his name for that of Mr Sturch's. At which Sir Henry said, 'Well, if Mr Sturch says it's alright, I suppose it is.'

The question of the army out of the way, the next difficulty was how to get enough money to go abroad and survive until the payment of the first instalment of the stipend in September. In 1959 banks were unaccountably keen on lending money, and I had noticed a newspaper advertisement inserted by Barclays Bank Ltd offering personal loans of up to £1,000, at a low interest rate and no security. So off I went to a branch of the bank at Highbury Corner where I knew my slum landlord deposited a large part of his ill-gotten gains. I asked if I might see Mr Goodbun, the manager, and told him that I wished to do business with his bank and open an account.

'And how much are you thinking of depositing with us?' the unsuspecting Mr Goodbun asked.

'That,' I replied, 'depends entirely on how much you are prepared to lend me!'

'And may I ask, Mr Hebborn, what your source of income is?'

'I'm an artist.'

'Oh, I see,' he said, recoiling as if I had said I was a leper. 'In that case I don't think that Barclays would be prepared to assist you. Unless perhaps you own a house or some other asset that you could use as surety.'

'But your advertisement said you didn't want any security,' I said ingenuously, adding that if Barclays were not people of their word I was very sorry, but I would be obliged to take my business elsewhere. This knowledge did not quite have the effect that I had imagined, and instead of grovelling for custom, a distinct look of relief spread over Mr Goodbun's honest features. And there the interview might have ended, had I not thrown down my ace, saying grandly, 'And when I take my business elsewhere I shall take my landlord's with it.' It would appear that slum landlords mean more to bankers than artists do because on hearing this, the bank manager's attitude changed at once, and he suggested that we might discuss the possibility of a small unsecured loan, not in excess of a hundred pounds, if only I would first explain what my connection with the landlord was. I told him that I was his trusted advisor, that he had implicit faith in my judgement in financial matters, and one word from me and Barclays would see no more of him or his money. To what extent Mr Goodbun believed my story I could not tell, but he did take it seriously enough to phone the landlord up and tell him that he had a certain Mr Hebborn in his office who was asking for a loan of a hundred pounds, and would my landlord be prepared to stand as guarantor. My landlord did not, I suspect, know what the word guarantor meant, and asked if I was an arty-type with a beard. On being told I was, he must have said something like, 'Yes, that's 'im, by Christ, I can guarantee 'im already', intending perhaps, that he could guarantee that I was really myself. Anyway, Mr Goodbun seems to have understood that he had said yes to guaranteeing the repayment of my loan, and opened my account a hundred pounds in the red – a colour it cheerfully maintained until 1963 when Barclays, not without ugly threats, decided to close it.

At this point, preparations for my departure were well underway. A hundred pounds was, however, very little to last from May to October, and I hit upon the plan of walking from Calais to Rome. Such a walking tour offered the advantage, not only of saving money on train or air fares, but also, if I slept out of doors, on accommodation. Furthermore, I could profitably occupy my time in sight-seeing and sketching. My first expenditure was for an old army rucksack – a capacious canvas bag with a complication of pockets, straps and buckles. I opened it, put it on the kitchen table, and began to stuff into it all that the well-appointed traveller might need for a four-month walking tour: camping stove, lamp, cutlery, plate and mug, pots and pans, candles, ketchup, sardines, books, sketching materials, compass, clothing, footwear, thermos flask, large sheet of green plastic (which served as both groundsheet and tent), balaclava helmet, bayonet, mosquito net, etc. The pack was so heavy I could scarcely lift it. How, I wondered, would I manage to carry such a weight from Calais to Rome?

The day of departure was bright and sunny, but Graham and I parted with tears in our eyes. The train left at 10.30 a.m. from Victoria Station. London's dreary sprawl of suburbs rattled past the window. I was going abroad. Abroad. It deserves a sentence to itself. Just imagine, everywhere and anywhere in the whole wide world, except, of course, for England, is abroad, and I was going there for the very first time. Leaving my rucksack to take the blame for obstructing the corridor, I made my way to the cosy Victorian-style dining car in whose atmosphere of velvet covers and linen cloths, brass lamps and crystal mirrors, sturdy crockery and weighty Sheffield, I treated myself to breakfast. Had I known then that I was about to exchange that glorious morning fare of bacon and eggs, buttered toast and marmalade, and cup after cup of thickly brewed tea, for a miserable repast known as a continental breakfast, I might perhaps have savoured that meal even more than I actually did. Lunch was on the boat ride from Dover to Calais. It consisted of five or six duty-free glasses of brandy and a white pasty object, triangular in shape, which had it not been clearly labelled 'cheese sandwich', I might not have known what to do with.

The English Channel is not called the French or even the Anglo-French Channel, and it is a curious fact that I did not feel that I had left England until I actually set foot in France. To a certain extent this must have been due to the boat being English, but what really told me beyond doubt that I was leaving my homeland was when, stepping off the boat at Calais, I found myself faced with a wall of foreign aromas. The most obvious was the smell of the Gauloises smoked by the porters, but there were hundreds of other less decipherable ones. These were mostly blended mixtures of the wholesome appetising aromas of a great cuisine: wine, garlic, herbs and spices, the smell of newly baked bread and freshly brewed coffee. I was plunged in a dense atmosphere of olfactory pleasure – sensuous and uniquely French. Passport formalities over, I picked up my monstrous rucksack and followed my nose out of the customs shed, into the town, along a narrow street and up a flight of steps into a café. This being my first meal on French soil, I thought I should eat something truly French. No Englishman would, of course, eat anything as slimy and disgusting as snails, but *escargots* are alright. They were served sizzling hot in butter, garlic and parsley. I ordered a half-litre of *vin ordinaire* but nothing was or could have been *ordinaire* that day. The main course was *extra-ordinaire* to me because the *légumes* were served separately from the *boeuf*. At home meat and vegetables invariably arrived on a single plate.

By now it was evening, and as I was to sleep in the open I went in search of a field. My rucksack, heavy in the morning, was doubly weighty now. My shoulders were hurting from the straps and my leg muscles were sore. Strengthened by the food and wine and with avid anticipation of continuing my grand tour in good form in the morning, I consulted my compass and, with only the occasional deviation to avoid hitting a building, struck out due north. The street lamps of Calais were soon behind me, and in the darkness I turned into what I judged to be a meadow where I stumbled across some bales of straw and with no further ado fell asleep. It was bright sunlight when I woke, or rather, was woken. There was a deafening roar and a racing car whizzed within inches of the top of my head. My bales of straw were part of a safety barrier set up around a race track.

As my intention was to walk to Rome, any reader with a sense of direction may be wondering why I was walking northwards from Calais. Well, a man called Eugene Fromentin is responsible for that. Fromentin was a successful French artist of the nineteenth century who is now less known for his paintings than for a book he wrote called *The Old Masters*. It is an acknowledged masterpiece of art criticism, and a copy of it, which Graham had given me, was in my rucksack. The Old Masters Fromentin discusses are Dutch and Flemish, notably Hals, Rembrandt and Rubens, and he explains that he wrote his book immediately on his return from seeing the work of those artists in the lands of their birth. This struck me as interesting. Are pictures, I wondered, like certain wines, better savoured in the place of their origin? Can the country in which an artist lived and worked tell us something about the artist himself? What I knew of Flanders I knew from Flemish art; could I learn about Flemish art from Flanders? I had only to walk a little out of my way to discover the answers.

I have never kept a journal, but now I rather wish I had. Bruges, Ghent, Antwerp, Brussels, Liège and Aachen are little more to me now than names, and yet I visited them all. I seldom forget a painting and remember having seen a number of fine ones but can no longer remember where. What does come back vividly is a memory of such physical discomfort as blisters, sore muscles, sunburn and diarrhoea – the result of getting myself accustomed to carrying my load for twenty-odd miles a day beneath a scorching sun (Europe was having one of its hottest summers for years), and sustaining myself on a diet of ever-changing novelty. Another unpleasantness was the great motorways of noise and smell, which I could not always avoid. I had decided to walk from Calais to Rome and this did not permit cheating by hitch-hiking. On the major roads, cars were constantly stopping to offer a lift, an offer which I suspect would, had it been accepted, often have been accompanied by a proposition of another kind. I met a youth of my own age who, when I complained of my blisters, said, 'I bet your feet aren't half as sore from walking as my penis is from hitch-hiking!'

So I tried as much as possible to take small, out-of-the-way roads, lanes and footpaths. One of these byways, somewhere between Brussels and Antwerp, led me through a tiny hamlet. It was growing dark and I was hurrying on to find a resting place in the fields when somebody called to me. He was leaning over and out of the lower half of the door, the kind that is used for stables. His face had the appearance of having been made out of a turnip, eyes and mouth roughly hollowed out, a peg for a nose, and flaps for ears. In his hand was a pewter tankard, and on his face a jolly grin which wrinkled up his glowing nose and turned his ruddy cheeks to shiny apples. From behind him came sounds of revelry, and when I answered his beckoning call I found myself part of a tavern scene that might have been painted by Adrian Brouwer. The taverner was a jovial, powerfully built man who could have better played the part of the village blacksmith, and, like his customers, was comically ugly. Making it clear that there would be no charge, he gave me a slopping tankard of beer and two hard-boiled eggs. The topers, who, I suspect, had never seen an even remotely normal looking human being in that hamlet of merry monsters, gathered around me as one would a great curiosity. They pointed out to each other my remarkable oddities, and treated me with the greatest hospitality, plying me with food and, more especially, drink. They even found room in my bulging rucksack for some excellent smoked sausage. We danced to music improvised by beating knives and forks on to tin plates and I was encouraged to do a Russian-type dance of a kind I have never seen danced before or since. This I did on top of a shaky trestle table which soon decided it had had enough of it.

Although my hosts' language was unknown to me, there was no problem of communication, and I was able to convey to them the idea that I was walking to Rome. Acquainted with this knowledge, the jolly taverner's great frame shook with mirth, and with many a sign of affection led me to understand that as his very best friend on earth he could not possibly let me face the perils of so arduous a journey alone, and loyalty and devotion demanded that he accompany me on my way. To underline the sincerity of his feelings and the seriousness of his intentions, he went to fetch a blanket in which to pack what he might need for the road. He was assisted in his packing by his customers. Those living caricatures of Breughel and Bosch threw into the blanket a number of three-legged stools, quantities of pots and pans, fire-irons, pewter jugs, some sorry looking pictures, a clock and a calendar. The greater part of the moveable contents of the tavern bundled up in the blanket, the taverner fetched a clothes-line on to which he strung a long row of saucepans and saucepan lids and terminated the row with a frying pan.

His friends and customers decided to see him on his way. The tavern was locked and left to darkness. It was a velvet night of stars and silence. At least it had been until we intruded ourselves on it.

Fig. 34: 'Jan Breughel the Elder', *Studies of a Man with a Scythe*, 1968, pen and wash. (Sold by Sotheby's, Amsterdam, 25 April 1983)

Now the silence had fled, the topers were singing a marching song and the taverner with his huge bundle of possessions on his shoulders was trailing the line of saucepans, lids and frying pan on the ground to make a fearsome clatter, and every now and then would dramatically point ahead of him and shout at the top of his raucous voice: 'A ROM! A ROM!' Then every one, including myself, would echo his stirring cry: 'A ROM! A ROM!' Making our clamorous way out of the hamlet we marched in single file along a flat strip of moonlight. To an observer from the side we would have looked like caricatures cut from black paper, or the whole parade some comic shadow show. We must have marched for over half an hour, and I was beginning to fear that my new-found friends might not have realised how far from Brussels Rome really is and I was perhaps taking them farther afield than they had bargained for. But then we came to another cluster of cottages and barns, and there, behind another stable-like door, was another group of revellers. Once more I was the centre of attraction, once more my oddities examined, once more plied with drink, but here my dear friend the taverner decided to abandon me to my fate and let me pursue my journey to Rome as best I might.

At about one in the morning the local mayor, who spoke a few words of English, invited me to stay at his mayoral residence. He wobbled and wisely wheeled his bicycle beneath what was to me, and doubtless to him, a double moon. Shortly we came to a relatively large and, unlike its owner, totally characterless house of brick. After days of sleeping rough I was rather looking forward to the comforts of a bed. 'This way,' said my host as he led me to the back of the house, through a cow shed and into a dung-filled outhouse. Here he tossed an armful of straw into a corner and indicating a hole which I might use as a lavatory without messing up the place, bid me good night.

The hangover the next morning was no great problem, and was walked away in an hour or so, but the memory of my drunken night in Flanders did not vanish with it. I had learnt that Flanders could indeed teach one something about Flemish art. It taught me more about Brouwer and similar artists than any picture gallery could have done, and now, should I sit down to draw or paint a tavern scene in the style of those little masters, there is one thing I can guarantee – the atmosphere is absolutely authentic.

Little more than two weeks had passed since I had packed my rucksack in London, and now I was in Cologne (Fig. 35) admiring its great cathedral and preparing to walk down the Rhine. The mighty river was then clean enough to swim in, and I would sleep on its banks and each morning wake myself up by rolling out from under my sheet of green plastic to make a splash. Strong swimmer that I was, there was no question of swimming against so strong a

Fig. 35: *A View Near Cologne*, summer 1959, watercolour (Collection of the artist)

current, and I would allow myself to be swept downstream for a few hundred yards, then clamber out and make my way back to my rucksack for whatever breakfast I might or might not have. The Rhine valley was, and I trust still is, very picturesque, and I made a series of line and wash drawings of its green mountains and old castles perched high above the great flow of water. There was the delicious *Rhein Wein* to be savoured, and I developed a taste for *leder hosen*, or more precisely what was contained in *leder hosen*. Only the other day I came across a postcard dated 19 September 1959, and addressed to me at the British School at Rome. It showed a charming view of Germany's great waterway and on the back of it is written 'Remember this place and our happy hours? Love Horst.' Yes, Horst, I still remember.

In France and in certain parts of Belgium I had been looked at askance for carrying a rucksack. The Germans, however, seemed to think there was something admirable about it, and everywhere I went I was greeted in the most friendly way. I picked up a few words of German (now forgotten), and would have liked to linger there between Bonn and Mainz, but Rome was calling, and every day saw me a little further south.

In Heidelberg, the famous old university town, I was lucky enough to find a beer festival in progress. This delayed me for three days. By then walking had made me extremely fit, and I could pick up my huge rucksack with one hand and swing it on to my back as easily as putting on a jacket. Some days I would walk as much as forty miles, others only two or three, but on I plodded. Stuttgart, Augsburg, Munich (what pictures there!), Salzburg and then in the general direction of the Alpine road to Lienz. Map-reading is not my forte, and I got hopelessly lost. I tramped for days across the Alps, right off the beaten track, with only my compass to make certain I was headed south. I passed through some ravishingly beautiful scenery. Magnificent mountain ranges, incredibly lush meadows and thick dark forests, long steep climbs, awe-inspiring descents. The tortuous paths that I took did not pass through towns or villages and I scarcely saw a living soul. But curiously, I did not feel alone. Now I know why wise and holy men seek such places for their meditation, for there, nature makes her presence felt and shows us how very unimportant in the great scheme of things mankind really is. The mountains of the earth have merely to shrug their shoulders to be free of the whole lot of us. They inspire worship and teach the virtue of humility. After six days of wandering in those splendid surroundings, with only a flask of wine and a few tins of sardines to sustain me, I found myself leaving the cool mountain heights and crossing rugged hills to descend to gentler slopes that led me to the narrow coastal plain of the then off-the-tourist-route provinces of Udine, Gorizia and Trieste. Somehow I had got into Italy without showing my passport! During my walk across the Alps I had time to reflect on a number of things. One was the wisdom of continuing my walking tour. Footsore, but not weary, it seemed to me that I could be using my time better than getting blisters on my feet, and resolved that on reaching a highway I would hitch-hike to such places as Venice and Florence and use the time I would save in enjoying the wonders that I knew those cities would contain. So putting my penis in peril, I thumbed a lift and by sheer good luck got a ride from an elderly German couple who were planning to spend two weeks in Venice, where many years before they had spent their honeymoon.

I have heard that it is a truly unforgettable experience to approach Venice for the first time from the sea. Certainly the road which I took from Mestre which takes one over the Ponte di Libertà and close to the railway station of Santa Lucia has little to recommend it except that one enters the city abruptly. And I must admit that there was something wonderful about leaving that everyday matter-of-fact road and parking lot at the *Stazione Maríttima* to suddenly find myself aboard a *vaporetto* in a magical world of waterways. Here was the city I knew from Canaletto, Bellotto, Guardi, Turner, Whistler, and many more, in itself an indescribably beautiful work of art which has possibly inspired more artists than any other city in the world. It would not, I imagined, be possible to sleep under the stars in Venice. So I was on my way to the *Ostello della Gioventù* on the island of Giudecca, the old Jewish ghetto. I had consulted a guide book to find out, not the quickest, but the most picturesque way. I need not have bothered – there is no corner of Venice which is not picturesque. As it was, I was taking the *vaporetto* along the Grand Canal to the Bacino di San Marco, with the idea of changing boats there and crossing over to the Giudecca. How I wished I could have afforded to hire a *gondola*. How pleasant it would have been to recline myself, a glass of chilled wine in hand, and be punted leisurely along between the marble palaces which lined my way. Palaces dating from the twelfth to the eighteenth century, with a predominance of those from the fourteenth and fifteenth, many of them bearing the arms of noble families. The beauty of these famous buildings lies not so much in their forms, lovely as they are, but in the way they both absorb and reflect light.

It was early evening; the day had been pitilessly hot. Now there was a bright blush of golden ochre on the tops of the buildings,

the best art of the present. It was not just *different*, it is very definitely better.

I spent many days in the *Galleria dell'Accademia* which without doubt houses the greatest collection of Venetian paintings in the world, and documents the story of the city's art from the fourteenth to the eighteenth century. Every art lover is familiar, if only through reproductions, with this great gallery's major pictures. Works by the so-called Venetian primitives such as Paolo and Lorenzo Veneziano, Michele di Matteo, and Michele di Giambono; followed by the fifteenth and sixteenth century painters, Carpaccio, Crivelli, Giovanni and Gentile Bellini, Cima da Conegliano, Mantegna, Tura, Sebastiano del Piombo, Giorgione, Titian, Paris Bordone, Palma the Elder and Younger, Bonifacio de Pitati, Tintoretto and Veronese; then the painters of seventeenth- and eighteenth-century Venice: Tetti, Strozzi, Ricci, Magnasco, Guardi, Canaletto, Zais and Zuccarelli – what a feast!

I am aware that my approach to these artists' work was radically different from that of most visitors to art galleries in our time. Perhaps as an over-reaction to the Victorian critic who tended to pontificate, there is a tendency nowadays for people to make no critical judgment whatsoever, but to accept indiscriminately every painting that is in an art gallery for no better reason than that it is there. To people with this attitude, pictures are not good or bad, they simply *are*: the ideas would seem to be an illogical extension of Alexander Pope's thought:

> All nature is but art unknown to thee,
> All chance, direction which thou canst not see;
> All discord, harmony not understood;
> All partial evil, universal good;
> And, spite of pride, in erring reason's sprite,
> One truth is clear, Whatever is, is right.

Their attitude is, however, a dangerous one because it does not admit of standards. By its anything-goes attitude, no painter is any better than any other painter, no age (except perhaps our own) any better than any other age. This is, of course, a reflection of the approach of the modern art historian, who with cold objectivity views paintings and other works of art as documents giving an account of the life and times of the men and women who made them. And from this point of view a miserable daub is just as important as a great masterpiece. The excrement that I threw about as a child in Station Road, Harold Wood, was incontestably as graphic a description of a child's frustration as the frescos in the

Fig. 36: *The Blindfolding of Cupid*, after Titian, 1961, etching made at the
British School at Rome (Collection of the artist)

Sistine Chapel are of a great artist's inspiration, the difference
being, I would argue, that as art, it was not as good. Likewise, I
believe that the neurotic, desperately extrovert and egocentric
works of art that characterise our century provide an admirably
clear indication of the mental and spiritual disorders of our time,
but, as art, leave much to be desired. My view was encouraged in
the Accademia. Wandering leisurely through its galleries, I was

rash enough to enjoy some paintings more than others. It seemed to me, for example, that Titian is a far better artist than Tiepolo. True, Tiepolo is as good an example of Rococo frivolity as Titian is of Renaissance rectitude but to my mind rectitude is a greater virtue than frivolity. Ultimately, I judge a work of art by the extent it moves me, and the depth of the emotion it moves me to. For instance, some artists like Rowlandson and Ghezzi amuse me, and as I like being amused, and they do it very well, I think of them as excellent. Other artists, such as the Tiepolos, do not exactly amuse me, but they invariably please me, delighting me by their inventions, exotic trimmings and novel viewpoints. So I count these painters too as wonderfully good.

A few painters, however, and Titian is among them, can move me to tears. Their pictures touch the chords of my deepest emotions and these painters are the ones that I regard as the very greatest. One picture which even in recollection brings tears to my eyes, is Titian's last work, before which I stood in the Accademia for hours, wondering by what magic a few coloured earths, oils and canvas can be combined to speak to the soul. Who with a crumb of sensibility could fail to be moved by such a work? The subject is the *Pietà*, but it is not the pathos of the subject itself that accounts for the funereal mood – I have seen some laughably bad *Pietàs*. No, the atmosphere is achieved by painterly, not illustrative, means. It is with the simplest of colours and grandest of forms that Titian involves the viewer's emotions. By saying that the mood of the picture is funereal, I risk suggesting it is a dreary joyless work, when in fact the scene of lamentation fills the viewer with exultation. It is all of the tomb, but the artist makes one conscious of the ultimate triumph of the spirit. Titian was nearly a hundred when he painted it, and the tremulous touch that speaks of the painter's own struggle with mortality is enough in itself to raise a lump in the throat. The great artist stands heroically between life and death with neither regret at the passing of one, nor fear at the coming of the other. It was this picture that he wished to be placed above his tomb, and no man could wish for a finer monument. To speak of Titian's last masterpiece in these pages is particularly relevant because a very considerable part of the picture was not painted by Titian at all. When the master died of the plague in 1576, the *Pietà* was incomplete and finished by his pupil and assistant, Palma il Giovane, who, with justifiable pride, wrote a bold inscription to that effect on the painting itself. The very presence of the inscription suggests that Palma's contribution to the picture was of considerable importance. Simply finishing off a part of the background and adding a few touches here and there to the figures would not warrant such a conspicuous statement to draw the viewer's attention to Palma's own work. Now, I defy any authority, however expert they may be, to separate Palma's work on this picture from Titian's own. There is no faulty drawing or poor colouring to speak of an imitator. Every touch is by a master and if it were not for Palma's inscription one would never suspect that any part of that magnificent work could possibly be by any hand other than Titian's own. Studying Titian's *Pietà* made me realise that it is possible, difficult certainly, but possible, to work so completely in another painter's manner as to make one's work indistinguishable from that artist's own. In other words when Berenson wrote '. . . the one thing the forger cannot do is to satisfy the standard of a specially trained taste, and to avoid betraying himself by some mannerism of his own which the experienced eye can learn to detect', the great man was saying something which is only generally, not invariably, true. But let us suppose that one *could* separate Palma's work on the *Pietà* from Titian's own, should we remove the pupil's additions and have only what is from the master's own hand? Of course not. To destroy a complete masterpiece just to have Titian's autograph fragment would be a heinous act of vandalism. My study of the *Pietà* also made me wonder how many other Titians Palma painted. As many as Titian made in the manner of his masters Bellini and Giorgione? Probably, but what does it matter; as far as I am concerned, the more Titians there are in the world, the better.

When I was not looking at paintings, I was drawing the city, and soon had a portfolio of Venetian views. Some of these I was able to sell then and there for a few lira to the tourists, but not enough. Money had become a pressing problem. My taste for *gran seole*, Comachio Valley eels, sole, mullet, sturgeon, lobster and shrimp (scampi are especially good in Venice) washed down with Soave had reduced my hundred pounds to little more than a hundred lira. I could no longer afford the luxury of a bed in the Ostello della Gioventù, and had moved my belongings to the Lido. This may surprise any reader who knows Venice, because the Lido is the most fashionable stretch of sand and sea in Italy. Like the French Riviera and Hawaii's Waikiki Beach, it is one of the world's most luxurious playgrounds, drawing wealth and glamour from all over.

When one got off the *vaporetto*, and walked down Viale Santa Maria, the Lido's main street, which runs past dozens of tastefully decorated hotels, cafés and pensions to the other side of the island to end at the wide stretch of sandy-white beach and blue water beyond, the wealth and glamour turned right. I turned left, and so instead of finding myself on the seaside boulevard, Lungomare Marconi, which curves its way past the Grand Hotel des Bains to a square formed by Palazzo del Cinema, where the famous film festival is held, and the Municipal Casino with its plush lounges, bars and great terraces, I found myself on a barren stretch of sand known as the 'gay' beach. Like so many gay places and faces, *la spiaggia gay* was really rather sad. Perhaps because of its proximity to the noise of the San Nicoló airport, there were none of the hotels, cabins and dressing rooms, lawn tennis courts, riding schools and golf courses of the Lido's smart side. There was only one building, an improvised shack, surrounded by litter, from which a good-looking beach boy with a marvellously *simpatico* grin, sold drinks and snacks. His name was Giulio. I made friends with him and would occasionally help him by running his seedy snack bar while he went to see his family or buy stock. It seemed that during my sojourn on the sand, he and I were the chief attractions of the squalid stretch of beach, for we were constantly being propositioned. But he was not homosexual, and I, generally speaking, was not interested.

One day, however, a little romance did come my way. It was midday, I was sitting alone in the middle of the square of shadow beneath the snack bar's tattered awning, drinking the half-litre of wine on which I had spent my last few lira, when looking out along the beach, I noticed in the far distance a dark speck materialising on the dazzling whiteness – it was moving, and moving fast. Soon it developed arms and legs, a head, a colourful short-sleeved shirt with shorts to match, dark sunglasses, hair and features; and in no time at all it burst into my shadow, and my life, with:

'Hi, I'm David, American painter!'

'Hi,' I echoed lamely, 'I'm Eric, have a drink.'

David was a man of my own middling height, about forty and bursting with vitality. Swigging down my wine as though there was plenty more where that came from, he asked:

'What are you doing tonight, Eric?'

'Actually I haven't made any plans.'

'Great, you're having dinner with me!'

David did not waste time.

In David I had a lively, interested and interesting companion. I liked him a lot and was intrigued by his worldly ways. He was bisexual. One day David invited me to go with him to visit an old girlfriend of his from the States. She had a wonderful home, full of modern art, on the Grand Canal called Palazzo Venier dei Leoni, and her name was Peggy. Somewhat older than David, whom she had met when he was an art dealer, handling among other artists Pollock and De Kooning, David had described Peggy to me as 'a fun loving gal', but now there was something sedate about her. Slim, dressed very soberly, her hair grey, her face lined, youth lingering only about her eyes, her demure manner made David's seem rather gross. She showed us her home which is now famous as a museum of modern art. The paintings and sculpture were arranged in an informal way. She had, for instance, hung examples of work by an ex-husband, Max Ernst, in her bathroom. It would be a cheap joke to say that that is where they belonged, but there would also be an element of truth in it.

I had not thought it necessary to tell David of my almost total disinterest (sexually speaking) in women and I got the distinct impression that in his ignorance he was trying to get Peggy and myself paired off for the evening, or was perhaps thinking of a threesome. In any case, when we came to Peggy's bedroom, he threw himself on to the leopard-skin bed-cover and kicked his legs up into the air in a most improper manner, as if inviting us both to join him; at which Peggy informed him that she no longer went in for 'that kind of thing'. As far as I was concerned, this was a relief to hear, but my relief was short-lived, for when we returned to her main terrace overlooking the Grand Canal, Peggy drew me away from David to admire a sculpture by Marino Marini. It represented a boy on a horse; the horse's head and neck had been modelled to suggest a phallus, and the boy's arms were sticking out at right angles to his trunk, as was his penis. Peggy put her hand on the bronze erection and said in a sultry sexy kind of voice, ill-suited to the sedate manner she had affected: 'Eric, the whole heat of Venice seems to concentrate itself on this spot.' With which she unscrewed the object, and to my horror, thrust it into my hand and invited me to kiss her. Thinking it impolite to refuse a lady, I gave her a gallant peck on the cheek and returned the metal penis with: 'I am sorry, Peggy, but this is a lot harder than mine is'. David, overhearing the remark, laughed, at which Peggy laughed as well, and for reasons known only to herself she put the sculpt phallus in her handbag.

The three of us then set out in Peggy's private gondola to eat supper in a restaurant in the Piazza San Marco which, for two painters and a patroness of the arts, was most appropriately called Quadri (pictures). The restaurant was luxuriously furnished and the food exquisite. I ordered risi e bisi which is a traditional Venetian soup served with rice and peas that once graced the table at all official banquets during the ancient Republic of Venice. And while David and Peggy spoke of their past, I quietly got myself merry on the Valpolicella and fantasised about what I felt sure was going to be my glorious future, where dining with millionairesses would be the order of the day. I also decided to write a letter to Graham telling him of my adventures abroad – a letter which needless to say never got written. One letter was, however, posted by me in Venice. It was on Royal Danieli notepaper and addressed to Britain's War Office; it read:

Dear Sirs,

Re your invitation to join her Majesty's Armed Forces

I regret to inform you that for the time being commitments abroad make it impossible to accept your kind offer.

I trust this will cause you no inconveniences, and looking forward to contacting you on my return to England

Yours truly,

Eric Hebborn

David moved in fashionable circles and must have known many influential people. No doubt this explains how he managed to get tickets for us, and at a moment's notice, for the world premiere at the Palazzo del Cinema of a film called *Some Like It Hot*. It starred Marilyn Monroe, whose well rounded performance failed to arouse me to any more enthusiasm than the riches and glamour of the audience of celebrities. Furthermore, the photographers' flashlights made my eyes feel sore. Poor David simply could not understand how I could be so totally unimpressed, and it would have been futile to explain to him how pathetic the whole tinsel show seemed to me after the true glories of Venice. I was much more thrilled by something else that my well connected friend wanted to arrange. He had a letter of introduction to Bernard Berenson, and promised to take me with him to meet the famous connoisseur. The plan was that we should make our separate ways to Florence, visit Berenson, and then travel together to Rome where David would rent a studio and prepare an exhibition. When, however, he phoned I Tatti, Berenson's home outside Florence, it was only to be told that while we would be welcome to visit the villa, the great man was too ill to receive visitors. As it transpired, Berenson was on his deathbed. Since David had really been more interested in adding yet another famous name to his long list of acquaintances than seeing 'old art', he decided to go straight to Rome. For myself, as I still had several weeks to pass before I could take up my scholarship, I thought there could be no better way of spending some of the time than in seeing Florence, more especially since the city was on my way. So having agreed that David would leave a message for me at the British School, we parted company with promises of taking up our friendship again in the capital.

Venice had sated me with beauty. I had feasted on more than delicious seafoods and *risi e bisi* and was still trying to digest a little of what I had seen. Now I was faced with an even larger plate of artistic delicacies – it was simply too much. Nevertheless, I did my best and spent the three weeks I had decided to stay in the city in assiduous sightseeing. And as time was no object, I worked out an itinerary involving a number of specific detailed trips which all began from the city's centre at the Piazza del Duomo where I would have breakfast, consisting of a version of the Roman *cornetto*, which I, as did many Florentines themselves, accompanied with a glass of good Chianti. Thus every day I would see the great Duomo, the *campanile* of Giotto, and the lofty cathedral of Santa Maria del Fiore (the largest church in the world after St Peter's in Rome) in the light of early morning. Few painters have succeeded in getting poetry out of the sun and shadow of noon; by far the greater number choose the hours close to sunrise or sunset to work their magic, Claude, Turner and Corot, to give some distinguished examples. The old architects were also very much concerned with the effects of light. Like the painters, they knew that the raking side-light of morning and evening throws volumes into relief, and they modelled the outside of their buildings to take advantage of this fact and much of the beauty of their work depends on subtle transitions from low to high relief which are best appreciated at the beginning or the end of day. Noon is for the enjoyment of the buildings' cool interiors.

Although Venice had not totally exhausted my capacity to view works of art with a fresh eye, I must admit that, much as I saw on my first stay in Florence, I absorbed very little. Any knowledge I may now claim to have of the city and its art I have gathered on subsequent visits. As it happens, I know exactly how many times I have returned to that city of marvels – seven. This is because on each visit I buy an ancient coin from a dealer who trades from what is literally a hole in the wall, just off the Piazza della Signoria, a hole scarcely large enough for him and his few drawers of stock. I am very happy with my seven souvenirs of Florence. Coins are small pieces of sculpture, and when one buys a Greek or Roman coin, one is buying a Greek or Roman work of art. It seems to me incredible that it is still possible to buy an ancient masterpiece for a hundredth of the price of a piece of modern sculpture that, more

Fig. 37: *A Corner of the Garden at the British School in
Rome*, 1960, drawing in oil paint on canvas in
preparation for painting. This underpainting was
carried out in the same technique as Titian employed
for the basis of some of his later works (Collection of
the artist)

often than not, is liked simply because it is modern. By its very
nature, modernism is a transient virtue, whereas the coins I bought
on the banks of the Arno give as much pleasure to me now as they
did to art lovers of the past and will to those of the future. I do not
know or care to know the names of the artists who made them; nor
would I mind in the least if a coin expert told me that my little collection is composed in its entirety of modern fakes. I did not buy
these works of art because they are old (there are some ugly old
coins, and any pebble is millions of years older), I bought them
because they are beautifully designed and executed. In this lies
their true value; a value few experts seem to appreciate and no
expertise can alter.

When I eventually arrived at the British School in Rome, I was not a little surprised to see a group of Nazi soldiers coming down the flight of steps leading to its entrance. They were dragging a wretched civilian who, from his English academic looks, I imagined was the Director of the School, then threw him into the back of an army truck. It was only on spotting the camera crew that I realised what was really happening. The neo-classical façade of the School, with its well proportioned Corinthian columns, was designed by Lutyens as the British pavilion at the International Exhibition in Rome of 1911. Lutyens' pavilion was so much admired that the mayor of Rome offered to present the land on which it stood to the British nation provided that it be used as a permanent exhibition centre. The British Ambassador, however, managed to persuade the Mayor that the building could be better employed as the home of an enlarged British School, then housed in the Palazzo Odescalchi. The School's building has three massive doors, but these are seldom flung wide, and when I rang the bell, only a small section of the great door on the right opened. The person who opened it was a long-standing member of staff called Augusto. He let me into the entrance hall, and sitting me down on a rickety chair, which I later found out was there for the comfort of Angelo the night porter, he explained in a mixture of broken English and what I later knew to be demolished Italian, that he could see I was starving, and that although the Schools were still shut for the summer, he was going to make me a luverly plate of spaghetti. He disappeared to the kitchen and I was left to contemplate my surroundings. The hall was large, stretching the whole length of Lutyens' colonnade, and had glass doors overlooking a spacious courtyard with a fountain in the centre of it – the work of John Skeeping, a former Rome scholar. On the far side of the courtyard was a bronze bust of Edwin Austin Abbey, a successful mural painter who in the early part of this century supplied the wherewithal to build the row of roomy studios against the arcade of which his likeness now stood. The plants and shrubs around the fountain were well tended, and on the whole I was favourably impressed with what was, starting in October, to be my new home.

The hallway itself was painted white and had no decoration beyond two portrait bronzes of former Directors: Bernard Ashmole and Thomas Ashby. I was studying these sculptures and was rapt in thought as to whether or not collars and ties give the sculptor less room for inventiveness than togas and other old-fashioned drapes, when I was startled by a thump on the back. Turning round, I saw that it had been delivered by a distinguished looking man in his forties, too neatly dressed to be an English scholar, with thick iron grey hair receding at the temples, who was grinning as though he had done something awfully clever. It was Bruno, the head of the School's staff. He had a mischievous look in his eyes, and I felt sure we were going to get on. He knew a little English and explained that part of his duties was that of being the School's accountant in charge of paying the scholars their stipends. My own stipend, I was informed, had been awaiting my arrival since the first of the month, and taking me to his office, Bruno handed me, if I remember correctly, three of those ever welcome 10,000 lira notes together with a letter. The letter was from David, and I took it to read in the night porter's chair while I awaited Augusto's spaghetti. It was a brief note telling me he had rented a studio for us both in a street called Via Margutta, and was looking forward to seeing me as soon as possible. Augusto reappeared and ushered me to the School's dining-hall. It is hard for big rooms to be cosy but this one was doing its best. It had a large fireplace with a thick carpet in front of it surrounded by large comfy sofas and there was a pianola and a hi-fi set; but what I noticed first were the huge refectory tables whose gleaming wooden tops were five or six inches thick. They were not antique, but they were friendly old things, and as I sat at one, eating my luverly spaghetti, all alone except for the solicitude of Augusto, who was as attentive to me as if I were a long-lost son, I thought of all the many distinguished artists and scholars who had sat at those tables before, engaged in what I innocently imagined had been friendly well-informed after-dinner conversation. I knew nothing then of the acrimony which all too often attends the discussions of the learned.

To my mind one of the chief attractions of the British School lies in its close proximity to the Villa Borghese, the earliest of the grand villas of seventeenth-century Rome, which was begun in 1605 by Cardinal Scipione Borghese, a nephew of Pope Paul V. The villa is set in a park and garden which have a circumference of four miles. Following directions given to me by Bruno and Augusto, I strolled through these magnificent grounds with their shady walks of old ilex on my way to find Via Margutta and David. I passed a lake, a riding school, fountains and statuary. It was sunset as I made my way towards the Pincio (Fig. 38), and emerging from dark lanes flanked by trees and shrubs framing marble busts of Italy's patriotic heroes, I was suddenly faced with a ravishingly beautiful view of central Rome silhouetted in purple against a vibrant sky of crimson and gold. After admiring the view for some minutes, I turned to my left and descended a ramp to the Villa Medici, which,

Fig. 38: *Sunset from the Pincio, c.* 1960, oil on canvas (Collection Joe McCrindle)

since it was bought in 1805 by Napoleon, has been the home of the French Academy. Little did I think then that one day I would visit the Villa Medici to view an exhibition of Old Masters to which I had myself made an important contribution. Continuing to the church of Trinita dei Monti, I walked down the famous Spanish Steps, which might be more justly called the French Steps, because the Trinita dei Monti was built by the kings of France, and the Piazza di Spagna below was originally known as Piazza di Francia. Wanting to catch David before he went out for the evening, as I knew he would, I hurried down the steps, but even so I could not help noticing that things had changed since Dickens's day when he spoke of the Spanish Steps as the meeting place of artists' models, colourfully dressed in their regional costumes trying to catch the attention of the foreign visitor with artistic aspirations. Now there were still people (males) trying to catch the visitor's eye, but for the purpose of importuning or, in gay slang, 'cruising'.

The foot of the steps was gay in the traditional sense. It sported a profusion of peddlers' carts bright with flowers, and in the Piazza di Spagna itself, Bernini's Fontana della Barcaccia, which represents a boat sinking into the ground, was on that hot evening surrounded by Romans and tourists seeking to cool themselves. The Piazza di Spagna and its environs has traditionally been the great tourist centre of Rome. It has also traditionally been the centre of the city's artistic community, and David, the up-to-the-minute modern American artist, friend of Pollock, Klein and De Kooning, by renting a studio in nearby Via Margutta, was being far more traditional than he probably knew, or would have cared to know. Artists had lived there since the late-sixteenth century, and for the next three centuries the Piazza di Spagna area gave hospitality to such distinguished foreigners as Rubens, Poussin, Claude, Angelica Kauffman, Robert Adam, Stendhal, Balzac, Liszt, Wagner, Thackeray, Hans Andersen, Byron, Keats, Tennyson, and now last, and in my opinion very definitely least, David and Eric.

When in October I took up the Rome Scholarship, I would

Fig. 39: *On the Aventino*, 1966, watercolour (Collection of the artist)

normally spend the working hours in my studio at the British School. The daily walks between the two studios were a great source of pleasure to me and I came to know the route between Via Margutta and Via Antonio Gramsci intimately. One morning of sun and gleaming ochre, of the kind which reminds one that Rome is not only eternal, but eternally young, I had a distinct feeling that the city was preparing to pull a surprise on me. There was something different about the now familiar sights. The Fontana della Barcaccia was spouting with increased vigour, the flowers at the foot of the Spanish Steps more fragrant, and as I bounded up the 137 steps I thought the famous *scalinata* seemed to ascend with even greater grace and charm. Today, the shaded fountain in front of the Villa Medici, the subject of one of Corot's most charming views of Rome, was so invitingly cool I could not resist dipping my hands in it and splashing water on to my face. While thus engaged, I was greeted by a Greek friend called Stavros, who was not feeling quite as chirpy as myself. He had been living with a good-looking Filipino artist called Tomas. They had been very much in love, but now, Stavros told me, their affair had come to an end. The cause of the rift was Tomas's cooking. Not that it was bad, on the contrary it was far too good. Stavros had become fat and Tomas's love for his once classically proportioned Greek diminished in inverse ratio to the width of his friend's girth. Stavros had scarcely finished his tale of woe when we were joined by one of his Italian acquaintances, a boy called Gianni, an eighteen-year-old of Sicilian extraction with the black curly hair, big brown eyes and full sensuous lips of Caravaggio's famous painting of the young Bacchus. And like Caravaggio's model, there was something sultry and wanton about him. He was made for bed, and his look told me that he had similar thoughts concerning myself. My knees went weak, it was love at first sight. Stavros recognised the signs at once and said: 'I'm going to leave you guys before you rape each other on the spot.' His prediction was not far from the truth. Gianni and I wasted no time. We seized each other by the waist and climbed to the Pincio where we promptly jumped into the privacy of a clump of bushes and fell into a frenzied embrace of an emotional intensity and turbulence that was explosive in its fervour, our impetus and fevered encounter reaching a climax of erotic resonance and rhythmic vehemence unknown to me before. It has been said that one feels more in love in Italy than anywhere else in the world, and that romance is as much part of Italy as its art and history. Certainly if one should fall in love there, one will not forget it.

One may, however, regret it, and looking back on my affair with

Gianni I realise that it brought me rather more pain than pleasure. This was not Gianni's fault. It was due to my own nature. During the months of our affair I looked upon Gianni with a delirium of excitation that alternated with fits of violent jealousy, caused by a monstrous possessiveness.

The rules of the British School did not permit the Scholars to have live-in friends and forbade visitors after eleven. But I was not going to let the School's regulations regulate my love life and introduced Gianni into the place as my model. The night watchman, Angelo, must have told the Director, John Ward-Perkins, that my model would often visit the schools in the evening and stay the night, and I was summoned to the Director's office to account for it. Although much criticised by some of the other Rome Scholars, especially the artists, Ward-Perkins was to me a very likeable and admirable man. He had the reputation of a first-rate scholar noted for his vital work in recording the archaeological remains of Southern Etruria. Less well known, to the artists at least, was that Ward-Perkins was also an authority on Roman architecture and engaged on what is still the standard work on the subject, and thus clearly much more interested in art than they gave him credit for. I was not, however, in Ward-Perkins's office to discuss these matters, and when he asked me about Gianni's staying overnight I made some feeble excuses about my model suffering from sudden attacks of violent headaches that made him incapable of doing anything other than jumping into the nearest bed until they passed. At this the Director gave me a stern look and said: 'Very well, Hebborn, but be careful, people *will* talk you know.' That evening there was a knock on my studio door. I hastily dressed, and opening the door only slightly, so that the visitor could not see my naked model posing with a full erection, I came face to face with Margaret Ward-Perkins. The thoughtful woman wanted to know how Gianni was feeling, and would he care for some aspirin.

The Director was quite right – people did talk. An anonymous letter was sent to the head of the Faculty of Engraving in London informing Sir Henry that I was keeping 'undesirable' company – whoever wrote it had clearly never been to bed with Gianni! Sir Henry told me that he destroyed the 'foul thing' without reading its full contents, but felt I should know that I had at least one enemy in the School. With few exceptions, such as Victor, the Rome Scholar in painting, and Paul, Rome Scholar in classical studies, the others were a miserable lot. There we were in the Rome of the *dolce vita*, a colourful city of warmth, of life, of fun, of sex, a place for young people to enjoy, if there was one. And what did those grey academic creatures from fog-bound Britain do but shut Rome's pleasure-loving way of life firmly out behind the great doors of Lutyens' façade, and nurse petty ambitions of getting their dreary selves home to a 'good' position as soon as possible.What was worse, they made virtues of their faults and faults of Italian virtues. If they were dowdily dressed they were discreetly attired; if an Italian was smartly dressed, he or she was being a show-off. When they were being aloof their behaviour was seemly; when Italians were friendly they were being forward, if polite, servile. For myself, and much to the annoyance of most of my fellow scholars, I was enjoying Rome to the full. And I loved the Romans, if for one quality alone – they hate hypocrisy.

The most obvious difference between the Rome of my youth and the city as it is today lies in the number of cars. In 1965, Georgia Masson wrote in *The Companion Guide to Rome* that an estimated number of 7,000 new cars came into circulation in the city every month. If we accept her figure as a true indication of the increase in traffic in those years, we can estimate that during my first year at the British School there were 420,000 fewer vehicles in the Eternal

Fig. 40: *On the Palatine*, 1966, oil on board

City, than when Miss Masson complained of Rome's already
chaotic traffic conditions. The air was cleaner, there was less noise
and confusion, one could eat outside at many more restaurants,
and above all it meant that people could promenade. Romans
adored promenading and they would dress up and go for a walk for
no other reason than to show themselves to each other. They did
this in the cool of the evening, and the smartest place to promenade
was Via Vittorio Veneto. The street had become the centre of
Rome's night life, and from sunset on summer evenings till one or
two in the morning, one could sit with friends at the tables outside
Rosati's, the Café de Paris or Doney's, and watch much of Rome's
fame, fashion and fortune stroll by. Many of the people one would
see were connected with the city's then thriving film industry. Most
of these people belonging to the cinema crowd whom I knew
personally were not famous.

A person I knew with connections in the film world was Eugene.
He was a thirty-five-year-old American writer, tending to plumpness, who had won an important literary prize for his first novel *The
Untidy Pilgrim*. Like most artists and writers, Eugene was hard up,
and to make ends meet, he had worked as an extra in a number of
films. Once, he told me, he had played the part of a nun in a Fellini
film, and said that Fellini used only men and boys for the nuns,
because real nuns have a masculine way of walking that only experienced, hence highly paid, actresses could convincingly imitate.
Eugene came from America's south, and liked to say that he had
left home in a flurry of cardboard boxes and turkey shit. He was
most entertaining and got along well with everybody. He greatly
enjoyed socialising and would give little soirées in a small apartment in Trastevere. Today, Trastevere is Rome's equivalent of
London's Chelsea or New York's Greenwich Village but in those
days it was not at all fashionable. Its honeycomb of narrow pas-
sages, from whose shade one would unexpectedly emerge into the
brightness of some great square such as Piazza Santa Maria, or
Piazza San Cosimato, was inhabited almost exclusively by working-class people who considered themselves the true descendants of
the ancient Romans, and although their claim is not always supported by the minimum seven generations of residence in the city,
they were nevertheless fondly referred to as the *romani romani di
Roma* (Roman Romans of Rome). They were a choice collection of
street-wise, sharp-eyed, quick-tongued characters, not unlike
London's Cockneys. High rents have now moved them to the
suburbs, but then Trastevere's shopkeepers, cabbies, masons, car-
penters and artisans followed the same *mestieri* in the same streets

and houses as their forbears had for generations. Characteristic of them were the cigar-makers living in a colony around Piazza Mastai. And it was not far from there that many an evening would find me climbing the steep flight of steps to a supper party given by Eugene in his tiny house, backing on to the rocks of the Janiculum which towered above it. The two small rooms were always crowded. Much of the space was taken up with books and magazines; and people occupied the rest. Many of those I met there were to play a role in my later dealings in the art-world. One was Joe, the owner of a small magazine with a big reputation called *The Transatlantic Review*, another was Tony, the Director of the Minneapolis Museum in Minnesota. Both these people appear in later pages.

Sometimes Eugene would bring a potential client to my studio in the School, and if they bought something or commissioned a portrait, it was agreed that I treated Eugene to a good meal. My favourite restaurant was Ranieri's in Via Mario dei Fiori, near the Piazza di Spagna. It is said to have been founded by a former cook of Queen Victoria. And with its sumptuous if not decadent atmosphere of great velvet curtains (complete with swags and tassels), gilt mirrors and chandeliers, something Victorian still clung to it. But Ranieri's was a little too quiet and sedate for Eugene who preferred such places as Al Re degli Amici, in Via Borgognona, or Alfredo's in Piazza Santa Maria in Trastevere, which were much frequented by the cinema crowd. One of the visitors Eugene brought to my studio was Principessa Topazia. This noble lady ran an art gallery in Trastevere. The *principessa* was an elegant, witty and worldly creature nearing forty. She did not like my old-fashioned work at all. She did, however, like me, and nor was I the only young artist that she liked. It was fashionable in those days for society women, kicking against the traditional restrictions imposed by their class, to like modern art and the young artists who made it. Here tradition counted for nothing, youth and novelty were both at a premium, and of the two I suspect it was youth that attracted them most. It was through Eugene and his connections that I got a commission to paint the portrait of Ingegnere Lerici, a man known to archaeologists for having developed a technique for exploring Etruscan tombs without necessarily breaking into them. Lerici's office, where I made the portrait of him, was a very swish affair in Via Veneto. It was decorated with some of the most impressive Etruscan vases I have ever seen and these seemed to me to make a very suitable background for the painting. The *ingegnere*, however, did not think so. He was old, immaculately groomed and monstrously vain. He was forever interfering, and as I refused to flatter him by ignoring the signs of his maturity, he hated the picture. It was never paid for, and when soliciting payment, I was told by his secretary that in a fit of pique Lerici had put his foot through the canvas.

In addition to the hosts of people I met directly or indirectly through Eugene there were those I encountered at the British School itself. Some of these were important visitors making an official tour of the place. So it happened that the School had the honour of a visit from the Prime Minister, Harold Macmillan. My studio had been tidied up for the occasion, and had been very thoroughly inspected by security people. As I was waiting for the great statesman to appear, the time seemed to lag and, without thinking of the consequences, I decided to carry on with my work. Surrounded by security men and journalists and lit by the flashes of a host of photographers, Macmillan entered the studio. He was tall and straight, a wonderfully impressive man whose presence alone commanded respect. Preparing to shake hands, I realised to my horror (as Macmillan himself must have done) that my hand was covered with paint, and consequently I hesitated to put it forward. Here was a potential snippet for the press: *Painter Refuses Handshake of Tory Prime Minister*. But Macmillan was not a politician for nothing, and he extended his hand in such a confident do-your-damnedest manner, that I could not refuse. It was probably the first time the Prime Minister had dirtied his hands for years. Nevertheless, he smiled and managed to say something complimentary about my drawings and paintings. He must have known more than most politicians about art because, indicating a copy I was making, he said: 'That's a Giorgione, isn't it?' This seems to have been the only remark he made in the School worth reporting. At least it was the only one that gave rise to a headline. If I recall correctly it was in the *Evening News* and read: *Art-lover Macmillan Spots Giorgione*. Another distinguished visitor to my studio was King Gustav of Sweden, the father of the present king. He was not fond of formality and was attended only by an elderly gentleman-in-waiting. I showed His Majesty a number of drawings among which was a highly finished study of a young female model in the nude. This was particularly to his taste, and he seemed reluctant to put it down. After a while his gentleman-in-waiting, looking daggers at the King, exclaimed in a mildly shocked voice, 'Your Majesty!' But he could not stop that most human of monarchs from feasting his eyes on the forms of the lovely young girl. So I said: 'If I may have the honour of presenting Your Majesty with the drawing, I should be delighted.' The gift was graciously accepted, and I was to see more of King Gustav.

It is hard, even for English people, not to be sociable over a good meal, and in my time the food at the School was excellent. This was especially true of supper. The cook, Pietro, would have nothing to do with *'quella roba inglese'* (that English stuff) and prepared local dishes for us. With the exception of the delicious pastas, which were with us all year round, the main dishes, or the *'secondi'* as they are called in Italy, were as seasonal as the weather once was itself. In spring, for instance, would come the *carciofi* (artichokes) *alla Giudea;* in summer *pollo alla diavola* (devilled chicken) with green peppers; in winter *agnello arrosto* (roast lamb). Some of what seemed to us as Pietro's exotic specialities were in fact common favourites among the Romans: *fettucine all'uovo* (handmade egg-noodles), *saltimbocca* (slices of veal and ham interspersed with sage leaves, and fried in butter), tripe *alla Romana.* There was usually a delicious well-seasoned salad on the table, and we ended the meal with fruit: cherries, peaches, melons, or grapes – whatever was in season. Or if preferred, cheese: *mozzarella, caciotta romana, pecorino, parmigiano vecchio* or *gorgonzola.* In short, we did ourselves well, and as the meal proceeded, the English reserve would to some extent dissolve and the conversation become more animated.

The people around the large refectory tables were a mixture of archaeologists, medievalists, artists, historians and those engaged in classical studies, and it was hard to find topics for discussion that would interest the whole company. For this reason there was a tendency to bring out some of the old feuds between the factions and give them a fresh airing. One of these disagreements arose from the artists' long-standing contention that the School should not be under the directorship of an archaeologist. As far back as 1932, Sir William Rothenstein had written: 'Up to now the head of the British School at Rome has been an archaeologist . . . One or two of us have felt that archaeologists are not the best people to look after the studies of painters, sculptors and engravers, especially in these days when all sorts of extreme abstract ideas are about, which settle like microbes in the student's brain . . . '

In this argument I did not share my fellow artists' point of view. As I have intimated above, I thought that the then Director, John Ward-Perkins, an excellent head of the School, who did his very best to understand and help the artists; if he failed in this respect, it was largely the fault of the artists themselves who did not try to meet him halfway. Furthermore, it might pertinently be asked if artists are the best people to look after the studies of archaeologists, medievalists, and classical scholars. Perhaps an art-historian might one day be an acceptable compromise, but meanwhile Ward-Perkins was doing an excellent job; and as the Executive Committee renewing his tenure had said: ' . . . the School's reputation has never stood higher than at present and . . . its success is in large measure due to the ability and energy of its Director.' In any case, I argued, the School is a centre of learning, and the Director must perforce be erudite, and until the unlikely event of an artist presenting himself who possesses erudition comparable to an Ashby or a Ward-Perkins, the Directorship of the School was best left to such scholars.

But my artist colleagues did not approve of learning. Indeed they made strenuous efforts to prevent themselves from getting to know anything of the great art of the past by which they were

Fig. 41: *Anthony Blunt, c.* 1979, pen and ink (Collection of the artist)

surrounded. The truth was, that for fear it might challenge their ideas about modernism, they did not want to be in Rome at all. This too was an old point of view. In *A Short History of the British School at Rome*, J. P. Wiseman writes: 'Ever since the twenties, the artists have chafed at being in Rome rather than somewhere more central to modern art', and quoting a passage from L. Whistler's *The Laughter and the Urn: The Life of Rex Whistler,* which refers to 1928, continues: 'Students anxious to make answer to the twentieth century were at a loss how to use a city where the century's contribution was negligible, or decreed by Mussolini. The painters, even if hardly aware of Post-Impressionism, would have been better off in Paris, the architects in Germany or America; the School seemed an anachronism. Why were they there? . . . Things were appearing to move so fast in the London art world that a year or two in Rome could seem an omission rather than a gain.'

The artists' argument that they would be better off elsewhere was an unnecessary one and reflected very badly on those who put it forward. In the first place, nobody had forced them to compete for the Rome Scholarship, and if they preferred to go to America or somewhere else, nothing except their own lack of initiative and drive was stopping them. Secondly, they were grumbling and procrastinating in a position where many a young artist with a belief in traditional values would dearly love to be, but from which, because of their refusal to pay homage to Almighty Modernism, they had been excluded.

But apart from the occasional airing of these and other perennial differences, there was normally a congenial post-supper atmosphere, and it was during these times that I might sometimes be heard holding forth and, with all the earnestness and confidence of my years, putting the problems surrounding art to rights. There was nothing which I did not know on the subject and if anyone dared to contradict me, I was quick enough to point out their error. In fairness to my young self, however, I must say that I did not take myself seriously – that was just an act. What I was doing was entertaining myself by seeing just how much nonsense I could talk without being seriously challenged. Usually it was quite a lot. This was largely because, due to their antipathy to learning, the artists knew scarcely anything about art other than their own, and the archaeologists and other scholars had only such general knowledge of art and its history as might be expected of the average educated person. My discourse would usually begin with some such absurdity as: 'All the great paintings in the world contain a horse.' It was amusing to watch the expressions on the faces about me as a brow wrinkled or frowned as if deliberating on the veracity or otherwise of the ridiculous proposition, a proposition which I would of course try to support. This was done by quoting any masterpiece I could recall which happens to have a horse in it, and ignoring all those which do not.

One evening in my cups, cheerfully giving a discourse on how the art of painting started its long decline with the invention of the brush, I found myself being regularly interrupted by a long-faced upper-class type who had endeared himself to me by keeping my glass filled from his own *fiasco*. He never interrupted rudely, but waiting for the right moment, would in the most courteous of educated tones gently tear my argument to shreds. Had I known I was crossing intellectual swords with one of the greatest historians of our age I might have had the good sense, or at least the modesty, to keep quiet, but as it was, with all the foolhardiness of youth, I put up as good a fight for my untenable argument as I could, and it was not until my opponent's *fiasco* was empty that I admitted partial defeat, grudgingly conceding that he 'might' have a point. Our art-centred conversation had sent our neighbours to bed and, sitting alone at the table, we introduced ourselves. My new acquaintance was Sir Anthony Blunt, Surveyor of the Queen's Pictures, and Director of the Courtauld Institute (Fig. 41). Although now over fifty, he still fitted to a large degree the description of him at the age of seventeen given by a school fellow at Marlborough: 'He was very tall and very thin and drooping, with deadly sharp elbows and the ribs of a famished saint: he had cold blue eyes, a cutaway mouth and a wave of soft brown hair falling over his forehead . . .'

We became friends, and our friendship was to span two decades, but although we were both homosexual and Anthony was certainly attracted to me physically, what fascinated me about him was his mind. My working-class background and the poor education attendant on it had not been conducive to cultivating my own intellectual powers, and I felt very conscious of my shortcomings. Now I had the advantage of following the workings of a really fine intellect at close quarters, and I was determined to benefit from the experience as much as I possibly could. We spent the greater part of our time together drinking and discussing Old Master drawings, and I learnt a great deal, not only about the drawings themselves, but what goes on in the minds of the experts who view them. Anthony was endlessly patient with me, and in spite of his great learning and brilliance, never once gave me the impression he was talking down.

Naturally, it was I who benefited most from our discussions but I

Fig. 42: *Preciosa and the Wind*, 1961, wood engraving, an illustration to a poem
by Frederico García Lorca (Collection of the artist)

do recall having helped him from time to time, especially when
speaking of technical matters. On one occasion, for instance,
Anthony showed me a print by Giovanni Benedetto Castiglione in
a technique which puzzled him, and I was able to tell him that it
was a soft-ground etching. He was very excited to learn this, and
explained to me that the invention of soft-ground etching had hitherto been attributed to Le Prince a century or so later. Anthony
published his discovery in *The Burlington Magazine*. Some people
might argue that it was really my discovery, but this is simply not
true. Anthony could have found out that the Castiglione was a soft-
ground etching by consulting any number of people conversant
with etching techniques, but it was he who had spotted that the
print was in an unusual technique for the artist, and after informing
himself on the matter, it was he who saw the historical significance.

I spoke to Anthony of my theory of there being common denom-
inators between all really good drawings – things independent of
time, place of production, or even of the artists who produce them.
As, however, the making of clear distinctions between the various
times, places and artists that have produced drawings and other
works of art is perhaps the art-historian's first consideration, my
idea was not very appealing to him. The eminent art historian did
not want the very foundation of his discipline questioned, and not
surprisingly dismissed the proposition out of hand. Realising that I
had presented the notion rather crudely, I changed my approach

and put forward the tentative suggestion that there are certain combinations of line which would seem to have a universal significance and others which appear to be the product of a particular age and become the common property of that time. This modified view found more favour with my learned friend, and after a long discussion, mostly about the second half of my proposition, where it was possible to speak of clearly dateable changes in drawing style, such as Leonardo's introduction of *pentimenti* (the draughtsman's alterations left visible), Anthony proposed that we might collaborate to produce a book on the subject. The idea was that I would use my practical knowledge of drawing to analyse the various styles and he would put such an analysis into a precise historical framework. But all that was in the future. Then and there in our first encounters at the British School, Anthony and I were little more than drinking pals, with our homosexuality and an interest in art as a bond between us.

If in this highly condensed account of the two years I spent as a Rome Scholar I have inadvertently given the impression that I did nothing in my days at the British School other than savour the joys of the flesh with Gianni, get drunk with Anthony, and socialise with David, Eugene and various princesses, I must correct, or at least modify it. For if I played hard, I also worked hard, and was fully conscious of being in Rome to study. More than once in these pages I have spoken of drawing as a language, and it was at the British School at Rome that I decided to write a serious grammar of it. As part of the preparatory study for this work, I wanted to find out what links there might be between drawing and verse. This was because I knew drawing at its best to be visual poetry rather than visual prose. As I was not a poet myself, it was necessary to learn something about writing verse, and for that purpose I made a translation of Federico García Lorca's book of poems, *Romancero Gitano*, which at the time had not, I believe, been translated into English in its entirety (Fig. 42). Mine was, however, really a second-hand translation because it was made from a dual text with the original Spanish opposite an Italian translation and it was the Italian which I understood better. Nevertheless, my Lorca translation taught me something about poetry and Italian at one and the same time and thus prepared me for my next project.

It occurred to me that if there really is some tangible connection between the poet's and the draughtsman's art, such a correspondence might become more apparent to me if I first studied the poems and drawings of one person in depth. If the visual and verbal works of art I was studying were the product of a single mind, I might reasonably expect to find some kind of correlation, and if I should, it was less likely to be a chance connection. As there have been hosts of poets who have made drawings, and hosts of draughtsmen who have written poems, there were numerous candidates for my study to choose from. The problem was, however, that these many artist-poets and poet-artists were mostly far better in one field than in the other. Lorca's drawings, for instance, are feeble in the extreme, and Turner's verses are better not spoken of. Occasionally a balance is struck: Blake is a notable example, and I might very well have chosen him for my in-depth study, except that to study an English artist in Rome seemed rather perverse. After giving the matter considerable thought, at length I decided on no less an artist than Michelangelo. Not everybody knows of the great painter and sculptor's verse and of those who do, few realise the extent and importance of it. Michelangelo wrote over 300 poems. He was a master of the Petrarchan sonnet form and has been called by one critic 'Petrarch's most distinguished follower'. In addition to his eighty-four complete sonnets he wrote madrigals, pieces in *terza rima*, and employed the *sestina* and other poetic forms. His work as a poet has the utmost variety: love poems, religious verse, pastoral and humorous themes, as well as epitaphs. In his own time, the great artist enjoyed a high reputation as a man of letters, and on his catafalque the muse of poetry was as prominent as those of painting and sculpture.

Being a Rome Scholar, I had the necessary qualifications to gain access to the autograph of Michelangelo's verse housed in the Vatican Library, where I was introduced by my museum curator friend, Tony. It was an unforgettable experience. The master wrote in a beautiful Italic hand, essentially the Cancellerescha of the great renaissance scribe Arrighi. Calligraphy is, as we know from the Chinese, a form of drawing, and here were wonderfully *drawn* as well as wonderfully written poems. What greater encouragement could I have had to continue my search for links between drawing and poetry! Incidentally, although Girardi's critical text of Michelangelo's poems was published during my stay at the School, I had not yet read it, and in consequence was surprised to note that some of the great artist's 'late' religious verses were written in the firm handwriting of his youth. Thinking that the best way to gain an intimate knowledge of Michelangelo's poetry would be to translate it into English, I began to wrestle with the poet's archaic Italian. Even Italians have problems with it, and it was to be years before I got anywhere with my translation, but here is one of my first efforts made at the British School. It is a sonnet written about 1511 and addressed to Pope Julius II who reigned from 1503 to 1513. The 'withered boughs' of the last line is an oblique reference to the family name of Julius, Rovere, meaning oak tree. I have written the poem out in a handwriting similar to Michelangelo's own (Fig. 43).

I was in my second year at the British School and had seen little of the environs of Rome. Joe, who in addition to being an editor was also an art collector, invited me to go with him to look at the work of a Chinese artist who lived in a mountain village called Anticoli Corrado, fifty miles east of Rome. He was in the company of a film star, whose name I forget, but remember he played Gulliver in Jack Sherls' *The Three Worlds of Gulliver*, which is said by E. Halliwell to have had 'neat trick work but less than absorbing screenplay'. Joe or Gulliver or both had rented a Buick saloon driven by a chauffeur with an impassive face which was meant to be saying: 'Speak freely, I'm not listening'. There was not, however, much conversation to overhear. Gulliver, who was unbelievably handsome and far too busy preening himself to talk, sat next to the driver and would

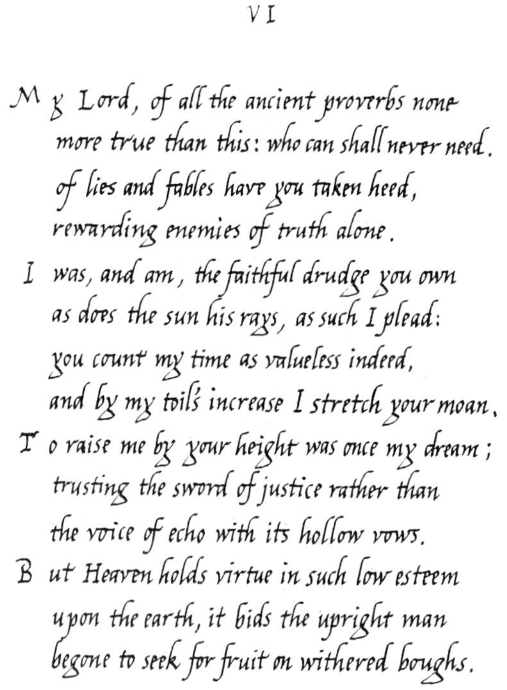

VI

My Lord, of all the ancient proverbs none
    more true than this: who can shall never need.
of lies and fables have you taken heed,
    rewarding enemies of truth alone.

I was, and am, the faithful drudge you own
    as does the sun his rays, as such I plead:
you count my time as valueless indeed,
    and by my toils increase I stretch your moan,

To raise me by your height was once my dream;
    trusting the sword of justice rather than
    the voice of echo with its hollow vows.

But Heaven holds virtue in such low esteem
    upon the earth, it bids the upright man
    begone to seek for fruit on withered boughs.

Fig. 43: Michelangelo sonnet translated and written out
by hand by the author, 1961

Fig. 44: *Gabriele*, pencil, squared up for transfer,1975.
At ninety-six Gabriele was at the time the oldest man
in Anticoli (Collection of the artist)

occasionally turn around to practise his gorgeous smile on Joe and
myself, who did not say much for fear of distracting him from his
performance.

We set out after an early breakfast with the intention of doing a
little sightseeing on the way. Taking the Via Tiburtina, we had
travelled for a little under half an hour when we came to a very
smelly place which made us look at each other with unjustified suspicion. It was called Bagni and a little beyond the smell of its sul-
phur baths was Villa Adriana, Hadrian's Villa, one of the largest
and richest of the Roman world. Now it lies in imposing ruins,
some of which I remembered having seen in the prints of Piranesi.
A villa in ancient times was clearly something very different from

that this charming old place was called Villa San Filippo and had once been the summer home of Pirandello and his artist son, Fausto, and had in its time given hospitality to such literary giants as Norman Douglas and D. H. Lawrence and, as village lore would have it, Princess Margaret.

The days of my *Dolce Vita* at the British School at Rome ended as they had begun – with a letter. It was from the Positano Art Workshop:

11 April 1961

Dear Mr Hebborn,

We are urgently looking for a qualified teacher of painting and drawing for our summer course (June 1 – September 30).

Your name has been given to us by David Porter, who recently visited the Workshop, and spoke highly of your abilities.

Please let me know as soon as you possibly can whether or not you would be interested in considering the job.

Yours truly,

Edna Lewis
Principal

In spite of its sense of urgency, and the fact that I never got the job, this letter nevertheless turned out to be a verbal time bomb which took a decade to explode. Meanwhile, I returned to London.

CHAPTER VIII

THE CASE OF THE COLNAGHI 'COROT'

'It is the misfortune of fakes that they are almost always defined by what they are not, instead of being valued for what they are.'

Mark Jones.

Not every sailor loves the sea, anymore than every garbage collector loves garbage, but if you are an artist deserving of the name you must and you do love art. You love it with a passion, and like all true loves yours is a selfless devotion – art means more to you than the satisfaction of your personal ambitions. This being so, whenever I come across a so-called artist who counts his career of greater importance than the furtherance of his art, I have no respect for him. I view him as I view a power hungry politician or a greedy businessman, i.e. as a pest. I must, however, thank one of these artistic pests (I shall call him Paul) who was largely re-sponsible for saving me from becoming despicable in the same way myself, for I too once harboured ambitions to rise in the ranks of the artistic establishment. I was only twenty-four when I was elected to the Royal Society of British Artists and, as a Rome Scho-lar, had the highest academic qualification attainable in art schools. On such a foundation, the steps up to becoming first an associate and then a full member of the Academy might easily have been accomplished if only I could have found it in me to go in for art politics like Paul. But let me tell the story of how it came about that this pest helped me to decide to have nothing to do with an establishment-type career.

On my return from Italy in the summer of 1961, I not only took up again my dealing activities, I also resumed part-time teaching in art schools. Apart from teaching anatomy and life drawing at

Walthamstow, I was in charge of the engraving department of Reigate and Redhill School of Art. One day on my occasional visits to the Academy, the Keeper, Sir Henry Rushbury, spoke to me of his intention to enlarge the facilities for studying engraving in the Schools. At that time whatever etching and engraving was done in Burlington House was carried out in a poky little room above the Schools' canteen, with little or no tuition or guidance and the barest essentials in the way of equipment. It was Sir Henry's idea to use some of the proceeds of the forthcoming sale of what was perhaps the Academy's most valuable single possession, the renowned Leonardo Cartoon, to forward his project, and employ a teacher. This was where I came into his plans; the Keeper had, he said, heard favourable reports of my work at Reigate and Redhill and would very much like me to occupy myself with the running of the Academy's new engraving department. It was a great honour for somebody as young and unknown as myself and, elated with the prospect, I accepted the proposal eagerly. Then came the trouble.

There were a number of older and better-known engravers than myself who would dearly have loved the job, and Paul, who was particularly adept in art politics, was determined to secure the position for a friend of his, an engraver whose name was much bigger than his talent, but who could be relied upon to support Paul in his own push upwards. To attain his ends Paul deliberately set about poisoning Sir Henry's mind against me. This he did by first cornering me and asking about my agreement with the Keeper. During the conversation he enquired in a casual manner as to how much I was going to be paid for the job. To which I answered that the fee had not been discussed yet, but it didn't really matter how much or how little I received. It was such a wonderful opportunity, I would accept anything the Academy could afford to give me. 'That's all very well,' Paul replied and, as if he had only my best interests at heart, continued: 'but you've got to live, and if I were you I wouldn't accept anything under twenty-five pounds a week.' I made no answer to this, but my so-called friend, pretending that my silence meant a tacit agreement with his view, went to Sir Henry, into whose favour he had spent years wheedling himself, and told the Keeper that he had heard me say I would not consider taking charge of the new Engraving Department unless I was paid at least twenty-five pounds a week. Understandably, Sir Henry took me for an ingrate who, instead of appreciating his good fortune in having the chance to show his worth, was thinking first and foremost of what he was going to get out of it. Sir Henry never spoke to me of the job again. When I found out through the grapevine of Paul's treachery I decided there and then that if I would have to sink to his level to advance myself in the art establishment, I was better off out of it. As it transpired, the loss of the post at the Academy was a blessing. Just imagine, I might have spent the rest of my life as bound to responsibility as any nine-to-five office worker. Where then the happy carefree years that actually lay ahead?

In the months immediately following my return from Italy, my teaching and dealing left me precious little time for seeing friends unconnected with those activities and, among others, I had neglected to keep in touch with Anthony Blunt. For this I was shamed by Anthony who, inspite of being probably the most important figure in London's art world at the time, with the endless duties and commitments that his high position entailed, still found time to send me a telegram which read:

WHY SO STANDOFFISH?
PHONE WEL 1074
A

When I phoned, Anthony asked me round for a drink at his apartment above the Courtauld Institute at 20 Portman Square. I had had no supper and the quantities of gin and tonic with which I was plied soon went to my head; as a result, on that evening, the first of many I spent in Portman Square, Anthony and I got as near to going to bed with each other as we ever would. Literally speaking we did go to bed together, because when I got to the stage of singing tuneless songs and telling excruciatingly unfunny jokes in an 'Irish' accent, the almost equally tipsy Anthony wisely suggested that I should stay the night. So after several nightcaps and 'ones-for-the-road' I was incapable of taking, we collapsed together on his bed, where our drunken condition, giving rise to what in some circles is known as brewer's droop, prevented us from doing anything other than sleep. The next morning Anthony was up first, and woke me with a cup of tea, two aspirins, and the news that my 'secretary' (Graham) had phoned to remind me of an appointment at eleven. We laughed at the pretence, but it was no laughing matter when I later tried feebly to explain to an angry and naturally disbelieving Graham that Anthony and I were just good friends.

After the famous Rachman scandal in the early sixties, things were getting too hot in England for slum landlords, and mine decided to sell up his real estate and emigrate to Australia. He had the landlord's collection, on which he had spent in the region of £10,000, carefully packed and heavily insured for the journey. He could well afford to do this because he was taking advantage of the Australian government's offer of a ten-pound ticket for 'desirable' immigrants. How he qualified I shall never know! I was, however, sorry to see my slum landlord go. Not because I had grown any fonder of him, but because I had failed to cheat him as I had set out to do. My plan had backfired. Many of the fakes I sold him could and did pass for real, and as I had not charged him any more for them than I would have asked for work in my own manner, he ended up making an enormous profit. With his departure for Australia, Graham and I had to look for other accommodation and rented a maisonette in Packington Street, which is not far from Canonbury Square, then only beginning to be fashionable, and Camden Passage, which was gradually making itself known as a centre for trading in antiques. And it was there in Packington Street that I decided to set up a limited liability company called Pannini Galleries Ltd.

My reasons for doing so were many. There was, for example, the advantage gained in regard to income tax, the profits being shared by Graham and myself in the form of salaries. Moreover, had I dealt as an individual I would have had a personal responsibility for debts in full. As it was, Pannini Galleries Ltd was responsible only up to the £1,000 of its capital, and those who had dealings with the company knew that it was to this subscribed capital alone that they could look for satisfaction of their claims. Because of the nature of my business, this was a very important consideration indeed, for it is the practice of respectable dealers to return the purchase price of a work of art to any customer who can prove beyond reasonable doubt that what they bought from them is a deliberate fake and I certainly didn't want to be any less respectable than the established dealers, and would gladly have taken back anything that a customer could demonstrate to be a forgery, but there would have to be a limit. Furthermore, I had noticed that some of the most reputable dealers were able to sell fakes with impunity simply by refusing to make a warranty. Well, as Mrs Buckle was fond of saying: 'What's sauce for the goose is sauce for the gander.' And if such firms as Sotheby's and Christie's could safeguard their interests in this way, so could I. In consequence, the receipts of Pannini Galleries Ltd carried among others these conditions of sale:

1. The Company shall not be bound by any warranty or conditions not expressly specified herein or agreed by the Company in writing. Personal opinions, verbal promises, or representations by our agents or servants are not binding on the Company.
2. Unless agreed in writing by the Company, as sellers, these contentions override stipulations by the buyer.
9. Goods sent are on approval for three days from receipt. During approval the buyers may consult other opinion on the goods, but not offer for sale. . . .
10. Goods are offered with all faults, errors of description, attribution or provenance and are sold 'as seen' by the buyer. The sellers make no warranty whatever.
12. The sellers retain the copyright and future use of any negative, photograph, transparency or block in their possession at the time of the sale.

This last condition was scarcely necessary, because by the copyright law, an artist automatically retains the reproduction rights of his work. Having made certain that I was not in any way breaking the law of the land, I went even further and imposed upon myself an unwritten moral code:

1. Never sell to a person who was not a recognised expert, or acting on expert advice.
2. Never ask a higher price than a similar work in my own style would fetch unless the higher price was established by the buyer.
3. Never make a description or attribution unless a recognised expert had been consulted; in which case the description or attribution would in reality be that expert's and not mine.
4. Never hit an expert with his acumen down. (It would not, for instance, be fair play to force an expert into a hasty decision over a boozy lunch).
5. Never bribe or in any way pay an expert for his opinion.
6. Never question an expert's opinion unless in conflict with equally expert opinion.

To have a moral code at all in the jungle of art dealing was something of a novelty, and it did not go unnoticed. Geraldine Norman was to speak of it later in *The Fake's Progress* in which she and her husband helped the well-known art faker Tom Keating to tell his story. Without mentioning me by name, she said she knew of a 'distinguished faker' who seemed to take an ethical stand and sold only to dealers or through salerooms. The argument was apparently that as dealers and saleroom experts earn their living on the strength of being able to distinguish the genuine from the spurious, the faker is perfectly within his rights to pit his wits against theirs, and should they be deceived, they should be prepared to take the consequences for what is in fact a professional lapse. In the same passage Mrs Norman refers to a dealer who bought from me regularly but when he moved over into the museum field was never offered any of my works again. This dealer I seem to recognise as Christopher White, a former director of Colnaghi's, to whom I sold a good number of drawings and who became the Director of Prints and Drawings of the National Gallery of Washington. Christopher was educated at the Courtauld Institute, and was a Director of Colnaghi's from 1965 to 1971. Author of numerous books, he is currently Director of The Ashmolean Museum, Oxford. Christopher's is, with that of Byam Shaw's and others, one of the names Mrs Norman was careful to suppress in her account of the Colnaghi scandal in *The Times*, a name which I see no reason to hide from the reader and which will appear elsewhere in these pages.

In the spring of 1963 the newly founded Pannini Galleries Ltd issued an illustrated catalogue containing twenty works including drawings attributed to the following: Whistler, Natoire, School of Mantegna, Sandby, Mola, Bartolozzi, Vanni, Tempesta, and Reynolds. Space does not allow me to discuss all of these drawings, so I shall speak only of the 'Whistler' – of how it came into existence, and how it led to the creation of a drawing which has long held a place of honour in the collection of Dutch and Flemish drawings housed in a great museum. The Whistler was not an original effort such as my portfolio 'Pinelli' or Colnaghi 'Corot', but one of three extremely close copies of an authentic Whistler I had bought from Appleby's for my old landlord, and replaced with a previous copy. Immediately after having made this second copy, I was, as is the case with all artists and recent work, too close to it to see it objectively, and had I had the time and the patience I might have done what Horace advised the young Piso to do with his writing: 'You, I am sure, will not say or do anything counter to the will of Minerva; you have judgement and sense enough for that. But if at any time you do write anything, submit it to the critic Maecins, and your father's and mine as well; then put the papers away and keep them for nine years. You can always destroy what you have not published, but once you have let your words go they cannot be taken back.' (*Ars Poetica*, trans. T. S. Dorsch.)

Unfortunately, our new landlords and other creditors would not wait for nine years for their money, and I had somehow to know whether my 'Whistler' might pass or not a little sooner than that, so I showed it together with the framed original to Graham. Being a talented draughtsman himself he had a good eye and I could rely on his judgment. His comment was that, were it not for the fact that he knew the original to be the one in the frame, he would not have been able to decide which was the real Whistler and which the drawing after it. This was encouraging, and Graham's comment set my mind working on another framed drawing in the Pannini Galleries' stock, and how I might replace it with an improved version, and again use Graham's fresh eye to test the result. The drawing in the flat brown wood frame of a kind popular with collectors in the twenties and thirties, which Graham had bought at auction from Hallet, Fox and White, was an attractive drawing of Roman ruins which was purported to be by Jan Breughel (1561-1625). Not only did it bear the signature of Breughel, but the drawing had been sold by Colnaghi's of Old Bond Street whose attribution to Breughel was clearly stated on the firm's label on the back of the frame.

Now the more I looked at this Breughel drawing the more I felt that it was not an original. There was something about it that spoke to me of an engraver's hand. In olden times the only way of reproducing drawings and paintings in quantity was to engrave them, and many engravers were extremely able copyists. For this reason there are large numbers of old engravers' drawings in existence – some made in preparation for an engraving, some simply for the sake of making a copy in its own right. All but the very best of these engravers' drawings can be distinguished from original productions by a certain lifelessness in the line. Every line is meticulously copied, but in the process something of the spontaneous touch of the creative draughtsman is lost. The reproductive engraver does not as a rule really know how to draw, and can therefore only reproduce the outward appearance of the lines. The result is not unlike that of somebody having copied a page of handwriting composed of characters they do not understand. They may have succeeded in giving the general appearance of the page, but if the text is of any length they will generally have made a slip somewhere, and in any case the writing will have lost its natural flow. This is because if the copyist is to reproduce the writing with any degree of accuracy he must write at a slower speed than the original writer; and one cannot alter the speed at which a drawn or written line is made without altering the character of that line. The reader may if he wishes test the truth of this statement for himself by writing out some phrase or other two or three times at different speeds; such as I have done below (Fig. 45).

Now, what it seemed to me about the Breughel drawing, was that in the copyist's attempt to be slavishly faithful to Breughel's original, the lines had been slowed down. Doubtless the copy was perfectly dependable, and if one saw it together with the original in

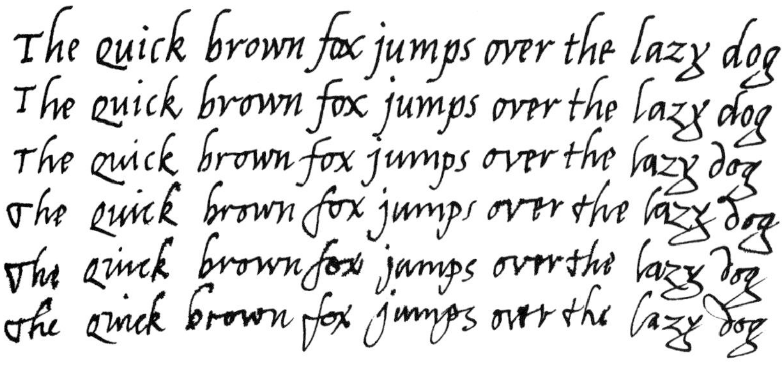

The quick brown fox jumps over the lazy dog
The quick brown fox jumps over the lazy dog
The quick brown fox jumps over the lazy dog
The quick brown fox jumps over the lazy dog
The quick brown fox jumps over the lazy dog
The quick brown fox jumps over the lazy dog

Fig. 45: Different speeds affecting the rhythm of the drawn line. Compare
carefully the first and last lines – the slow and the quick

photographic reproduction only, one would probably not be able to note the difference. But as it was, a trained eye could detect a slower line, and one lacking in the variation of pressure that a spontaneously drawn line has. Having decided to my own satisfaction that what Pannini Galleries owned, in spite of what Colnaghi's label stated, was not an original by Breughel but a copy, I wondered if it would be possible to make a copy of this copy in which the lines were speeded up, i.e. draw the lines at the same speed that Breughel had originally drawn them, rather than that of the plodding reproductive engraver. Thus in a sense recreate the original. As you may imagine this was not going to be easy. The new drawing would have to be an absolutely exact copy save for an additional quality of line so subtle that it would be discernible only to the most expert eye.

To make a perfect, indeed a more than perfect copy, it was imperative that there be not the slightest difference in any of the materials employed. First of all, the paper would have to be identical with that on which the engraver's copy was made. This is because the particular texture of a sheet greatly affects the kind of line one is going to get. Then there was the ink to consider – in this case bistre (here my memory may be at fault because I notice that Graham or I described the drawing for one of Pannini Galleries' advertisements as being in sepia) and in the background a touch of blue which to be consonant with the supposed age of the drawing must have been pure lapis lazuli. Eventually, I found a suitable sheet of sixteenth-century paper of the right texture and tone. It was the fly leaf of a book I had to pay twenty pounds for in Foyle's antiquarian book department in Charing Cross Road. In the early sixties one could buy mediocre Old Masters already made for half that price. So to cut my losses, I carefully replaced the fly leaf with another sheet of period paper and resold the book to Mr Seligmann for ten pounds.

As for the bistre and lapis lazuli, I had the good fortune to discover an eighteenth-century paint-box in Louis' stock (Fig. 46) containing a large amount of both these pigments as well as of sepia. The box cost me eighteen pounds, a very modest sum when one considers that the contents were to make drawings presently valued at hundreds of thousands of pounds. The proper materials in hand, I prepared to set to work. I sized the old paper to prevent the ink from spreading and pegged it to a clothes line to dry. This had to be done because size is glue, and if the sized paper had simply been laid down to dry it might very well have stuck to whatever surface it was in contact with. When the size had dried I tested

Fig. 46: *Materials of the Faker's Trade* – in the centre is shown an eighteenth-century paint-box bought from Louis Meier. In it can be seen a glass pestle and slab for grinding the dessicated colours contained in the paper envelopes below. The vellum-covered books contain blank paper from the sixteenth and seventeenth centuries. On the bottom of the pile on the left will be noticed a book with part of the vellum removed to provide the support for a drawing in the manner of Parri Spinelli (1387-1453). In the lower right-hand corner are two oak galls of the kind used in the preparation of 'old ink'

the sheet to see how it took the ink, and when satisfied there would be no tell-tale blotting of the lines, I dampened the paper, attached it to a drawing board by putting gummed paper around the edges, and left it to dry. This process stretched the paper and made it as flat as could be.

The next part of the procedure was to take the old Breughel copy out of the Colnaghi frame in such a way as to be able to replace it with my version without leaving any sign whatsoever of the frame having been tampered with. The back of the frame had been sealed against dust with a stout sheet of brown paper. This I carefully steamed off and put aside. I had then to patiently remove the little nails holding down the backing board. Each slightly rusty nail would later be returned to the very same hole from which it had been removed and nestle its head in the selfsame groove in the board that it had occupied for the thirty-odd years since Colnaghi's frame-maker had first knocked it in. Extracting the engraver's copy of a presumably lost Jan Breughel from its mount I attached it with a little scotch tape to my drawing board – to the left of my blank sheet of old paper. Taking up a powerful magnifying glass I spent an hour or so making a meticulous examination of every stroke of the old engraver's pen. As I did so, I asked myself questions such as: in the original from which this copy was taken, in what order were these lines executed? For the copyist had not, I suspected, copied the lines in the same sequence that Breughel had originally drawn them. The reader who is not a skilled draughtsman may not think that such a change of order could be of the slightest importance, but in fact the sequence in which the lines of a drawing are put down is vital. This is because of the rhythmical nature of good drawing where one movement leads naturally to another. If one changes the order in which the lines are made, one changes the rhythm. Again the reader may better understand what I am speaking of by making a comparison with handwriting. If you were to copy a specimen of writing by imitating the letters in a random order you would later have difficulty in linking them up with a convincing flow to the writing. Let us imagine, for instance, that you are copying Breughel's signature. Naturally you will copy the letters of his name in the same sequence as the artist wrote them. You would not I imagine begin by copying the r, the u, the h, and the l, and try to fit in the remaining letters. This is because you know how to write, and should you also know how to draw (by which I mean considerably more than most people mean by the phrase), and you were to set about copying a Breughel drawing, you would also know the proper sequence of his lines. You would know which are construction lines, which the correcting lines, and which the final strokes used to strengthen or stress the essential movements. Having satisfied myself that I had understood the order in which Breughel had created the lines in the lost drawing from which the engraver's copy had been made, I rehearsed the drawing time and time again, both in my mind and lightly with a dry pen over the old copy. But I was too tired to start the re-creation of the lost Breughel that day. So I rested my eyes and brain and waited for the following morning, when fresh and bright, with the drawing I was about to make deeply etched upon my sub-conscious, I picked up my pen and set to work.

To make the first marks of a new Old Master, knowing that one tiny slip could cost you a small fortune in wasted materials, is a nerve-wracking experience and it was not until I had sipped a tot of brandy and drawn a few lines in Breughel's manner on a scrap of note paper that the stage fright vanished and the connection be-tween the conscious and the subconscious was unblocked. Obli-vious of my actual surroundings, I found myself sitting on a stone in front of the ruins of the so-called temples of Venus and Diana at Baia on a bright clear morning over 300 years ago. Time was halted. Hours must have passed but it was as if I had breathed the drawing into existence in a moment. The differences between my 'Breughel' and the engraver's copy from which I had worked were subtle in the extreme. The strokes of the pen were identical save for the ineffable quality of touch. Whereas the old version was im-personal as though it were the product of a copying machine, my own had, I hoped (and I am not ashamed of using the word), the authentic touch of a draughtsman's hand. But as I have suggested above, one cannot trust one's judgment about one's own work until a certain amount of time has passed since it was made. So, I put my handiwork into the Colnaghi frame and, carefully sealing it up so that there was no suggestion that the frame had ever been opened, waited for Graham to come home to get his opinion. The 'Breughel' (Fig. 47) hung in its usual position in the front room, and in the course of the evening I drew Graham's attention to it, saying that I had been studying it very carefully, and thought that for all its attractiveness it might be a copy. What did he think? Graham looked at it attentively, and after a few moments unsuspectingly said: 'It doesn't look at all like a copy to me. In fact the more I look at it the better it seems.'

At this point I have to confess to doing something that even now makes me feel uneasy. I remembered a story told of Lord Duveen of Millbank. Duveen came from a family of antique dealers, and before he took to dealing exclusively in Old Masters, he had gained a good knowledge of other antiques. And one day to put his knowledge to the test an uncle of his stood Duveen in front of a shelf of valuable old porcelain mixed with near perfect imitations, and putting a walking stick into his hand told him to smash all but the authentic pieces; which he did. I would now consider Duveen's an act of vandalism because copies and imitations have their own value and can serve many purposes. They can, for instance, record lost originals, show how an artist or craftsman viewed a previous age to his own, or simply function as works of art in their own right. But in those days, in Packington Street, a part of me still shared the popular myopic view that copies and fakes are somehow unethical, and thought that Duveen had dealt with the spurious porcelain as it deserved. With this ridiculous attitude, totally inconsistent with my own faking activities – I destroyed the old engraver's copy. I tore it to shreds and flushed it down the lavatory. Supposing I was mistaken and it was not a copy. Had I destroyed a genuine Jan Breughel and replaced it with a wretched modern fake? I hope not, and I don't think so. Nor apparently do the experts, because my effort was to make its way through the hands of Colnaghi's 'again' and to New York's Metropolitan Museum where for over a quarter of a century it has enjoyed the reputation of being one of the museum's most important Flemish drawings.

Delightful duality, sometimes known as diabolical duplicity, is a glorious game. It is played like this. The experts know you for an ignoramus of the first order. They buy from you a work of art which in your ignorance you have failed to recognise for the master work it is and attribute it to a famous artist. You later hear others prattling with ridiculous deference both about the work of art (which of course you have made) and the clever expert who discovered it; while treating you with indifference or even scorn. So you take the skin off human foibles, and examine them at your impish hidden ease. A game for sly rogues indeed. To make delightful duality worth playing one must choose worthy opponents. Just as there could be little satisfaction in scoring a goal in the absence of a goalkeeper, so it is that to sell a master drawing to someone lacking the necessary expertise to make a proper appraisal of it is at best a hollow victory. In other words only the experts are worth fooling, and the greater the expert, the greater the satisfaction of deceiving him.

One of the very finest connoisseurs of our time is James Byam Shaw, CBE. Born in 1903, Byam Shaw's accomplishments are too numerous to list – he had a distinguished education and joined Colnaghi's in 1934, where he became a Director from 1937 to 1968.

Fig. 47: 'Jan Breughel the Elder' (1561-1625), *The Temples of Venus and Diana at Baiae*, 1963, pen and wash with touches of blue watercolour (sold to Colnaghi's; at present in the Metropolitan, New York)

Amongst his other activities, he was Associate Curator of Pictures at Christ Church, Oxford (1973-1974) and is an acknowledged expert on the Old Masters, having published numerous books and catalogues on them, notably Guardi and Tiepolo.

One could not wish for a better opponent to play delightful duality with than him! But before describing one of a number of games in which I have had the honour of matching myself against the great scholar, I would like to stress the point – and there is no tongue in the cheek – that I have the utmost respect for Mr Byam Shaw's learning. I owe much of my own knowledge of drawing to our little encounters, and if he has made the occasional slip, so have I, and this in no way diminishes either his rank as a connoisseur or my own as a draughtsman. A good expert may on occasion be permitted a mistake, just as a good singer may sing a wrong note, or a good goalkeeper let in a goal, all without incurring eternal damnation. It was sometime in 1963 before his retirement as a director of P. and D. Colnaghi and Co Ltd of 14 Old Bond Street, the illustrious firm of art dealers whose name so often appears in these pages, that I showed him a pencil portrait of a child in the hope that he would attribute it to Corot.

The choosing of Corot was again, like the choosing of Byam Shaw, dictated by the idea of challenge. I knew that the drawing would have to be of very exceptional quality if Byam Shaw was going to associate it with this particular artist's name. The reason was that there have been more imitations of Corot than of any other artist in history, in consequence of which even genuine Corots of unknown provenance are normally dismissed. The attitude of the average dealer and collector was that of the Berlin art dealer, Paul Cassirer, who, according to Sepp Schüler in his book *Forgers, Dealers and Experts*, states that after the First World War he was offered some 200 'Corots' by soldiers returned from France. 'There might have been one genuine work among them,' he says, 'but I didn't dare to take it.' The drawings wrongly described as being by Corot are unbelievably numerous. In the early part of this century, a certain Dr Jousseaune claimed to own between 2,000 and 3,000 sheets from the master's hand, boasting never to have paid more than 110 francs each for them. After the doctor's death, these drawings gave rise to a scandal which has been described by René Huyghe as 'one of the most amazing swindles of the day'. In 1928, the Jousseaune collection was exhibited in London, and the following year a catalogue published in which many items were designated as 'from the artist's collection'. The story went that they were the contents of Corot's studio at Coubron, and that the master had bequeathed them to a certain M. Gratiot – one of the many friends with whom the painter stayed on his prolonged sketching tours. It was the old trick of creating a false provenance. The poor quality of the work could be explained by suggesting that the drawings were simply 'studio scrapings'. The old trick seems to have worked, for when the collection was dispersed, some of the drawings were bought for important public galleries both in England and America. The deception was exposed in 1929 by Eugène Bonvy. Such was the number of 'Corots' in circulation at one time that Forain made a popular cartoon depicting a young woman urging an artist to take his work around the galleries, saying: 'Come on, dear, get your portfolio and we'll sell the dealers some Corots.'

The production of pictures in Corot's style has truly been described as an industry. It began after the master's death and the dispersion of his atelier in 1875. In 1887, a Corot imitator named Vernon was tried in court, and this led to an immense traffic in 'Corots' being uncovered. In 1888 no less than 235 'Corots' were sent to France from one Brussels workshop alone – there were even a number of such workshops, or 'schools' as they were called, engaged in the mass production of the French artist's work. No wonder with so many 'Corots' of dubious authenticity in the world that there is not a collector today, however innocent, who would not question a Corot 'find'. Unless, that is, it were of such good quality that it demanded to be given serious consideration. But who, we may ask, would or could determine those intangible, ineffable virtues of drawing that we call quality? Why, an expert of course! For only an expert, and a very good one at that, can truly appreciate the subtleties of a fine drawing. It would be pointless to try to dispose of a master work in uninformed circles. To try to convince a Joe Bloggs, who couldn't tell a Corot from a carrot, of its worth would be virtually impossible. And even if one succeeded it would be as despicable as passing the fabled buck to a blind man – like all games, delightful duality has its rules. Being a newcomer to the Corot industry I had the advantage of being able to study the work of pioneers in the field, and so avoid some of the pitfalls that had led to their exposure. The typical Corot imitation is as much an insult to the viewer's intelligence as it is to the great painter's talent. It is more often than not a landscape feebly attempting to simulate the silver, sylvan atmosphere for which Corot was justly famous. This is done by blurring and smudging, without any regard to serious drawing. I also had the opportunity of studying what is thought to be a Corot drawing in the original. It hung on the walls of Anthony Blunt. He had bought it in a junk shop in his Cambridge days for four shillings and sixpence. Naturally, Anthony knew of the enormous number of imitations in circulation, and knowing his cautious nature, I very much doubt he would have risked a penny more on the drawing. Even Anthony did not trust his judgment on the matter of Corot, and it was not until he had obtained the favourable opinion of a Corot expert that he felt his four and sixpence well spent. The Blunt drawing is typical of the French artist's studies of serpentine trees with feathery foliage such as are normally imitated, but unlike the weak imitations I had seen, it had a certain natural vitality which spoke of a real draughtsman. Whether or not that real draughtsman was Corot I do not pretend to know.

My attitude to the drawing was that of Vollard's to a picture brought to him for appraisal. The story is told by Sepp Schüller. 'The painter Maurice Vlaminck relates that one day, while he was in the shop of Vollard, the art dealer, in Paris, a respectable looking man came in, with a picture under his arm, and asked Vollard what he thought of it. Vollard examined the work with interest.

'"It's very good," he said. "I like it very much. It's very fine."

'"But do you think it's an original?" the man asked.

'"Original?" Vollard exclaimed. "My dear Sir, you can't expect me to guarantee that the painting is by this, that or the other artist or that it's not a modern copy. It looks well over 300 years old. But I couldn't possibly tell for certain." He smiled enigmatically. "Why not consult my colleague across the way? He's got a brass plate up, with "Art Expert" written on it.'

This story illustrates a number of things. It will be noticed that the raconteur feels it necessary to tell us that the unknown man was 'respectable looking'. But if he not been respectable looking, what possible difference could it have made to the authenticity of the picture under his arm? Are we supposed to imagine that some of the genuineness of his well tailored sleeve rubbed off on the painting? The truth is that the judgment of works of art is all too often coloured by our knowledge of their owners, and in consequence is lacking in objectivity. The book in which I discovered Vlaminck's anecdote contained a fascinating photograph of an expert examining a painting in the style of Rubens through a pocket magnifying glass. He scrutinises a detail of a splendid over-life-size head of the drunken Bacchus. The inebriated deity gazes back at him through the glass as if to inspect the credentials of this wretched mortal who dares to question the authenticity of a god. The caption reads: 'A genuine Rubens or a forgery?' This painting turned up in the possession of an *unemployed man* and the experts disagree about its authenticity. The italics are mine. All of which leads me to imagine that had the Blunt Corot belonged to let us say Rose Molly Marchand, instead of the Keeper of the Queen's Pictures, the Corot expert might have come to another conclusion, and Rose Molly would have lost her four and sixpence. Vlaminck's Vollard anecdote is also characteristic of the situation in the art world today insofar as it points to the reliance of the collector and dealer on the expert. Naturally, the inexperienced collector is fearful of acquiring a forgery, and although the dealer may have his own view, he will normally refer such a collector to an expert for a definite opinion. It is the expert's job to eliminate the risk of the amateur being landed with a fake.

That then was the role in our game of Byam Shaw – to eliminate the risk of Colnaghi's customers acquiring a forged work. As his opponent it was my aim to thwart him in his intentions. To do this, I was not simply going to hope that he would err in his judgment. Indeed my plan depended on his displaying his knowledge and intelligence to the full. And supposing that Byam Shaw would think logically, I tried to anticipate his reasoning, and be, as it were, one step ahead. His thoughts would, and should, I imagine, go along these lines:

1. It is an attractive drawing in the style of Corot.
2. It is not a copy of a known Corot drawing.
3. It does not belong to any of the known groups of forgeries.
4. It bears no false signature or sale mark.
5. It compares favourably with a number of drawings known with certainty to be by Corot.
6. Although it is in no way copied or adapted from it, the drawing is closely related in style to a picture in the Fogg Museum, Harvard University.
7. The sitter appears in the same position in a painting by Corot in the Louvre. But the present drawing can hardly be a copy from the Louvre picture, because the painting has no lines to copy, and a copyist would be obliged to draw it in his own drawing style. It is inconceivable that an imitator could have so thoroughly assimilated Corot's personal 'handwriting' as to draw freely in it while remaining faithful to the formal content of the picture.
8. It shows no sign of having been artificially aged, and the paper is of a kind employed in Corot's day.

Taken together, the above factors tend to suggest that the drawing is by Corot and that it is a preparatory study for the Louvre picture.

The stratagem was not, however, worked out at once, and as an opening move in this first game with Byam Shaw, I toyed with the idea of presenting a landscape drawing. Not one of the obvious kind

Fig. 48: Corot?, *Portrait of Henri Leroy*, pencil

of Corot such as the sketch in Anthony's collection but of the sort
that the artist had produced at an earlier period. I made it in black
chalk on blue paper (not a typical Corot combination). The nineteenth-century paper had the watermark of the Italian paper
makers, Fabriano, and suggested to me a study of the *campagna
romana*, the countryside around Rome with which I was to some extent familiar, and where Corot had made a number of very beautiful works. This first attempt produced an effective drawing, but not
one to suit my purpose. Quality and subject-matter apart, there
was not a strong enough link with Corot. True, the paper and style
should have suggested a French artist working in Italy during the
first half of the nineteenth century, but because of the number of

Fig. 49: Corot?, *Portrait of Henri Leroy*, pencil (one of these by kind permission
of the Fogg Art Museum, Harvard University)

such artists, and the reluctance of modern experts to put forward
the over-exploited name of Corot, I felt that it was not worthy of my
distinguished opponent's consideration. Even so it seemed a shame
just to throw the study away, so I took up a piece of chalk somewhat different in its blackness to the actual drawing and wrote on
the landscape study C.P. These might be the initials of a score of
French artists of the last century, but when they are found on blue
period paper there is an irresistible tendency to imagine that they
stand for Camille Pisarro. And this is in fact what Joe erroneously
thought when he spent a few pounds more on it than was his
custom. He did this in spite of the warning of no less (there couldn't

be) an authority than my adored Miss Marie Grey of the Old Curiosity Shop, who had said that it was her considered opinion that C.P. stood for Constable Pinxit.

Once having recovered from my disappointment at having to sell a perfectly good 'Corot' as a doubtful Pisarro I set to work to make a copy on modern paper of the Corot drawing in the Fogg Museum, Harvard University. The purpose of the copy was to familiarise myself with the master's portrait style sufficiently well to make an original drawing in it. It might perhaps amuse you to test your own abilities as a connoisseur, and decide for yourself which of the two photographs (Figs 48 or 49) represents a detail from the original. Even if you happen to be Joe Bloggs in person, you will still have a fifty-fifty chance of being right. Look carefully, take your time, and seek the hesitant line of the copyist as opposed to the strong sure line of Corot. The answer is given at the bottom of the page. Now, having read the solution, look at the two drawings again and you will suddenly notice how poor my version is, how faulty the construction, how harsh the modelling, and all sorts of ghastly errors which escaped your notice before. But what if I should now tell you that the answer at the bottom of the page is wrong? Perhaps you had better look up the Fogg drawing after all. Should you happen to have a copy of Paul J. Sachs' *Modern Prints and Drawings* (Alfred A. Knopf), no date (*circa* 1959), you will find it reproduced in full on plate 18 with the following caption:

> COROT, CAMILLE, Portrait of Henri Leroy, DRAWING, PENCIL *c.* 1835 10¾″ × 9⅞″, Fogg Museum, Harvard University
>
> 'Drawing', said Corot, 'is the first thing to seek, then the volume.' I illustrate his genius in black and white not by one of his romantic etched landscapes but by this serious, moving pencil portrait, a drawing in which there is a complete absence of any calligraphic trick; a drawing which renders a mood miraculously. The child reminds me of a youngster on the Rue de Bac, Paris, who each evening, years ago, solemnly stepped out of his parent's tobacco shop and with wide open eyes and never a smile handed me my evening paper. He seemed like Henri, too serious, too delicate for his tender years. He lived on the very street where Corot's mother had a milliner's shop and where Corot was born.
>
> To appreciate this subtle drawing there is no need to consult x-ray, ultra-violet light, or any of the other modern, scientific aids often used to bolster insensitive vision. In this instance, however, there is an amusing side to what was revealed by the ultra-violet light. Then only could one read an inscription on the reverse of the blue mount which enframes the drawing. The sentence not only identifies the little sitter but expresses the wish that the drawing remain in the family, never to be sold.

Answer: Fig 48

I have included the above quotation because it is a good example of the drivel that experts tend to talk when they are obliged to go beyond factual description. For myself, I am prepared to believe Mr Sachs when he says that the drawing is in pencil, measures $10\frac{3}{4}'' \times 9\frac{7}{8}''$, and is in the Fogg. Nor do I see any reason to doubt him when he says it is by Corot (although I must admit that my estimate of his knowledge of drawing would rise dramatically were I to discover he had really made it himself). But beyond such simple facts and the totally irrelevant gossip about Corot's mother owning a milliner's shop in the street where Mr Sachs once bought newspapers from a boy who happened to look like Henri Leroy, the famous connoisseur tells us nothing. But worse than that, his words are designed to intervene between us and a direct experience of Corot's visual statement. They set out to pre-condition our reaction to the work. Look how cleverly he first introduces the word 'genius', with its vague connotations suggesting superhuman talent and qualities of the mind. This is to make us approach the little study with unnatural awe and set one of the most approachable artists up on a pedestal. Mr Sachs then informs us that the drawing is 'serious' and 'moving', and renders a *mood* miraculously. All this is nice to know, but what does it really mean? Surely it's just waffle, but it is not harmless waffle, because it is urging us to look for these intangible verbal qualities instead of approaching the work with an open mind and letting the drawing speak for itself. The simple fact is that drawing is a visual language, and cannot and should not be translated into verbal terms. If anybody wishes to know anything about drawing, let them draw. The great connoisseurs of the past were draughtsmen: Vasari, Rubens, Rembrandt, Reynolds, Lely, the Richardsons – draughtsmen and collectors all. When conferring a doctorate on Paul J. Sachs, Yale University justified its thus honouring a Harvard man in these words: 'Connoisseur, collector of works of art, teacher, counsellor, you have inspired a generation of art gallery directors and curators with your generosity, wisdom and standards.'

Needless to say, I did not study Corot's drawings by reading what the experts had to say about them, but by following the artist's visual statements with a pencil in my hand. Although my version of the Fogg drawing is a copy, it is not a slavish one. I have not tried to copy the drawing line for line. That would merely have been a mechanical achievement of little worth in an age when almost perfect facsimiles can be made. No, what I attempted to do was to look through Corot's drawing, as if it had been drawn on glass, and see again little Henri Leroy in my mind's eye, drawing him in a style closely following Corot's. Having thus familiarised myself with Corot's vision and method of communicating it, I was now prepared to make an original work with some of the virtues I admired in the Fogg drawing. I have forgotten where and how I obtained the old paper, but I suspect it came from one of the albums of blank paper acquired from Mr Seligmann of Cecil Court.

Corot's life was dominated by his friendships. Visits to friends and landscape painting expeditions were normally one and the same thing. One friend, with whom he regularly stayed on his never-ending tour of France, was a certain M. Robert, a magistrate of Mantes. M. Robert had three sons, two of whom, Louis and Maurice, Corot painted: a portrait of Louis holding a whip when he was three in 1840, and Maurice with a trumpet in 1857. Little Louis did not survive except in art, and his portrait was eventually bequeathed to the Louvre by his brother Maurice, together with other works which had belonged to their father. These included his own portrait and the decoration of the magistrate's bathroom at Mantes, with its Italian scenes, this last being destroyed during the Second World War. It was the portrait of Louis Robert (Louvre inventory F.2601. Fig. 50) which provided the subject matter and inspiration for the Colnaghi 'Corot'. The painting was available to me in a photographic reproduction which, because of the picture's small scale (11½″ × 8″), was almost the same size as the original.

Perhaps when I say that the Colnaghi 'Corot' is not a copy of the Louvre picture I shall be misunderstood. After all, does it not show the same child in the same position? And are not such details as the costume and lighting taken directly from Corot's painting? Yes, but a true copy can only be made in the medium of the original. Corot's picture is composed of areas of colour without lines, and to restate those areas of colour in linear terms requires translating them. And the process of translating automatically excludes the possibility of copying. This is why engravings after paintings are not considered copies. An engraving, say, by Marcantonio Raimondi after a painting by Raphael, is not considered to be a copy of Raphael but an original engraving by Marcantonio Raimondi. But what about the drawing style, is not that copied from Corot? No. The Colnaghi 'Corot' is in a style of drawing that Corot sometimes employed, but that style does not belong exclusively to him. It is a style much used in the nineteenth century, being employed on occasion by artists as widely differing as Géricault and Bonington. It is the style of an age. Just as draughtsmen of the Renaissance may be said, broadly speaking, to have had a style in common, so did draughtsmen of the nineteenth century. And as Braque wisely said in 1953: 'A style in

Fig. 50: Corot, *Portrait of Louis Robert*, 1840, oil on
canvas (Louvre)

common indicates authenticity, mere resemblance a counterfeit.'
To sum up: it was my aim to make an original drawing, not a copy
or an imitation of another drawing. This original drawing was to be
in a style which Corot had used, and to be of a subject that Corot
had depicted in another medium. The drawing was intended to be
good enough to be mistaken by a first-class connoisseur as really
and truly being by the French master himself. How far I may have
succeeded in these aims would be for Byam Shaw to decide, but
before taking my effort to Colnaghi's for his consideration I thought
it might be wise to test its effect on other intelligent viewers first.

To this end, I had my unsigned 'Corot' framed, and hung it in
the hallway of the maisonette Graham and I had rented for eight

pounds a week in Packington Street not far from the Angel and Camden Passage with its antique shops. It was towards the end of March 1963 when I was visited by an important dealer in master drawings from New York called Helen Sieferheld. Her name was familiar to me from her regular advertisements in *The Burlington Magazine*. She was in London for important sales of Old Masters and was looking for fine drawings generally. The American dealer was accompanied by Edward Lucie-Smith, the well known art critic, broadcaster and writer. Business at Packington Street was by appointment only (how embarrassing it would have been to be caught in the very act of making yet another exciting discovery), and when the dealer and critic knocked on the door, my plan of action had been carefully rehearsed. It was arranged that Graham should open the door and on the pretext of my being engaged on the telephone, keep them waiting in the hallway for a few minutes. Having come for the express purpose of looking for good drawings, it was to be supposed that while waiting to be shown the more important drawings in stock, their professional eyes would wander over the minor works on the walls of the entrance, and alight in an act of joyful recognition on the Corot. When, however, I finally decided to come down the stairs to greet them, they made no mention of my portrait of Louis Robert. Had they been so clever as to spot at once that it was a worthless fake? Helen Sieferheld and Edward Lucie-Smith were shown into the tiny living-room to look over the drawings I had for sale. Among them was a vigorous sketch of *Medea Contemplating the Murder of her Children*. It was in pen and sepia ink and pencil corresponding in description to a drawing I bought only a few days before, on 20 March, in Sotheby's (Lot 15). The drawing I bought as a birthday present to myself. It was by George Romney. But the drawing I was about to sell to Helen Sieferheld was by Eric Hebborn – the actual Romney had been hidden away, otherwise the two were identical. Edward Lucie-Smith was attracted to a 'Reynolds'. Not one of my best efforts, but then Reynolds himself was by no means always good as a draughtsman. The sketch was apparently *for*, rather than *after*, the artist's well-known full-length portrait of 'Lady Crosbie'. Although I very much doubt that Sieferheld or Lucie-Smith are as happy with their purchases in the early nineties as they were in the early sixties, they may console themselves with the fact that they did not spend very much money, and as genuine Hebborns their drawings have gone up in value immensely.

Clutching their newly acquired treasures the expert couple stood again in the hallway to say goodbye to me, and (for a few years) their money. I tried to detain them there with small talk, hoping that at any moment one or the other would notice and comment on the pencil portrait of Louis Robert. At length, unable to endure further indifference to my 'Corot' I swallowed my pride and drew their attention to it.

'What do you think of this?' I asked, taking the picture down and handing it to them.

'It's a sketch of a child,' said Helen Sieferheld with remarkable accuracy.

'Yes,' confirmed her art-critic companion. 'Who could it be?' Understanding Lucie-Smith to be asking who the artist might have been rather than the identity of the child, I thought I might drop a clue, and said that the drawing did not seem to me to be English –

'French perhaps?'

'Perhaps,' said Lucie-Smith and with no more ado my intelligent viewers departed. To have elicited so little response, no more than if I had shown it to Joe Bloggs, was not a very propitious start for the Colnaghi 'Corot'. But reflecting that Sieferheld and Lucie-Smith were not infallible, and encouraged by their having purchased my 'Reynolds' and 'Romney', I did not lose heart, and hoped that I might yet find a more appreciative audience.

The time had come to make the next move in the game of delightful duality with Byam Shaw. I rang up Colnaghi's and made an appointment to see their drawing expert. I explained that I had a pencil drawing of a little girl which somebody had suggested might possibly be by Degas. This white lie was intended to convince Colnaghi's of my total ignorance on the subject. Remembering that paintings and drawings in the possession of respectable looking people are more authentic than those in the possession of out-of-work looking people, I took care to groom myself and, putting on an expensive suit, which according to Peter Greenham, is the sign and symbol of an artist's waning powers, phoned a cab, and made the first of many visits to the premises of P. and D. Colnaghi and Co. Ltd of 14 Old Bond Street, experts and valuers, established 1760. There was no one called Colnaghi in the firm now, nor had there been for nearly two centuries, but nevertheless the present directors were very proud to trade under the name of those long-since-dead brothers, who once bought pictures for George III. I understood their feelings perfectly. How proud I was to represent J. C. Corot and Co. Unlimited, even though the firm was not founded until 1875. Furthermore, I argued, if artists like myself can benefit from the reputation of dead artists, why shouldn't dealers benefit from the reputation of dead dealers?

Colnaghi's occupies a large, sober-looking terraced building of nice proportions dating from the firm's foundation. Its main feature is a clock which sticks out over the street. Colnaghi's clock told me I was a few minutes early for my appointment, so I took time to study their window. It contained only one painting, which looked to me like a Karel du Jardin, but it had no label on it or any price tag. There is nothing to be gained in the art trade by the little dodges of window display that draw impressionable shoppers like you and me into a department store. All Colnaghi's premises did on the outside to promote its business on the inside was to admit the customer with a kind of stately geniality. Once inside, the visitor was met by a young lady of charming manners, whose purpose was to make one's movement about the galleries easy, the opportunity for examining the stock unhurried, and the impression of the firm's solidarity profound. Every action she made, every word she spoke, the effortless handing of a catalogue, the calling of Byam Shaw on the in-house phone, seemed designed to express the reposeful solvency of the business, its ample reserves, its princely rank among merchants, its resolution to stay in the trade not for an age but for all time. Colnaghi's was not a shop. On its premises things were regularly bought, and things were regularly sold, but not as in a shop. Normally, both parties to every transaction were understood to be cultivated ladies and gentlemen who knew their stuff. So sales talk was of no use there, nor was haggling. In vain would one look for a ticket on a painting saying something like: 'Genuine hand-painted original, over a hundred years old, two thousand pounds only.' Warranty was unnecessary, authenticity and fair prices taken for granted.

As James Byam Shaw entered the gallery from a side door, I was thrilled to meet the great scholar whose work I so much admired. He was just as I had imagined. A soft-spoken, gentle soul, whom a lifetime spent in the study of beautiful things had refined, so that he had about him that air, as ineffable as it is unmistakable, of a cultivated man. He had a way of holding himself that spoke of long years bowed over books and papers, was slight, his manner natural and unforced. 'So sorry to have kept you waiting, Mr Hebborn, let us look at your Degas upstairs, shall we?' He led the way through the side door from which he had emerged to a lift which took us to an upper room with windows looking over Old Bond Street. The room was lined with books and reminded me in its polished wood and leather of the larger library of the Royal Academy. Here, clearly, was a very remarkable collection of reference books. Knowledge is the dealer's greatest asset, more important even than money, and these handsome volumes were not mere decoration; they were tools, instruments for making and breaking attributions. Between their covers lay the labours of generations of scholars. Exhaustive and, it must be admitted, sometimes exhausting studies of all the major, and perhaps more important, many of the minor, European masters, constantly to be consulted for the correct description of the works of art passing through the illustrious dealers' hands. But the room was not just a library. The leather topped 'desks' or 'tables' were in reality chests of drawers containing Colnaghi's valuable stock of Old Master drawings which, with the possible exception of that of Hans Calmann in Bruton Place, was the most important on the London market.

Undoing my parcel I laid the now unframed 'Degas', the 'Corot', or the whatever it was going to be, down in front of Byam Shaw for his perusal. He examined it carefully, in the unhurried way that I have grown to associate with people who really understand drawings. Almost sick with nervous excitement I awaited my opponent's first move. What was he thinking? Had he started to reason along the lines that I had hoped and planned? He turned the drawing over, held it to the light, put it down again. And then the words I was hoping for:

'Well, it's certainly an attractive drawing, though quite honestly I can't see the remotest connection with Degas. Corot might be a closer guess, but as you are probably aware, the problems surrounding the paintings and drawings of Corot are such as to make more than a tentative association with his name at this stage unwise. What I suggest is that you leave the drawing with us for further study, and if it is what I suspect it may be, Colnaghi's would be prepared to make you an offer for it.' Delighted to know that I was talking to somebody who knew his stuff, I gladly agreed to allow my opponent to take his time – study the Corot literature, consult experts more intimately connected with Corot studies than himself, and so arrive at a considered opinion.

'How long do you think you will need to come to a decision?' I asked.

'Two or three weeks should be sufficient,' he replied, 'but whatever the outcome, it is a drawing of considerable quality, and I am grateful to you for having brought it to our attention.' I could have kissed the man (I was not as British by now) but decorum dictated a polite thank-you for his having taken the trouble to look at the work, and I went my way.

Then came the wait, the seemingly interminable wait. Drawings, even elaborate ones can sometimes be made in a few hours, but discussion of them can, as these pages prove, continue for years. Byam Shaw was no doubt comparing my handiwork with every Corot portrait drawing he could trace. He would have shown the portrait of Louis Robert to those specialists in the field whose opinion he respected. Furthermore, he would have looked again and again at my drawing with a critical eye – it is amazing how what may seem a good drawing at the first viewing can sometimes, and quite suddenly, reveal its weaknesses later. I once heard a man boast that he had never gone to bed with an ugly woman, adding wryly: 'I've only woken up with them.' And many a collector could say that they had never bought a bad drawing, only disposed of them! Poor Byam Shaw. He could not possibly have known it, but he was playing a game which, ironically, he could only win by making a false move. All the time he thought logically and correctly he would be obliged to follow the path of reasoning I had mapped out for him and be forced, however reluctantly, to admit that here, in spite of all the fakes on the market, was a real Corot. I was banking on the man's knowledge, intelligence, and sensibility to quality and hoping he would not disappoint me by making a slip. In a number of later encounters with my preferred expert where the bones of contention were Venetian (Byam Shaw thus playing on his home ground) I would sometimes win and sometimes lose. When I lost I was much more pleased than had I won against some of the lesser authorities. This is because I felt certain that Byam Shaw had arrived at his verdict with sound reasoning from which I could learn. Whereas even if minor experts might sometimes come up with the right answer, they dismissed my work for the wrong reasons. In other words they did not really know, and had simply made a lucky guess.

Three or four weeks passed before I got in touch with Byam Shaw. He asked me if I would like to visit him again at Colnaghi's, as he had some news for me concerning the portrait of Louis Robert. Passing once more beneath the clock in Old Bond Street, into the gallery and up in the lift, I found the 'Corot' laid on a table, and surrounded by books with markers in them. 'Well, Mr Hebborn, we have taken some trouble to check your drawing. It has been compared side by side with original drawings, as well as photographs of originals. Furthermore, I have shown it to specialists, and have satisfied myself that it is a drawing by Corot. The market, however, and here is the problem, has been so flooded with imitations of this particular artist, that it will not be easy to persuade a collector on ocular evidence alone of the work's authenticity. As far as I understand, the drawing has no provenance that might help us to trace it back to Corot, and without a signature the evidence of its authenticity rests in the eyes of the few people capable of seeing it. Fortunately, one of the firm's customers, an American lady, agrees with me about the portrait and has made an offer. Naturally enough, in view of the difficulty of reselling the drawing under the name of Corot she has proposed a speculative price. In consequence of which we could not give you any more than . . . . ' The price escapes me, although it was certainly well within a hundred pounds. But if Colnaghi's had only given me the price of a cup of tea for the Corot I would have been overjoyed. My plan had worked. I had sold a drawing of my own, to one of the greatest authorities on drawing of our age, who had judged it on its merits alone to be a Corot.

This particular round of delightful duality would certainly have amused Corot himself. He was only too pleased when his followers' work was mistaken for his own, and has even been accused of encouraging the counterfeiting of his work. A well-known story is told of how a pupil asked him to criticise a painting which the latter had made. Corot praised the picture but felt it could be improved with a few touches here and there, and without thinking twice added them. The pupil was delighted and full of admiration exclaimed: 'It is so much better now that it is really more yours than mine. Surely there would be no harm in your signing it. I'd love to own a painting of yours!' At which Corot duly added his signature. Of the subsequent history of the Colnaghi 'Corot' I know nothing. It was not mentioned in the newspapers' accounts of drawings sold to the firm, and perhaps was not thought to belong to the group of drawings then attributed to me. In answer to my request to trace the drawing for inclusion in this book, the present director of what is now called Colnaghi Drawings informed me that the firm has kept no record of the transaction. I wonder why? The fact that it went to America is, however, amusing, because of a famous witticism which goes: 'Of the 700-odd proved originals by Corot, 8,000 are to be found in America alone.' Now it has 8,001!

My decision to give up an establishment-type career coincided with Graham's graduation from the Royal College and as he had made no particular plans for what to do in the future, he, like myself, considered that of the few possibilities on offer, Pannini Galleries Ltd was the most interesting. So it was that we became art dealers on a full-time basis. As art dealing is an international trade, Graham and I realised that we need not perforce stay in London. True, the great capital was a highly important centre for buying and selling works of art, but like any other market place, the dealer need only visit it on market day. In our case we needed only to attend the few major London sales of Old Master drawings throughout the year, and the rest of the time we might spend wherever we pleased. This was especially true since we had planned to issue further catalogues of our stock, and consequently would not have to rely entirely on customers dropping in to see us. And so it was, after much weighing up of the pros and cons that sometime in 1964 we decided to move Pannini Galleries to Rome. Pleasant memories of my *dolce vita* years were of course instrumental in choosing Rome the Eternal City for our home from home, but there were many other reasons for the choice. One was the then lower cost of living in Italy (now the other way round), another was the climate – the winter before we left was one of the bitterest on record – a third was the cheap wine. But as artists, we didn't need excuses to live in one of the world's most beautiful cities, and our only regret was that of going to live so far from our London friends.

The financing of the move came from the sale of two 'Johns' made especially for the purpose. I cannot now recall to whom these particular 'Johns' were sold – as it was never my intention to write a book about my dealing activities such records as I possess have survived by chance, and any document I may once have had concerning the sale is lost. They were not the 'Johns' sold by Christie's mentioned earlier, nor had they anything to do with the drawing sold on my behalf by Sotheby's on 14 December 1966, lot 237, catalogued as being by Augustus John OM RA For by 1966 Pannini Galleries was well established in Rome. My suspicion is that the removal 'Johns' were sold directly to a company which had over the years bought a number of my drawings in the manner of this artist, and were, if I remember correctly, the purchasers of the Sotheby 'John' just mentioned. Anyway, whoever bought the 'Johns', in the early summer of 1964, the proceeds of the sale took Pannini Galleries Ltd and its two directors, Graham and Eric, to Rome.

CHAPTER IX

A TALE OF TWO CITIES

'If the counterfeit were a good one, I should be delighted. I'd sit down straight away and sign it.'

Picasso.

The Eternal City had changed very little during my absence. There were more cars, and the cost of living had risen, but essentially it was the same enjoyable city of the senses that I had left nearly three years before. Eugene had moved from working-class Trastevere to a grand *palazzo* in Via delle Botteghe Oscure, the street of the gloomy shops, now widened and no longer corresponding to its picturesque name which was, incidentally, the name used for the little magazine which foreshadowed Joe's. This street is not very far from Piazza Venezia, considered by the Romans themselves to be the city's centre. His move was not, Eugene told me, the result of having come into money, but because he had discovered that to be behind in paying a high rent is no more distressing than being in arrears with a low one. Moreover, fortune tends to knock more often if one's door is in a good area. In short he was still broke, but broke in style. So I lent him 10,000 lire and invited him to lunch at Gigetto's, a restaurant in Rome's Jewish quarter, next door to the Portico d'Ottavia, originally built by Quintus Metellus in 149 BC, one of the many facts of Roman history which makes us all feel young. Gigetto's is one of my favourite restaurants, and what I like most on its menu is the *zuppa di pesce alla Romana*. This is a huge serving of all kinds of fish: *morena, pescatrice, cappone, scorfano*, ink fish, octopus, and *scampi*, all cooked in a fish stock, and flavoured with parsley, tomatoes, and celery added to sautéd garlic and anchovy. It is served in an all-but-overflowing bowl with a slice of toasted bread, and is piled high with succulent mussels and clams still in their shells. A dish to remember, and in itself a good enough reason for returning to Rome.

As we happily made our way through our mountainous lunch and a litre of Frascati, Eugene gave me news of himself and what had happened in the Rome that he frequented. He was full of Fellini, whom by now he had got to know personally. The great film maker was, said Eugene, shooting a new film called *8½*, and employed him as one of a number of unofficial casting directors. Then there was an acquaintance of his, a Canadian photographer who had been commissioned to make a book of photographs of Greece. Eugene was to accompany him and make a short explanatory text. In the event, when they returned with the photos and text, Eugene and the photographer fell out over money matters. Roloff argued that as he had shouldered Eugene's travelling expenses out of his own pocket, he had no further obligation. This nettled Eugene, who, knowing that the photographer had kept no record himself of what and where he had photographed in the Aegean Sea, snatched away his manuscript and rushed out of the room with: 'Well, honey, just let me tell you what your book's going to be called – *Guess Where in Greece!*' I told Eugene of Pannini Galleries Ltd and asked if he could perhaps help me to find a suitable apartment from which Graham and I could run the business. He said that he knew of nothing then and there but was certain that with his Roman connections there would be little difficulty. But as chance would have it, it was not Eugene who was to find the new premises of Pannini Galleries Ltd. No sooner had we finished our lunch and said goodbye outside the Portico d'Ottavia than I encountered Peter, an ex-Rome scholar. He had been the Scholar in engraving for 1960 and was an amiable character who had been kind enough to give up some of his time at the School to teach me the craft of etching.

Now he was going to be kind to me again. When he learnt that Graham and I were staying in a *pensione* while looking for an apartment to rent, he told me that we might have the use of a place that was only a few steps from where we were standing – a charming little studio flat that he was looking after for a friend who would be away for a couple of months. It was situated on the other side of the Portico d'Ottavia, and overlooked a group of ancient ruins standing before the great Roman theatre known as Teatro Marcello. Nothing could have been more to my taste, and I gratefully took Peter up on the offer. 'You're welcome,' he said. 'Let's go to my flat and have a drink to celebrate your return to the city of the soul.' With this he led the way along the road, and took a turning on the right which led to Piazza Mattei where the famous Fontana delle

Tartarughe stands – one of the most delightful fountains in the whole of Rome. It was made in 1585 by Taddeo Landini probably after the design of Giacomo della Porta, and gets its name from four little tortoises that are being supported to drink in an upper basin by four lithesome youths of bronze with dolphins spouting water into marble shells. Taking an alleyway running along the side of the oldest palace of the group built by the rich and powerful Mattei family in the sixteenth and seventeenth centuries we came to a small square called Piazza Paganica. There we entered the great *portone* of number 13, and climbing ninety-nine marble stairs found ourselves in Peter's flat.

It was a huge sprawling place of fourteen rooms. From the windows overlooking the palace's courtyard, one enjoyed picturesque views over the rooftops of old Rome, and one window framed the dome of Sant'Andrea della Valle, the splendid baroque church known

Fig. 51: *The Dome of Sant'Andrea della Valle*, seen through
a window of Piazza Paganica, 1966, red chalk
(Collection of the artist)

Fig. 52: *Interior of the flat in Piazza Paganica*, showing the
dining-room decorated with copies by the author of
Pompeian frescoes, 1967, oil on board (Collection of the
artist)

to opera lovers as the scene of the first act of *Tosca* (Fig. 51). From the
kitchen window one looked down upon Piazza Mattei and the charming fountain we had just passed. Peter explained that he and a group
of friends rented the grand but ramshackle place for only 30,000 lira.
But now he and his flatmates had decided to return to England and in
a few weeks the apartment would be vacant. Looking around I realised that if the rooms were renovated and a proper bathroom
installed, here, apart from the inconvenience of having no lift, were
impressive premises for Pannini Galleries Ltd. And so it was to be.

Graham and I moved into the studio flat in Via Portico
d'Ottavia where we stayed until September when we took over
Peter's apartment in Piazza Paganica. Our furniture and pictures
had still not arrived and this gave us the opportunity to see to the
renovations without the place being cluttered with possessions. The
construction of the new bathroom and the renewal of the electric

Fig. 53: 'Giovanni Benedetto Castiglione', *The Assumption of the Virgin*, 1966,
pen and wash (one of a number of drawings sold through Edoardo)

wiring we left to the professionals, whereas the painting and decorating we did by ourselves (Fig. 52). It was an enormous undertaking, and there were many times when we wished we had called in painters of a different genre to ourselves. We did, however, have some help from a young woman called Janet, a close friend, who had been a student of mine at Walthamstow and a fellow student of Graham's at the Royal College. We had agreed Janet might stay with us in Rome in return for some assistance in running the business. But without stock or the materials to produce any, for several months there was no business to run, and we devoted our time to making the apartment as attractive as our energies and fast diminishing funds allowed. Eventually our furniture and other possessions arrived and we began to furnish our new home and resume business. We then advertised our presence in Rome with an exhibition for which purpose we hired a gallery in Via dei Coronari, a street known for its antique shops. The exhibition was entitled *Italian Views from Breughel to Bermann*. Bermann was a distinguished stage designer and a keen collector of Old Master drawings. He was also a prolific draughtsman. At that time he was an elderly man, but he still managed to make a drawing a day, and the two that he lent us for the show were most attractive. The exhibition was a reasonable success, but none of the more important drawings, such as my Breughel, found a buyer.

For a year or so, Pannini Galleries Ltd dealt mainly in minor prints and drawings, mostly views of Italy that I would buy on my regular trips to London. Our chief customer for the prints was a dealer called Plinio Nardecchia, with a very inviting shop in Piazza Navona next to the Church of Sant' Agnese in front of which stands Bernini's Fountain of the Four Rivers which is the chief glory of the most picturesque of all Roman squares. Our main outlet for the minor Old Master drawings was Edoardo Fiorani, with a shop in Via del Babuino, near Piazza di Spagna. Both Plinio and Edoardo were pleased not only to buy from us, but to sell on our behalf. Thus Pannini Galleries had two shop windows in good parts of town (Fig. 53). Plinio is a very knowledgeable print seller who had been in the business all his life, but although a dealer of many years standing, Edoardo's knowledge of drawing was no more than it should have been. One day, for instance, I sold to him a copy I had made of a drawing by Canaletto, and the next day I received a telephone call from him asking for his money back. 'By all means, Edoardo,' I said, 'but what's the matter?' Whereupon he explained that he had done some research on the drawing and discovered that it couldn't be the original Canaletto because the original was in the possession of a certain English collector called 'Signor Windsor Castle'.

Apart from Plinio and Edoardo with whom we had regular business, there were many others with whom we had the occasional transaction. One of these was Sestieri of Piazza di Spagna. Carlo and Marcello Sestieri were very important picture dealers indeed, perhaps the leading dealers in Rome. It was a family business, founded by the brothers' grandfather who made his money selling antiquities from Pompeii. I was introduced to Carlo and Marcello by Tony Clark, who helped them enormously in selling what at the time were rather difficult pictures to place – works by then unpopular unwanted artists from the seventeenth and eighteenth centuries whose work is now greatly appreciated, such as Luca Giordano and Sebastiano Conca, the latter being one that Tony had made a special study of. There was always a bottle of chilled champagne

Fig. 54: *Narcissus*, 1967, Rennaissance bronze
authenticated by Sir John Pope Hennessy and
sold to Sestieri, Rome, 1967

waiting at Sestieri's for Tony, and any visitor he might bring along, such as myself. Although I knew the Sestieris over a number of years I sold very little to them. This was mainly because most of their major outlets for important pictures in England and America were known to me, and there was no point in using Carlo and Marcello as middlemen. I did, however, sell a number of bronzes through the brothers.

Occasionally newspapers have referred to me as a sculptor, which is in fact one of my activities, and I shall be speaking of it later. My preferred medium is bronze, and it was a highly important renaissance bronze that I sold to the Sestieris in my first transaction with them. Even though I say it myself, it was an exquisite little sculpture. Moreover, I could sell it with absolute confidence because it had been authenticated by no less an expert than John Pope Hennessy. I had met Pope Hennessy at one of Joe's parties at 33, Ennismore Gardens, and was friendly with a student of his called Fred. And it was over lunch with Fred and himself off Kensington High Street that I showed him my little bronze. He studied it very carefully and told me that there were very few other casts of the subject, *Narcissus*, one of which was in the Wallace collection (Fig. 54). He gave me a complete history of the piece straight off the cuff. I was quite impressed. Incidentally, sculpture, of all forms of art, is the most easily faked (perhaps copied is a better word). This is because one can take casts of originals, and the copies do not differ from the original in the slightest. We may take for instance the famous horses on the façade of San Marco in Venice mentioned above. True, with bronze there is normally a slight shrinkage in the cooling, making detection of the cast by measurement possible. But even this is not an insurmountable obstacle for the ingenious forger.

In the spring or early summer of 1965 I approached Colnaghi's with my 'Breughel' *Temples of Venus and Diana* (see Fig. 47), asking them, if interested, to make an offer for it. So it was that after accepting their offer I received the following letter from the firm:

19th July 1965

E. Hebborn Esq.,
Pannini Galleries Ltd.,
Piazza Paganica 13,
Rome, Italy.

Dear Mr Hebborn,

Thank you for your letter of the 12th July. I am glad to hear that you have agreed to accept our offer of £200 for the Breughel drawing, and have arranged for a cheque to be sent direct to your banker.

I shall be in Rome at the beginning of September, and would very much like to come and call on you and see what drawings you have in stock – will you be there?

With kind regards,

Yours sincerely,

Christopher White

Colnaghi's sold my 'Breughel' almost immediately to a Mrs Carl Seldon who donated it to the Metropolitan Museum, New York. What Colnaghi's asked I do not know. I imagine that it was considerably more than the price they gave to me.

How I know anything at all about the subsequent history of my 'Breughel' is because, on a cold but sunny morning in January of 1973, I went to Villa Medici, where so many years before I had met my Caravaggio-esque lover, Gianni, to see an exhibition called '*Il Paesaggio nel Disegno del Cinquecento Europeo*' ('Landscape in European Drawings of Sixteenth-century Rome' – 20 November 1972-31 January 1973). It was a very important exhibition indeed, and among the 157 exhibits were drawings by such renowned artists as Raphael, Giorgione, Titian, Fra Bartolomeo, Hans Baldung Grien and Albrecht Altdorfer. The magnificent collection had been brought together by borrowing the treasures from the greatest museums and collections in the world: the Rijksmuseum, Amsterdam; the Staatliche Museen, Berlin; the Musée des Beaux Arts, Copenhagen; the Uffizi, Florence; the British Museum, London; the Metropolitan Museum, New York; the Louvre, Paris; and the Boymans Museum, Rotterdam; all contributed their finest examples of sixteenth-century landscape drawings. It was a wonderful experience to see so many master drawings shown in such a beautiful setting, and my own pleasure was not a little enhanced when I came across a wall of drawings arranged around my 'Breughel', which acted as a centre-piece. When I looked my handiwork up in the catalogue I read the following (my translation).

Jan Breughel, the Elder
Brussels, 1561–Antwerp, 1625

118. THE TEMPLES OF VENUS AND DIANA AT BAIAE. Pen and brown ink, with brown and blue washes.
H.O, 262; W.O, 194. Inscribed in pen to the left: T. Diana; and at top centre T. Venere.
Prov: acquired in 1965; the gift of Mrs Carl Seldon.
Inv. 65209
Bibl.: Cat. Exh. Florence, 1966, p. 33, no 18.
Exh.: New York, 1970, n.2

The dates attached by Jan Breughel to the drawings during his sojourn of several years in Italy allow us to fix the time of his stays in his major ports of call. In 1590 he was in Naples, from 1592 to 1595 in Rome, and later in 1595 in Milan where he entered the service of Cardinal Federico Borromeo. The landscape shown here is not recorded in the study of M. Winner of the artist's drawings (*Zeich-nungen der Aeltern Jan Breughel*, in 'Jahrbuch der Berliner Museen', II, 1961, pp. 190-241); but was added in 1966, by C. van Hasselt and A. Blanket, to the list of drawings of the Italian period (Cat. Exh. Florence, 1966, p. 33). In the foreground stands the temple of Venus and in the distance to the left, the temple of Diana at Baiae, near Naples, in the state of ruin in which they were to be found at the end of the sixteenth century. E. Haverkamp Begeman does not exclude the possibility that the drawing could be by the son, Jan Breughel the Younger, who visited Italy in 1622; however, the sureness of the cal-ligraphy and the vigour of the style of this study links it more closely with the well known series of ancient monuments by Jan Breughel the Elder.

New York, Metropolitan Museum of Art, Department of Drawings.

It is, of course, scarcely surprising that the 'Breughel' was not in-cluded in M. Winner's learned paper of 1961 – it did not exist! The 'Breughel' was the first of my many transactions with Christopher White who was then in the process of taking over the reins from Byam Shaw as Colnaghi's drawing expert. He had formerly been on the staff of the British Museum and had a distinguished track record.

When Christopher turned up in Rome in September I had been busily preparing for his visit. Knowing that he was an authority on Dutch, German and Flemish drawings I created among other things for his perusal a design for a frontispiece in the manner of Rubens. I later had the satisfaction of seeing this discovery on his own wall. He had clearly liked it so much he had kept it for his personal collection. It was about this time that I made the drawing in the manner of 'Mantegna' (Fig. 55). It is a carefully thought out composition showing the *Lamentation of the Three Marys over the Body of the Dead Christ*. As I could not expect the experts to be so rash as to attribute a newly discovered sheet to Mantegna himself, I did not follow his style exactly but aimed at making the study suffi-ciently Mantegnaesque to be attributed to the school or circle of the great artist. I enjoyed making the 'Mantegna' and took a great deal of trouble over it. It is not a copy, nor a patchwork of pieces taken here and there from Mantegna's work but an original work, the main purpose of which was to analyse the artist's drawing style. When I had completed it in genuine old materials, I damaged it by cutting it to an irregular shape and gave it to Graham to restore.

Fig. 55: 'School of Mantegna', *The Lamentation of the Three Marys*, 1965, pen and brown ink (sold to Colnaghi's *c*. 1967)

Being rather pleased with the result it was signed on the left-hand side with my initials. The collectors' marks were added together with an inscription 'Andreus Mantegna' and an appointment with Colnaghi's was arranged. To put myself in the right mood to play the part of the successful dealer I flew to London first class, where as usual I stayed with Anthony and his friend John in Portman Square. Drawings from the fifteenth century of any kind are rare, and important drawings from the period excessively so. So I knew that the discovery of an imposing composition such as my lamentation scene, even if judged to be the work of a follower of Mantegna (which of course it is) would arouse some interest. I was not, however, prepared for the kind of reception it got at Colnaghi's.

As I have mentioned elsewhere, I do not approve of rushing experts into a hasty decision and as was my custom, I left the drawing with the firm for a few days for inspection. When I returned with expectations of either picking up my 'Mantegna' or a substantial cheque I was met not by one expert, but by three. There in the upstairs library and showroom of Colnaghi's were Christopher White, James Byam Shaw and John Baskett, all directors of the firm. A trio of experienced experts and dealers to whom the handling of important works of art was a matter of course, but I could tell that they were in their British way particularly excited about this acquisition. They tried to hide their enthusiasm by discussing the damaged condition, and the over-optimistic inscription, but as the Italians say, '*Chi disprezza compra*' (who criticises buys), and it was not long before I left them with smiles on their faces and a four-figure cheque in my pocket. No doubt they *now* claim that they always had their doubts about the Mantegna, but writing out a cheque for it seems to me a curious way of having expressed them.

Again I would like to invite the reader to play a little game of connoisseurship. Experts tell us that the forger invariably betrays himself by some personal mannerism which gives to all of his work a certain stamp, so that his various works purporting to be by different artists and from different periods all have a family likeness. This being the case, my 'School of Mantegna' in the manner of a fifteenth-century master, must bear an uncanny resemblance to my 'Corot', my 'Breughel', my 'Pinelli' and every other 'Old Master' I have ever made. With this in mind, look again at my copy of the Corot (Fig. 48) with which you are already familiar and compare it with my 'School of Mantegna'. Can you see the similarity? You can? Well done! You possess just the kind of imagination that will get you places in the museum world!

So far I had sold my new Old Masters to or through a very limited number of people, Colnaghi's, Christie's and Sotheby's being the chief ones. A select group perhaps, but restricted nevertheless. So I started to look about for other outlets. On principle I could only deal with the best dealers and experts, and the field was narrow. There was only one dealer who had a stock of Old Master drawings approaching that of Colnaghi's in London and that was Hans Calmann of Bruton Place. I have heard Hans described as 'overbearingly autocratic', and maybe he was, but he had an eye for quality and in spite or perhaps because of his arrogant faith in his own judgment, some of the very best Old Masters on the market passed through his hands. Having studied Hans' character from a distance, that is watching his behaviour in the sales rooms, and listening to stories about him from people who had had dealings with him, such as Anthony, I came to the conclusion that he was a man who enjoyed the thrill of the chase. To have a work of art served up to him already vetted by experts (for whom, by the way, he had a healthy disrespect) was nowhere near as interesting to him as the making of a discovery. He had endless tales of how he had discovered, shall we say, a Rubens in a country sale catalogued as an Etty, or recognised a Greek bronze of the head of a youth in spite of its having been fitted on to a Victorian bust, and so on. Knowing this about Hans I decided not to approach him, but let him discover me. If I was one of his discoveries I felt I would start our relationship with a great psychological advantage. So I left a trail for him to follow which led to Piazza Paganica.

Hans occasionally came to Rome on the look-out for fine drawings, and when he did so he usually went to see what my old friend Edoardo had in stock. Learning through the grapevine when Hans was expected, I left a folder of not very exciting drawings for Edoardo to show him. Among them, as if it were there by chance, I put a photograph of the 'Mantegna' that I had sold to Colnaghi. On the back of the photo I wrote: Collection, Pannini Galleries Ltd., Piazza Paganica 13. 'So that's where Colnaghi's got that remarkably fine *quattrocento* drawing from,' thought Hans. 'I must look these people up, perhaps they have something else of museum quality.' And so it was that one sweltering afternoon I opened my door to a panting and sweating Hans, who had, in spite of his sixty-

Fig. 56: *Hans Calmann*, 1972, pencil. Preparatory study
for the bronze on p. 331 (Collection of the artist)

Fig. 57: 'Jan Spaekert', *Biblical Scene*, 1967, pen
and wash (sold to Hans Calmann; turned up
in an advertisement in *The Burlington Magazine*,
November 1969)

odd years, taken the ninety-nine steps without a pause. He was a
Jew and an impressive man, well over six feet tall, with a big
hooked nose and large protruding ears (Fig. 56). Although he was
out of breath he never stopped talking. What he was saying was,
however, not easy to grasp because added to the irregular breathing was a strong German accent struggling with what was intended
at first to be Italian. His heavy-lidded eyes darted everywhere as he
made a professional appraisal of what everything around him was
worth.

I phoned down to our local bar in Largo Argentina, and in a few
minutes, a remarkably pimply youth in a white jacket, with a tray
of cold drinks precariously balanced on one hand held high above
his head, had bounded up the stairs as easily as he might have

Fig. 58: 'Peter Paul Rubens', *The Entombment*, 1967, pen and wash (sold to Hans Calmann)

moved on level ground. No matter how many times a day this boy was summoned he never seemed to tire. Hans sipped iced tea, I drank beer, and together we looked through the stock of Pannini Galleries Ltd. It was a very mixed bag. Not all the drawings were fakes, only the more interesting ones; and as Hans had a sure eye for quality he had soon sorted out a pile of my work. While he was doing so he had confidently and almost confidentially told me what every single drawing was, as though I had never seen it or, for that matter, any other drawing in my life before and had better learn something about my stock before the next customer came, in case they took advantage of my ignorance.

One of the drawings I sold to Hans on his first visit to Piazza Paganica later turned up in a dealer's advertisement in *The Burlington Magazine* of November 1969. I mention this drawing (Fig. 57) not for any artistic merit it may have, but because its history is a clear example of a dealer's desire to find a name for an unattributed work at all costs. In this case the dealer chose the name of Jan Spaekert, an artist I have not heard of before or since. I had no particular painter in mind when I made the drawing. All I had aimed at was an Italianate drawing from the seventeenth century by a northern artist acquainted with the work of Michelangelo. Well, I suppose if Jan Spaekert ever existed he may fit the bill, but it is rather odd that I should have made a drawing in the manner of an artist totally unknown to me. The first drawing of any real importance that I sold to Hans was a drawing of *The Entombment* (Fig. 58) which, after removing the misleading inscription 'Van Dyck fecit', he ascribed to Rubens. This was soon followed by many others and over the next decade Hans was to buy heavily from me but that is a story for another chapter.

Members of the British and American art world like Anthony Blunt, Ellis Waterhouse, Tony Clark, and John Maxon, Director of the Chicago Institute, were all regular visitors to Piazza Paganica, and all but John Maxon were buyers not only of 'Old Masters' but also of my own work. In 1965, I produced a book called *Lottatori Americani* (Fig. 59), containing twenty-four original etchings on the theme of American style, catch-as-catch-can, wrestling. Anthony, Ellis and Tony all bought copies. Moreover, Anthony some years later showed his volume to Seymour Slive, the Director of the Fogg Art Museum, Harvard University, who also purchased a copy, and on receipt, sent to Anthony the following letter of appreciation, which Anthony forwarded to me:

Fogg Art Museum
Harvard University, Cambridge, Massachusetts 02138
28 February 1972

Dear Sir Anthony,

Eric Hebborn's Lottatori Americani arrived in perfect order, and my wife and I want to thank you for procuring a copy of it for us. The etchings make a magnificent book. The more we look, the more we find and the more pleasure we receive. I can't make that statement about the work of many contemporary artists. There is hope! I would be grateful if you would tell Mr Hebborn he has put us deeply in his debt.

With all good wishes,
Seymour Slive

Tony Clark had secured a copy of my book for the Minneapolis Institute of Arts, and in their *Bulletin* Vol. LV. 1966, p.74, is to be found the following entry:

ERIC HEBBORN
American, 20th century
Group of twenty-four bound etchings,
Lottatori Americani
Gift of The Henfield Foundation, 13862-13885.

Fig. 59: *Wrestlers*, 1965, line and wash. This is a
study for one of the etchings in *Lottatori
Americani* (Collection of the artist)

It will be noticed that even when cataloguing perfectly genuine
works, mistakes can happen and I have changed nationality. On
the same page of the *Bulletin* is the name of David Hockney, but
here the editor has made no mistake and David is correctly stated
to be English. This situation is ironic, for if any British artist
deserves to be an honorary American it is certainly not myself, but
David. I had known David in London. He was a close friend of
Graham and Janet, with whom he had been a fellow student at the
Royal College, and had on occasion visited our place in Packington
Street. I admired him, not only as an artist, but as a person. One of
the qualities I admired was that he knew what he wanted. Having
decided, for instance, that the source of his inspiration was
America, unlike some of the Rome Scholars I had met, he did not
waste his or anybody else's time by applying for a scholarship he

had no use for. On the contrary, with the same refreshing straight-forwardness which is the hallmark of his work, he simply packed his bags and flew to the States. It was one of David's American friends who unwittingly led me to make or rather, remake a Hockney.

The American's name was Ferrill. On the strength of being a friend of David he had got to know Graham, Janet and myself and joined us for several months in Piazza Paganica. On his bedroom wall was a drawing given to him by our mutual friend. Hockney drawings were at the time only beginning to rise in price and Ferrill, apparently placing little value on it, had unceremoniously attached the unframed drawing with a thumb tack.

So little did Ferrill appear to value David's gift that when he went away he left the Hockney behind. But as it turned out he cared for the drawing more than we imagined, for some two years later when Hockneys were worth a small fortune, he wrote to remind us that he had left in our safe-keeping his most treasured possession, and if any harm had come to it we would pay dearly for our neglect. The Hockney was still in its place, but now the yellowed, flyblown sheet was in tatters. Time, which had increased its value with one hand, had destroyed its condition with the other. What was to be done? Doubtless the astute reader will already have guessed. The only difficult thing about the operation was matching the coloured pencils or crayons David had used. I had none in my studio. The Old Masters didn't use such bright and cheerful colours, but modern school children do, and eventually I found just what I wanted in a tobacconist who also stocked school supplies. But I did not destroy the battered original, and somewhere in the world are two Hockneys, identical save for their condition.

Here are some tantalisingly brief entries in an old memorandum made while I was in London on business from 27 April until 15 June 1966:

```
April 27  Fiumicino 11.45
May   3   Lunch Christopher White, Chez Victor, 1 o'clock
May  11   Christopher Powney (a dealer in Old Master drawings)
May  12   Marie and Louis, 6 at the shop
May  20   Craddock & Barnard (dealers in prints)
May  26   Phone Colnaghi
May  27   Marie, the flat 8.30
June  2   O'Nians (dealers in Old Master paintings and drawings)
          Christie's, see Brian Sewell
June  8   Lunch Joe, Fortnums 12.30
June 13   Supper Brian Sewell, meet 7.30
June 15   Airport
```

On Tuesday, 18 April 1967, Christie's sold on my behalf in their sale of Important Drawings by Old Masters a drawing which I had made in the German manner of the sixteenth century. As a great number of old German and Swiss drawings bear imitations of Dürer's well-known monogram, I put it on my production as well. The drawing was catalogued as follows:

Circle Of Hans Von Kulmbach
81. *A Soldier Holding a Standard*, seen from behind, with a bay in the distance – bears Dürer's monogram – pen and brown ink – 11⅜in. by 8¼in.

Collection: Nathaniel Hone (L.2.793)

Only two days after the sale of the Hans Von Kulmbach-type drawing at Christie's on 20 April 1967, Sotheby's sold a drawing of mine that was to cause themselves, Colnaghi's, and the Pierpont Morgan Library of New York considerable embarrassment. The drawing represents *A Pageboy with a Lance* (Fig. 60) and was said by Sotheby's experts and consultants, notably Richard Day and Philip Pouncey, to be by Francesco del Cossa, a Ferrarese painter, first mentioned as an artist in 1456, and who died in Bologna in 1477 or 1478. The drawing was illustrated in Sotheby's catalogue, and Cossa's name given in full. As it was then the custom to illustrate only the most important drawings in a sale and we have noted elsewhere, that by giving Cossa's name in full the auctioneers were convinced that the drawing was really and truly by that artist, it is clear Sotheby's were proud of their 'Cossa'. In fact, when writing to me to suggest a reserve of £1,000, Mr Day told me that 'although not the most valuable drawing in the sale' (there was an important Castiglione put in by Sir Kenneth Clark), 'it is by far the most attractive'. The attribution of the drawing to Cossa was supported by its similarity to a drawing tentatively given to be by that artist in the British Museum (1946-7-13-212), (Fig. 61). The British Museum drawing was known to me from the catalogue of the fourteenth- and fifteenth-century *Italian Drawings*, compiled by A. E. Popham and Philip Pouncey, published by the Trustees in 1950.

Putting my Pierpont Morgan 'Cossa' side by side with the British Museum Cossa, from which, to a large extent, it derives, we may note a number of differences. We have the same boy, in the same costume, but there is no question of one being copied from the other. In the first place the two poses are entirely different. The British Museum drawing shows the attractive young model with

Fig. 60: *A Pageboy with a Lance*, 1967, pen and ink (sold
by Sotheby's, 1967; now in the Pierpont Morgan
Library)

Fig. 61: Attributed to Francesco del Cossa, *A Pageboy
Holding a Staff* (*fl.* 1456-77), pen and brown ink with
traces of red chalk near the lower margin. (This
drawing in the British Museum was the inspiration for
Fig. 60)

his heels together, the weight mostly taken by his left leg, and looking down to our right. In contrast, the Pierpont Morgan drawing
presents the youth with his feet apart, the weight on his right leg,
and his head tilted upwards to the viewer's left. But the differences
do not end there, for there are also important divergences in style.
The British Museum Cossa is more delicate in touch; a finer line is
used and there are fewer signs of the draughtsman's having made
revisions. Naturally, those who assume that art derived from
former art is almost by definition inferior to its prototype will judge
every deviation I have made from the British Museum Cossa as a
failing on my part, but this is not necessarily the case. Certainly my
drawing lacks some of the virtues of the British Museum sheet, but
then the British Museum sheet lacks some of the qualities of my
effort. Take for instance the boy's stance; the *quattrocento* artist has
given to the pose a gentle, reflective quality. The lad is quite un-
selfconscious, his attention focused on what it is he is taking from
the purse suspended from his belt. In my version, on the other
hand, the young man is striking an attitude. He is posing and getting a little bit tired of it. One can imagine him saying to the artist:
'Haven't you finished yet? Can't I go and join my mates?' The first
is full of exquisite poetry, the second speaks of the pent-up vitality
of a youth, who, like Herrick of Maldon, would rather be running
wild than dressed up in the finery of a page at court. In short, the
two drawings are saying different things, and to denigrate my effort
because it is not putting forward the same notion as the British
Museum sheet is to criticise it for what it is not, instead of appreciating it for what it is. As we all know, comparisons are odious and
even if the Pierpont Morgan *Page Boy* is not quite as good as the
British Museum's, the fact that it is not pure gold does not make it
ipso facto total dross.

Among other differences of style I have alluded to above, we may
note that my drawing has more *pentimenti* (changes of mind) than
the older drawing. This is especially noticeable in the figure's right
hand and right thigh. This is because I used a different method.
Close to the lower edge of the British Museum drawing are traces of
red chalk. These in all probability are all that remains of a preparatory underdrawing in which the draughtsman tried out his
idea. When he was satisfied he drew the ink lines with certainty on
top, thus eliminating any need for further revision. The Pierpont
Morgan drawing was drawn directly in ink, thus the alterations
show. The ink used was not made up from an old recipe, as I had
done with the Met's 'Breughel' and was to be my regular practice
in my mature years as a faker, but was simply Pelican sepia ink

bought off the shelf in an art store. Unfortunately, it had an uncon-vincing shine to it and this gave rise to a little scraping down with a razor blade – a ruse that was mentioned by the curator of the Pierpont Morgan Library, Miss Felice Staenfle, who after the drawing had been in the Pierpont Morgan Library for well over a decade was quoted as saying '. . . the manner in which the ink had aged began to look more like the careful work of a razor blade than the passage of time'.

In fact I had made a far worse mistake in regard to my *Page Boy* than using modern ink and scraping it down with a razor – a gross mistake which I shall speak of in another chapter when discussing some of my shortcomings as an apprentice forger. My own mis-takes, however, were as nothing compared to those of the experts. For instance, how on earth could Philip Pouncey (who, as Assistant Keeper of the department of prints and drawings in the British Museum, had with A. E. Popham catalogued the Museum's Cossa) have agreed to cataloguing the Pierpont Morgan drawing in Sotheby's sale as Francesco del Cossa in full, when the entry for the Museum's catalogue only very cautiously attributes the British Museum drawing to that artist: 'In the Fenwick Catalogue tenta-tively ascribed to Foppa, this drawing appears rather to be Ferrarese. The structure of the face and in particular the slightly protruding eyelids call to mind Cossa's types. The quality is per-haps just good enough to allow of its being placed under his name. If not by Cossa it might be an early work by Roberti.'

Is it logical to state that a work of art is definitely by a certain artist on the basis of its resemblance to a work which is only pos-sibly by that artist? Apparently Mr Pouncey thinks it is.

My own carelessness can to some extent be explained, but not excused, by the fact that I did not foresee that my 'Cossa' would ex-cite the interest that it did. For me it was only one of a large num-ber of essays in the manner of the Old Masters that I was making in preparation for a full-scale analysis of the art of drawing seen as an ancient and alas almost dead language, the grammar of which had remained largely unchanged since man's appearance on the earth. Should any of my essays fool the experts, I merely took it as proof that I had done my homework, and if by so doing I had made some money it was always a welcome bonus. Once, however, I had made a drawing, I no longer took it very seriously, and in the early days was extraordinarily careless about the ageing and creating prove-nances and so on. For this reason the two collectors' marks on my 'Cossa' are far from being perfect. This in spite of the fact that it is much much easier to fake a collector's mark than it is to fake a drawing; one merely has to take a photograph of an original and give it to a professional seal cutter, and that is that. But I was so cavalier about the whole matter that I would sometimes just draw collectors' marks freehand in watercolour just for the fun of it, and their sheer decorative value. That the Richardson and Reynolds marks on the Cossa were fake was noticed almost immediately. Hans, for example, mentioned it to me, only shortly after the sale, little suspecting that I knew already. So it really is surprising that from Sotheby's the *Page Boy* went to Colnaghi's for £1,700, and from them, for a larger, but undisclosed amount, to the Pierpont Morgan Library where for thirteen years it was to remain unquestioned.

On 26 March 1968, Christie's held a sale of Important Drawings by Old Masters. Lots 139 and 140, a Pontormo and a Castiglione, were two of my efforts which Graham had consigned to two of Christie's representatives in Rome. One of them, Luisa Vertova, had assisted Bernard Berenson in the production of his *Drawings of Florentine Painters*, and although the Pontormo was shown to a number of other experts, including Anthony Blunt, it was probably she who catalogued Lot 139 (Fig. 62). At the risk of being tedious, I give the lengthy catalogue entry in full. First because it gives the reader a description of the drawing, and second because it shows

Fig. 62: 'Jacopo Carrucci detto il Pontormo', detail of *A sheet of studies*, 1968, red and black chalk (sold through Christie's, 26 March 1968)

that the diligent Vertova, in discovering my sources, must have done her homework. It may also serve as an indication of how much research is sometimes involved in the making of what may appear to the layman as little more than a hasty scribble.

THE PROPERTY OF A GENTLEMAN
139. JACOPO CARRUCCI, IL PONTORMO
A Sheet of Studies: left above, two studies of a boy's head tilted backwards; centre, study for a Madonna, half length, seated holding the infant Christ; nude, his right arm resting on her left shoulder; right, a nude male figure, three-quarter length, turned to the right, his arm extended and his head turned facing the spectator – red chalk (the study of the Madonna and Child is in black chalk) – 18¼in. by 13½in.
Collection: Conte di Bardi (L.336)
This hitherto unpublished drawing is closely linked with the genesis of Pontormo's 'Madonna and Child with Saints Joseph, John the Evangelist, Francis, James, and John the Baptist', commissioned according to Vasari (Vol. VI, p. 258) by Francesco Pucci (d.1518) for the family chapel in San Michele Visdomini, Florence. The larger study of a boy's head appears to be a preliminary idea for the head of the infant John, the smaller an indication of the placing of his arm and shoulder. The larger male nude repeats, more dramatically, the attitude of the studies from the Corsini sketch-book which Rearck, *The Drawings of Pontormo* 1964, Nos. 53-56, connects with the *putti* holding up the curtain over the Madonna and Child. The sketch for a Madonna and Child could be a first idea for the group in this altarpiece, although it is more closely connected with a Madonna with Infant Saint John now in the Paggio Collection at Varramista, near Florence.

For all the blurb, and the then high price of 1,400 guineas the 'Pontormo' is not one of my happiest performances. In later years I was to do far better work in the style of this artist, but to repeat the Chinese sage: 'A journey of a thousand miles starts with the first step'. Lot 140 is a far better drawing; this time in the style of Castiglione (Fig. 63). It was catalogued as follows:

140. GIOVANNI BENEDETTO CASTIGLIONE
140. A Young Oriental and His Horse – brush and red-brown wash – 13in. by 8¾in.
Compare the drawing at Windsor, executed in pen and brown ink, brown wash (illustrated in Blunt, *The Drawings of G.B. Castiglione and Stefano della Bella ... at Windsor Castle*, 1954, No. 45, plate 19). This has additional figures on the right – a man with a lamp, possibly Diogenes, addressing the Oriental – and shows the horse facing the spectator.

Castiglione is an artist that I have studied very closely indeed. Although his is not a name known to everyone, as say Picasso's is, he is one of the great innovators of drawing style and technique. His influence on French eighteenth-century art was profound. Fragonard's drawings, for instance, are, in terms of handling, extremely close to the Italian's, and Castiglione's invention of soft ground etching and use of the monotype have indirectly affected the work of hosts of nineteenth- and twentieth-century artists. In addition to the thirty-seven 'Castigliones' which are still undetected in museums and important private collections throughout the world, I have produced nine, such as Christie's *A Young Oriental and His Horse* whose authenticity is being questioned. The problem involved in imitating the Genovese artist, stems from two things: he is a great virtuoso, hence any hesitancy will at once betray the follower, and, being fond of experiment, his drawing materials are often unusual and difficult to match. It was this last point which caused me the most trouble. At the time of making Christie's 'Castiglione' I knew the artist's work only in reproduction. My first introduction was through Anthony Blunt's catalogue of the Castigliones at Windsor. In that volume I noticed that a number of the most beautiful works were drawn with brush, and with what Anthony described as 'red' oil paint, used alone or in combination with 'green' oil paint with an occasional touch of blue. If one doesn't want to make one's 'Castigliones' look as if they were made yesterday, the technique of using oil paint on paper poses the problem of what to do with the oil which spreads out into the paper on either side of the line, no trace of which can be seen in the authentic Castigliones. The answer to this is relatively simple – one drains the oil out of the paint by spreading it on blotting paper before using it, and employs a volatile medium in its place. Petrol would probably be the ideal substance, but as I cannot abide the stench of the stuff, I used the purest of turpentines, an extract from the pine tree. But pleasant as the smell of turpentine is, it has the disadvantage from the faker's point of view of attaching itself to newly applied paint for quite a long time, and even the most trusting of experts might grow suspicious of a drawing, supposedly dating from the seventeenth century, which still smelt of it. After a number of experiments I found that the quickest way of ridding my 'Castigliones' of the unwanted aroma was to wash them in detergent and hang them to dry in the open air – pegged out on a clothes line among the more conventional washing of my neighbours. As for the 'red', in my first efforts I used burnt Siena, but this I later discovered was really rather too red, or what we painters call too

Fig. 63: 'Giovanni Benedetto Castiglione', *A Young Oriental and His Horse*, 1968, brush and red-brown wash (sold by Christie's, 26 March 1968 for 1,400 guineas)

warm, but as I had not seen any originals, or even coloured re-productions of Castiglione's drawings, I was working in the dark and this excessive redness made it all too easy for the experts to sort out eventually my early experimental Castigliones. I soon dis-covered that Castiglione's 'red' was more closely matched with burnt umber, and his 'green' with raw umber, and the so-called redness and greenness of the colours was the result of contrasting the warm and cool earth colours in such a way as to enhance and intensify their relative chromatic value, that is, making the burnt umber appear relatively red and the raw umber relatively green.

But whatever its demerits, my early *Young Oriental with His Horse* was considered to be a fine drawing and fetched, like the Pontormo, over 1,000 guineas. In discussing the above two drawings in later years, journalists quoted Christie's as having said that they had consulted Anthony Bunt, and it was he who had 'authenticated' them. In defence of Anthony, Brian Sewell stepped forward and said that all Anthony had done was to give some rather general and vague advice to Christie's in-house expert: 'All I think is that he has said, "If this drawing is all right you had better look in the direction of so and so . . . " Much as I approve of Brian's loyalty to our old friend, now that Anthony is dead, I can see no reason for hiding the truth. Anthony was definitely responsible for the Castiglione attribution. I know this because he had admired it on my wall in Piazza Paganica saying it was his favourite kind of Castiglione, even going so far as to offer to buy it. Moreover, I was staying with Anthony when the drawing was with Christie's and he told me that he had vetted it for the auctioneers but that there had been considerable discussion as to the authenticity of the Pontormo. The experts in the field were divided, but he did not, however, confide in me to which camp he himself belonged. As quoted in the *Sunday Telegraph*, Brian also alludes to these doubts, but goes too far when he says: 'Ever since the two drawings came up, there was not a dealer in London who was convinced they were right – either of them.' Surely if no dealer at all had believed in the drawings, they would not have fetched the high prices they did. Furthermore, if Christie's had doubted even for a moment that the Castiglione was not authentic, they most certainly would not have chosen it for inclusion in the *Christie's Review of the Year 1967-68*(p.49). Christie's annual *Review* is a handsome book recording the choicest items that have been sold in their rooms during the twelve months prior to its publication. That the auctioneers had selected my Castiglione out of the hundreds of Old Master drawings that they must have sold in the year 1967-68, for the honour of a place in this volume is proof enough of the esteem in which the drawing was generally held.

Home life in Piazza Paganica was becoming strained. Graham and I were managing to irritate each other so often and over so little, that it was a relief to be out of each other's company. Much of Graham's initial irritability was, we discovered later, due to the onset of hepatitis. Both he and Janet went down with this condition. Fortunately, being young and fit, they quickly responded to the treatment prescribed by the doctor, a lady called Doctor Jeans. Even so they were in delicate health for months. But in spite of being unwell, Graham, through the good offices of Eugene, was offered a walk-on part in a new Fellini film. He was so thrilled that no advice from Doctor Jeans could keep him at home. Happily, working in the film turned out to be good therapy, and he was soon his old self again. Now it was my turn to be ill. A bout of pneumonia. After pumping me full of antibiotics, Doctor Jeans said that what I needed on recovery was to get away for a while from Rome's

Fig. 64: *In the Doria Pamphili Park*, 1966, oil on canvas (Collection of the artist)

centre which was traditionally unhealthy. It was a delightful prescription which as soon as I was strong enough caused me to take my paints and go landscape painting in the park of the Doria Pamphili family on the Janiculum. What a park it was! I say was because since it became public, in the seventies, neglect and vandalism have robbed it of much of its former magic. When I first knew it, the gardens had to my eye just that right balance between art and nature, the formal and the informal, the classic and the romantic to attract the artist. This was to some extent due to the marriage of two kinds of garden design. Originally, it was laid out in the manner of formal Italian gardens and then converted to the English landscape style. How often I walked round its nearly six-mile circumference admiring its villas, a triumphal arch, a great lake, a valley in which deer still ran, a baroque fountain (one of Bernini's) and what is known as the 'theatre'.

One day I was painting a view of the 'theatre' (Fig. 64) when I was interrupted by the voice of a woman coming from behind me. 'Sheep shit! That's what we're living in, Willy, sheep shit!' (The Pamphilis, to whom the park still belonged, had flocks of sheep roaming the grounds as a convenient way of keeping the grass down.) Then, as the owner of the voice came nearer she looked over my shoulder at my painting and said, 'I say, that's jolly good. Did you know that Corot painted a picture from this very spot, in pre-cisely the same afternoon light when the mellow tones show to such advantage? Where else would one find a typically Baroque subject providing inspiration for an artist of the Romantic School? Willy! Willy! Now please be a good dog, and come here!' The pitch to which she raised her voice to call her dog seemed to have put a strain on her heart, and to my alarm she collapsed at my feet where she lay motionless, her eyes shut. I'm not at all good in cases of emergency, but I don't as a rule panic, so I tried to remember what one is supposed to do in such cases, and vaguely recalling some-thing about making sure that any very tight clothing around the neck, the chest or the waist is loosened and turning the patient on their side I was about to attend to these matters, when the lady opened one eye, and whispered: 'Not to worry, I'm only play acting. It's Willy, you know, if he thinks his meal ticket is dead he suddenly becomes all concerned, and runs back at once.' And sure enough Willy was soon licking his mistress's face in the most solicitous way.

Getting to her feet the lady introduced herself as Babs Johnson. She's known to the world by her pen name, Georgina Masson, the author of *Italian Villas and Palaces*, *Italian Gardens*, a biography of

Queen Christina, and her best-known work, on which she was working when I met her, *The Companion Guide to Rome*. Babs lived in the park in a converted stable which she rented from the Pamphilis. She had decorated it charmingly. Although by no means a rich woman, she had excellent taste and I seem to remember her little home was once the subject of an article in *House & Garden*, illustrated with photographs taken by herself. She liked to entertain, and was a great, if unusual, snob. She used to say that she only frequented two types of people – the titled and the talented. And this claim was largely true. She was well acquainted with the Roman aristocracy, and her parties, to which I had the honour of being invited, were as well peppered with *principi* and *principesse* as they were with distinguished scholars and intellectuals. One of her regular guests who had the distinction of being both titled and talented was King Gustav of Sweden, whom I had met at the British School.

The king's talent and passion was for archaeology, and it was this burning interest that led him to spend so much time in Rome. It was clear from his cheerful and totally relaxed manner that His Majesty loved the informal evenings he spent in Babs' modest home, surrounded by people with the same or similar interests on an equal footing. Babs usually gave a buffet supper and the king would serve himself, and balance his plate like everybody else. When he spoke of archaeological matters he spoke as a scholar. He was no dilettante and had he not been a king he could very well have made a living out of his interest. There was something very special about Babs. I was never quite able to define it, but it had something to do with hating humbug and saying things as they are. I remember, for example, her presenting the Principessa Doria Pamphili to King Gustav with, 'May I introduce my landlady?'

Soon the Principessa and her English husband, Frank Pogson, were to be my landlords as well. This was thanks to a charming young couple called Reynolds. The husband, Michael, was a Rome Scholar who had grown to love Rome and was trying as hard as he could to make a living there, and so put off his return to England. The couple had rented a small flat in the gate house of the park, where Graham and I would sometimes visit them. When at the end of August 1965 the impossibility of making ends meet drove the Reynolds back to England, I took over their place as a studio at a rent of 40,000 lira a month. The gate house of the Doria Pamphili park stands at the busy road fork where Via San Pancrazio and Via Aurelia Antica meet. The din of the traffic was tremendous, and had it not been for the Pamphili grounds extending behind it, it would not have been a pleasant place, but as it was, the beauty of its setting making up for any amount of din. My studio was on the first floor. Above me lived a Russian called Tolstoy, who claimed to be related to the renowned novelist. He worked as a translator at FAO (Food and Agriculture Organisation of the United Nations). His English and Italian were flawless, with not the slightest trace of a foreign accent, and apparently he spoke seven other languages with equal mastery. We would occasionally meet on the narrow staircase and pass the time of day. There was, however, something about him which made me uneasy – he seemed to me unreal, and what he had to say contrived. A little after I had moved in, he invited me up to his place for a drink. His small two-roomed flat replicated my own on the floor below, but his was crammed as full as could be with antiques and antiquities, some real, some not. He showed me a row of Etruscan vases, pointing out that he had chosen them for their height so that their rims formed a line sloping down at regular intervals. It was perfectly obvious to me that they were all fakes but he apparently did not know this, and thinking it rude to tell him, I merely said that I found it extraordinary that one could have any choice of size in ancient pots, at which he told me that he bought exclusively from a *tombarolo*, a professional grave-robber who knew what Tolstoy was looking for and regularly dug up just what he wanted. This sounded to me unbelievably naïve for a man of his intelligence and I began to suspect that Tolstoy was playing games with me. He was really trying to test my knowledge expecting me to say something like 'Come off it; these are fakes'. But why?

As I like to work in daylight, it was unusual for me to linger in my studio after dark, but one evening I did and was surprised to note that a light was flashing on and off in Tolstoy's bathroom window at intervals, suggesting morse code. Looking across the Aurelia Antica from the gate house I could see the lights of the Russian Embassy and no doubt if Tolstoy was flashing a message it could easily be seen from there. But why use a flash light when one has a telephone? Was it because Tolstoy's phone was being tapped? My upstairs neighbour was becoming more and more of a mystery man. I also had a telephone in my studio, and I wondered if perhaps that too had been tampered with. According to a spy thriller I read called *The Berlin Memorandum*, one can tell if a phone has been tapped because a moment after picking up the receiver one hears a click – and when I lifted my phone I did hear a click. Things were getting curious indeed.

Then the strangest thing of all happened. I was painting a picture, commissioned by a dealer, in the style of a great northern master, which I was anxious for nobody, not even Graham to see, when there was a knock on the door. Hurriedly covering my work with a canvas made especially for the purpose, I opened the door to Tolstoy who was carrying a portfolio. He explained that he had bought a series of old prints in a junk shop and as I knew something about engravings, perhaps I could tell him what they were. When he opened the portfolio I could hardly believe my eyes, for there was a complete set of an excessively rare series of engravings by Marcantonio Raimondi (1480-1534). These were the twenty licentious subjects Marcantonio had engraved after designs by Giulio Romano, illustrating lewd sonnets by Pietro Aretino and entitled *The Loves of the Gods*. Marcantonio was imprisoned for his share of the work, and the Pope ordered the destruction of the prints, which seems to have been efficiently carried out, and as far as I knew there was only one complete set in the whole world. According to Bartsch, *The Loves of the Gods* is so rare that at one time its very existence was doubted. He himself had seen only the first plate of the set of twenty (B231). Passavant, in his additions to Bartsch's catalogue of Old Master prints, describes the entire suite, and states that Mariette, the great French collector, had possessed a complete set, which he supposed to have entered the Bibliothèque Nationale, but he says, 'all searches have proved in vain'. Other than that, some fragments exist in the British Museum. Now here was Tolstoy calmly showing me a complete set in fine condition, which he claimed to have found in a junk shop. Holding each print up to the light I checked to see if it was on the right paper. It was. There was no doubt they were genuine. I told my neighbour what the prints were and expressed my amazement at his good fortune, but I knew instinctively that these rarities had not just turned up. They must have come from some great national collection and were on loan to Tolstoy for the purpose of putting my knowledge to the test, but again, why?

Tolstoy scarcely spoke to me after this incident, and very shortly left his apartment. When he went the click on my phone went with him. What was really going on I never found out for certain, but it is my suspicion that it had something to do with my friendship with Anthony. At the time, of course, I had not the slightest idea that Anthony had already confessed to being a Russian agent, and as I have never meddled in politics myself, I had no reason to suspect that I was worth investigating. It now seems to me possible that somebody somewhere, knowing of my connection with the Fourth Man, and wondering at the coincidence of my moving in below another agent (if that is what Tolstoy was), was checking my credentials. Was I really an artist and a dealer in antiques or had I been planted to watch their 'agent's' movements? It may be pure fantasy, but the clicking of the phone, the flashing of the light, Tolstoy's unreal behaviour, and his sudden access to the excessively rare prints were not.

The great pleasure that Graham and I got out of 'Pamphiliing' as Tony called our frequent outings to the great park on the Janiculum, made us think that perhaps we should, if only at weekends, get away from the hustle and bustle of Rome completely. This led us to rent a studio in the mountain village of Anticoli. The studio was large and light, but it was almost impossible to heat in the winter. Furthermore, being in the village it was not always as quiet as we could have wished, and it was not long before we began to look for another place. Normally, we took our meals in the trattoria where I had first eaten in Anticoli with Joe and the film star, Gulliver, run by Renzo and his wife Quirina. It was Renzo who told us that Villa San Filippo was for rent. Moreover, he had for many years been the gardener at the villa, and said that, if we were interested, he could arrange with the owner, Dottore Antonio Carboni, to have the keys, and show us the place. I have mentioned elsewhere how attractive I thought the villa was as seen at a distance, and a closer inspection only confirmed me in my view.

We took a steep stony footpath leading us first through an ancient olive grove and a vineyard. Beyond the vineyard was an outcrop of rocks covered with moss and shaded by bay trees. Set in the rocks was an old ironwork gate which Renzo unlocked and we found ourselves in an avenue of box that, by the height of its towering hedges, must have been well over a hundred years old. We later discovered they had been planted in the last century by the builder of the property, a grand-uncle of the present owner, Monsignor Loreto Carboni, who had been an overseer of the Vatican Gardens. The avenue ended in a sunny ramp and curving steps sweeping up to the high perched house from where we looked down on its terraced gardens. Now all was neglect, and yet one could see by the well established plants and their skilful arrangement, that this was a garden that had been tended with love and devotion for a very long time. Renzo pointed out with a gardener's pride, some of the features that he himself had created under the guidance of a Signor Macpherson and a Signor Lyons whom he referred to collectively as the 'Macapersons', both British. Apparently the villa had a long history of British tenants, all keen gardeners. There was a Lady Spicer, who lived there for many years before the war, and then immediately after the war an English colonel took over the place, then came the 'Macapersons', who had only two years before left the villa and bought a magnificent property in Tuscany. The interior of the villa was, although of no great distinction, straightforwardly rustic with great beamed ceilings, brick floors, large fireplaces and beautiful old doors with their original handmade fittings. Behind the house, and beyond a circular *giardino segreto*, of which, before the time of Lady Spicer, Pirandello had himself painted a picture, was what made the place for me an absolute must. It was a spacious, well-lit artist's studio. Graham was as taken by the charm of the place as I was, so I went at once with Renzo to sign an agreement with Dottore Carboni.

Carboni was an elderly military man, an army doctor. He was a stickler about money matters, and made no secret of the fact. 'Signor Eri,' he said, '*Lei può pagare il deposito, ora, o subito, o immediatamente come vuole Lei.*' (You may pay your deposit now, or at once, or immediately, just as you wish.) So it was that Pannini Galleries which had started life in 1963 in Packington Street in Islington, and had survived for four years in Rome was in the spring of 1968 transplanted to the fertile ground of Anticoli Corrado where it was to flourish for a further decade.

CHAPTER X

THE GOLDEN DECADE

'He also copied drawings of the old masters so perfectly that his
copies could not be distinguished from the originals, since he smoked
and tinted the paper to give it an appearance of age. He was often
able to keep the originals and return his copies in their stead.'

Vasari on Michelangelo.

In the summer of 1968, Anthony Quinn and Anna Magnani were
on location in Anticoli. The film was Stanley Kramer's *The Secret
of Santa Vittoria*, and was based on a novel by Robert Crichton of the
same title. Santa Vittoria is an Italian hill town described in the
book as:

> . . . one of those clusters of houses which can be seen from any main
> highway, a huddle of gray and white shapes pressed up against the
> side of a mountain as if they were sheep fearful of falling off it, which
> they sometimes do. Some are unreachable except by mule or on foot
> or by military vehicles, and the towns are as isolated on their
> mountains as any island in the sea.
>   The people have no tradition of outsiders and no procedures for
> handling them. They are not hostile, but they are suspicious and
> afraid of them. History has proved that to talk to strangers sooner or
> later leads to trouble or ends up costing money, and so history has
> rendered them incapable of telling truths to outsiders. They don't lie,
> but they never of their own will provide the truth. There are people in
> Santa Vittoria who are capable of denying knowledge of the town
> fountain when it can be heard bubbling behind their backs.

Anticoli and its people fitted this description so well that plus the
place's greater proximity to Rome it was preferred over the actual
Santa Vittoria as the location to shoot the film – a huge production
– and for three months Anticoli was given over to being a film set

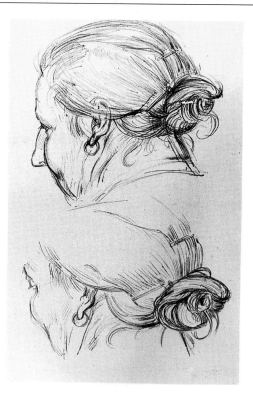

Fig. 65: *Sandrina the Cook*, 1975, pencil. This is
a study made for a large painting in the
church of Santa Vittoria in Anticoli (Collection
of the artist)

and many of the villagers to being extras. The film gave a boost to
the village economy, for in some way or another everybody made
money. Rooms, houses and flats were rented for exaggerated sums
to the film company's employees – the actors and the technicians.
The pay for participating in a single crowd scene was more than
some of the villagers earned in a month, and then there was com-
pensation money for removing one's television aerial (the film was
set in the forties) or car, or any other anachronism you might own.

Graham and I also made money out of the film. By now San
Filippo had been completely renovated, a central-heating system
installed, and the charming old place furnished with good antique
furniture, Persian carpets, and fine *objets d'art*. Renzo had been rein-
stated as the gardener and had restored the grounds to much of
their former well tended loveliness. In a sense the villa was Anticoli's Manor House. Certainly it was at the time the grandest house

in the district and we ourselves took to living in a style in keeping with our surroundings. In addition to a gardener, we had a cook (Fig. 65), a maid and a driver. The villa made such a good impression on the film's director, that Kramer at first thought of staying there himself, and we agreed to sublet it to him. In the event it was the author Robert Crichton who was actually to spend the summer in Villa San Filippo, for Kramer found the villa too far from the set – that is to say from the Piazza. Having worked so hard on getting our home into good shape, we decided to take advantage of the situation and sublet at ten times what we were paying Dottore Carboni in rent. The idea was to put the rent money towards a luxurious holiday, lasting the three months of the filming, which would not only refresh us but keep us away from the hubbub that the film set called Anticoli was bound to become. There was no pressing business to attend to. The restoration of San Filippo had not been the only work I had been engaged upon, and the sales of my new Old Masters had been excellent. So on all accounts we deserved and could afford a holiday. The place we decided on was Positano, on the Amalfi coast.

Fig. 66: 'Boucher', *Mythological Scene*, 1967, black chalk heightened with white on blue paper (sold to Hans Calmann)

275

Just before leaving, some time at the beginning of June, I received a further cheque from Hans, being the proceeds from the sale of a 'Boucher' (Fig. 66) that he had made on my behalf. This black chalk drawing heightened with white seems to have perplexed him, and his doubts about it were the exception that proved the rule of his total confidence in his own judgment. The following letter from him some weeks before the sale clearly reflects an unusual uncertainty on his part, while at the same time revealing his unwillingness to accept the judgment of others. It also shows that I was leaving the description of the drawing entirely up to him.

Perridge House
Pilton
Shepton Mallet, Somerset

8 April 1968

My dear Hebburn [sic],

I have looked at your drawing for the last few days but I cannot say I am the wiser for it. It is not at all the drawing where you can rely on your hunch, it needs checking up against other existing material and that I can only do in London. What speaks for the drawing is that it is not the type done by Boucher for selling, but who knows why he or a pupil might not have made a copy for some particular reason.

Shall I keep the drawing till I am back in London, that is early in May and report to you then? I would not like to buy it from here with nothing to consult.

Boucher drawings are always a doubtful proposition, what with innumerable copies and fakes and some appalling experts. I am not particularly versed in them, it is not really my taste.

However, as to business, I might be able to sell the drawing for you as a pretty decoration, in case I should be unable to convince myself that it is a proper Boucher – let me know your price, or wait till I know more about the drawing.

The garden is marvellous at the moment, and when the sun shines as he did the last few days, it is not at all cold. We really need some warm rain now. Hope to show you the place one day.

Sincerely yours

Hans Calmann

Hans was in fact to show me Perridge sooner than he or I knew, but first I was to have the holiday which was to greatly affect both Graham's and my own future, for it led to the breaking-up of my long attachment to him and my falling in love with a person who was to fill my life for the next twenty years. The place we decided to holiday in was Positano, and the reason we were going there and

Fig. 67: *Edgar*, 1971, pencil (Collection Edgar Alegre)

not elsewhere was, of course, because I had come to know the place as a result of Edna Lewis's letter inviting me to teach there. Graham had for some time been sexually tired of me, and was constantly looking about for change – even girls. And at the beginning of this holiday he told me frankly that it would be no holiday for him if he could not have his freedom in the matter. There was nothing I could do but to agree, or else live the life of a person sick with jealousy, forever anxious, wondering where and with whom my partner might be and, worse still, knowing that even when Graham was with me he might really be wishing he was elsewhere. Naturally, I warned him that if he had his freedom then I should have mine. Moreover, as I was not happy about sharing my life with somebody intent on sharing theirs with as many takers as they could find, if I were to meet somebody I particularly liked I would cultivate their company.

To condense what could be turned into a novel, Graham had his fling, and I turned for solace to a handsome young oriental called Edgar (Fig. 67). We had exchanged glances on the beach, but our actual meeting was in a discotheque called not over-subtly 'The Black Banana'. He was an excellent dancer and when he was on the

Fig. 68: 'French School, eighteenth century', *Study of a Man Leaning on a Ledge*, 1969, red and black chalk (sold to Colnaghi's in 1969)

Fig. 69: 'French School, eighteenth century', *A Young Man Lounging*,
1969, red and black chalk (sold through Sotheby's, 2 December
1969)

floor he attracted a lot of attention. I was at the bar with an English girl called Pauline, one of the many hippies who invaded Positano that year, and she seemed to know everybody. 'Who,' I asked, 'is that Chinese boy with such finely sculpted features?' In answer she shouted out across the dance floor 'Edgar, you've made a hit. This bloke's called Eric!' As it turned out Edgar was not Chinese, but Filipino. We got along wonderfully right from the start and I soon discovered my new companion was not only attractive and charming, but also highly intelligent, and well educated with a degree in English literature. So to borrow a phrase from the newspapers on the subject – Graham moved out and Edgar moved in. The people and the events of that unforgettable summer in Positano could in themselves fill a book. There was Rudy and Vallee, a hippie couple who lived above the village in a shepherd's hut which they shared with a goat, a pig, a monkey, a fox and six hens. Vallee was an artist and one could recognise her girlfriends because she was given to tattooing moustaches on to them. Then there was Shawn, a brilliant American guitarist who wore his hair like Jesus, gave concerts on the beach, and later was to make a name for himself; Laura, a Neopolitan *contessa* whose family produced Pope Paul IV, and who, though now in her seventies and crippled with arthritis, still busied herself designing clothes. This incidentally is one of Edgar's many talents, and Laura and he joined forces to produce a highly successful fashion show at Positano's smartest hotel, the Sirenusa. Then of course there was my old acquaintance Edna, and the people who ran and attended her art workshop such as Peter and Eugene. In short, lots and lots of interesting people all in a small space, and all intent, each in their different way, on having fun.

In London, the salerooms and other dealers were still kindly working on my behalf. For instance on 9 July, Christie's sold for me a William Rothenstein, Lot number 69 in their sale of English drawings. The proceeds from these sales would not, however, be paid to me until a month had elapsed from the date of the auction, and as my high standard of living was burning holes in my pockets I hit on the idea of making a stop-gap drawing, break my vacation for a couple of weeks, and take the drawing to Hans at Perridge, who, if he liked it, would give me cash there and then. So I phoned up Hans and told him that I had what appeared to be a fifteenth-century drawing and might I bring it to him for his opinion. He was of course only too pleased to see something that might turn out to be a valuable addition to his stock. We made an appointment in Bath, the nearest city to his home, for the following week. So far so good, but what about the fifteenth-century Old Master? At that

Fig. 70: 'Giovanni Benedetto Castiglione', *Shepherd and Shepherdess with their Flock*, 1969, brush drawing in red oil paint (sold to Colnaghi's)

point it only existed in the mind, which is of course where all drawings should begin, but surprisingly few do. My suitcase contained a number of old sheets of paper, and suitable pens and inks that I had packed with the idea of the occasional practice session to keep my hand in. So taking care to lock my hotel room door, I shifted the dressing table to the window for light and, having arranged my materials, set to work. I was working away from sources, that is to say I had no reference books with me, and what I drew came entirely from my memory and imagination. The paper I used was part of the same sheet on which I had drawn the Pierpont Morgan Library's 'Cossa'. This was very foolish of me because if the two drawings should ever be placed side by side, the fact that the two drawings purporting to be by two different artists from different schools, if not different periods, were on identical paper could raise doubts about the authenticity of both of them. But as it seemed at the time that the chances of this happening were remote, I determined to take the risk. After about three hours of intensive work the drawing of a standing saint, really and truly by a follower, if a rather late one, of Mantegna was complete. It only remained to stress it and give it some other signs of age and it was ready to be taken to Perridge in Somerset.

I went with Edgar, to whom England was a new experience. We

put up for a night in Bath, where Mrs Calmann collected me to take me to nearby Pilton while Edgar went sightseeing. Perridge House is a large country residence, basically Georgian, set in magnificent grounds with views over unspoiled acres of Somerset pasturage. The garden with its croquet lawn, ancient monkey- puzzle tree, water garden and many other beautiful features was Hans's pride and joy and, with the help of two gardeners, he kept it in immaculate condition. 'What would you care to do first?' asked my host, making for the French windows leading into the garden. 'See the garden or show me the drawing?' Needless to say I elected to be shown the garden. And a great pleasure it was. Being a keen, if not very knowledgeable or efficient gardener myself, I was genuinely appreciative, and Hans's own enthusiasm brought into relief a side of his nature very different from the one I had seen in London and Rome. Gone was the autocrat with a tendency to bully, and in his place an affable kindly person taking a simple delight in his beautiful surroundings. Our shared joy in the garden seemed to form a link between us, and from then on Hans dropped his rather old-fashioned formal manner towards me and we were on first-name terms.

Coming in from the garden we sat in a conservatory full of tropical plants and comfortable furniture, where Hans asked if he might see the drawing I had brought for his opinion: '*Quattrocento*, Eric, difficult to place, but it's somewhere around Mantegna. Not good enough for the master himself, but too good for Foppa or Parentino. What are you asking for it?'

'Well, not knowing to whom it could be attributed I don't know what to ask. I got it reasonably and will accept what you think is a fair price,' I said. Reaching for his wallet and taking out his cheque book, Hans asked: 'Two thousand alright?'

Two thousand pounds in 1968 for a few hours work was very alright indeed, and gave me ample means to return with Edgar to Positano and continue having a good time. It was decided that we should stop on our way in Paris to see some Filipino friends of Edgar. While in Paris, I thought I might take a look at the gallery of Geneviève Aymonier, an important dealer in Old Master drawings who regularly advertised in *The Burlington Magazine*. The two most important drawings in her stock at the time were a large drawing in chalk and watercolour attributed to Frans Snyders (an assistant of Rubens) and a pen and ink drawing by Parentino. As I had made the Snyders myself and I must confess to a certain pride in it, I was not tempted to buy it, but the Parentino was a different matter. Madame Aymonier was asking the equivalent of £700 – less than half of what I had just sold one of my own in a similar vein for. So, thinking that I would have the pleasure both of handling and studying a genuine *quattrocento* work for a few weeks and selling it to Hans at a good profit, I changed some of my pounds into francs and paid Madame Aymonier her price.

In thinking I would sell the Parentino to Hans I was mistaken. Unknown to me the drawing had been through one of the London salerooms only a short time before, and although nobody doubted its authenticity it was generally considered mediocre. So when Hans turned down the only authentic drawing I had ever offered him, it was clear that he preferred my productions over the real thing. Experts will tell you that such situations arise because a forger must always, even if he is unaware of it, imbue his work with the taste of his own time, and consequently his forgeries appeal to his contemporaries more directly than the originals. But this argument does not hold water. In the first place Hans did not approve of the taste of his time, and had he sensed something modern about my productions he would have disliked them for it, rather than preferring them over originals. Secondly it simply is not true that the style of an artist's work always reflects the time in which it was made. This is just one of those nice cosy theories of convenience which give the scholar the agreeable feeling that some way or another fakes are always detectable. The unpalatable truth is, however, that although it is true that fakes often, even mostly, reveal themselves by the stamp of the time in which they were made (which of course makes the forging of contemporary work the easiest thing in the world), this is by no means always the case and it is possible for the master forger to escape the hallmark of his age. I know this statement is bound to shock the art historian, for it undermines that fundamental principle in the study of art, according to which a particular style arises from specific conditions operative at a particular moment in time and can no more return than the time which produced it can return. If things were otherwise, it would be to the scholar as if two plus two had ceased to make four, and his pet theories hitherto established on unassailable truth had been torn from their roots. But let him reflect that it is only by the constant re-examination of the principles upon which his discipline is based that any real progress can be made.

In the autumn of 1968 I rented for Edgar and myself a *pied-à-terre* in perhaps the finest street in old Rome, Via Giulia, named after Pope Julius II who created it as part of an unrealised plan for a grand new approach to St Peter's, and was in the latter part of the sixteenth century the most fashionable street in the city. Some of Italy's greatest architects were connected in some way or another in the design of its palaces, Sangallo, Bramante, Raphael, Borromini, and even Michelangelo. In fact the place I rented was only a few steps away from an arch dripping with vines which is all that remains of Michelangelo's design for linking the Palazzo Farnese with the Farnesina across the Tiber. Our *pied-à-terre* was in an old building opposite the magnificent seventeenth-century *palazzo* designed by Borromini for the Falconieri family and appropriately decorated with a large falcon's head. For 40,000 lira a month we had a room of moderate size, a kitchen, a bathroom, and a small courtyard. The place had only recently been restored, or more correctly, modernised, and only the vaulted ceiling of the principal room spoke of its probably sixteenth-century origins.

One of the great advantages of having this tiny flat in Via Giulia was that the beauty and historical interest of the old street had attracted a number of antique dealers to open shops there, so that after Via del Babuino it was, with the possible exception of Via dei Coronari, the most important centre for trading in antiques in Rome. This meant that I had numbers of potential clients passing my door every day. One customer, to whom I regularly sold drawings from my flat in Via Giulia, was Italo. He had been introduced by Guido, one of the dealers in the street. Italo was a private collector, but he had all his purchases vetted by experts. It was to him I sold the genuine Parentino, and a number of my own productions. One of these I recall quite clearly. It was a largeish Gianbattista Tiepolo in red chalk on blue paper heightened with white. The reason I remember it is not because it was particularly good, on the contrary it was rather poor, but because I had not copied or adapted one of Tiepolo's works, but of all things an engraving by a British artist called Mortimer. This artist had come so heavily under the influence of Tiepolo that all I had to do was to translate his engraving, representing an oriental wearing a turban, into something resembling the style of the Italian master without in any way changing the pose or costume of Mortimer's work, and it passed for a typical Tiepolo creation. What I had done was to look beyond the Mortimer to the kind of Tiepolo which had inspired it.

It was in the Via Giulia flat that I made two drawings somewhat in the manner of Watteau. No attempt was made to make them deceptively like the French painter's work, for no matter how well I might have made such 'Watteaus', the experts are nervous about adding newly discovered drawings to that great artist's oeuvre, and I did not want my efforts to be branded as fakes, because as fake Watteaus they would be valueless, whereas being simply in the manner of Watteau, they would be appreciated (like the 'Boucher' sold through Hans mentioned above) for their decorative value. The drawings are in black and red chalk on fine eighteenth-century paper. Christopher White liked the one I showed to him and bought it on behalf of Colnaghi's, who exhibited it in their summer exhibition of Old Master and English drawings, May-June 1969 (Fig. 68). The catalogue entry reads:

> FRENCH SCHOOL eighteenth century
> 44 *A Man with his legs crossed leaning against a Ledge*
> Red and black chalk, 352 × 218
> In style close to Watteau, but not by him.

Well, apart from the 'French School' and the 'eighteenth century' it's a perfectly accurate description and it is a sign of the esteem in which such descriptions by Colnaghi's are held in the trade that it was cited by Sotheby's when they sold the drawing's companion in a sale of Fine Drawings by Old Masters on Tuesday, 2 December 1969 (Fig. 69):

> FRENCH SCHOOL, 18th CENTURY
> 193 A YOUNG MAN LOUNGING – inscribed 'Watteau' – 14⅞ by
>   7⅞in, 378 by 201 mm
>   black and red chalks
>   A similar drawing was recently with Colnaghi
>   (Exhibition catalogue, May/June 1969, No. 44)
>   See illustration

The Colnaghi catalogue of their summer exhibition 1969 contains two other examples of my handiwork also bought from me by Christopher – lots 19 and 21. Number 19 represents Colnaghi's first purchase of one of my numerous 'Stefano della Bellas', and is described:

> STEFANO DELLA BELLA 1610-1664
> 19 *Death carrying a Child*
>   Pen, brown ink and grey wash over black chalk, 332 × 208
>   Preparatory study for the etching (de Vesme 89)

Naturally, the drawing is in reality not a preparatory study for the etching but rather a drawing after it. This does not, however, mean that the study is copied from the etching. Copying the etching would involve reproducing the print line for line, whereas there is not one line of my drawing which is copied, and that is why it maintains the freedom of an original drawing, which indeed it is – the only thing which seems to worry the experts being that it is an original Hebborn rather than an original della Bella. The third and last drawing in Colnaghi's catalogue of summer 1969 (Fig. 70) which must now be attributed to myself, has the following impressive catalogue entry:

> 21 GIOVANNI BENEDETTO CASTIGLIONE, called
> IL GRECHETTO *c.*1600-1670
> *Shepherd and Shepherdess with their Flock*
> Brush drawing in red 233 × 390
> Collection: N. Hone (L. 2793)
> The subject was a favourite one with the artist and the present drawing can be compared in both theme and style with a group at Windsor (A.F. Blunt, The Drawings of G.B. Castiglione & Stefano della Bella in the Collection of H.M. The Queen, London, 1954, nos. 110-21, pl.9), which are described there as early works before 1645. Their characteristic feature is a very firm linear technique, often with bold hatching and with little shading. In general, a strong red is used, sometimes tending to orange.

It always amuses me to see my 'Old Masters' on show, and when I saw this 'Castiglione' beautifully framed and hanging in Old Bond Street, I could not help but smile at the memory of it hanging with its fellows earlier that year on my washing line in Italy exuding a wholesome smell of turpentine. The three drawings just mentioned from Colnaghi's summer exhibition of 1969 had been made in Villa San Filippo and taken to London with a number of others including a 'Poussin'. The story of the Poussin did not, however, really begin in Anticoli Corrado, but in Portman Square.

Twenty Portman Square is a Georgian terraced house, which, like its companions, owes its distinction not to any lavish show of costly materials but rather to the combination of humble brick, tile and timber, in agreeable proportions. Between the years 1932-1990 this handsome building housed the illustrious art history department of London University which is named after the multi-millionaire Samuel Courtauld who had the honour of paying for it. In the sixties, the Courtauld was immensely important in the art world because, unlike the American universities of the time, it placed considerable emphasis on the 'art' (some would claim 'science') of connoisseurship and it was more often than not the great American museums would turn to the Courtauld for guidance when faced with a thorny problem of attribution or authenticity. The director of the institute was my friend Anthony, Surveyor of the Queen's Pictures, who was at the apex of his long and distinguished career with a reputation that seemed impregnable.

The Courtauld under Anthony has been described by Christopher Wright, art historian and former student of Blunt's, as a 'benevolent despotism'. Well, the 'benevolent despotism' was closed for the day and I was obliged to put down my cumbersome parcel of Old Master drawings and engravings on its doorstep and fumble for the keys. During my frequent visits to London, I stayed with Anthony, whose flat was on the top floor. Thus, having entered the house and carefully closed the door behind me, a process involving a good deal of key turning in what I imagine would nowadays be considered a highly unsophisticated security lock, I crossed the vestibule and turned right to take a tiny rattling lift that had been squeezed into the well of a dingy back stairway. Had I not been burdened with my parcel, I might have turned left and climbed the splendid main staircase, whose elegance originated in the mind of no less an architect than Robert Adam and whose painted decoration had been carried out by Angelica Kaufmann.

Entering the flat I deposited my parcel in the spare room and went to find my host. Anthony, shirt-sleeved and slippered, was in the sitting room, his favourite armchair surrounded by piles of

Fig. 71: 'Giovanni Battista Ghisi (*fl.* 1498-1563), *Trojans Repelling the Greeks*, engraving after Giulio Romano (Collection E. Hebborn)

Fig. 72: 'Nicolas Poussin', *Study of an Ancient Helmet* – recto, 1969, pen and ink (sold to Hans Calmann, 1970)

books, magazines and manuscripts, all to be studied, reviewed or corrected, this being his way of relaxing from a hard day. He was, as I have mentioned elsewhere, a tall man of frail appearance, now sixty years old. His long wrinkled face was of that uniquely English stamp which the upper classes, to whom such faces usually belong, term distinguished, and which the lower classes refer to as being horsey. A stroke had partially paralysed its right-hand side, which scarcely moved unless he was annoyed. On these occasions the semi-frozen half of the upper lip would take to twitching, eloquent of pent-up feelings that his charming educated voice and gentle aristocratic manner would scarcely have conveyed. I recall Anthony once priding himself on being able to deliver a withering rebuke by merely raising an eyebrow. This revelation was doubtless intended to fill me with fear and trembling of ever crossing him.

But on the rare occasions during our long friendship on which I can remember having done so, it was not the dreaded eyebrow but the involuntary twitching of the lip that forcibly told of his displeasure. The rooms of Anthony's flat had once formed the servants' quarters – hence their access to and from the backstairs. Nothing beyond their relatively modest proportions had remained to remind one of the menials they originally sheltered. Now they had been transformed into a home of quality and comfort. To say that the flat was luxurious is not to tell a lie, but one should not conjure up an image of ostentation, for its occupant was not only a great scholar and a first-rate connoisseur, he was also a man of consummate taste, being, if the word has any meaning at all, an aesthete. The sitting room, which overlooked Portman Square, was neither precious nor pretentious. The antique furniture, rare books, oriental carpets, master paintings and drawings, were all of the finest quality, but it was as much in their arrangement as in their selection that their owner showed his finely tuned sensibilities. For these valuable objects had been combined to produce a comfortable and relaxed atmosphere in which their monetary value seemed totally irrelevant. Thus, one could appreciate Anthony's art collection in an intimate way, a way difficult in the impersonal surroundings of a museum, and impossible in the commercial climate of the market place.

His private collection was a clear indication of his extensive interests, for few indeed are the historians who have covered the field of art as widely as Blunt. The catalogue of the Sir Anthony Blunt Collection, held at the Courtauld Institute Galleries in 1964, lists seventy-six items by or attributed to artists as separate in time and spirit as Giorgio Vasari, André Derain, Gianlorenzo Bernini, William Blake, Pierleone Ghezzi and Sir Edwin Landseer. But of all the many artists that he had studied and written on with authority, there was one that held a very special place, not only in his thoughts but in his heart – the French seventeenth-century genius, Nicolas Poussin. 'I first became interested in Poussin as a schoolboy in the early twenties. My dissertation written for a fellowship at Trinity College in Cambridge, to which I was elected in 1932, was largely concerned with Poussin's ideas about painting, though it spread out into a wider field; and although I have inevitably been led to work on other subjects, Poussin has always remained my first love.' Yes, Anthony loved Poussin and it is not surprising that this artist should have figured in his collection. The catalogue mentioned above lists four drawings by Poussin of which two are of particular interest here:

Fig. 73: Detail of *Study of an Ancient Helmet*, p. 288

No. 57 A bride led by a woman
No. 58 Drawings after Fragments of a Roman Altar.

These two drawings were to prove an inspiration for a new 'Poussin' illustrated in Fig. 72. But I am jumping the gun and we must return to the director's flat in the Courtauld, where Anthony and I are drinking inordinate amounts of gin and tonic which he has recalled from their daytime exile in the broom cupboard. For it must be admitted that the then Director of the Courtauld and Surveyor of the Queen's Pictures loved his gin and tonic almost as much as he loved Poussin, but did not care to advertise the fact until after six. Anthony was aware that my visits to London tended to coincide with Christie's and Sotheby's sales of important Old Master drawings. What he was not aware of was that I attended the sales to see how much my own work was fetching and to study the other drawings in the sale with a view to emulating them in the future. Sometimes I would buy a lot I needed for study purposes. In any case, Anthony was always keen to have a look at any new acquisitions I may have made during my stay. And at some point in the evening our conversation went something along these lines:

A. 'Was your bid at Sotheby's successful?'

E. 'No, it was knocked down by Colnaghi's for five hundred guineas.'

A. 'Incidentally, what did the little Salviati fetch?'

E. 'Hold on a minute, I'll get the catalogue from my room. (I leave the room returning shortly clutching a sales catalogue and a pile of Old Master prints.) Let me see . . . the Salviati was lot number . . . ah, here we are . . . it fetched a hundred and fifty . . . Here, I thought you might like to see some engravings I bought from Craddock and Barnard.'

I made it a must to visit Craddock and Barnard Ltd, print dealers with premises near the British Museum, each time I went to London. They invariably had a large selection of prints from all periods and their prices were very reasonable. That day I had bought from them a group of prints by the Italian engraver Marcantonio Raimondi and his School. Such prints were not at that time popular with collectors and could be had for a pittance. For myself they were especially useful as source material for drawings in the manner of various renaissance draughtsmen, and I bought them in quantity.

Among the prints was one by Giovanni Battista Ghisi. It represented the Trojans repelling the Greeks (Fig. 71). This overcrowded composition, its many figures wearing a variety of ancient armours, was of particular interest to Anthony. Putting down his glass, and getting up from his armchair, he padded across the room and took down from the wall his Poussin, *Drawings after Fragments of a Roman Altar* (mentioned above). Bringing the drawing over to where we had been looking at the prints, and seizing on his momentarily neglected glass, he spoke of Poussin's close attention to archaeological details and how he had gained his knowledge not only by drawing directly from ancient sculptures (as would seem the case with the Blunt Poussin) but also by making drawings after details of engravings by the school of Marcantonio Raimondi. He cited a drawing by the master, in the collection of the *Ecole des Beaux Arts* in Paris after one of Marcantonio's followers, Nicolas Beatrizet. Could it be, wondered Anthony, that Poussin had used this particular Ghisi print as source material? Would I allow him to keep the engraving for a few days to do some research? What he

really meant was would I save him the trouble of visiting the British Museum prints and drawings department. Naturally I agreed to do this, and so as not to detach Anthony from his glass, I put down my own and offered to put his Poussin back on the wall. As I was engaged in hanging up the drawing, my eye wandered towards its charming companion, *A Bride led by a Woman* (mentioned above). This drawing, I recalled, had been sold to Anthony by Hans Calmann, who charged him ten pounds. Now ten pounds, even in those days of modest prices, was a ridiculously low sum for an authentic and attractive Poussin. Since Hans was a 'client' with whom I was now on friendly terms, I knew him far too well to imagine that he had taken pity on the 'poor scholar' (Anthony's misconception of himself), and had generously declined a handsome profit for the advancement of learning. The truth is that Hans

Fig. 74: 'Nicolas Poussin', verso of Fig. 72, pen and ink. Note how the iron in the ink has eaten through the paper with 'age' so that the recto shows through

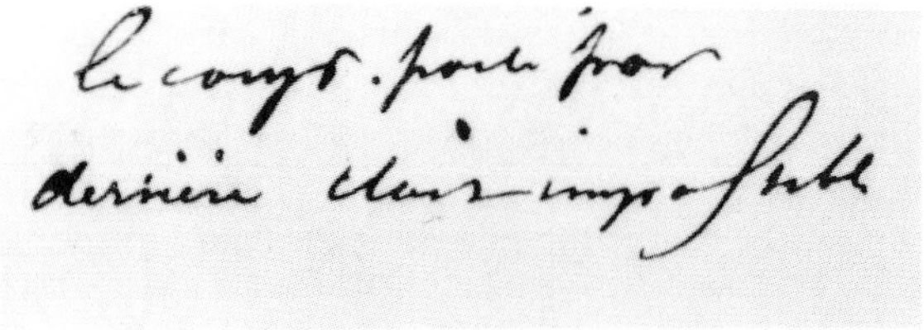

Fig. 75: Inscription on a drawing by Pierre d'Angers
used as a model for the handwriting on the verso of the
'Poussin' drawing

had failed to recognise the drawing as a Poussin, and Anthony had
not thought it in the least bit necessary to point out his oversight
until the treasure was safely in his own possession. Needless to say,
when Hans finally learned of his mistake and loss of profit, he was
not exactly delighted, and from then on nurtured a grudge against
Anthony. Nor did my host throw any oil on those troubled waters
by dismissing a Poussin in Hans's stock as not having 'the remotest
connection' with his beloved artist. With the passage of time, the
rift between the two authorities was only to widen.

It was while reflecting on the differences between Anthony and
Hans that I was suddenly struck with an idea of producing a
Poussin that would put to the test the knowledge and sensibility of
the rival experts. I would make a drawing that was close enough in
style to Poussin for Anthony to take seriously, but not so close that
he would accept it as being really and truly by the master. This
done I would merely have to show the drawing to Hans, tell him of
Anthony's doubts, and he would be fully convinced that Anthony
had made yet another blunder, a blunder he might this time turn to
his own advantage, and buy it. Several days had passed before
Anthony returned the Ghisi engraving, telling me that he had indeed found a connection between the print and certain drawn
studies by Poussin, but, he mentioned in passing, it was a curious
fact that in all his long experience he had never been able to establish a definite link between Poussin's completed paintings and his
studies made from the antique or such engravings as the Ghisi.
In the light of what was to follow, this statement was to prove
significant.

During the days in which Anthony had been studying the Ghisi,
I had also been doing some research and, whether by chance or
diligence, had discovered an undeniable link between the Ghisi and
a painting by Poussin that Anthony had apparently overlooked.
The fact is that the helmet of one of the soldiers by the side of the

Lord's cross in Poussin's *Crucifixion* is very close in detail to that appearing on the head of a warrior on the extreme right-hand side of the Ghisi *Naval Combat*. Now, although there is the remote possibility that Ghisi and Poussin were drawing from a common source, it is much more likely that Poussin had drawn his inspiration for his Roman soldier's helmet from the Ghisi engraving. It therefore suggested the former existence of a drawing made by Poussin from the Ghisi print, and later used by him when painting the *Crucifixion*. Since this postulated drawing appeared to have perished, I determined to lend a helping hand to the art historian and reconstruct it. Hence the case of the Poussin helmet (Fig. 72).

At this point the reader must bear with me while I talk shop, that is, speak of technical matters. But I do so only to show some of the problems involved in the making of a reasonably convincing reconstruction of a lost work of art. In this instance I had decided that, although the drawing was not intended to be anything more than stylistically akin to Poussin, it was to be physically indistinguishable from a drawing that had been made some 300 years ago. That is to say it was to be technically, thus chemically, perfect. There would be no way in which scientific tests could prove that it had not been made in Poussin's day. Fortunately, my portfolio of old paper contained a sound seventeenth-century sheet that had once served as the fly leaf of an insufferably dull religious tract, the title of which I have mercifully forgotten. In the preparation of paper intended for writing or drawing in ink, it is given an application of glue, or 'size'. Without this the paper is absorbent and any ink applied to it blots, or 'bleeds'. With age, the sizing deteriorates. If the paper has been subject to damp, the old glue is attacked by various kinds of fungus which, if left unchecked, eventually destroy the fibres of the paper itself. If, on the other hand, the paper has been left dry, the sizing will lose its elasticity and slowly disintegrate leaving the paper too absorbent for use. But however the old glue may have vanished or been made ineffectual, if we are to draw on centuries-old paper without leaving a tell-tale bleeding line, we must first give the paper a fresh application of glue. This glue should be of natural organic substance. It is true that scientific analysis can determine with a rough degree of accuracy the age of glues. But since restorers of books, prints and drawings are sometimes obliged to strengthen old papers with fresh size, the discovery of fresh glue in an Old Master drawing is not proof positive that it has been made recently. What is more, in a technically perfect reconstruction of the kind I was about to make, no trace of the new sizing was to be left!

Upon my return to Anticoli I immediately started work on my 'Poussin'. Having prepared a glue according to the time-honoured recipe given by Giotto's pupil Cennino Cennini in his celebrated *Libro dell'Arte*, and applied it three times to the paper (for several weak coats are more effective than one strong one), I turned my attention to the ink. In the course of over thirty years of activity I have collected a large number of recipes for ink, but have in practice employed no more than twenty. This is because the inks used by the Old Masters mostly fall into these groups: bistre, sepia and gall. Bistre ink comes from soot collected in a chimney where willow logs have been burnt; sepia comes from the cuttle-fish; gall ink is made from oak galls. These inks can be complicated to make, and I have many times used modern surrogates. By far the greatest number of Poussin drawings were made with bistre. But as I was not interested in making an altogether typical Poussin, I decided on using oak gall ink. Living close to a small wood which boasts splendid old oaks, I collected as many galls as I could find on the ground and I ground them to a fine powder with my kitchen mortar and pestle. This I mixed with rain water, adding to the mixture some filings taken from a rusty old nail, and left the concoction to evaporate to the right consistency. Should any reader wish to make some gall ink for themselves, here is an old recipe:

> Put into a quart of water two ounces of right gumme Arabick, five ounces of galles, and three of copras. Let it stay covered in the warme sunne and so will it sooner prove good incke. To boyle the sayd stuffe together a little upon the fire would make it more speedy for your writyng: but ye enboyled yeldeth a fayrer glosse, and longer indureth. In stead of water wine were best for this purpose. Refresh your incke with wine, or vinegar, when it wareth thicke . . .

> From *The Petite Schole* by Francis Clement, 1587.

The first difficulty was not small. How to draw like Poussin. Even Poussin did not learn how to draw like Poussin without years of practice. For just as no one could play the violin in imitation of Ughi unless they had first learned to play it rather well, so it is that no one can draw an imitation of a master draughtsman without being a pretty good draughtsman himself. Long years of practice added to arguably a solid art school background had given me some proficiency in the art, and I could at least claim to understand the visual language Poussin used. But now, I had to learn his dialect, his accent, his pitch, his almost imperceptible inflections and mannerisms, subtleties that he himself may not have been aware of.

In this, I was in much the same position as an actor who has to study the speech and movements of a character before giving a convincing portrayal. The drawing was not to be a copy or a variation of an already existing Poussin, but an original effort saying something that he might have said, in approximately the manner in which he might have said it.

Having never attempted a Poussin drawing before, it was necessary to rehearse it a number of times before committing it to the valuable period paper. Every draughtsman knows the kind of stage-fright that a blank piece of paper can induce. Imagine then the tension of facing a virgin seventeenth-century sheet, taped on a board, virtually irreplaceable, and which may even have cost as much as a lesser, but authentic, drawing from the same period. Although I have produced hundreds of drawings in almost as many styles in my attempts to understand something about the mystery of drawing, I have never overcome this trepidation.

The subject was to be a plumed helmet largely in the style of Poussin and taken from a detail of a helmet on the right-hand side of the Ghisi *Trojans Repelling the Greeks* (Fig. 73). The drawing was not to be, in any way at all, a copy, but an adaptation. The flowing plumes, which are so unlike the stiff quills of the Ghisi, were inspired by a fragment of a cartoon, sold by Christie's on 26 March 1968, Lot 67. It was from the school of Raphael and showed the head and shoulders of a young soldier wearing a helmet surmounted by a griffin. The subject matter was to be refracted through the mind and hand of another artist, that artist being not altogether me but in large part Poussin. Now, while it is conceivable that an imitator may be skilful enough to follow the hand of a former artist, for that hand has left a visible, tangible trace, how can he possibly make the necessary step back in time to enter the mind of that artist? Such a feat is not quite as miraculous as it may at first seem. The truth is that every mark a draughtsman makes is a reflection of his mental state. Their hand works in obedience to their mind. If one truly understands the marks of a drawing and more particularly the meaningful relationships between those marks, one is in mental contact with their author, no matter how far remote in time and space. This requires great knowledge and sensibility, not clairvoyance. It is no more than can be reasonably expected of a connoisseur.

The drawing is virtually complete but there is something not quite right with it. The trouble is, it is a little too much like Poussin for my purpose, and despite the unusual ink, Anthony might be tempted to add the drawing to the master's oeuvres. What is to be done? Further deviations from Poussin's usual style must be introduced. But what? Cross-hatching! A form of linear shading built up of two or more sets of parallel lines crossing each other, the tones achieved largely depending on the amount of paper that remains uncovered. Poussin rarely shaded with the pen, preferring to do so with a brush charged with diluted bistre. When he did use the pen, he normally shaded with just parallel lines. I remember having seen, however, in a sale at Sotheby's 21 March 1963, Lot 96, a Poussin drawing of the *Holy Family* with uncharacteristic and extensive cross-hatching, and there are other examples. Even so, Anthony will certainly be on his guard if he sees cross-hatching in a supposed Poussin. So in the hatching goes. But even the 'out of style' shading is not conclusive proof against the drawing, for it is not unusual for artists to experiment from time to time with techniques and modify their methods. Therefore, I must introduce other discrepancies.

I remember that Anthony is bilingual, speaking French with the same fluency as English. He has given lectures on Poussin in the artist's native tongue. Supposing then, there is an inscription on the verso in faulty French? Anthony will surely notice the error and further doubts will arise in his mind. Hence the inscription in an old hand: *peut mesurer le soleille et la lune*, the spelling of *soleille* being incorrect (Fig. 74). I had seen a drawing by Pierre d'Angers with some puzzling inscription and patterned my enigmatic inscription after his calligraphy to give the character of French handwriting, even though its style was really late eighteenth-century (Fig. 75). This misspelling is not in itself evidence of the drawing not being by Poussin, because in the seventeenth century spelling was not standardised as it is today. But a number of such irregularities and Anthony's doubts will turn to certainties. Above the inscription, a somewhat self-consciously Poussin-esque profile, and an optimistic attribution in still another hand on the recto, and the drawing is ready for ageing. To be successful, ageing requires very considerable skill and nicety of judgment. There is a tendency for the inexperienced to overdo it, and as a corrective to this I have sometimes underdone it. In the present case I think I can justifiably claim to have carried out the ageing process in the *giusta misura*. Being really and truly from the seventeenth century, the paper needed no stressing, bleaching or tinting to simulate age. The ink, however, although chemically indistinguishable from inks used in Poussin's day, had not amalgamated with the paper as it would have done had it really been in contact with it for over 300 years. Furthermore, magnification would reveal no disintegration that truly old

Fig. 76: 'Giovanni Battista Piranesi', *Preparatory Study for an Etching*, 1969, pen and bistre (sold to Hans Calmann; now in the National Gallery of Denmark)

inks do, something like the cracks in old paint. The new sizing had also to be washed away. The work of centuries would have to be carried out in a matter of hours. Let it suffice to say that it involved the cunning application of moisture, heat and a corrosive.

The following year, 1969, packing the Poussin into my suitcase, with three 'Johns' for Arthur Tooth, the 'Castiglione', the 'della Bella' and the Eighteenth-century French School for Colnaghi which I have mentioned above, a 'School of Dürer' for Hans Calmann, and various minor 'Old Masters' for the salerooms, I set off for Fiumicino airport. Enjoy screeching across the heavens, thousands of feet above sea level without so much as a thread to connect one to earth? I thanked God it was over and that I should soon be cruising on *terra ferma* in an old-fashioned English cab, with only an occasional honk to announce its leisurely journey backwards in time to 20 Portman Square.

When I had deposited my bag of mischief in my room, reclined myself on the sofa in the sitting room with my gin and tonic and the conversation with my host was well underway, I brought up the subject of the Poussin. This may very well have surprised Anthony, because, whereas I would normally show him any work of art that I had acquired in London, I never sought his opinion of the drawings I brought over from Italy, although more often than not, my prospective buyers would bring the 'Old Masters' to the Courtauld for Anthony's opinion. For instance, he was the recognised authority on both Stefano della Bella and Benedetto Castiglione, and had prepared the catalogue of their work in Windsor Castle. Consequently, any drawing in the style of these two artists was certainly going to be shown him. Sometimes my name would be mentioned as the source, and then he would ask me why I had not consulted him directly. On at least one occasion, I had thoughtlessly left some drawings on the desk in my room where Anthony had chanced upon them. And naturally, when staying with me in Italy he would see the new drawings on the walls. But in spite of these exceptions my general rule was never to show drawings to Anthony for fear of compromising his position. This 'Poussin', however, would be shown to him, because he was almost certainly going to dismiss it as the work of an imitator.

So I fetched the photograph of the helmet drawing and handed it over to Anthony. I did not show him the original straight away because, although no expert worth his salt will make a firm attribution on the basis of a photograph, they will go so far as to judge from the print whether the work of art is of sufficient quality to warrant an inspection of the original. Therefore, should Anthony be interested enough to see the original, it would be a strong indication that his first impression had not been totally unfavourable. After a few minutes of silent contemplation he laid down the photograph with the words, 'It is not at all typical of Poussin, but it could be right. Do you have the original?' On being shown the actual drawing, he again fell into rapt silence. After a lengthy scrutiny he announced that he was not at all 'happy' about it but would like to study it further and might he show it to Professor Rees Jones? For many years in charge of the technology department of the Courtauld, Rees Jones was an internationally recognised expert on the conservation of paintings. Connoisseurs seldom have scientific tests made on a drawing unless they are seriously worried about its age. Why he should have been worried about the age I didn't know. I imagine that the divergences from Poussin's normal style had already led him to think of a follower. The eighteenth-century handwriting may have suggested the possibility of the follower belonging to that period. But whatever his reasoning, Anthony must have felt that he could not date the drawing on stylistic

Fig. 77: Giovanni Battista Piranesi (*fl.* 1729-78) *Part of a Large Magnificent Port used by the Ancient Romans*, etching and engraving, Focillon 122 (Collection E. Hebborn)

grounds alone. He was on the right track! But how far would he follow it?

I spent the few days that I had to wait for the answer making myself some money by launching the contents of my suitcase on the London art market. The 'Johns' were particularly well received at Arthur Tooth and Sons Ltd and one of them was included in their exhibition *British Paintings 1900-1971* held in their Bruton Street gallery from 20 April to 15 May 1971. The catalogue entry reads:

> 27 AUGUSTUS JOHN Child's Head
>   drawing 12' × 13' a/2

Although it was among those items in the show that Tooth's thought worthy of illustrating, their cataloguing of it was careless. First of all the drawing was not just a head, it was a bust with an indication of hands, secondly it was clearly recognisable as a portrait of John's son Robin. Christie's did not 'like' one of the drawings that I left with them, which was not surprising since I did not 'like' it myself. The 'Castiglione', the 'della Bella' and the eighteenth-century drawing were considered a welcome addition to Colnaghi's forthcoming exhibition. At Bruton Place, Hans gave his usual enthusiastic reception to yet another 'Calmann' drawing. So, my 'Old Masters' found good homes and I would return to Italy a few hundred pounds better off than when I left.

When Anthony returned the Poussin, he told me that it was his considered opinion that it could not be by the master. It was, he added, extremely rare for a Poussin to have cross-hatching of the kind used on the helmet, the French inscription contained a spelling mistake, and the drawing of the profile, although in the manner of Poussin, was too feeble. He then mentioned the ambiguous drawing of the lower part of the helmet where it is not at all clear whether or not it is an added leather ear flap. If it is, why on one side only? Or perhaps it is a continuation of the metal upper part that has been largely consumed by time. In which case, it is to be supposed that the artist was drawing from an antique helmet. Why then the fresh plumes? He had me stumped there!! Apparently, the drawing had passed whatever scientific tests it had been subjected to with flying colours, and had been judged to be genuinely old. On the whole Anthony too had passed the test very well. But to have failed to notice the connection between the helmet of the drawing and that of the soldier in Poussin's *Crucifixion* was, for an expert with his intimate knowledge of Poussin's work, curious in the extreme. Regardless of the authenticity or otherwise of the helmet drawing, it does point out an undeniable connection between a painted work by Poussin and an engraving by Ghisi. Since Anthony had only recently studied the print, the appearance of a drawing purporting to belong to the series of drawings after such prints should have led him to find the motif in the Ghisi at once, and his familiarity with the *Crucifixion* should have led him to connect the two. His oversight is inexplicable.

All that remained for me, to bring my plan to completion, was to find a propitious moment to show the drawing to Hans Calmann and hope that he would buy it. My little 'Poussin' would not in itself be sufficiently interesting in terms of money to warrant getting in touch with Hans again then and there. I would have to return to Rome to wait for the right psychological situation, and offer the Poussin with a drawing of greater importance. An early Italian *Head of a Youth*? Although I had no particular artist in mind, the master that was to come into the experts' minds was my trusty old friend Francesco del Cossa who had previously inspired the much-publicised *Pageboy with a Lance* drawing, now at the Pierpont Morgan Library. Suffice it to say at this point that this latest 'Cossa', representing yet another good-looking youth, was admired by no less an authority than the art-dealer David Carritt, famed for his discovery of the Tiepolo frescoes in the Egyptian Embassy in London, which Calmann cynically claimed everyone had long known about except the 'experts'. Carritt also discovered a picture by Roger van der Weyden of *St. Ivo*, later sold to the National Gallery of London, and later presented by the art historian Christopher Wright in his recent book, *The Art of the Forger*, as a work painted not earlier than 1959.

It was not until the summer of 1970 that I sent a photograph of the 'Cossa' *Head of a Youth* to Hans. His reaction was immediate. He would fly to Rome at once. From the Hotel Excelsior in Via Veneto, he phoned me at my villa in Anticoli. Would I bring the Cossa to him the next morning? So it was that on a hot July day in 1970, Hans Calmann was waiting, cheque book at the ready, in the posh and exclusive surroundings of the Hotel Excelsior's first-class lounge. Young Hebborn was to bring what promised to be another magnificent drawing, a museum piece, the kind of work that makes its own price. 'Clever boy, no background to speak of, but a good eye. With a little guidance he might make something of himself yet . . . but what's holding the wretched fellow up?' The answer was the maître. Although I was wearing a perfectly respectable jacket, I did not have a tie. And so, not properly dressed to enter the holy-of-holies known as the first-class lounge, I was obliged to wait in the foyer while Signor Calmann was *chiamato*. Decently attired in a yellowed linen suit, whose quality alone had made it survive from the forties, Hans was every bit as imposing as his surroundings. It must be admitted though, that were it not for his impressive manner, one might have found something comic in his appearance. The outline of his paunch seemed to be the arbitrary result of a cushion stuffed up his shirt, and this, combined with his flap ears and very Jewish nose, gave so strong an air of Pulcinella that only respect for the man himself could keep one from laughing.

Away from the business pressures of London, Hans was in his most expansive and self-assured mood. Looking down on me from his over six-foot height, he patted me gently on the shoulder. 'Don't worry my boy, I don't mind at all going to the other lounge.' He was being magnanimous. I was completely at my ease for half the battle was already won. 'Delightful little drawing,' he beamed with the independence of spirit that allowed him to make up his own mind without reference to others. In all the many years I dealt with Hans, I can recall very few occasions on which I have seen him hesitate for more than a few moments before pronouncing his Berensonian Yes or No.

'It is a Cossa, you know,' he announced, and offered to buy it in half-share. (When he later sold it for several thousand pounds, my work was handsomely rewarded.) And now, for the Poussin.

'Hans, I don't imagine you'll be interested, but I have brought another drawing with me. Anthony Blunt has already seen it and feels it is not quite "right",' with which I handed him the helmet drawing. A moment's pause, a glance at the verso, and the triumphant voice declared: 'It's perfectly alright!! Charming drawing. Nobody but Poussin could have done it. What are you asking for it? Have another drink my boy.' Then, changing to a rather pitying tone, 'Poor Blunt. Such a gentle creature . . . But on Poussin?? . . . my dear Eric, remember this: never underestimate the stupidity of others.'

An artist whose work I admire immensely is the eighteenth-century engraver, architect and antiquarian, Giovanni Battista Piranesi, who is perhaps best known for his views of Rome. Incidentally, this remarkable man, who in his working life is credited with having produced over 1,300 etchings, mostly large and full of detail, still seems to have found time to create some fakes. Visitors to the recent exhibition at the British Museum entitled 'FAKE?' were able to admire a splendid example of his abilities as a forger in the form of a huge 'ancient' vase in marble. In reality it is a highly imaginative 'reconstruction' of a vase that never existed in anti-

COLNAGHI'S

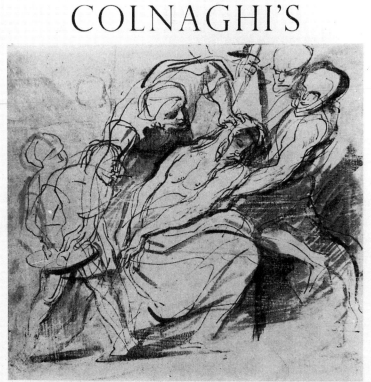

SIR ANTHONY VAN DYCK (1599-1641)   Pen and ink with brown wash, 261 x 287

EXHIBITION OF OLD MASTER AND ENGLISH DRAWINGS

June 3rd to June 26th

14 OLD BOND STREET, LONDON WI

Telegrams: 'Colnaghi, London W1X 4JL'   *Telephone: 01-493 1943*

cxlvi

Fig. 78: 'Van Dyck', *Christ Crowned with Thorns*, 1970, pen and ink with brown wash. Full-page advertisement in *The Burlington Magazine*, May 1970 (sold in 1970 to Colnaghi's, who later sold the 'Van Dyck' to the British Museum)

quity. To create it Piranesi has taken a few fragments of genuinely ancient sculpture and combined them with seventy per cent infill of his own imagining. Piranesi seems to have had similar ideas about faking as myself, and from 1767 onwards operated in Rome as a

Fig. 79: 'Jan Van Huysum', *A Flower Piece*, 1970, black
chalk and grey wash with watercolour (sold to
Colnaghi's)

dealer. He was particularly patronised by the wealthy British
travellers on the Grand Tour, and the British Museum's magnificent
vase was sold by him to the English collector, Sir John Boyd. Perhaps there is therefore some warped kind of poetic justice in the fact
than an Englishman should fake the work of an Italian faker who
took the English *milordi* for a ride. However that may be, Piranesi
has been the object of much study and emulation on my part. In
all, I have produced about twenty-five important 'Piranesis', and
perhaps as many again minor sheets. Of this number only one of
any importance has definitely been attributed to me, and perhaps a
further nine tentatively ascribed to my hand by a few authorities in
the field. As it is not, generally speaking, my intention in this book
to make the expert's task any easier, I am only going to mention
here the single important 'Piranesi' which has been positively given
to me. This drawing (Fig. 76) was for a number of years held to be

the preparatory study for the etching, *Parte di ampio magnifico porto all'uso degli antichi Romani*, Focillon 122 (Fig. 77).

It is well known that preparatory studies for works in other mediums, such as painting and etching, are more lively than the finished work, and it is this fact that helps the expert to recognise a genuine study for, as opposed to a copy after, the finished work. The copy lacks the spontaneity and freshness of invention that the creative artist gives to his work when dashing down his hasty lines in the first burning heat of inspiration. 'All forgeries,' writes Max Friedlander, 'quite apart from their other shortcomings, can be detected by their pedantically anxious execution. The forger can never let himself go and follow his natural inclinations. He must coldly calculate, painfully pick his way and squint in all directions. He can only hope to succeed if his copy is exact. Every time he yields to a personal impulse he takes a serious risk.' Once again the reader is invited to play the connoisseur and compare my Piranesi (Fig. 76) to the print from which it derives (Fig. 77) and view it in the light of Friedlander's words. Does my forgery like 'all forgeries' reveal itself by its 'pedantically anxious execution'? Can you see me squinting in all directions, painfully picking my way, knowing that I can only succeed if my copy is exact, and being careful not to yield to any personal impulse? Well, I very much doubt if you can, and I am going to blow my own trumpet and state categorically that this drawing has all the freshness and spontaneity that one would expect to find in a preliminary study. Like most of my productions, the Piranesi is not a copy, but an original drawing taking up the theme of the work which inspired it, and developing it in a way that I imagine the original artist might have done himself. Let me see if I can make myself a little clearer by trying to explain what was going on in my mind when one day in the spring of 1969 I took up a large sheet of thick eighteenth-century drawing paper, and with some bistre prepared from a packet of desiccated ink discovered in an eighteenth-century paint box, set to work to make this ambitious 'Piranesi'.

Looking through the reproductions in the Focillon catalogue of the master's engravings, I was struck by plate 62 (Fig. 77), not because it was any more beautiful than the others, but because of a number of weaknesses in the generally grandly conceived mixture of etching and engraving. The first thing that disturbed me was the lack of breathing space around the edges. The design seems to have been cropped to fit into the measurements of a smaller sheet of copper than such a design really required. Copper plates suitable for engraving are and were in Piranesi's time expensive items. There is a story traditionally told of the artist who was rumoured to be impulsive and sometimes even so violent that, having encountered his future wife while he was sketching in the Forum, and learning that she would bring with her a dowry sufficient to buy the copper for an edition of etchings, he terrified the poor girl and her parents into consenting to a marriage within five days. True or not, this story makes the point that for an engraver as prolific as Piranesi, the cost of his plates was not a negligible matter, and what I imagined from the cramped design of the etching under discussion was that the artist had adjusted his design to fit a copper plate of different proportions to his original drawing. The plate seemed unduly square for Piranesi's concept, and what had once been a design of greater breadth had been squeezed into its limits to avoid wasting an otherwise perfectly good and expensive sheet of metal.

If I was right in this surmise, then it postulated a lost drawing by Piranesi of the longer oblong proportion the artist normally preferred. This drawing like my reconstruction of it would have been more spacious than the print. There would have been room to exchange the miserly strip of water at the bottom of the print for a more generous expanse of the element which is the *raison d'être* of the architecture of any port, however grand. Then too there would be no necessity to introduce the framing device on the right hand of the print which creaks like an old theatre cut-out and spoils the sweep of the curved building behind. A wider expanse of sky, a slightly more dramatic, if equally illogical, perspective, and we have an interesting variation on Piranesi's design and one which may even be nearer to the artist's original conception than the print. In other words, it was not my intention to copy Piranesi's print but to see if I could improve on its design, and see through the rather mechanical engraved line back to the master's first free uninhibited sketch. In this attempt to improve on my model I was following the advice with which Joshua Reynolds concludes his sixth discourse, delivered to the students of the Royal Academy in 1774: '. . . consider them [the Old Masters] as models which you are to imitate, and at the same time as rivals with whom you are to contend.'

Whether or not my effort rivals Piranesi on his own ground is not for me to say, but before it was known to be a genuine Hebborn, it had its admirers. The first was the director of the Minneapolis Art Institute, Tony Clark. Tony saw it in Via Giulia and was highly impressed by what he called its 'organised freedom'. He even suggested that he might buy it for the Art Institute, but I was not at all keen on the idea – museums are mostly slow to pay up – so I said that the drawing was already sold. The next person to express great admiration for my 'Piranesi' was Hans. I had first sent him a photograph, and when he had shown interest I sent him the actual drawing, which was no simple matter. On the face of it the drawing was an important work by a great Italian artist and the Italian government would not have granted an export licence. And as there was no way in which I could have convinced their experts that I had made it myself – it bore no signature but every line was signed Piranesi – the only thing to do was smuggle it out of Italy which, because of its large size, was not easy. One does not fold Old Master drawings, and even rolling them up is best avoided, so I gave it to a friend of mine who was used to smuggling. His name was Martin and he normally earned his livelihood smuggling gold from India. All went well and in due course I received the following communication from Hans:

> Perridge House
> Pilton
> Shepton Mallet, Somerset
>
> 15 August 1969
>
> My dear Eric,
>
> You will have heard from my bank and from your friend, that he delivered the drawing safely to my son. But I am rather ashamed to remember suddenly, that I have not written to you. There are a few mitigating circumstances, the house full of elderly visitors, who had to be humoured, plenty of technicalities in the garden, etc. etc.
>
> The drawing is really imposing, there has not been a proper preparatory drawing for a print in the market, as far as I can remember and there are very few extant anyway. I suppose they got lost or destroyed in the process of print making.
>
> Who knows what it is worth. It may be too large for some, others might prefer a capriccio made as such. But surely size and the fact that it is for a definite print will make it more attractive for different clients. A drawing of such calibre creates its own customer, I always maintain – and I shall tailor the price according.
>
> I am happy to have such a marvellous work by one of my favourite masters and thank you very much again.
>
> Yours,
> Hans

The above letter was soon followed by another which gives some idea of how rapidly prices were rising for Old Master drawings since my 1963 sales of £100-£200 Gainsboroughs.

Perridge House
Pilton
Shepton Mallet, Somerset

19 August 1969

My dear Eric,

My mistake: I spelt your name with a u instead of an o, so the bank cabled back to London, but I hope it is cleared up. Sorry about this and sorry to have to ask you for an invoice in due form, the Bank of England insists on it. So please write on your note paper and give it some date *previous* to the sending of the drawing. You know the sort of text, addressed to me, and then: to a half share in a drawing by Giovanni Battista Piranesi, Lire 6,500,000.

Add to the bottom 'the drawing will be sent to you by messenger, owing to its size'. It is silly, but we have to keep the officials happy.

The main thing is that the drawing is here in all its beauty and that you got your money.

Incidentally, the bill is only for the satisfaction of the Bank of England, nothing whatsoever to do with anything else.

All the best,
Hans

At the time, 6,500,000 lira was somewhere in the region of £4,300, which means that the 'cost' price to Hans and myself was as far as he knew £8,600, so when he later sold it to the National Gallery of Denmark for £14,000, he had made £2,500, whereas I, as the creator of the work, had made the handsome sum of £11,300. For once the tables had been turned and it was the artist not the dealer who had the larger slice of the cake. Even so, the high price Hans obtained was to seem relatively low compared to sales of my later Piranesis, a number of which were to fetch over £100,000.

In January 1970 I was again staying with Anthony in Portman Square, and perhaps this is the moment to introduce the reader to Anthony's live-in friend, John. John was Irish and an ex-guardsman who was said to have been very handsome in his youth, but when I met him he was middle-aged, and slightly puffed from drink. He worked as a jeweller's assistant in Burlington Arcade, and dealt in jewellery as a sideline. He had a ready wit and could be good company. Being no intellectual, his interests were confined to sex and money – with time, exclusively to money. And it was John's overwhelming interest in money which led him to suggest that he act as my agent in London. It was through him that I sold a drawing which caused quite a stir in Old Bond Street, and was later bought by the British Museum (Fig. 78). Beyond asking him to get what he could for it and take ten per cent commission, I did

Fig. 80: 'Augustus John', *Dorelia*, 1970, pencil

not discuss the unattributed drawing with John. This was because I knew that he could easily get expert opinion – Anthony would direct him to the appropriate authority. Whoever the expert consulted was, they seem to have been convinced that the work they were looking at was by Van Dyck and, with this grand attribution to give him confidence, John did something I could very well have done myself – he offered the drawing to Colnaghi's where, according to him, he had great difficulty in persuading Christopher to buy it. And it was only after much persuasive sales-talk of the kind he had mastered selling jewellery in Burlington Arcade that he managed to get the princely sum of £200. Remembering that prices for good Old Master drawings had risen sharply, and assuming that Christopher would not have bought the drawing unless he thought it was a real Van Dyck, we can be sure that however stingy he may have been feeling that day, he would certainly have offered a fairer price for it than £200. Clearly jewellery dealers are no more honest than art dealers, and I had been cheated. I was, however, compensated for the loss of money by seeing my drawing as the centre piece of Colnaghi's Summer Exhibition of Old Master and English Drawings, 1970. As the Van Dyck was considered the most important work in the exhibition it was reproduced as the frontispiece of the catalogue and described as follows:

22 SIR ANTHONY VAN DYCK 1599-1641
The Crowning with Thorns
Pen and ink with brown wash, 261 × 287

A preparatory study, which has only recently come to light, for the painting of *The Crowning with Thorns*, formerly in the Kaiser-Freidrich Museum, Berlin (G. Glück, Van Dyck [Klassiker der Kunst]. Stuttgart, 1931, pl.48), which was executed during his first Antwerp period, before he went to Italy in 1621. Three other compositional sketches, in the Victoria and Albert Museum (H. Vey, *Die Zeichnungen Anton van Dycks*, 1962, no.72, pl.98), in the Fodor Collection, Amsterdam (Vey, no.74, pl.100), can be connected with the painting. All four drawings differ considerably in detail both from one another and from the painting. The present drawing, which is the freest in execution and the farthest from the painting, would appear to be the earliest of the group. Frontispiece.

'The freest in execution' – what now of Max Friedlander's statement that all forgeries can be detected by their 'pedantically anxious execution'? The Van Dyck was not my only drawing in Colnaghi's show, for catalogue number 35 was also made by me (Fig 79). Again, it was honoured with an illustration and was described thus:

35 JAN VAN HUYSUM 1682-1749
A Flower-piece
Black chalk and grey wash with watercolour, 451 × 370

As the following review in *The Burlington Magazine* (June 1970, p.410) suggests, Colnaghi's exhibition was an important one:

An enormous exhibition of drawings is being held throughout the month of June at Colnaghi's, this year combining English and continental drawings. So varied is the fare, one hardly knows where to start, or where to end. It always seems to me to be more sensible to refer in this column to a few items only, instead of to try and convey the whole range of the exhibits, but this does mean omitting the mention of many drawings which have some pictorial, topographical, or sentimental appeal. One loves drawings for so many different reasons: the Van Huysum flowerpiece, for instance, is quite uninteresting as a subject, but one's imagination is caught by the way the artist converts these ordinary flowers into a Baroque flourish as though like flames they were licking the frame above them. Bainborough Castle must have been drawn innumerable times in the nineteenth century and one hardly wishes to see again what it looks like, but seldom can it have been made the excuse for such a delightfully fresh sunlit landscape as by Frederick George Cotman in 1891. The churches, villas and farm buildings by Tiepolo are quite trivial, and yet what picturesqueness he infuses into these walls by a twist to the brush! Bison converts his antique frieze into a Tiepoloesque fantasy by the application of pink and grey washes. I have picked out some charming objects. But Colnaghi's offer us, not charm only, but also grandeur; drawings which make no attempt to seduce us, but point a warning finger at us, to remind us that art is also made of sterner stuff. Into this category come the Van Dyck *Crowning with Thorns*, a study for the painting in the Kaiser-Friedrich; Le Sueur's Carthusian Monk connected with a series of paintings of 1645-47, and an Annibale Carracci scene of hanged men, which as draughtsmanship is not particularly distinguished, but casts such a strange light on his character, that he should have made such a merciless study of them from the death (the catalogue says from the life), swaying there on their gallows. I must also record a Thomas Jones drawing of *Nemi* (1777) done very shortly after his arrival in Italy; a large group of drawings from a Chinnery sketchbook; an early John Linnell (1814) of a Derbyshire landscape; a beautiful Keene full-length of a Spanish model; a Bonington choir screen in Amiens Cathedral; a Cecco Bravo red chalk *Angel*; an imposing Primaticcio *Venus seated by an urn* – but already by listing too much I have betrayed my good resolutions.

This review was written by *The Burlington Magazine*'s editor, Benedict Nicholson. Mr Nicholson obviously approved of my work, for not only did he put both of my contributions to the exhibition in his selection of thirteen drawings to be mentioned out of the 142 items Colnaghi's were showing, but he also placed them at the head of the two categories into which he divided the exhibits. That is, he placed the 'Van Huysum' at the top of his list of 'charming objects', and the 'Van Dyck' tops his list of the drawings made of 'sterner stuff'. One wonders if had he known at the time that these two drawings were modern what his opinion of them would have been. Would he still have thought them the best drawings in the show? This of course we shall never know, but there are a number of things in his review which, to me, speak well of Mr Nicholson as a connoisseur. First is his statement that: 'We love drawings for so many different reasons'. It is so refreshing to hear somebody in the art world confessing to love his subject, instead of looking at art as some terrible chore, and always grumbling about its problems and difficulties, rather than simply enjoying it. Then there is his healthy disrespect for names – note how he dismisses a work attributed to Annibale Carracci, who is doubtless one of the most famous (justly so) draughtsmen of all time, as 'not particularly distinguished', and at the same time enthuses over something by a certain Frederick George Cotman, whose fame, if he has any, has certainly not spread beyond a handful of collectors. But perhaps because he was kind enough to single out my work for special mention, I am biased in Mr Nicholson's favour.

The Van Dyck and the Huysum were hanging together on Colnaghi's walls for the whole of June 1970, plenty of time for the experts to see any 'uncanny resemblance' between them, but apparently nobody did. Curiously enough I see a truly uncanny resemblance between my Van Dyck and No.18 in the illustrated catalogue (a Guercino), made all the more uncanny by the fact it is not my work at all. What happened to the Huysum I do not know, but the Van Dyck was sold to the British Museum for an undisclosed amount which we may be sure was a considerably higher sum than the £200 which, according to John, was all Colnaghi paid him for it.

Fig. 81: 'Giovanni Battista Piranesi', *Study for an Etching, c.* 1963. Sold by Hans Calmann and in process accumulated a signature

Another exhibition I went to see in the summer of 1970 was at Roland, Browse and Delbanco, actually of 19 Cork Street, but who, because of the added lustre, gave their address as 19 Cork Street, Old Bond Street, London W1. Again this was an important exhibition and was entitled 'Roland, Browse and Delbanco 25th ANNIVERSARY EXHIBITION, Drawings of Importance of the 19th & 20th Century'. The exhibits were by such illustrious artists of modern times as Bonnard, Degas, Delacroix, Forain, Guys, Klee, Kokoschka, Matisse, Millet and Picasso. There too was a Hebborn (Fig. 80), but catalogued as:

>No.52 Augustus John 1878-1961
>Pl.48 Dorelia
>   Black chalk 20¾ × 15 in
>   Signed. c.1909
>   Ex. Coll.: Eric Hebborn

I have never fully been able to assimilate Hans Calmann's advice about never underestimating the stupidity of others, and the incompetence of certain dealers still amazes me. Take for example the above catalogue entry. It is perfectly understandable that the gallery attributed the drawing to Augustus John, because it looks

Fig. 82: 'Giovanni Battista Piranesi', *Study for an Etching, c.* 1963. Sold by Hans Calmann

315

exactly like one of his works, but how in heaven's name can a competent expert mistake a pencil drawing for one in 'black chalk'? But at least Roland, Browse and Delbanco gave the provenance correctly, and if they had done the same with the Sickerts, Mintons, Whistler, Picasso, Degas, and other modern masters that they had bought directly and indirectly from me over the years, it would now be easy to trace a substantial proportion of my relatively few essays in impressionist and other modern styles.

Meanwhile, life at San Filippo was very enjoyable. Edgar and I were extremely happy together, we lacked none of the creature comforts, and had a host of friends. Both of us enjoyed entertaining, and, having domestic help, we thought nothing of giving garden parties for twenty to thirty people, and there were occasions when we entertained as many a hundred. We took infinite pains over the preparations, and served our guests the best of everything. Mostly we were lucky with the weather, and the beauty of the garden was perhaps the most important single factor that contributed to everybody's enjoyment. Our usual guests like Moyra and Manfred lived locally, whereas Ivo, Carlo and Renata were connected in some way or another with antique dealing in Rome, and then there were those whom Edgar had met while working in the theatre. These last – Tiffany, Renato, Farid, a colourful crowd of flower children – were performing in the Rome staging of the musical *Hair*, for which Edgar had also successfully auditioned. It would be pleasant to indulge myself in setting down here a more detailed account of those happy days of partying with our friends in the lovely surroundings of our charming old home, on those days when Edgar and I would say as Horace said: 'Today is the day to drink and dance on, dance then, Merrily, friends, till the earth shakes . . . ' But I suspect such reminiscence would be of more interest to myself than the reader, and will therefore return to the principal theme of these pages – faking.

Hans had some difficulty selling the 'Cossa' drawing that I had taken with me to show him together with the Poussin at the Excelsior and seems to have been left with it for about a year. The difficulty arose not so much from the drawing itself, which was generally considered to be most attractive, but from my having shown it to experts other than Hans, one of whom had cast doubts on its authenticity. The drawing was in pen and ink, and represented the head of a youth. Cossa had not actually been in my mind when I made it, and I was thinking just of some artist working in the north of Italy towards the end of the fifteenth and the beginning of the sixteenth centuries. In this case it was not in any way at all

Fig. 83: 'Parri Spinelli', *A Standing Saint*, 1970, pen and brown watercolour on vellum (sold to Colnaghi's, then to Denys Sutton for £14,000)

copied or adapted from anything. I simply thought my way back to the Renaissance, sat down in the *bottega* of a master whose speciality was for painting marriage chests and drew one of his young apprentices. When I had completed the little study, which as I remember was finely worked, I thought it might be interesting to know what I might have made, and took it for examination to the British Museum. The authority who looked at my effort was the head of the department of prints and drawings, John Gere. Nobody could have been more helpful, and I knew at once that he was impressed by the drawing. He went to endless trouble to compare my study side by side with all the relevant *quattrocento* masters in the museum. Nor did my drawing always suffer from the comparison. Some of the museum's drawings, although doubtless authentic, were in terms of quality below the standard I had set myself. Mr Gere seemed to share my unexpressed opinion, but was puzzled. Here was a drawing of quality which fitted nowhere in the scheme of things. Was it Paduan? Florentine? Venetian? It simply did not fit, and yet it was good. 'May I keep the drawing to study for a few days?' he asked. And so, according to my self-imposed rules of conduct, I left the drawing with the keeper of the department of prints and drawing to examine in an unhurried way. When, after a week or so, I returned to pick it up together with an expert opinion, John Gere told me that in the meantime he had consulted Philip Pouncey on the matter. It will be remembered that Pouncey was the expert who, with Richard Day, was responsible for 'authenticating' my Cossa *Pageboy with a Lance* in Sotheby's, three years earlier in 1967. This time, however, it seems that Mr Pouncey was not at all convinced of the authenticity of my 'Cossa', and Mr Gere told me that he (Pouncey) did not think it was right, 'not right', in the jargon of the art world meaning fake.

Now, whenever an expert expresses an opinion, I try to examine their arguments asking myself if their reasoning is sound. In this I am rather like the school teacher who counts the pupil's arithmetical answer valid only if the workings leading up to it are correct. Pouncey had nothing to go on except the drawing itself and what was there in that drawing to tell him that it was made yesterday? The materials were old and the actual drawing style was stylistically correct, but something was not right for Mr Pouncey, what was it? After pondering this question for a few days I hit on what satisfied me as the answer. What Mr Pouncey did not like was that the drawing failed to fit into his preconceived ideas of what *quattrocento* drawing should be like, it did not relate closely enough to any of the extant material. I should have followed an existing model. There was no room in his mind for the idea that the handful of well recorded drawings surviving from the *quattrocento* might be only a tiny proportion of those actually made, and if by some miracle the lost works were suddenly to reappear, their many departures in style from those we actually possess today might, by the same logic as his, lead us to call into question the authenticity of all the *quattrocento* drawings now known to us. In other words, Pouncey was right in thinking my 'Cossa' was not from the *quattrocento*, but his reasons for thinking so did not convince me. This being the case, instead of tearing the drawing up as a failure, I offered it to Hans. In doing so, I did not hide from him the fact that perhaps *the* world authority on early Italian drawings had doubted its authenticity. On the contrary I gave every detail of my visit to the British Museum and the resulting expertise. And this accounts for some phrases in the following letters:

Perridge House
Pilton
Shepton Mallet, Somerset

16 December 1970

Dear Eric,

All good wishes for Christmas and the New Year – happiness, health and prosperity.

Thanks for the postcard from Africa, I am glad you enjoyed yourself, I wish I were in a warm climate. It is not really cold here though, just wet and wintry. No definite progress with our drawing yet, however nobody believes that it could be anything but 1500. We should be grateful to Pouncey. I showed the head to David Carritt, who without any influence from me came to the same result as I: Ferrara, one of the Schifanoia masters. As it is I am asking £5,000, if I should be able to give the drawing a definite name, instead of 'near Cossa' we might ask more.

I enclose photos of two Piranesis, slightly too large, to amuse you. Not our size, but our quality. I have even got a third one, and hope for yet another.

Do the same as I, carry on. The appetite for good drawings is still growing, on minor ones some blight.

As ever,
Hans

The photographs of the two small Piranesis (Figs. 81 and 82) did indeed amuse me – I might have made them myself. Here is Hans' second letter after the sale of the 'Cossa'. It would appear that he had eventually got a good price for it the following year and I had written to congratulate him.

39 Bruton Place
Berkeley Square, W1

20 October 1971

My dear Eric,

Many thanks for nice letter – I do appreciate such kind compliments. Sometimes one can vanquish blindness and stupidity, at least we succeeded with the Cossa.

Now the Christie's dates I gave you were wrong. Their sale is on 25 November and Sotheby's (not very interesting) two days later. So we will be back in London on Monday 22nd at the latest.

We will be at the Gritti Palace Hotel in Venice from October 24 to 31. Cannot say where we will be after that, but letters c/o Leonardo Lapiccirella, Lungarno Vespucci 18, Firenze will reach me sooner or later.

See you soon, I hope,

As ever,
Hans

1970 was such a busy year that I have almost forgotten to speak of Christopher White's visit to Anticoli, which led to a very important drawing indeed coming on to the market. It must have been late September or early October when Christopher visited San Filippo with his wife Rosemary, and, if I remember right, their young daughter. I have now forgotten the daughter's name but she struck me as being a very bright young lady. This opinion was borne out by a story Christopher told me. Apparently, the little girl knew something about her father's profession, and possibly mine too, because one day she wrote a letter to Christopher which she took the trouble to draw stamps on and push through the letter box. The letter enclosed a childish sketch, and read: 'Dear Daddy, I have just made this drawing, is it by Dürer?' It was a beautiful sunny day, and before having lunch in the garden, Christopher looked through Pannini Galleries Ltd's stock. Among the drawings which interested him were a study of a child's head in black chalk in the manner of Van Dyck, and *Busts of Two Men*, a drawing which Christopher thought to be by Sperandio. I recall him looking very closely, and for some time, at the 'Van Dyck', but he did not buy it. (Eventually this drawing was bought by Hans who said it was a study by Rubens of one of his sons). Christopher did, however, buy the 'Sperandio'. I asked very little for it because I did not imagine for a moment that the experts would take it seriously. Unfortunately, I was wrong in this supposition and it was this 'Sperandio' which was to be the cause of exposing the Pierpont Morgan 'Cossa'

320

as a forgery. Again, as with Hans's *Standing Saint*, I had been foolish enough to use a piece of the same paper for the 'Sperandio' as I had employed for the making of the 'Cossa' *Page Boy*. My faulty reasoning had been that the probability of the two drawings being brought together was too slight to worry about. And had I been correct in my assumption about my 'Sperandio' not being good enough for the experts to take seriously, no doubt it and the Pierpont Morgan sheet would never have been seen together, but, far from dismissing the Sperandio, the experts thought it so important that it ended up being bought by the National Gallery of Washington.

There is no doubt in my mind that Christopher, who is really more expert on the Dutch, Flemish and German schools, before he sold the 'Sperandio' to Washington, would have consulted other experts. So the question arises in my mind why did they give thumbs up to the feeble 'Sperandio' and thumbs down to Hans's high-quality 'Cossa' of a *Youth's Head?* The answer is, I imagine, for the very same reason that the Pierpont Morgan drawing was originally 'authenticated': for like that work the Sperandio can be compared with an undoubtedly authentic drawing, insofar as period goes, in the British Museum (1936-10-10-16) whereas Hans's 'Cossa' stands alone, with only its quality to commend it. On that autumn day in 1970, in Villa San Filippo, when Christopher had been shown the drawings in Pannini Galleries' stock and made a selection from them to buy for Colnaghi's, I brought out for his perusal a photograph of a drawing I had made on vellum in the manner of a late *trecento* and early *quattrocento* Italian painter called Parri Spinelli (Fig. 83). This artist was of particular interest to me in my studies of the development of drawing styles, because he is perhaps the earliest draughtsman to make use of *pentimenti* and, in this respect, foreshadowed Leonardo. A clear example of Spinelli making a very definite alteration while leaving his original thought visible underneath is to be found in the British Museum (1895-9-15-480, verso).

Christopher was impressed by the photograph and would have liked to see the original, but I did not want him to have sight of it right there and then, because as this was an exceptionally important drawing, I wanted him to take the photograph to London first, look up the literature on Spinelli, compare the photo with the works normally given to the artist, and generally brush up his knowledge of this painter from Arezzo, so that when he saw the actual drawing his eye would be sharpened. This was in accordance with my self-imposed rule of never hitting an expert with his acumen down. So I invented a story about the Spinelli being in a private collection in Switzerland, but if after studying the photograph in London Christopher was still interested, then I would arrange to take the drawing to him at Colnaghi's. Christopher wasted no time and in a few days I received the following telegram.

LONDON 16/10/70 ORE 18

DRAWING ON VELLUM APPEARS TO BE FLORENTINE ABOUT 1400 NEAR TO PARRI SPINELLI IN VIEW OF QUALITY AND DATE WE WOULD DEFINITELY BE INTERESTED BUT IS IT POSSIBLE TO SEE IT? DOES PHOTOGRAPH MAKE IT LOOK DARKER AND MORE IMPRESSIVE? VERY BEST WISHES.
CHRISTOPHER

How I responded to this communication I have no record, but it seems from the following that I had other business to attend to connected with Colnaghi's.

P. & D. COLNAGHI & CO. LTD.
(ESTABLISHED 1760)

14 Old Bond Street
London, W1X 4JL

CJW/EB

22 October 1970

Eric Hebborn, Esq.,
Italy.

Dear Eric,

Thank you so much for your letter which arrived this morning. I was delighted to hear about the Vanvitelli and much look forward to seeing it when you bring it over. It is good news that it looks very much better in the original. I was not quite certain from your cable whether you wanted us to send the whole purchase price or only half. As you will realise we have sent the whole amount but since we owe you some money for the drawings I bought from you the other day, either outright or in half share, I will work out our account and send you a copy in due course.

The more I look at the vellum drawing, the more convinced I feel of the attribution to Parri Spinelli or at least the whole group are by the same hand. Certain doubts have been raised about whether the attribution to Spinelli is correct. I do not think this matters too much as drawings of that date are so rare. Moreover, the recent catalogue of early Italian drawings includes them under Spinelli's name. If you are able to get the drawing and bring it to London, so much the better but I would be very sorry to lose it because the owner would not allow it out of his possession, which I think is quite possible. As you have seen it, and in view of your comments, I would be prepared to trust

Fig. 84: *Edgar*, 1969, bronze (Collection Edgar
Alegre)

your judgement and buy it with you on the strength of the photograph. The price if I remember rightly, was in the region of £7,000.
The only alternative I can think of, would be if the owner would allow
me to see it in Zurich. I can easily go over there for the day. I leave the
whole matter in your hands, as I have complete trust in your judgement
of the quality and condition. It would be a most exciting acquisition.

The cold has descended on London and we think longingly of our
warm days in Rome. I have just collected the photographs I took at
the villa which further revives our happy memories. I am so pleased
Charlotte is coming out to dinner with you. We very much look forward to seeing you in London. We have a spare bed which you would
be most welcome to use. Do let me know if you would like to stay.

With very best wishes from us all to you and Edgar.

Yours ever
Christopher

Fig. 85: *Louis*, bronze, 1971 (ex collection Marie
Grey)

At this point, an unscrupulous person would simply have pocketed
Colnaghi's money without giving them the chance of examining the
original, but for all my faults I can claim to have a sense of fair
play, and I would not allow the firm to buy in the dark and certainly not on my judgment. The decision as to what the drawing
was had to be left to the experts. And so it was that once again I
packed my bags with Old Masters, and flew to London.

Leaving the 'Spinelli' with Christopher, I told him that the
owner had agreed to let the drawing out of his possession for two
weeks, during which time Colnaghi's might study it at their leisure.
A fortnight was in fact ample time, and after Christopher had taken
it to the British Museum to compare the vellum drawing with their
Spinelli and collected the opinion of other leading experts, he
decided to buy a half share in it at £3,500, a cheque for which
Colnaghi's made out to me there and then. But even with

Fig. 86: *Peter*, 1971, bronze (ex collection John
Gaskin)

Colnaghi's cheque in my pocket, I felt some misgivings over the
matter. These stemmed from my knowledge of the rather careless
technique I had employed in the making of my Spinelli. What had
happened was this. First of all I had made a number of rough pencil sketches on scrap paper to work out the pose of the saint and the
general arrangement of his draperies. When satisfied that one of
them might do, I very carefully developed the drawing in the right
ink on genuine fourteenth-century paper, but I was not happy with
the result. It was stiff and archaic, and although these are qualities
that could be ascribed to many of the drawings housed in museums
that are ascribed to Spinelli, I thought I could do better. Unfortunately, however, I had used up the only sheet of fourteenth-
century paper I had at that moment. Then it occurred to me that in
Spinelli's day vellum was as common a support for drawings as
paper, nor did it cost any more. True there were no extant

drawings by this particular master on vellum, but there was no reason why he might not have used it. Moreover, any discrepancies in the style of my drawing from the known examples of the artist's work could be explained by this variation in technique. The vellum that I had at hand was taken from the binding of an eighteenth-century book, and as real vellum is prepared from animal skin, and hence was once alive, it could theoretically be dated by the carbon 14 dating method. Added to this, in my impatience to set down the drawing before inspiration faded, I did not take the trouble to pre-pare the correct ink, and as my former supply was finished I simply used Windsor and Newton watercolour, which the slightest appli-cation of moisture would have at once removed. Christopher had mentioned to me his intention to have the drawing, which was badly cockled, treated by the restorers at the British Museum, and I was afraid that once the 'Spinelli' was thoroughly examined by the scientific department as a necessary step towards its 'restora-tion', the late date of the materials would be discovered, and Colnaghi's might want their money back. This being so, I thought of giving the old firm some of its money back at once. So pretending to have got a discount from the fictitious owner in Zurich, I sent Colnaghi a cheque to soften the blow should the drawing be discovered to be a dud. This ruse gave rise to the following:

P. & D. COLNAGHI & CO. LTD.
(ESTABLISHED 1760)

14 Old Bond Street
London, W1X 4JL

CJW/EB

22 October 1970

Eric Hebborn, Esq.,
Italy.

Dear Eric,

Thank you very much indeed for your letter. We were delighted to hear that you were able to get a reduction on the price of the Spinelli drawing. You must have done some persuasive bargaining. Thank you very much for your cheque for £670. We are also grateful for the receipt in duplicate so that we can send your share of the proceeds to you in Rome. Now that I know the drawing is ours, I will take it up to the Head Mounter and Restorer at the British Museum whom I have asked to undertake the mounting of the drawing.

I am enclosing a photograph of the Claude drawing so that you can show it to your prospective customer. I will keep it reserved for you so perhaps you would very kindly let me know as soon as you have some sort of decision.

I will certainly let you know of any developments at Portman

Square. Unfortunately we did not see them yesterday as Anthony wanted to postpone his visit until next Sunday. We greatly enjoyed seeing you. Do come again soon and as I said, there is always a bed available.

With very best wishes.

Yours ever,
Christopher

When I next saw my Spinelli it was beautifully restored and mounted. Apparently the British Museum's restorer had found nothing wrong with it beyond mentioning to Christopher that his job had been made particularly difficult on account of the 'fugitive' ink. What a relief it was to hear that! All that now remained was for Colnaghi's to find a purchaser and there would be more revelry in San Filippo. The buyer was not long in turning up in the person of a very distinguished art historian, Denys Sutton. This scholar had been the editor of *Apollo* since 1962, and was the art critic of the *Financial Times*. He had also been art critic for *Country Life* and sale-room correspondent of the *Daily Telegraph*, as well as a visiting lecturer at Yale University and a fine arts specialist at UNESCO. He organised the exhibitions of 'Bonnard' and 'France in the 18th Century' at the Royal Academy, and his many publications included magazine articles, catalogue introductions and books on painters and painting. Apart from his critical studies of Titian, Velázquez, Whistler, Toulouse-Lautrec, Rodin, Derain, and other artists, he had published Richard Wilson's *Italian Sketch-Book*. So you see, my Spinelli went to somebody well equipped to appreciate it and one who was prepared to pay £14,000 for the pleasure of owning it. Half of the sum came to me, which together with the £2,830 I had already received brought my earnings on the deal up to almost £10,000.

It was with Colnaghi's money that Edgar and I went for a splendid holiday in Morocco from where I sent the postcard for which Hans thanks me in one of the letters quoted above. We stayed in a de luxe hotel that had, we were told, once been a royal palace. Originally designed along indigenous lines, it had a great central courtyard where one could escape the African sun and walk in the shade of orange trees and enjoy the splash and sparkle of fountains, and from its Berber tower one had a fine view over the *medina* of Marrakesh. During the Second World War it had been the residence of the American Vice-Consul, to whom in January 1943 Roosevelt and Churchill paid a visit for no more warlike a purpose than that of watching the sunset on the Atlas Mountains. This idea was from Churchill, who had happy memories of a visit to Marra-

Fig. 87: *Baron Edmond de Rothschild*, plastalina,
1972, preparatory study for the portrait in the
Knesset (destroyed)

kesh in the winter of 1935-36 – he described the place as 'the Paris
of the Sahara' where all the caravans had come from Central Africa
for centuries to be heavily taxed *en route* by the tribes in the
mountains and afterwards swindled in the Marrakesh markets, receiving the return, which they greatly valued, of the gay life of the
city, including fortune-tellers, snake-charmers, masses of food and
drink, and the largest and most elaborately organised brothels in
the African Continent. I cannot vouch personally for the brothels,
but otherwise little had changed in the intervening years. The old
palace had obviously been enlarged and was now equipped with a
huge swimming pool around which we noted much wealth and
glamour escaping the rigours of a European winter. We ourselves
spent most of our two-week vacation sightseeing, dressed up in kaf-
tans, mingling with the crowd in the *souk*, posing for snapshots on

Fig. 88: *Baron James de Rothschild*, plastalina,
1972, preparatory study for the portrait in the
Knesset (destroyed)

reluctant-looking camels, being driven over the Atlas Mountains in
air-conditioned cars to see the desert, and visiting certain 'blue
people'. We thoroughly enjoyed ourselves and were most grateful
to the experts and dealers who had made our little holiday possible.

There was, however, work to be done. Apart from more Old
Masters, there was my own work and other studies to attend to.
Moreover, I was beginning to receive commissions for portrait
sculpture. It all began with a bronze head that I made of Edgar
(Fig. 84). This portrait was admired by many visitors to San
Filippo, including Anthony, Marie, and a friend who was a neighbour of ours in Via Giulia called Peter. Peter was the first to commission a portrait, and for many weeks he was a regular weekend
guest. He sat for his portrait on the front terrace of the villa. He was
a patient model, and it was pleasant working out of doors, which

seems to me a sensible thing to do with sculpture, because one sees one's work under various changes of light, so avoiding the distortions to which working in a light coming from one direction only too often gives rise. The next person to give me a commission was Marie. She wanted to have Louis' likeness (Fig. 85). There was no question of Louis coming out to Italy to pose. He disliked travelling intensely and it was with the greatest reluctance that he consented to make an occasional visit to his own family in Switzerland. So it was arranged that Louis should sit for his portrait in the crowded front room of 65 Gordon Mansions. A space had been only partially cleared in the centre of the room and the objects preventing the entrance of daylight removed from in front of the windows. My sitter posed in a chair dating from Elizabethan times which was no more than a few sticks of timber joined together in a most rustic fashion with no regard for the comfort of the sitter, but it had a fine silken patina and Louis was fond of it. The model, like the sculptor, was knee deep in a sea of old maps and prints on which floated the flotsam and jetsam of ancient history: boxes of Egyptian scarabs and jewellery, heads broken from Tanagra figures, Etruscan vases, Roman lamps, etc. etc. Working under such conditions, where one could hardly move for fear of damaging some precious relic of the past, was, to say the least, difficult. In fact I decided that I would have to do most of the work away from the model, in Italy. With this in mind I confined myself to making preparatory drawings from as many different angles as the cramped conditions allowed and making a rough model in plastilina – life-size, and with the principal measurements established on it.

Marie objected to the lock of hair which fell down over Louis' face, and let it be known she did not wish to see it immortalised. As, however, the lock seemed to me a very important feature of the likeness which would also give an interesting movement to the design, I went against her wish. Some months later, when I invited Louis and herself to see the finished bronze, which Anthony kindly allowed me to show in the handsome surroundings of his study in the Courtauld Institute, Marie wondered from where I had drawn the inspiration for the falling lock of hair, as Louis had not, and had never had, such an appendage. The truth was that she had cut it off, and very recently, because my old friend kept moving his hand to where the lock had for so long hung, his face still wearing the expression of surprise and disbelief that one imagines was Samson's under similar circumstances. There was, however, no arguing with Marie; if she said Louis had never had a lock of hair falling down over one eye then that was that. In all other respects both she and

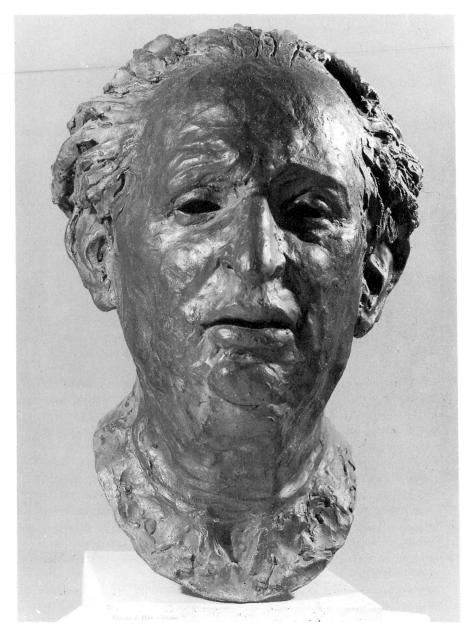

Fig. 89: *Hans Calmann*, bronze, 1973 (Collection John Calmann, photographed from artist's copy)

Fig. 90: *Raymond*, bronze, 1973 (Collection
Peter Stubbe, photographed from artist's copy)

Louis approved of the bronze and after I had made a promise to
remove the offending lock of hair, a promise which everybody
tacitly understood was not to be kept, the portrait was removed to
the chaos of 65 Gordon Mansions, out of which it had grown.

In the autumn of 1971, I made a bust of a handsome call-boy
named Peter (Fig. 86). This work was commissioned by three of his
regular customers, all rich men. One was the owner of a well-
known restaurant and night club, one a West End jeweller, and the
third was Anthony's live-in friend, John. John and Peter stayed at
San Filippo during the process of drawing and modelling in preparation for the bust. They were joined for a week by Anthony who
said some very flattering things about the portrait I was making,
and I think it was this bust that impressed him enough to obtain for
me a commission to make posthumous portraits of two distinguished members of the Rothschild Family.

Sometime in May of 1972 I received an invitation from Mrs
James Li de Rothschild to have tea with her in her palatial town
house, in St James's Place, to discuss the commission. It was a

In order to make the Rothschild paintings from the uninspiring photographs without copying them, I made models of the heads and so was able to choose which angle to paint them from (Fig. 87 and Fig. 88). I painted them, if not from the life, at least from the round. This work was carried out during the summer of 1972, and the paintings were delivered in September of that year. The following letters from the baroness to Anthony and myself show that they were well received.

11 September 1972

Dear Mr Hebborn,

I don't know how to tell you the immense relief and pleasure the sight of your pictures has given me – I do think it miraculous how you have conveyed the impression of idealistic will power in both portraits. I cannot think how you achieved this from the photographs provided (some of which I hear with regret never reached you).

Please do accept all my thanks.

Yours sincerely,
Dorothy Li de Rothschild

Fig. 94: 'Stefano della Bella', *Negro on a Horse*, 1974, pen and brown ink and grey wash (sold through Christie's, Rome, 12 November 1974)

The Pavilion
Eythrope
Aylesbury

6 October 1972

My dear Anthony,

Have just got back from Israel and heard you have been back in hospital for about a week – I do so hope this will tie up all the loose bits of your inside and that after a *proper* convalescence you will really begin to feel the benefit of all you have gone through.

No answer of course, but I think you will be glad to know that the pictures looked really well in the Knesset, and the new Yemenite speaker hit the nail on the head when he said he was at first startled but in no time at all began to realise the superb characterisation of both the pictures – unfortunately, Mrs Gad, who is responsible for all inside decoration, was away, but I am confident she will get suitable frames for them. They are just the right size and can hang side by side on one panel. All affectionate good wishes from Marie and myself.

Dollie

More commissions came my way and portrait sculpture began to take up much of my time. One commission was from Hans's son John, who wished to have a bronze of his father (Fig. 89). Hans posed in the garden of Perridge House, and as with Louis' portrait, I made numerous drawings and a life-size model, from which to work up the final bronze. Mrs Calmann, Gerda, would occasionally come to watch the progress of the plastilina model. As the process of modelling, in contrast to that of carving, is one of building up by addition, the first stages of a modelled portrait are skeletal – one starts, if one knows one's job, with the bony structure, leaving the features until last. Gerda was disappointed and lamented the fact that I had not done justice to Hans' great Jewish nose, and protruding ears. When, however, I delivered the completed portrait it seems to have been generally liked and on 7 May 1973 John wrote me a kind letter in which he said: 'Thank you for making such a good head of my father. I like it very much and it is going to stay in my collection. Everyone who sees it (or *nearly* everyone) likes it, Daddy also does, but can't live with himself!'

The phrase '*nearly* everyone' suggests that Gerda was still not happy about the portrait, but she was not the easiest of people to please. I recall standing with her before a magnificent sunset and asking her if she did not think it wonderful. 'No,' she said, turning her back on it, 'it reminds me of blood!' More portrait sculptures were to follow. There was one of a Mafia boss, where I produced my preliminary studies closely watched by four silk-suited gunmen.

Another was a posthumous portrait of a working-class youth who had fallen off a high scaffolding into a cement mixer, and whose mother felt that the proper way of using the insurance money was to spend it on giving the young man a splendid tomb fit for a prince. Then there was the bust of Raymond (Fig. 90) which I personally like because there seems to be something Pergamon about it, and several others.

My work as a portraitist in no way diminished the output of 'Old Masters', and in the summer of 1972, at the very same time as I was

Fig. 95: 'Fra Bartolomeo', *Standing Saint Viewed from Behind*, 1974, pen and brown ink (sold through Christie's Rome, 12 November 1974)

busy on the Rothschild portraits, I was also exhibiting in Colnaghi's exhibition, 'Drawings by Old Masters, June 27-July 29'. A reproduction of one of my contributions to the show (*A Huntsman*, in the style of Stefano della Bella, Fig. 91) appears in the *Supplement* to *The Burlington Magazine* of June of that year as one of the 'Notable Works of Art now on the Market'. A further mention of this drawing together with two of its fellows is made in the following issue of *The Burlington*, July 1972, p.484, this time in a review of Colnaghi's exhibition by Benedict Nicholson: 'Stefano della Bella is shown in three feathery drawings of horsemen, where movement is conveyed by grey wash and by different positions of riders' arms and horses' legs. The very uncertainty of the location of the limbs helps along the liveliness.'

This is perceptive, but Mr Nicholson's list of my 'Stefano della Bellas' in Colnaghi's exhibition is, however, not quite complete, and the catalogue entries are as follows:

2 STEFANO DELLA BELLA 1610-1664 [Fig. 92]
A Young Boy teaching his Dog to Beg
Pen and brown ink with grey wash. 120 × 136
A preparatory study in the same direction for Stefano's etching (de Vesme 98). There are two other studies connected with this print, one formerly in the collection of the late Carl Winter and the other in the Uffizi (Inv. no.795f).

3 STEFANO DELLA BELLA 1610-1664
A Negro Cavalryman
Pen and brown ink with grey wash. 239 × 212
This is a particularly fine study, possibly connected with Stefano's series of eleven etchings (de Vesme 270-80) depicting Polish, Hungarian and Negro cavalrymen.

4 STEFANO DELLA BELLA 1610-1664
A Huntsman
Pen and brown ink with grey wash. 162 × 290
A preparatory study in reverse, with notable differences, for Stefano's etching (de Vesme 759) of a stag hunt, one from the series of nine hunting prints. There is another study for this print in the Pierpont Morgan Library (J. Bean and F. Stampfle, Drawings from New York Collections, vo. II, no.88, repr.) in which the stag has been clearly drawn into the composition and the position of the huntsman's arm has been changed. Other studies connected with this print are in the Uffizi (Inv. no.454) and the Royal Collection at Windsor (Inv. no.464a).

5 STEFANO DELLA BELLA 1610-1664
A Horseman wearing a Turban and a flowing Cloak
Pen and brown ink with grey wash 125 × 103

Fig. 96: *Child on a Rocking Horse*, bronze, 1978, illustrating the sense of
movement to be achieved by repetition of certain lines in the manner of the
pentimenti of the Old Masters, notably Stefano della Bella. Compare with
Fig. 91 (Collection of the artist)

The history of these drawings began with a visit to Craddock and
Barnard in May 1971. The firm had in stock a large number of
original etchings by della Bella in a nineteenth-century edition at a
very reasonable price and I bought them for study. There is no
better way of studying a print, a painting, a sculpture, or any other
visual work of art than making a drawing of it. I do not mean by
this producing a *copy* of it. This is a point I have made a number of
times before, but it is of fundamental importance to understanding
what is an original drawing after something, and what is a copy or
an imitation, so I make no excuse for repeating myself. A drawing
after something which is not a drawing cannot be a counterfeit of
that something. If, for instance, one makes a drawing of a piece of
sculpture, one has not made a fake piece of sculpture, or any kind of
imitation of it, one has, for better or worse, made an original
drawing. So I made a series of about twenty-five original drawings
after, or in some way related to, della Bella's etchings and in his
own manner. I used, with one exception, seventeenth-century
paper, and chemical tests made later by Dr Julius Grant failed to
detect anything to prove them modern.

About half of the group I took to London, and while staying with Anthony in Portman Square had left them on a side table in my room where he chanced upon them. 'Do you think they're right?' I asked. 'It seems to me that one of them is on eighteenth-century paper.' This was in fact true, but Anthony examined them and found nothing wrong with them. When he asked what I intended to do with them, I mentioned an appointment for the following day to show them to Colnaghi's. Unknown to me at the time, Anthony then phoned Colnaghi's and advised them to buy. Christopher had by now left the firm to take up the position of Curator of Prints and Drawings at the National Gallery of Washington, and in his place was a very young man called Adrian Ward Jackson. Because of his lack of experience, I am pleased that he bought on Anthony's advice, for there is no satisfaction in deceiving the neophyte.

Colnaghi's sold many of my della Bellas before their summer exhibition. One of the purchasers was the dealer Yvonne Tan Bunzl who subsequently resold one to the National Gallery of Canada. Somehow or another this young woman found out the source of the Colnaghi drawings, and came to visit Anticoli in the hope of finding more Old Masters. In this she was not entirely disappointed and went home with a 'Pinelli' self-portrait, an 'Andrea Boscoli' myth- ological scene and a 'Bernardo Castelli'. Recently, she presented to the British Museum a drawing of mine in della Bella's manner of *Diana the Huntress*. Apparently, she felt that the Museum's exhibi- tion 'FAKE?' was somehow lacking in 'authentic' Hebborns, but as I pointed out in a letter to the organiser of the show, Mark Jones, the Museum has no shortage of my work, and if they did not care to show it, while hinting that I might be the author of a pathetic scrib- ble by some bungler, described as an Englishman living in Italy and graced with the title of the 'Maestro dei Riccioli', we must look for a reason other than shortage of material. Another lady to visit me in Anticoli looking for Old Masters was Luisa Vertova, one of Christie's drawing experts. She struck me as a very nice person in- deed, and we spent a most pleasant day together enjoying luncheon in the garden and talking shop. She was at the time looking for mat- erial to include in one of Christie's sales in Rome. Exactly what she found in Villa San Filippo is recorded on the receipt she gave me:

Hebborn Drawings
Received 22 V 1974

Fra Bartolomeo	– Apostle
Cigoli	– Capture of Christ
H-Robert	– Roman Ruins

Bertucci	– Equestrian Monument
Galeotti	– (illegible)
Empoli	– Mother and Child
Mola	– Half-naked woman
Solimena	– Death of St Francis
Castiglione	– Flight into Egypt
Gabbiani	– Diana
Anonymous	– Allegorical Figure
M. Tesi	– Architectural Project
Cambiaso	– Holy Family [Fig. 93]

Luisa Vertova

These drawings came up for sale at Christie's Rome on 12 November 1974 where together with yet another 'Stefano della Bella' (Fig. 94), they fetched in the region of £12,000. Incidentally, the 'Fra Bartolomeo' (Fig. 95) had been offered to Hans who had refused it because it was not important enough. I quote him from a letter of 6 November 1973, where he also mentions my large 'Piranesi' sold to Denmark:

> ... The photo makes a good impression, though a firm judgement is impossible without seeing the original. But even if we assume it is by Fra Bartolomeo, what is a Fra Bartolomeo price for it? It is too small for the great collector or the museums and probably too dear for the small collector.
>
> Has not the owner anything better? I am a bit chary of small fry now, as you know.
>
> There is a splendid Piranesi at Christie's on the 27th, a Pompeii one and so rather abstract. Ours was more attractive ...

In addition to portrait sculpture and Old Masters, I was working on sculptural groups from imagination, and many of these were exhibited in a one-man show in the West End in November of 1978. The owner was known for his philistinism. He made no proper contract with the artists he showed. Instead he produced a 'letter of agreement' wherein the sculptor or painter was required to accept the most unfavourable terms, whereas he himself could, after having taken a deposit against expenses, cancel the show without warning and without having to give reasons. It was not unlike the old publishers' agreements prior to the activities of the Society of Authors, which now to a large extent protects writers' interests.

The show was called 'Relationships' (8-30 November 1978) and in spite of my bad relationship with the gallery, was reasonably successful – I eventually received a cheque for £20,000. Under the title 'Moving Figures on a Sculptor Who Breaks Through the

Boundaries of Time and Space', the art critic Emanuel Cooper had this to say about it:

> Romantic sculpture with its accent on realism and sweetness and light came into its own towards the end of the 19th century. In many ways the work of Auguste Rodin marked the peak of this style; his famous figures such as 'The Kiss' and 'The Thinker' or 'The Burghers of Calais' followed in the tradition of Michelangelo and the Renaissance artists. The public was amazed at the naturalness of the sculptures which even brought accusations that the modelling looked too real and that it was cast from life. Eric Hebborn is a sculptor who works very much in the same style – but with a difference, for his figures are much more freely modelled. When Rodin wrote that 'Michelangelo freed me from academicism' it is also evident that though strongly influenced by the styles and methods of Michelangelo and Rodin, Eric Hebborn has also freed himself from the romantic context of modelling in clay and casting in bronze.
>
> Hebborn's exhibition, 'Relationships' at the Alwin Gallery, Grafton Street, London W1 consists of bronze figures some over 5 feet tall, all on various sorts of relationship – a theme which recurs in various ways throughout the exhibition. His subject is the human form – some are handsome male figures, alone or in pairs, others are children, but all lure the eye on, only to bring it to a startling halt. Each sculpture is not only concerned with the relationship between the various parts, whether they are two figures or not, but also with time itself. For example, the child on the back of the rocking horse is shown in multiple images as if the eye had acted like a camera and made several exposures. The horse has a second skeletal-like head, and the child leaves repeated bits of its body behind. A period of time is suggested and we do not know if the child is rocking forward or back.
>
> A male acrobat doing a hand-spring is also shown in several positions. From one head and pair of arms, two bodies emerge – the horse has two heads and eight legs shown in several positions. Hebborn has studied traditional Italian bronze casting and has introduced his own innovations. The sculptures are still but movement is cleverly suggested – the relationship between time, space, and figures is expressed. Other pieces suggest movement in different ways.
>
> One torso of a handsome male some 4 ft 6 in. high shows sensitively modelled details – features, muscles and buttocks – with a space between the front of the body and the back. Constantly we are reminded that this is sculpture and not reality, and is concerned with air and space around the pieces, which is controlled and defined with great skill.
>
> Surprisingly, this is Hebborn's first one-man show in London and the honesty of the modelling, the monumental quality of the work and the sheer force of the movement deserves much success.

It is always nice to receive compliments, but it is not just vanity that makes me quote the above piece. Emanuel Cooper has been perceptive and highlighted some of the influences on my work that derive from my study of Old Masters, and which I have used to my own ends. He mentions Michelangelo and Rodin, and certainly I have looked closely at these masters, but it was not from them that I conceived of the idea of multiple images in sculpture. The idea derives from my study of the *pentimenti* in Old Master drawings which we first discover in a definite form in Spinelli, and which found its most famous exponent in Leonardo, and from then on became common property. One artist who used *pentimenti* as more than a method of trying out different poses and positions, one who grasped the latent potential in this device for the introduction of the time element into drawing, is my old friend Stefano della Bella – and it was this and other aspects of his work which had led me to make so large a number of drawings in his manner.

A comparison between my version of Stefano della Bella's print of a huntsman (Fig. 91) and my sculpture of a *Child on a Rocking Horse* (Fig. 96) will make clear how I have adapted what I derived from della Bella to my own purpose. In my sculpture I have translated the drawn *pentimenti* into bronze. As far as I know this is an innovation, it has no precedent and can be claimed to be original.

So much happened on all fronts during those happy, productive and lucrative years which have been the subject of this chapter that I might have used the available space to write of entirely different works and events. In regard to my faking activities, I might have spoken at length of a 'Rowlandson' bought by The Witt Library and a 'Guido Reni' which I presented to the same institute because I had damaged it too much to make it saleable, a 'Lorenzo di Credi' silverpoint (made with the handle of a Georgian teaspoon) that the Barber Institute hankered after, but found difficulty in raising the funds for, an entire collection of 'Old Masters', which I arranged to be planted where Hans could discover them, and numerous lots which passed through Sotheby's, Christie's and other salerooms. I have, for instance, receipts from Christie's, one dated 20 April 1972, listing no less than thirty-four 'Old Masters', and another dated 11 April 1973 accepting for sale three 'Pinellis' and one 'Castiglione'.

As for events in my personal life, I might have written of my travels to Greece, Malta and Southeast Asia, the buying of a holiday home on an island off Sicily and a property in Trastevere in Rome, the life and death of a favourite dog called Emma Pinxit, of other one-man shows, including an exhibition of sculpture in the romantic surroundings of the Villa Gregoriana in Tivoli and a large retrospective at the British School at Rome, and much much else. But fearing to presume too much on the reader's patience I shall bring this sketchy account of my golden decade to an end.

CHAPTER XI

THE UNMASKING

'Art historians are not so superfluous after all. If they didn't exist, who would there be to explain, when we are dead, that our bad pictures are forgeries?'

Max Liebermann.

Gentlemanly and discreet, with faces like silver teapots, the better art dealers and auctioneers around London's Bond Street have long maintained their immunity from the scandals of the art world. Circumspection is the motto, coupled with a standing policy – among members of the British Antique Dealers Association – to refund the price of any fake. Therefore, when the biggest art forgery scandal in years came to a head in London last fortnight, the embarrassment was acute.

So began an article in *Time* magazine on 13 September 1976. The scandal had nothing directly to do with myself, but as the affair may be seen as a prelude to my own story of even further embarrassing the gentlemen 'with faces like silver teapots', I shall quote more from the article.

At a press conference, a rubicund, white-bearded cockney painter and restorer named Tom Keating, 59, revealed that over the past twenty-five years he had flooded the art market with anywhere from 1,000 to 3,000 pastiches of the work of dead artists, ranging from 17th century Dutch to Constable to German Expressionists. He was, Keating blithely admitted, a terrible faker. Anyone who sees my work and thinks it genuine must be around the bend. Moreover, Keating said, he did not mean his phonies to pass close tests: before setting to work he would scrawl 'fake', 'Keating' or a suitable rude word on the blank canvas, in lead-based paint which would show up under x-rays. Nevertheless, many of the works ended up in leading galleries and auction rooms, where, endowed with signatures and solid pedigrees, they were sold for even more solid prices . . .

Keating was a jolly likeable man who became something of a folk hero, but as he himself says, he was a total amateur as far as faking was concerned, and felt that his works were so bad that no one should have been taken in. This of course makes one wonder about the abilities of the experts who vetted his work and the dealers who handled them, like the Leger Galleries of Bond Street. How embarrassing to be duped by bad fakes rather than good ones. But one step forward in such an argument is – if the fake is good enough, no expert need blame himself for having been deceived – a view defended in an article discussing my own fakes which appeared in Rome's *International Daily News*, 12 March 1980: 'Done on authentic paper of the 15-16 centuries with ink and carbon above any suspicion, they are effectively the work of a true artist who has been able to fit himself into the style of the various masters he has imitated, and therefore no responsibility marks the experts of the auction houses who examined them before the sale.'

Doubtless much of the fascination that fakes seem to arouse in the layman emanates from the pleasure of seeing the experts fall flat on their faces. It is not my purpose in this chapter, however, to poke fun at them – that would be too easy, and in the end help no one. I am not an anarchist. Once I was chided by a friend for being a 'drop out', to which I replied, 'No, I'm not a drop out, I'm a stand aside.' There are, in my opinion, many things wrong with the art world, things which reflect the maladies of the world in general, and standing aside from it one can view the failings with greater clarity and objectivity, and so perhaps suggest some remedies. So while it is my aim to criticise the experts, I am conscious that if such criticism is to have any value, it must be constructive.

But before saying some hard things about the people who claim to be authorities on fine draughtsmanship, a distinction should be made between dealers and gentlemen, connoisseurs and scholars, and all of these people and a true expert. The difference between a gentleman and a dealer is simply this: with the rarest of exceptions to prove the rule, they are mutually exclusive. One cannot enter deep into the ungentlemanly muck and mire of art dealing and keep one's hands clean. Count Antoin Seilern, both an aristocrat and a great collector, knew this instinctively and would not admit into his house any picture dealer, however grand, except by the tradesmen's entrance. Unlike dealers and gentlemen, connoisseurs and scholars are not mutually exclusive, and a person may be both, but it should be borne in mind that one does not guarantee the other. One may be a connoisseur without scholarship, or a scholar without connoisseurship. This last point accounts for how, for instance,

Ellis Waterhouse, fine scholar that he undoubtedly was, could, after having just finished writing an important work on Gainsborough, have fooled himself over my study for *The Blue Boy* – he simply lacked, at least at that moment, the eye of a connoisseur.

But what distinguishes the real expert from the person – dealer, gentleman, or otherwise – who is both a scholar and a connoisseur? The answer to this is that the true expert is not only a scholar and a connoisseur, he has also been initiated into what the Italians quite rightly refer to as the *mestiere* (the craft) of art. They know art from the inside, they know how to use the artist's tools themselves and have themselves created pictures. In contrast, the average experts of today are excluded from the profoundest knowledge of art because they cannot themselves read and write its language. They are visually illiterate and their knowledge of art is limited to externals. In this they resemble a librarian who cannot read or write the language of the books he has to arrange and catalogue, and who in his ignorance groups them according to their colour, size and weight. Imagine one of his index cards:

No. 44

Blue Book
Size 10 ins × 6 ins
Number of pages 200
Weight 12 ounces

Acquired in 1908. Its charming pale colour compares favourably with an undoubtedly genuine volume in the Twit Library. But the coarseness of the paper has led Professor Fulldim to suspect that it may be spurious.

Some of the scholars' catalogue entries seem to the educated eye scarcely less ludicrous. But in suggesting that the modern authorities on drawing should at least know the rudiments of the art in which they profess to be experts, it should not be thought for a moment that I subscribe to the essentially philistine doctrine that artists alone can truly understand the work of other artists, or as Oscar Wilde puts it: 'Artists, like Greek gods, are revealed only to one another.' All I am saying is that the true expert on master drawings knows drawing from the inside out, not just from exterior measurable and catalogueable things. To understand a master drawing one does not have to be a master draughtsman oneself, any more than one has to be a great poet to appreciate a great poem. But if you cannot even read, poetry good or bad is meaningless to you. Similarly, if you cannot draw, the virtues which distinguish fine draughtsmanship from lesser work will be lost on you. True, even the non-draughtsman can up to a point recognise the subject-matter of a drawing and learn to recognise the various techniques, styles, periods, and learn parrot fashion the names and the dates of the artists, but when they know all these things they know perhaps five per cent of what it is necessary to know about drawing before one can claim to be a real expert. The other ninety-five per cent is what counts, and yet on the slender basis of a five per cent knowledge of their subject, the greater number of the so-called experts of the world set themselves up as unquestionable authorities.

In order to show some of the blunders of the authorities who examined my early work it will be necessary first to mention my own shortcomings. There is a little jingle which I read somewhere attributed to Dürer: 'Who looks for dirt would look no more if first he swept before his door.' Well, although I am looking for errors of judgment, rather than dirt, the same principle applies, and many such errors can be laid at my own door. Some of them are so gross that one wonders how even the dimmest expert could have deceived themselves. Take for instance the *Young Oriental with his Horse* which sold at Christie's for 1,400 guineas in 1968 (see Fig. 63). As a drawing it is not bad, it shows a far greater knowledge of Castiglione than most authorities on the artist have, it has not been copied from anything, and is thus an original work of art. Nevertheless, one does not have to be a Bernard Berenson to see that it is not as old as the seventeenth-century paper upon which it is drawn. 'Why' is a very good question to ask when examining drawings. This is because draughtsmen of any worth do not make marks without reasons, and if we ask ourselves in this instance why the horse's left hind leg is scarcely indicated we get a revealing answer. The animal's leg has been left as a mere indication because the draughtsman was avoiding the damage already existing on the old sheet of paper. If the paint was drawn over the holes it would have coated the thickness of the paper around the missing areas, giving proof positive that the artist was using a sheet of paper already damaged by time. But the skirting round the decayed area is in itself clear enough evidence of the fact that the seventeenth-century paper had not been employed by a seventeenth-century draughtsman. There are also more subtle errors in this 'Castiglione' of mine. The Genovese master was a great *animalier*. He had a profound knowledge of the structure of the animals he drew, whereas at the time of making this drawing I had not yet made a thorough study of the anatomy of the horse, and the shank of the animal's hind leg is too long. The muddled drawing of the young man's left hand is the result of trying too hard to correct what might perhaps have been better left as a faulty, but at least fresh, first indication, but such an error can be discovered in the works of better draughtsmen than myself. We cannot expect every expert to know the anatomy of the horse, nor can we blame them for passing over a small fault in a generally satisfactory drawing, but not to see the obvious avoidance of old damage is indefensible.

It has already been mentioned how careless I was in my early days in the making of collectors' marks, and this should have led to the early recognition of many of my productions. Although it may be argued that false collector's marks, like false inscriptions, can and do exist on genuine drawings, when an unrecorded work turns up with no provenance other than a demonstrably false one, surely that work should be looked at very closely indeed. It is my use of clumsily executed marks which should have led to the discovery that the Pierpont Morgan 'Cossa' (see Fig. 60) was spurious long before the fifteen years it actually took to discover the fact. The exposure of this drawing is worth studying in some detail. Not only because it led to the doubting of a whole group of my productions, but it gives an insight into the reasoning of the experts. First of all it must be remembered that the lone forger is challenging not one but an army of authorities. To make its way to the Pierpont Morgan, the 'Cossa' *Page Boy* had to pass the scrutiny of three sets of experts: first those of Sotheby's, Richard Day and Philip Pouncey; then those of Colnaghi's, John Baskett, James Byam Shaw and Christopher White; and finally those of the Pierpont Morgan Library itself, Miss Staenfle and her colleagues. If we are to believe the newspaper account, it took 'months of patient detective work' to provide convincing proof that the 'Cossa' was a fake. So let us examine the arguments which eventually convinced Miss Staenfle, the curator of the Pierpont Morgan and an acknowledged expert on Old Masters, that the *Page Boy* was in fact modern.

According to the newspapers, her suspicions were first aroused by Conrad Oberhuver, an Austrian, who at the time was Curator of the National Gallery of Washington. This scholar had himself bought drawings of mine from Colnaghi's, a work attributed to 'Sperandio' and allegedly another 'Cossa' (perhaps this was really the 'Cossa' I sold a half share in to Hans Calmann). Studying his purchases side by side, Mr Oberhuver was alarmed to discover that the drawings resembled each other, and instead of displaying the hands of two separate masters belonging to different schools, they both showed the flowing line of one and the same artist. In addition to this, there was a similarity in the preparation of the paper suggesting to Mr Oberhuver that both drawings had been 'washed' to

simulate age. It is impossible to comment on Mr Oberhuver's remark that his two drawings bore an 'uncanny resemblance' to each
other without knowing for certain which of my efforts the National
Gallery's 'Cossa' is. Quite possibly he is right, but one does wonder
why he did not make this observation before he spent public money
on the works rather than after. Similarly, why did he not notice the
'washed' look (if washed look there was) prior to making the acquisitions? Mr Oberhuver confided his belated misgivings to Miss
Staenfle and suggested she might take a closer look at her *Page Boy*.
Again one cannot help wondering why she had not given the drawing an exhaustive scrutiny before she bought it over a decade
before. Nevertheless, better late than later, she took Mr
Oberhuver's advice and *The Sunday Telegraph* tells us that when
Miss Staenfle looked at 'Cossa' with a 'doubting eye': 'It was suddenly obvious to her that it was "not right". There were visual and
stylistic faults in the pen and ink drawing: the pen was too flowing,
and the manner in which the ink had began [sic] to (age) look [sic]
more like the careful work of a razor blade than the passing of the
years. Although the head was still good, there were notable weaknesses in the lines around the legs and the figure's right hand . . .
The treatment of the paper also revealed the washed look that Mr
Oberhuver had noticed in Washington.'

The above clearly indicates how lacking in objectivity Miss
Staenfle was. In the first place, an objective viewer does not bring a
'doubting eye' to a drawing any more than they bring a credulous
eye. A doubting eye is a biased eye. And from her biased viewpoint
it was suddenly clear to her that the drawing was full of faults. How
the head managed to remain good is hard to imagine when so much
else had altered for the worse. We know of course that the drawing
had not changed in the least, and it was Miss Staenfle's reaction to
it which had radically altered. The seed of doubt had been sown by
Mr Oberhuver and she was looking through spectacles of mistrust.
She dared no longer give herself up to unqualified admiration of the
drawing but stared 'with gloomy and anxious suspicion', determined to trace evidence of fraud. Such an attitude would have
distorted her appraisal of any work of art genuine or otherwise. An
indication of the extent to which her judgment was influenced by
her colleague in Washington rather than a critical examination of
the 'Cossa' carried out with an open mind, is furnished by the report that she was also able to detect the washed look noticed by Mr
Oberhuver in his drawings. If true this was amazingly perceptive of
her, because in her 'Cossa' there could not possibly have been a
washed look to detect. As the paper I had employed was genuine

old paper dating from the 1400s, it would have been ridiculous for me to risk giving the game away by unnecessarily simulating age. The only reason I could possibly have had for washing the drawing would have been had I used one of the methods of 'ageing' the ink which involves soaking the paper in some bleaching agent; but as Miss Staenfle herself noticed, the ink lines had been 'aged' by friction with a razor blade. Therefore the washed look which might better be called the Washington look, was about as real as the emperor's new clothes – and although she had come to the right conclusion, she had done so with the kind of wrong reasoning which in other instances has led to the rejection of genuine work.

Once it had been established to Mr Oberhuver's and Miss Staenfle's satisfaction that the drawings they had bought for their museums were fakes, they informed Colnaghi's, who, realising that all three disputed drawings had come from me, were not a little worried that perhaps the other drawings they had acquired from the same source were also spurious. This led them to request from their customers the return of my work for inspection. Lining the drawings up, and using the doubting eye method, they discovered to their acute embarrassment that all the drawings bore the by now familiar 'uncanny resemblance' to each other, the washed look was everywhere, as was the flowing line and numberless errors in draughtsmanship. At this point Colnaghi's panicked, and on 9 March 1978 very foolishly made a statement to the press which was quoted in its essentials in *The Times* of 10 March and which was to prove as damaging to themselves as it was to me.

> About eighteen months ago, it came to our attention that the authenticity of a group of Old Master drawings which were purchased by two former directors of this gallery between eight to ten years ago, from one source and over a number of years, is now doubted. The present directors of Colnaghi's therefore decided to contact all the present owners of these drawings bought from this company and recall them for examination.
>
> Scientific tests failed to prove that any of the drawings are forgeries, but in some cases where the owners have requested it and the consensus of expert opinion has been against their authenticity, Colnaghi's have refunded the purchase price in accordance with long standing custom.

Again we find a sign of the experts' subjective approach. It is contained in the phrase: 'Scientific tests have failed to prove any of the drawings are forgeries.' Surely one cannot be said to have failed at something one has not attempted to do. Science, in its aims at least, is impartial, and the scientist involved, Dr Julius Grant, certainly would not have set out to prove that the drawings were fakes. In the manner of all reliable scientific investigators he would have made his tests and collected data without prejudice. He would have entertained no preconceived notion of what his empiric observations might or might not prove. As it turned out his data neither proved the drawings false or genuine, but unlike our experts Dr Grant was not influenced by matters such as the drawings' provenance, the opinion of others, whether his reputation would be affected for the better or the worse by his decision, or any other extraneous considerations of the kind which blur the judgment of all but the finest experts.

It was not scientific tests which failed to prove any of my drawings were forgeries, it was Colnaghi's experts. Miss Staenfle's 'doubting eye' had spread like an epidemic. Having failed to find conclusive proof of forgery, they turned to Dr Grant hoping that science would do their job for them and although the scientific evidence he provided was not acceptable proof of the drawings' authenticity, one suspects it would have been highly acceptable had it proved the works false. This lack of objectivity also works the other way. When the experts want to find something genuine they exchange the doubting eye for the credulous one. Thus when, for example, it would be a feather in their caps to make the acquisition of a Cossa or a Van Dyck or some other important work for a museum, then they tend to discover virtues rather than defects in the item offered to them. That is of course how they came to acquire my work in the first place. The doubting eye disease, an ailment Wilhem Bode spoke of as a 'fashionable complaint', which manifests itself after any sensational disclosure concerning art forgery, and which might well be called 'forgeritis', spread to the salerooms, as can be judged from this notice in *The Times*:

> DOUBTS OVER ATTRIBUTION DEPRESS ART SALES
> Both the bigger sales at Christie's yesterday were assailed by doubts over attributions. After the article in *The Times* yesterday a drawing attributed to a follower of Andrea del Verrochio of a *Youth's Head* was withdrawn from sale.
> The auctioneer announced: 'Following the unsubstantiated rumours that have circulated concerning this drawing we have advised the owner it would be best to withdraw it. In our opinion the drawing is of the period implied by the cataloguing.'
> The drawing had been estimated to fetch £10,000 to £15,000 . . .

In making the matter public, Colnaghi's used me as a scapegoat. They did not admit to having in any way made an error of judgment themselves. For fear of committing libel they made no mention of my name in their press release but sub-text was this: 'It's all the fault of that nasty Eric Hebborn in Rome, who year after year has offered us duds without telling us what they are. Expertise is no proof against villainy. We're very sorry and, as gentlemen, we have given the collectors their money back. Furthermore, we promise never ever to have anything to do with that scoundrel in Italy again.' Their aim was to deflect blame from themselves by suggesting that I am a criminal. I can hear someone protesting, 'But you *are* a criminal!' Not a bit of it. There is nothing criminal in making a drawing in any style one wishes, nor is there anything criminal about asking an expert what he thinks of it. 'But what about gaining pecuniary advantages by deception?' My answer to this is that I can see no reason why I should give my work away. Furthermore, I can truly claim never to have asked or received sums of money for my Old Masters in excess of what an artist of my reputation can command for his own work. The pecuniary advantages were gained by the dealers, and for this reason I object to being considered a criminal. However much some people may confess to a sneaking regard for rogues I do not happen to belong to the fraternity – let them save their sneaking regard for the dealers. Moreover, if Christie's, Colnaghi's, Sotheby's and other important merchants who have handled my work really think that I am a crook, why do they not press charges? The answer which comes first to mind is of course that they do not want to rock the boat, and no doubt this is true, for as London art dealer and specialist in nineteenth-century paintings David Gould said about the Keating affair: 'There's an awful lot more that hasn't come out and won't come out. You don't want to rock the market. Faith in the market is a very delicate thing.' Brian Sewell also made this point in a letter dated 31 July 1981 telling me that if my story should be aired, 'it is the connoisseurship of experts that will be in the dock, not you,' and continued with:

> As for Christie's, Sotheby's and Colnaghi's – it may surprise you to know that Julian Stock has for many years put the point that you have had a raw deal from the trade, and he is very defensive of you: Francis Russell maintains, quite properly, that it would be impossible for one single draughtsman to have produced all the drawings that are attributed to you, that nothing more than rumour surrounds the attributions, and that the gossip is damaging not only to you, but to the trade as a whole. Colnaghi's now employ no one from the days of your association with them, and their present status in the market place is about as low as it can go.

But fear of damaging the trade is not the only or even the most important reason for the dealers and experts not putting me in the dock at the Old Bailey. The truth is they have no case.

Some years ago I read a book which gave an account of the life and crimes of characters who have been termed 'aristocrats among crooks' – the confidence tricksters. It spoke of 'Count' Caliostro, the infamous eighteenth-century mountebank whom Carlyle called: 'The quack of quacks, the most perfect scoundrel that in these latter ages has marked the world's history . . . Really a liar of the first magnitude, thoroughly paced in provinces of lying, what one might call the king of lying.' It also spoke of such rogues as 'Count' Lustig who, apart from selling the Eiffel Tower not once, but twice, managed to con Al Capone and live to tell the tale. But the author steered clear of the art fakers, for the reason that the full flavour of their craft can only be savoured by the experts; otherwise it was made plain that they were worthy of inclusion among the typical (it might have said the 'genuine') swindlers. The attitude is a common one. The man in the street, our old friend Joe Bloggs, views a forged work of art in precisely the same way as he views a forged banknote. And in a way one can understand his view, for in our society works of art are generally equated with money, and the first thing one is likely to be asked about a picture is: 'How much is it worth?' On the other hand, Joe Bloggs is not the person to consult if one wants to get to the truth about the status of works of art which are labelled fake, because if Joe is a thinker at all, he is a shallow one.

So let us do what more serious intellects do, and approach the subject by first examining our terms. What is it that we really mean when we attach the word 'fake' to a work of art? One would imagine that, having used the word so often in these pages, I should have no problem whatsoever in defining what I mean by it, but in fact this is not so. Nor am I alone in finding it hard to say what, if anything, corresponds to the description 'a fake'. This explains why the British Museum's exhibition of 'false' art was entitled *Fake?*, the question mark indicating the difficulty, if not the impossibility, of giving a straightforward answer. Now, it is the way of the kind of thinker we are trying to emulate to examine difficult questions to make certain that the problems standing in the way of a satisfactory answer to them do not stem from the question itself. That is to say they examine the question's validity to determine whether or not it is worthy of consideration, and one of the things they look for is a false premise, assumption or supposition. For instance, were I to inquire: 'What is the length of a unicorn's horn?', I would have erroneously supposed the actual existence of the mythical animal, and consequently there is no reason why anybody should take my question seriously. Similarly, when we ask, what is a fake drawing or painting, we are assuming that drawings and paintings can be fake. Should this assumption be false then our question may be dismissed, never to be seriously posed again. But can drawings and paintings be fake? Surprisingly, the answer is no.

To make this point plain I quote a passage from a book that the late Lord Clark described as one of the most brilliant books on art criticism he had ever read – *Art and Illusion* by Sir Ernest Gombrich:

> Logicians tell us – and they are not people to be easily gainsaid – that the terms 'true' and 'false' can only be applied to statements, propositions. And whatever may be the usage of critical parlance, a picture is never a statement in that sense of the term. It can no more be true or false than a statement can be blue or green. Much confusion has been caused in aesthetics by disregarding this simple fact. It is an understandable confusion because in our culture pictures are usually labelled, and labels, or captions, can be understood as abbreviated statements. When it is said 'the camera cannot lie', this confusion is apparent. Propaganda in wartime often made use of photographs falsely labelled to accuse or exculpate one of the warring parties. Even in scientific illustrations it is the caption which determines the truth of the picture. In a *cause célèbre* of the last century, the embryo of a pig, labelled as a human embryo to prove a theory of evolution, brought about the downfall of a great reputation. Without much reflection, we can all expand into statements the laconic captions we find in museums and books. When we read the name 'Ludwig Richter' under a landscape painting, we know we are thus informed that he painted it and can begin arguing whether this information is true or false. When we read 'Tivoli', we infer the picture is to be taken as a view of that spot, and we can again agree or disagree with the label.

From which it follows that it is the labelling, and only the labelling, of a picture which can be false, and contrary to popular belief there is not and can never be a false painting or drawing, or for that matter any other work of art. A drawing is as surely a drawing as a rose is a rose is a rose, and the only thing that may possibly be false about it is its label – its attribution. What a relief this truth should be for the art world! No longer need the expert, the collector, or anybody else worry about fakes. The term can be expunged from the art lover's vocabulary. All we need worry about now is educating the experts to attach the right label: 'Tom Keating in the manner of Samuel Palmer', 'Michelangelo in the manner of the antique', 'Andrea del Sarto in the manner of Raphael', 'Anonymous twentieth-century artist in the manner of Claude', and so on.

No crime, no fraud has been committed, prices are adjusted accordingly, and all those people who could not possibly afford to own a work by their favourite master can have something very close to it at a fraction of the cost without feeling either guilty or deceived.

To give two examples, one of correct and one of incorrect labelling from the British Museum, I would like first to cite the museum's copy by Rembrandt of a drawing by Mantegna. This work is correctly labelled as Rembrandt after Mantegna. But let us suppose it was labelled as being by Mantegna himself, would it then become a fake – a fake Mantegna? No, for as we have seen drawings cannot be fakes, it would still be perfectly genuine but now with a false attribution. Another drawing in the museum (see Fig. 78), which unaccountably was not included in their exhibition 'Fake?' – which, incidentally, contained no genuine Hebborns, a fact which led Yvonne Tan Bunzl generously, but unnecessarily, to donate one of my 'Stefano della Bellas' she had bought from Colnaghi's to the collection – has been falsely labelled twice. In the first instance as 'Sir Anthony Van Dyck', and then as 'a modern fake'. The proper label should be of course 'Eric Hebborn in the manner of Van Dyck', for regardless of its quality, it is no more a fake than Rembrandt's drawing after Mantegna is a fake. Indeed, not only is my drawing not a fake: it is not, as the Rembrandt is, even a copy.

What brought down the curtain on the embarrassing scene in Bond Street of the late seventies, which was threatening to explode into a full-scale scandal, was my letter to *The Times* of 17 April 1980 which again stresses the importance of descriptions and points the finger at the true culprits:

Attributions of drawings
From Mr Eric Hebborn

Sir,

Re Geraldine Norman's article 'art establishment rumpus boiling up over drawings thought fakes' of March 3. The case of the drawings that have passed through my hands, and whose attributions have been doubted, raises some interesting questions that few appear willing to discuss. The newspapers seem far too interested in exaggerating Professor Blunt's negligible part in the matter, and show that I am a brilliant draughtsman, to ask to what extent the dealers and experts are to blame for the whole affair.

Instead of stressing how clever the possible imitations are, it might be more rewarding to examine the abilities of those who made the attributions and on whose advice large sums of public money were spent. In short, the first question that might sensibly be asked is: who are the people responsible for the false descriptions (always assuming that they are false) that turned the unattributed drawings offered for inspection by myself, into the possible fakes that Christie's, Colnaghi's and Sotheby's are responsible for marketing? The answer to this question might very well lead to the unmasking of some fake experts.

Yours faithfully,
ERIC HEBBORN

At this point in our version of the Vincent Van Blank story we are short of a villain. Vincent is playing the prima donna, he refuses to be called a criminal, or wear his mask, and is adamant about his work not being fake. Nevertheless, somebody has got to play the villain's part, and be unmasked, otherwise our tale will be as anti-climactic as if Agatha Christie should forget to tell us whodunnit. Fortunately we have two candidates for the role, the expert and the dealer. The former is guilty of making false descriptions, and the latter of making money from such false descriptions. Personally, I do not think that the expert suits the part of the villain very well. After all we have no reason to suppose he is not acting in good faith. Furthermore, those of us who love the art of the past owe an enormous debt of gratitude to the poor scholar I have elsewhere so cheerfully maligned, for in spite of the severe handicap of not being sufficiently versed in the creative side of the visual arts, and having to rely too much on the rough and ready principles of his discipline, it is to his labours that we largely owe the survival and conservation of our great cultural heritage. His very occasional lapses in ethical conduct would seem to result from keeping bad company. Berensons who mix with Duveens do so at the risk of their integrity. But on the whole, the expert is a good guy, sometimes a little bit too self-important perhaps, but no villain. So we are left with the only other candidate for the rogue's role – the dealer. I apologise for the type-casting, but we shall see below exactly how villainous the art dealer can be.

In the newspaper articles following Colnaghi's press release are references to a 'group' of Old Master drawings which I sold, and whose authenticity had been questioned. According to the *Sunday Telegraph*, this group was composed of twenty-five works. Anybody who has been patient enough to follow me to this point must consider twenty-five to be a very low estimate indeed. One only has to reflect that the group of Stefano della Bellas alone came to around that number. Then there were whole collections made for Hans, and parcels of drawings delivered to the salerooms. Having kept no

precise records, it is not possible to give the exact number of new
Old Masters that I put on the market during the fifteen years between the appearance of my first Johns at Christie's in 1963 and
Colnaghi's press release in 1978, but estimating it at the low rate of
one a week, it comes to well over 600. To be absolutely certain of
avoiding exaggeration, and to make a round figure, let us say 500
drawings in the style of the Old Masters had been put into circulation. Out of those 500, only twenty-five had been seriously doubted,
and all of those twenty-five had passed through Colnaghi's, Christie's,
Sotheby's and Hans. None of the drawings that I had channelled
through other dealers had, as far as I knew, been questioned, and
this and other considerations made me wonder if I had not given
the experts too easy a task. They had discovered the group of
twenty-five drawings were not right, not by any cleverness on their
part, but from my own errors of judgment, not only of method, but
also of marketing. The drawings I put into sales under names other
than my own had passed as genuine. Then there was the fact of my
increasing competence. By the late seventies I can claim to have
gained considerable mastery of the art of making new Old Masters.
Now there was no more scraping with razor blades, no crude collectors' marks, no Washington look, or stylistic discrepancies for the
expert to recognise my work: it was then totally indistinguishable
from the real article, unless I wanted it to be otherwise.

Taking all these things into consideration, I decided that even
though I had been exposed as a 'forger', I could and would continue with my activities until I had put on to the market a further
500 'Old Masters'. If they got through, then I would know for certain that my theories about drawing were right, that is, it is possible
to escape the influence of period, place, and one's own personal
mannerisms, and enter mentally into the timeless world of art from
which the best artists draw their inspiration. This time I would
avoid the mistakes of my apprenticeship and, keeping a low profile,
make sure that none of the works could be traced back to me.
Although sometimes, however, it would amuse me to take a
genuinely old drawing into a saleroom giving my own name, and
watch the expression of disdain on the expert's face as he turned it
down. These instances further convinced me of most experts' lack
of objectivity. The years passed and the Hebborn affair was re-
legated to the archives. It had just been a flash in the pan, a handful of clever fakes, but now the experts had a dossier on them, they
could recognise the hand and should any more turn up they would
soon be spotted. Little did they know how many of my works they
were still handling, and how many more were yet to come.

To put the experts even further off the scent, I made a series of drawings which caricatured my early unsatisfactory productions. I called these drawings my 'red herrings'. It was a doubly appropriate name because I purposely made the ink for them unusually red. I also let the ink bleed, put too much careless energy into them, and exaggerated my early mannerism. Even so, with all these faults, some of the first ones passed through the salerooms and elsewhere at relatively good prices. After two or three years, however, the prices dropped, and I knew that the experts had been alerted to a certain kind of 'fake' which they happily imagined to be the product of my waning talent. Now they felt safe – Hebborns were easily identifiable. That the experts were really on the lookout for red ink is confirmed by this article by the saleroom correspondent of *The Times*.

> A fake Rembrandt drawing of startling quality has been sent for sale at Sotheby's. Having valued the drawing at about £10,000 to £15,000, Mr Julian Stock, director of Sotheby's drawing department, was about to start advertising the sale of this treasure when he realised his mistake . . .
>
> The fake came to Sotheby's from America with a note saying that it had been in the Harewood sale. A quick comparison with the photograph in the Christie's catalogue appeared to confirm that. The two must be compared for several minutes, with great care, for the difference to become apparent . . .
>
> The red ink appears to provide a key to a flourishing little business in manufacturing Old Master drawings. 'I was surprised when the drawing arrived,' Mr Stock said. 'I had come to recognise that ink, and believed it was the sign of a modern fake. The fact that the drawing had been in the Harewood collection appeared to prove me wrong.'
>
> The discovery that the Rembrandt also turns out to be fake confirms his previous suspicion of the ink. All the other drawings in this ink seen at Sotheby's were Italian, mainly Venetian. There have been several Guardis, both Francesco and Giacomo, and several Tiepolos, both Giovanni Battista and Domenico.

It seems that all drawings in red ink had become suspect, and it is rather ironic that the copy of the Rembrandt which led to my knowing of the success of my red herrings, was not by me at all, nor were the Venetian views. How handy for the experts – three different forgers all using easily identifiable red ink.

Having lulled the unsuspecting experts I set about slowly to prove not only my theories, which I plan to make the subject of a serious book on drawing, but also to disprove the six pet theories with which connoisseurs frequently deceive themselves:

1. The forger always betrays himself by personal mannerisms.
2. The forger always lacks freedom of execution and originality.
3. A forgery is always of lower quality than an original.
4. Forgeries always reveal the taste of their time.
5. Forgeries only get through in troubled times.
6. Where ocular evidence fails to uncover forgery, scientific examination will succeed.

If we exchange *always* for *sometimes*, the first four of these cosy theories are sound. An artist working in the style of draughtsmen of the past may *sometimes*, even often, reveal his authorship by personal mannerisms, lack of freedom, poor quality, and the sign of his time, but not *always*, and if he is sufficiently able, *never*. There has already been suspicion cast in this book on the adequacy of these comforting notions. There is for instance no mannerism linking the Pierpont Morgan's 'Cossa' to the British Museum's 'Van Dyck', there is no lack of freedom in the National Gallery of Denmark's 'Piranesi', some of my 'Johns' are better than many of that artist's own drawings, and I defy anybody to find anything particularly twentieth-century about the National Gallery of Washington's 'Sperandio' or the Metropolitan Museum of New York's 'Breughel'. As for number five on the list of the experts' favourite theories about fakes – that forgeries only get through in troubled times – this is an absurdity based on a few instances when fakes did happen to get through in troubled times, notably Van Meegeren's Vermeers during the Second World War. My own productions have circulated during twenty-five relatively peaceful years.

The last of the cosy theories which argues that science can substitute connoisseurship in the matter of detecting fakes is as fallacious as it is widely held. In the *Enciclopedia dell'Arte Garzanti*, under the heading of *Falsificazione* comes this welcome news for the collector (my translation).

> ... today chemical analysis, the spectrograph, the radiograph, and microscopic examination can come to the aid of unmasking forgery, a premeditated crime by almost every legal system. There exists to this end the most complicated and sophisticated techniques: from the so-called geological clock (potassium – 40, uranium – 238, rubidium – 87) which allows one to establish the age of the materials involved due to nuclear transformation which acts upon the composition of such materials until the work of art is saturated with elemental particles. This method is particularly effective for determining the age of oil painting, where advantage is taken of the characteristics of white lead. The radioactivity of this element is in fact dramatically increased with age – it suffices therefore to measure the radioactivity of

lead based colours, in particular flake white, to establish whether, for example, a painting was made in this century or hundreds of years ago. Furthermore, in this century, industry, nuclear experiments and the poisoning of the atmosphere in general, have increased the level of C-14 in organic substances (paper, canvas, linseed oil, etc.) to the extent that it is possible to determine with precision paintings made after the Second World War.

These words of comfort were written in 1973. In some of my drawings examined by Doctor Julius Grant, an analytical chemist, five years later, I had employed oil paint containing linseed oil and white lead, nevertheless it was not possible for the investigator to establish that the works were modern. The unwelcome truth is that scientific methods for examining objects of art are still in their infancy and even if, one day in the future, they are perfected, they will only ever be able to prove a work fake, never that it is genuine.

But to return to my plans for continuing to try the experts. Subjective at the best of times, I could not expect them to approach the small group of drawings they had condemned as fakes with anything even remotely approaching an unbiased attitude regarding their artistic merits. Clearly they had never read Gombrich and nobody had told them that strictly speaking fake works of art do not exist, and the very word fake set up in their minds only derogatory vibrations – much as the very name of the Devil sets up in the minds of the superstitious, fearful vibrations, even though they have no proof of the Lord of Darkness's existence. Their attitude now was: 'O, they are just fakes, so they cannot be any good, at best they are rather clever, but no one would be fooled by them now.' Moreover, since they 'knew' them to be 'fakes', they put them into the pigeon hole in their minds reserved for 'fakes' and forced them into conformity with the preconceived concepts established by authorities on the subject. For example, if Max Freidlander says 'The forger can never let himself go', then these Hebborns lack spontaneity, and what looks like spontaneity is really only a cunning simulation of it. These things being so, to prove my theories beyond doubt it was necessary for me to start all over again and produce another set of Old Masters which had no traceable connection with myself. There could be no more phoning up Colnaghi's and making an appointment, or bowling into Sotheby's and asking them what they thought of my latest efforts – such authorities would have to handle my work without them knowing the source before I could be certain that their opinion was not totally biased.

Opportunities for putting my new productions on to the market were not slow in turning up. No sooner had my letter to *The Times* squashed the scandal caused by Colnaghi's press release than I was contacted by any number of dealers commissioning 'Old Masters'. Mostly they did this by telephone. After I had identified myself, the voice at the other end of the line would say something like: 'Mr Hebborn, I wonder if you could help. I have a client for a Guercino. Do you think you could find one for me?' To which I would reply that I would see what could be done and ask the caller, who seldom gave his real name, to ring back in a couple of weeks or so to find out if I had been successful in my search. If I had it would be arranged to deliver the drawing and collect the money, which has the going price of my watercolours – around £200 in the late seventies, to £1,000 in the late eighties. To hide the identity of these mysterious dealers, the usual method was to leave the drawing at the desk of one or other of the de luxe hotels in Rome with the dealer's alias written on the parcel and pick up an envelope with my name on it containing the cash or sometimes only a promise to pay next time – presumably after they had successfully marketed the work. Where the greater part of my productions – about 500 in all – which I made in the decade 1978-1988 have ended up I do not know. The market seems to have an endless capacity for absorbing them. Occasionally I see one in an auctioneer's catalogue or a dealer's advertisement (Fig. 97). Sometimes the figures they fetch are astronomical. Between £80,000 and £150,000 seems to be the range of my best efforts. It gives me some satisfaction to note that the museums are still buying them and I look forward to the recent acquisition notices in their bulletins with the same eagerness as some people await the football results. Obviously the dealers who put this large body of 'Old Masters' on to the market knew exactly what they were handling, but I very much doubt whether any of the drawings was correctly labelled as for instance: 'Eric Hebborn in the manner of Federico Barroci', or even 'Late follower of Castiglione', or whoever the artist happened to be.

Let me tell the story of a dealer who handled thirty of my creations which, because they were not intended to pass the most stringent tests, I can reveal without jeopardising the success of my major productions. Again, it all started with a phone call. This time, however, the caller did not hide his identity. He asked if he might come to see me on a matter concerning some 'Old Masters' he was anxious to acquire. It was a wet and chilly evening in the spring of 1985. The fifteen-year lease on Villa San Filippo had expired, and I was warming myself with wine and a roaring log fire in the inglenook fireplace of the new home which Edgar and I shared.

Fig. 97: 'Gian Domenico Tiepolo', *Pulcinalla Abducted by a Satyr*, pen and sepia and grey wash, 1985, advertisement printed in the Italian art magazine *Antiquariato*, March 1986. Note that the shanks of the back legs of the horse have deliberately been drawn too long

It was in many ways similar to San Filippo and only about two kilometres away. We had restored and enlarged an old farm building in a wonderful unspoiled setting close to a group of ancient oaks – not only beautiful, but to me, useful for their galls. Daylight was failing and I was glad to be comfortably home. Edgar was usually with me at this hour, also enjoying an early evening sip, and I was wondering where he had got to when there was a tap on the door. On the step stood the suave, well-dressed and well-mannered dealer. My visitor wiped his Churchs on the doormat and I recognised at once the dealer in him. His steely eyes were wandering about the room to appraise its contents. His professional gaze was noting the portrait of Sir Peter Lely over the fireplace, the Bassano on the wall opposite, the Persian rugs, the collection of books, bronzes, antiquities, a Dutch seventeenth-century coin cabinet, a great seventeenth-century oak cupboard from France, and many other, not terribly valuable, but attractive old things, all of which he immediately translated into cash. He did this in order to estimate how much I was worth, and consequently how much or little he would offer for my services. Taking from him his cashmere coat,

I studied him as much as he was studying the room. My overall impression was beware, here is a smooth operator.

Seated in the inglenook, glass in hand, he came straight to the point of his visit. He was, he said, looking for an album containing a hundred or so Old Master drawings of 'decorative value' only. Playing hard to get, I responded to the effect that I no longer dealt in old drawings.

'I have a client who is prepared to pay *molto bene*,' he said between sips of wine, '*very well indeed*, shall we say thirty million lira?' This was about £15,000, which if divided by 100 came nowhere near the price of one of my watercolours.

'Well, even were I still dealing I doubt very much if I could find a hundred Old Masters at that price.'

'*Va bene*, Eric, how about looking for a smaller collection – let us say forty to fifty.'

Now we were getting a little nearer the mark, so I countered by suggesting that twenty to thirty might be a more realistic figure. In Italian we have a formal and an informal way of addressing one another: we call strangers or acquaintances *Lei* and friends and intimates *tu*. And as he and I had only just met we were using the formal *Lei*, but at a certain point he said in the most charming manner that as he was certain that we were soon to be the very best of friends would I permit him to address me as *tu*. Having dealt with rogues before, I knew very well that he was just buttering me up. Friendships are made in Italy no quicker than anywhere else, and his attempt to put our relationship on a friendly informal level at once was just a trick to put any dealings we might have, or agreement we might make, on an equally friendly and informal basis which he could and would abuse at the first opportunity. Nevertheless, pretending not to have seen through him, I played along and we were soon *tu*-ing each other in the friendliest way imaginable, and as glass after glass of wine went happily down he became less cautious about speaking of the 'Old Masters' it was to be my purpose to 'find'. When I mentioned there might be technical problems standing in the way of discovering so many period drawings, he said cheerily, 'Oh, old paper? I can supply plenty of that.' After a little more bargaining it was agreed that he should pay me one million five hundred lira each for the drawings (about £750) and anything he made above a hundred per cent profit would be divided between us. As I knew that all the money I would ever see for my work was what was paid on delivery, I stipulated that no drawing was to go out of my possession without being paid for in cash – definitely no cheques. So shaking hands on the deal, he had one for the road – which in Italy is called *staffa* (stirrup) and frequently accompanied with the recital of an old adage which may be rendered: 'Ne'er take the road, or rain and shine, Unless thy lips should taste of wine.'

No sooner had he left than I was surprised by a rustling coming from inside the seventeenth-century French cupboard, and suddenly one of its doors swung open to reveal a smiling Edgar who, knowing that I tend to forget what has been said or done when I have been drinking, had hidden himself away to overhear my conversation with the dealer. We had no secrets from each other, and he frequently acted as my memory. 'What a slimy piece of work that one is,' he laughed, as he stepped out of the cupboard. 'You

Fig. 98: 'Giovanni Domenico Tiepolo', *Scene from the Story of Antony and Cleopatra*, 1985, pen and wash over pencil

should have tripled your price.' A few days later the dealer returned with a large quantity of old paper of all periods from the fourteenth to the nineteenth century, but with a predominance of sheets from the 1700s. Wanting to test his knowledge, I asked him if he would be kind enough to write on each sheet its date. This he did with very few mistakes. He had, I learned, also been a customer of Louis and Marie, and toiled through the piles of prints and drawings in the Old Curiosity Shop. With the old paper, he also brought many books, reproductions, photographs and other source material – including some originals. Among the photographs were a number of very crude pastiches of works by the Tiepolos, and the presence of these gave rise to my first suspicions that this dealer's knowledge was not what it should be. He also brought for my use some bottles of modern glistening brown ink and sticks of fiercely black and red crayons. How on earth, I wondered, did he expect me to make anything even vaguely resembling an Old Master with that rubbish! Moreover, his attitude was irritating me. He spoke as if his was the brain and mine was the brawn. He was the expert who knew all about the subtleties of period and style and I was a numbskull who had somehow acquired a certain manual skill, a knack with chalk and pen that required no more intellect than the wielding of a pick axe. I felt that he was presumptuous, and given half a chance would be telling me how to draw. However, I said nothing and permitted him to think that he was fooling me with his half-baked knowledge, suave manners, and feigned friendliness.

The first batch of drawings I made for him included a 'Gianbattista Tiepolo', two 'Giandomenico Tiepolo's (Figs. 97 and 98), a 'Palma il Giovane', a 'Guercino', a 'Vanvitelli', and a 'Castiglione'. Although these followed the manner of the various artists closely, I purposely introduced some defect in style or technique, so that in fact he was getting the 'decorative' drawings he had pretended to want. When they were lined up for inspection he was pleased with all of them excepting the 'Guercino'. He was quite right, it was really very poor. For some reason or another – and I am sure this will please the world expert on the artist, Denis Mahon – I have never been able to make an entirely satisfactory 'Guercino'. And this is most odd because his pen and wash style is one that is very much akin to some of my own drawings, and the seventeenth century is one I feel at home in (Fig. 99). Furthermore, I have studied him assiduously. It seems we all have a blind spot somewhere and 'Guercino' is mine. Anyway, it was agreed that the dealer need take only those drawings he was happy with, and I committed the 'Guercino' to the flames. I was paid in cash as I had requested, and he went back to his home to await a telephone call announcing that I had discovered yet another batch of new 'Old Masters'. On our meeting he arrived with another group of original drawings, some to serve as models, and others in need of restoration. Since we were friends it was understood I was to undertake restoration work free of charge. Together with these drawings I was surprised to find he had returned my 'Gianbattista Tiepolo' and 'Luca Cambiaso' – they had been ruined. The dealer, or somebody at his behest, had soaked them in a chemical solution of some kind which had turned the paper to a most unconvincing shade of mauve, and so stressed the ink that the drawings were no longer legible. I was furious: 'What the hell has happened here?' I fumed.

'I was only trying to make them look older, they looked too fresh,' said the dealer nervously.

Fig. 99: *Study of a Figure*, 1974, pen and wash. This drawing is in the author's own manner but the long flowing lines are not unlike those sometimes found in Guercino (Collection of the artist)

'You bungling idiot,' I yelled back, 'don't you know that if the paper is really old, you don't go about artificially ageing it! And in any case how dare you presume to play around with my work?'

'Alright, Eric, calm yourself,' soothed the dealer as he put the table between us. 'You can easily make them again.'

'Like hell I can! If you're so damned clever you can do it yourself!'

He was full of apologies, but I was still angry and made it quite plain to my new friend that in future he would decide whether or not the drawings were to his satisfaction before taking them away, as they could not be returned, or exchanged, and most certainly not remade.

When I had sufficiently cooled down I showed him my new discoveries, which included among others a 'Marco Ricci' landscape, another abortive attempt at a study by 'Guercino', a large and very important figure composition in the manner of 'Antonio Guardi', and a small Venetian view after Giacomo. He took them all except the 'Guercino' which again went up in smoke. Once more he paid for them in cash. That is, with the exception of the 'Giacomo Guardi', and this shows how *faccia tosta* (thick-faced) he was. Even after my having made it clear that he was to decide on the drawings before taking them away, he asked if as a special favour he might have the 'Giacomo' on approval until his next visit. He told a sob story about having a child with a drug problem, and how hard it was for him to raise the money for the drawings, but for a friend he had *'fatto l'imposibile'* (done the impossible). Foolishly I wavered in my resolve, and was never paid, nor of course ever saw the 'Guardi' again. The dealer's visits to Anticoli during the summer of 1985 were frequent. As a rule he would arrive mid-morning, decide on the drawings, and then I would take him to lunch at Renzo's *trattoria* in the village. Over the meal he would discuss what he was going to do with the collection of decorative drawings he was acquiring. Apparently, it was to go up for sale in the autumn, and to encourage me to produce as much work as possible he would reiterate his promise to give me fifty per cent of all profits after he had doubled his money. On one occasion he asked me if perhaps I had anything I would like to put into the sale on my own account. As it happened I had a series of twelve original drawings by Raphael Mengs after heads in Raphael's Vatican frescoes. They were large drawings for which there was no wall space in the new house. I consigned these to him with an important little Venetian drawing of an old man's head which had been in the collection of Sir Robert Mond – it was probably from the workshop of Gentile Bellini. As we were friends he gave no receipt.

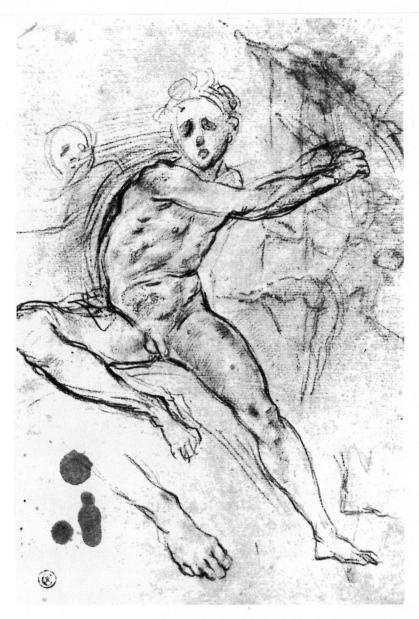

Fig. 100: 'Jacopo Carrucci detto il Pontormo', *Study of a Young Male Nude*, 1985, red and black chalk. The collector's mark is drawn in black watercolour. The stains in the lower left-hand corner were added after the drawing left Anticoli. They are not very convincing insofar as they have conveniently managed to fall where they do no damage. (Sold on 25 November 1985)

Fig. 101: 'Francesco Mazzola detto il Parmigianino', *Saturn and the Nymph Philira*, 1985, pen and wash heightened with white on red prepared paper (sold on 25 November 1985)

Fig. 102: 'Giovanni Boldini', *Portrait of a Lady*, 1985, black chalk

ANTIQUARIATO/ASTE

**Disegni: richiesti
ritratti e figure mitiche**

Dalla Salome del
Maestro di Leyden (119
milioni e mezzo alla
Christie's) allo "Studio
del giovane nudo" del
Pontormo battuto a 138
milioni da Salamon
Agustoni Algranti di
Milano. Risultati buoni
alla Finarte di Milano.

Maestro di Leyden (1494-1533), "Salome offering the
head of John the Baptist to Herod", 1500 ca, inchiostro nero e acquerello bianco e grigio, 19,9×15,5 cm
(Christie's, Londra, 13 dic. 1985)
(19,7/29.600.000) **119.400.000**

Giovan Battista Piazzetta (1683-1754), "Ragazzo che tiene
limone", gessetto bianco e nero su carta azzurra, 39×30,8
(Christie's, Londra, 12 dic. 1985)
(74,2/123.700.000) **426.700.**

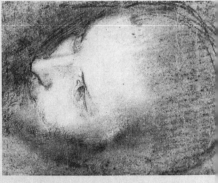

Federico Barocci (1528 ca-1612), "Testa di S. Francesco, che guarda a sinistr
gessetto nero, rosso e bianco su carta grigia, 21,3×27,5 cm (Christie's, Lond
13 dic. 1985)
(9,8/14.800.000) **31.200.**

Jacopo Carucci detto il Pontormo (1494-1556), "Studio di giovane nudo ed
altre figure", 1520-22, gesso rosso e matita nera, 40×28 cm (Gallerie Salamon
Agustoni Algranti, Milano, 25 nov. 1985)
(S.R.) **138.000.000**

◁Giovan Battista Piazzetta (16
1754), "Giovane con cappello e fl
to", gesso nero e bianco su ca
applicata, anticamente, su pergar
na, 38×28 cm (Finarte, Milano,
nov. 1985)
(12/14.000.000) **20.100.**

Gaetano Gandolfi (1734-1802), "Giovane donna", sanguigna, 41,5×28 cm (Finarte, Milano, 26 nov. 1985)
(5/6.000.000)   8.000.000

Francesco Londonio (1723-1783), "Scena pastorale", matita, 20,5×27,5 cm (Finarte, Milano, 12 dic. 1985)
(1,5/2.000.000)   4.100.000

△
Scuola Svizzera, "Portrait of a young man wearing a hat, in profile", 1521, gessetto nero, 38×28,7 cm (Christie's, Londra, 13 dic. 1985)
(S.R.)   184.900.000

△
Jean Dominique Ingres (1780-1867), "Portrait of the Hon. Mrs. Fleetwood Pellew, later Lady Pellew'", 1817, matita, 29,7×22,2 cm (Christie's, Londra, 13 dic. 1985)
(S.R.)   597.400.000

Francesco Mazzola detto il Parmigianino ▷ (1503-1540), "Saturno e la ninfa Filira", penna, inchiostro nero e acquerello grigio su carta preparata in rosa, 32,6×18 cm (Gallerie Salamon Agustoni Algranti, Milano, 25 nov. 1985)
(S.R.)   25.300.000

◁ Luca Cambiaso (1527-1585), "La fuga di Enea e Anchise", penna e inchiostro bruno, 39,5×26 cm (Finarte, Milano, 12 dic. 1985)
(3/4.000.000)   4.100.000

Fig. 103: Double-page spread from the Italian art magazine *Antiquariato*, March 1986, showing the 'Pontormo' and the 'Parmigianino' together with the prices they realised at auction

Over a period of about ten weeks I had discovered about thirty 'Old Master' drawings for him. Among the most important were: an imposing study by 'Tintoretto' squared for transfer, a 'Pisanello' study of an eagle's head, a sheet of studies by 'Bandinelli', a study of figures by 'Longhi', a study of a male nude by 'Pontormo' (Fig. 100), studies by 'Parmigianino' (Fig. 101) a number of minor masters including a Boldini (Fig. 102) and of course numbers of both the 'Tiepolos' to use up the eighteenth-century paper. All of these may be demonstrated to be modern, because as suggested above they were made as decorative items with no intention to pass a proper examination. Nevertheless, as the prices they fetched at auction show, the dealer did succeed in fooling people with his false labelling. Figure 103 reproduces a double-page spread from *Antiquariato*, March 1986, giving the prices realised by two of my works sold at the Gallerie Salamon Agustoni Algrante, in Milan on 25 November 1985: 138,000,000 lira for the 'Pontormo' and 25,300,000 lira for the 'Parmigianino'. A total of about £95,000 – not a bad return on an outlay of only £3,000. Incidentally, the portrait of a young man wearing a hat in profile, sold at Christie's as early sixteenth-century on 13 December 1985, on the same spread, although not by me is also modern. The hat has been copied from one genuine period-drawing and the date from another. Furthermore, the model bears a distinct resemblance to the young man in the Metropolitan's disputed La Tour, *The Cheat*. In spite of the dealer's enormous profit, far above a mere hundred per cent, he seemed to have forgotten the half share he had agreed to give his friend Eric. In fact he seemed to have forgotten his friend altogether. And as I had not heard from him for some time, I thought I might visit him, say hello, and pick up my Mengs and Venetian School drawing or the money they had made at auction, together with the payment for the Giacomo Guardi.

The dealer had moved house. Now he lived in a spacious villa set among vineyards and which commanded splendid views over the city. It was sumptuously furnished, and a new wing had just been completed to house my friend's valuable library. But surprisingly in spite of these evident signs of affluence, according to the dealer things had not gone at all well. Although Byam Shaw had authenticated all the Venetian drawings, rival dealers had cast doubts on their authenticity. Nor were my Mengs really by Mengs. And as for the Guardi and my early Venetian drawing he had no record. Nor was there any mention of sharing with his friend any profits, so I returned from my visit empty handed and have never been contacted by the dealer again. Well, such is the way of the world, and such is the way of certain dealers, gentlemanly and discreet, with 'faces like silver teapots'.

EPILOGUE

As with Vincent Van Blank, in early life I knew poverty and hunger. Also like him, I later knew comfort, and in my golden years even luxury. Unlike him, however, I have never considered myself a misunderstood genius, or for that matter a genius at all. No one asked me to become an artist, and the world does not owe me a living.

It may please some experts to learn that I am no longer working in the manner of former artists. Now there are long-standing projects of my own to bring to a conclusion: a book on the language of line, the text of which is entire, but requires much work to complete the illustrations; a translation into English verse of the complete poetical works of Michelangelo, which again textually exists, but which I would like to see produced as a visually satisfying work; a version of *The Epic of Gilgamesh* rendered into English verse and accompanied with notes, illustrations, and commentary. This last mentioned work I use as a source book for paintings and sculpture, and have already produced it in the form of a handwritten and illustrated manuscript, which could if anybody was interested be turned into an edition. So if granted a few more years I shall not lack for interests. As for the present, I have got to the age when one pays for youthful indiscretions. Excesses have brought me to failing health. But like the happy voluptuaries of Ancient China, contentment is an axiom of my philosophy and I would not exchange my life for another. And when pleasure, from life or art is finally denied to me, it will be time to go.

It is normally the way of writers who tell the tale of Vincent Van Blank to end with a little advice to the collector, and in deference to the form I shall do the same. The first invariable rule is never invest in art – *buy* it! Money wrongly invested will sour your interest, but money paid for something you really enjoy (and people who do not enjoy art have no right to own it) is always money well spent. And should one day some stuffy expert try to spoil your pleasure by informing you that you have bought a fake, point to Sir Ernest Gombrich's observations on page 357 of this book and tell him or her in no uncertain terms that there is no such thing as a fake, only fake experts and their fake labels. And lastly, do not for a moment allow the pleasure you derive from your acquisition to be lessened by wondering what it is not instead of positively enjoying it for what it is. Who knows, perhaps you own a genuine Van Blank.

Italy
April 1991

right

a